A Man of Two Flags

Happy Birthday

Pelesie

Mikey

A Man of Two Flags

The story of Jozsef Bukkhegyi

Jozsef Bukkhegyi with Sydney Lewis

A Man of Two Flags is a work based in fact, enhanced by fictional elements. Some names and identifying details have been changed to protect the privacy of individual lives and experiences.

Book and cover design by E. K. King

Dedication

To Those Who Never Surrendered

Bukkhegyi

Foreword

Jozsef Bukkhegyi, was an intelligent and perceptive man. He read constantly, always learning. His ability to see a few steps ahead and think on his feet was uncanny. He was "street smart," which was one of the few things he boasted about.

As a boy, I felt especially close to my pop. He traveled, but he was home a lot too. We had many chances to talk and spend time. When the opportunity was there, I was ready to listen, and thankfully, I was a good listener. He'd lock into a gaze — his eyes an all-knowing, piercing, deep blue — and talk. Sometimes for a very long time. He'd talk during our Saturday morning dump runs, or at the lake-house or standing in the kitchen. I learned about his childhood, his involvement in the Hungarian Revolution in 1956, how he had to escape from Hungary to eventually join the U.S. Special Forces. He talked about his time in North Korea at the 38th Parallel, the bitter cold, capturing North Korean intelligence officers. Survival. All of it. He talked about his family, his friends growing up, German soldiers, Russian soldiers, all the things that happened in war, and peace time — such great loss humanity can inflict on itself. He talked about his parents — his father was an officer of the *Red Devils*, an elite special force comprised of horseback swordsmen. Their motto was *Take No Prisoners.* Pop would joke, "It would tire out the horses if they took prisoners."

Understanding at a very young age that he suffered from what we now identify as PTSD. Whenever things got dicey, as they can in families, I was able to sense why life for him wasn't always easy, and why he had a hard time with certain American concerns, such as the need for Levi's jeans or Timberland boots, and American pastimes such as watching professional sports, which he thought was frivolous. He taught me fishing, shooting, camping, how to play chess, and other things not all American boys are exposed to by their dads. I felt far more lucky than frustrated. I absorbed useful life survival skills; not of a military nature, but just how to get along with other people. Even a little about negotiation. He told me that I had the knack of a survivor, a sort of tenacity. I've never forgotten that and think of it often during difficult times.

My pop witnessed horrific things throughout his childhood, and heard about terrible events firsthand from family members and friends. Survivors of the WW2 Holocaust, his townspeople brought their experiences back to their small town outside of Budapest. Certain relatives and so many family friends never made it home. Later, he saw childhood friends turn into KGB-style secret police, committing atrocities on fellow countrymen. To survive, he had to do things that would haunt him for the rest of his life. "I had to make a choice, Dani," he'd say. "It was gonna be them or me. I wasn't ready to go yet. I had too much to do."

I still hold the memory of exactly when he first began revealing the intensity of his traumas. I was twelve. Mom and my brother weren't home that morning, and I'd been following him around as young sons tend to do. Over the course of the morning, he'd seemed more and more troubled. That would happen on weekends off and on when his mind was free to reflect. It was early afternoon when we walked into the kitchen, and standing there, I reached up to put my hand on his shoulder and said, "Are you okay, Pop? As we stood there, he reached into the cabinet where he kept a jug of Vin Rose for making *Fröccs*, a Hungarian wine spritzer. He made a drink, slugged it down, made another, and stood leaning against the counter. He began to talk about some of what he'd seen and experienced, first as a child, then as a fighter in the Hungarian Revolution, and about how he'd survived being hunted by the KGB and secret police. My sense was to let him unwind it all. Let him get it out. I wanted to soak in his experiences, to learn from them. These were defining moments. From then on, he knew he could talk to his son. He'd find no judgment or overreaction to unpleasant topics, and I'd try to ask the right questions. And though I was young, I could handle it. He could talk and that was something he needed to do. To just let it out.

"I have nightmares that the ones I sent to meet their maker are coming after me," he'd said that morning. I took notice of the disturbed expression on his face. His expression hardened when he added, "They had it coming, but still…I see them coming for me." I'd known better than to ask, "How many?" The number wasn't something he wanted to share.

That was almost 40 years ago. We had many of those conversations from that point on. He never for a moment glamorized violence, death, or the taking of a life. "Dani, the guys that brag about how many heroic things they did, how many enemy they killed, never even fired a rifle in their life." He didn't need to explain, it was clear what he meant. He was a fair man, too, without prejudice of any kind. He'd experienced the intolerance of ignorant young men directed at him in the army and had no patience for narrow-minded people of any ilk.

Little sayings of his are in my head, to this day. "Dani, there is no use for dead hero." "Work smart, not hard." "It's okay to be a trash collector, just be the guy that owns the truck." He was charismatic, funny and quick with a joke. Whether with family or friends, either here or during trips to Hungary, he would hold the room for long stretches. When he was young and vibrant and healthy he would tell stories, keeping his audience entranced and entertained, or even scared out of their wits — as was the case when telling ghost stories on Boy Scout camping trips, or rolling on the floor in laughter with a group of drunken college friends at the lake-house. He had a certain charismatic endurance, at times fueled by liquid enhancement, that could put his audience completely in the moment he was describing. At least that's how it felt to me.

I was lucky to grow up knowing that if something, anything, needed to be fixed, it would be fixed. There was always a solution. If I complained because I didn't have something I wanted but didn't need, he'd say things like, "You've never been hungry. You have shoes. You can go to school tomorrow. You can go to church with your mother, or to any church you want to go to. You and your brother have your own rooms. We have two cars. A dog. A cat. A home with a fireplace..." "I know, Pop." Thing is, I really did know. Now, in mid-life, I have it. I know it, Pop. I'm grateful.

On my daughter's high school graduation day, he stayed home — in West Groton, Massachusetts, where he'd lived since his release from serving in the US Army Special Forces and the CIA. My parents' house was far away and very different from Pop's earlier life in Hungary. While he rested in bed, we went to the graduation, had a gathering at home and embraced the goodness of the day. The absence of my pop was felt by all. He had become quite ill. That night I went to bed feeling a combined sensation of pride and the anticipation of a huge loss. My daughter was entering a new phase of her life, and my dad's time with us was drawing to a close. My head was spinning with the events and significance of the day; my daughter, my dad — her childhood, my childhood. Eventually I drifted into a dream state. My pop and I were in an American Legion type hall occupied by a group of old ladies sitting on metal chairs. Maybe it was a bingo night. Festive music played and the environment was happy. He got up out of his chair wearing his familiar work-around-the-house jeans, wiggled his rear end, looked back at me…and walked toward the front of the room and out the door. I awoke, and immediately knew. Pop had passed. It was fitting for him to leave this realm like that, in the form of flesh and blood and attitude. I counted to myself as I awoke, 3, 2, 1, and my cell phone rang. It was my brother: "Dani, Pop is gone." "I know John, I'll be there soon." Soon after, I pulled into our boyhood driveway to be with pop, my mom and my brother. That was a very hard morning.

My pop began work on this book in the early 90's. This is *his* story about much of his life, most of which is true and accurate. The reader can determine the parts that work a bit of historical fiction into the mix. This version was adapted from an original very long manuscript, which he'd revised a few times. Sydney Lewis, an old soul and now a dear friend, met with my pop, mom, and myself several times. She spent time interviewing him and emailing questions till the end of his time here. After he passed, she continued asking for details and insights. Syd has been instrumental in keeping my promise to my father: "We will finish the book." A sincere debt of gratitude for her work here. It means the world to me and my family, and I can't think of a better way to honor the man.

I am lucky to have had Jozsef Bukkhegyi as my father for 45 years. This is his story.

Looking Back

Jozsi Budai peered at the clock. It was one in the morning and he was too restless to sleep. He rose, careful not to disturb his wife, and made his way to the kitchen, where he grabbed a glass and a bottle of *palinka,* and careful to avoid the creakier spots, silently made his way down the stairs to his workroom in the basement.

Although his mind had been racing this night, overall, in many ways he felt at peace. He and his wife were healthy, enjoying their life and home. He had work he still enjoyed, household projects to tend, the love of his family, the comradery of his friends. He did not have a fortune, nor did he need one. Jozsi's attitude had always been: if you lose it all tomorrow, well, at least you had it today. And who knew what tomorrow would bring. The rug beneath his feet had been pulled away too many times to trust that this day or the next would be anything at all like the ones that came before. He embraced each distinct day, fully confident that he could charm, reason, bullshit, or fight his way through whatever difficulties might appear in the next. He had little fear of illness, pain or death, which had always been as tangible as the big oak tree in his yard, simply a feature of life's geography.

Jozsi reached under the green glass shade of the lamp in the center of his work table, switched on the light, and smiled at a photograph of Dani, then five, thumbtacked above the shade. In it, his little boy stands in the yard wearing a cowboy hat, holding high a small metal statue of a rearing horse, and grinning. Jozsi had lost track of the horse, but thought he'd packed it away. Now that Dani was going to be a father he'd have to dig it out and give it to him. Eventually, he'd risen to look for it.

He was proud of his son: solidly standing on his own two feet, beginning his own family. The good news had come over the phone, Dani too excited to wait and announce it in person; they'd kept the news secret until they'd passed the three-month mark and now were ready to share their excitement. "My boy, my boy," Joszi had repeated as he'd absorbed Dani's words. He was more than ready to be a grandfather, had in fact eagerly anticipated being given that moniker since the day of Dani's wedding.

From a high shelf Jozsi pulled down a mahogany box, a foot long, half-a-foot wide. He poured himself a drink and opened the box. He didn't think the horse was in it, but it had been a very long time since he'd looked inside and he was feeling sentimental, or as close to that as he ever came. Jozsi removed a small stack of photographs, fanning them out on his worktable — a series of shots of World War Two soldiers standing with their loved ones. It had been years since he'd seen them, but he remembered each with a start of recognition. As a boy, he'd studied them and felt as though he'd actually known all of the people pictured. There sat a young man with his look-alike younger brother. In another, a man wearing a helmet, rifle in hand, stood in a yard with his family, a farmhouse in the background. And there, one of his favorites, a tall man with wire rim spectacles, his arm around a woman in a polka dot dress, her face betraying worries she strove to disguise from the camera. He'd grown adept at disguising emotions and perhaps it was that photo that first cued him to the value of convincingly controlling your expression.

He then took out a small tin box and lifted the lid. He pulled out a piece of shrapnel he'd found in Hungary and ran his fingers over its strange inscription, then drew it close to his nose, inhaling the metallic scent. Along with the smell came a raft of images — the land where he'd found the shrapnel; the warmth and comfort of Bandi, the horse who'd been with him when the bombs fell; the Toth family and their farm; his own family and the house he'd grown up in. A world away in time and space, he thought, and yet now present in this basement. He reached in again, to the far-right corner of the box and gently unfolded a small piece of black velvet. He smiled at the whistle it held, placed it to his lips and blew in the tiniest of breaths, just to hear the sound. He felt his father's love surround him.

Jozsi took another stack of photos, ones from his life in America. He shuffled through them, lingering over one of he and Ann standing behind Dani costumed as a cowboy. Halloween. They stood in the yard next to a pile of raked leaves. He had his arm around Ann, her hand rested on Dani's shoulder. A picture of contentment. He sipped *palinka,* rubbed his eyes, sighed. Ann had suffered because of his choices, and so had Dani. Long ago he'd come to understand a certain truth: life is joy, life is suffering. Looking back, he knew that if he had his whole life to live again, he'd end up making the same choices. He'd done things, taken actions that caused him shame, things he couldn't quite forgive in himself, but he'd learned to accept the weight of those actions. After all, he was still alive. He accepted the haunting dreams, the stabs of guilt at pain he'd caused others, the ugly memories that arose unbidden. Just as he accepted the blessings of his current life: a grandchild coming before the next Christmas, a wife he loved, a home in a country he'd come to feel part of. He could not say that he deserved any of these things after all of the destruction and hurt some of his actions had caused. He could not be the judge of his worth, he could only accept the reality of his existence. And tomorrow he had work travel to California to arrange, wood to chop, and a reading lamp to rewire as he'd promised his wife. He was a man of his word, Jozsi thought, at least that. As was Dani. And though his son's life had so far been far easier than his own, he hoped for Dani, in whose spirit he saw his own fierce will to survive, the same eventual peace in acceptance at what life delivered. You are who you are. You face what you find. You make the best of it.

1

Korea

Jozsi had lost count of exactly how many mosquitoes he'd smushed since laying his weary, aching body down in the dank cave. He took care to smush and not smack when returning them to God. That was how his mother always described the slaughter of small pests: sent back to God. But who could know? Was there a special place in heaven for ants, termites, flies? Who could know, really? And would the satisfying clap of skin on skin ricochet around the cave, bouncing off rocks to land in the ear of someone who might want to send Jozsi himself back to God? Which was exactly why he smushed rather than smacked. He and Laci were tucked out of sight, about 200 yards from the officers' quarters of a sprawling North Korean base camp on a hot, sticky night. Being discovered by a hive of angry North Koreans in this godforsaken land was not a happy option. Should they be caught, these two strapping Hungarian lads would definitely be sent back to God, by way of smacking, smushing, and excruciating rounds of torture. That they weren't American would not matter: fight as an American soldier, die as one.

Their surroundings were barren: few trees, little vegetation, rugged rock formations. They'd come to respect and even appreciate the ubiquitous mountains of Korea. At times the crevice caves were their only shelter from winds that galloped the mountains like crazed Huns, searching for warm blood to freeze in the winter and sane minds to addle in the summer.

Jozsi didn't yet know the full geological history of the mountains, their sharp ridges visible from most anywhere he ventured in the vicinity of the 38th Parallel where he and his comrade-in-arms, Laslow Botlo, were stationed. Laslow, known to all as Laci, didn't much care about learning geological details. He'd heard all he needed to know about the North Korean mountains, and what he'd learned was a refrain: do not camp directly under their ledges…ever. The layers of stone were vertical — look closely, you could see the razor-sharp rims that gave

Laci bad dreams in which North Korean soldiers pressed his whole body against their jagged edges. The dreams always ended with Laci lurching awake, heart pounding, nerves momentarily wrecked, images of sliced boiled beets in his head. By now, both men, Jozsi, 25, Laci two years younger, had been shellacked by exposure to human misery and death; they feared the mountains more than their enemies.

Jozsi noted that mountains comprised of horizontal flat layers had more dignity and poise than the ones currently in view. The kind of mountains they'd grown up with did not collapse without warning, as occasionally happened in North Korea when the summer winds raced north off the Pacific Ocean. When vertical layers of stone met rainy, humid, full-thrust summer winds, they greedily collected moisture along their surfaces. Water trickled into the crevices and clung there, waiting to be joined by even more torrential downpours from fall monsoons. In winter, the winds fully and forcefully shifted, coming south out of the Asian interior, brisk winds spreading bitter cold and snow across the higher mountains in the northeast. Inside the vertical ledges, the water would freeze, year in, year out. It was not unusual for a 500-foot high stone mountain to crack apart, divide, and collapse. If you happened to be camped underneath, your troubles were over. Laci announced he would rather hold onto his troubles, and on this the two agreed.

But now it was nearing the end of August and they had spent many hot hours wading fully clothed through an endless black, grassy swamp. It was so black they couldn't see beneath the surface. If there were snakes, they felt no slithering; leeches they cavalierly plucked off their clothes. Laci, edgy from another bad dream and not enough sleep, agreed Jozsi should be the point man. You had to pay attention because you never knew if your next step was going to bring you down one foot or eight — the swamp bottom followed no logic known to man. Jozsi's eyes scanned back and forth, hoping to spot tree shoots. Shoots grew out of denser ground. This lessened the risk of finding your mouth filled with swamp water following a sudden drop that sunk you so low in the murk you vanished from view.

At the far edge of the swamp, they lingered, sweating through more hours until darkness came full and they could risk crossing the border. Jozsi muttered, "Even if this mission shits the bed, you realize we're known as the most fearsome Hungarians around."

Laci's long narrow face wrinkled in confusion, "What the hell are you talking about?"

"The Zips have discovered our special gifts," he said. Zip a shorthand for Zipperhead, the slur Americans used.

Laci looked toward his crotch and winked at Jozsi.

"No, you idiot, I mean the gift of aiming." Jozsi mimed a trigger-pull. The two were known to spend hours taking pot shots at the border guards, knocking them out of commission more often than not. "I've heard the word is out that when anyone gets hold of 'those two Hungarians' — meaning you and me, Laci, in case you're not following — they're to hang us by the balls. Payback for all the soldiers we've popped in the head. But you won't have anything to worry about."

"I won't?" he said hopefully.

"They can't hang you by the balls…too little." Jozsi waved dismissively in the direction of Laci's privates. Laci gave him the finger.

"Hey," Jozsi shrugged, "passes the time." They quieted down to watch and wait. In the three years since they'd first met — Jozsi fleeing Budapest as the Russians and their tanks stormed the city, crushing all hope of freedom — he and Laci had spent hundreds of hours together; sometimes in silence, more often carousing, scheming, spying, and somehow surviving. They were a good team: Jozsi the brains, Laci the up-for-anything companion — not by any means dull-witted, but content not to be a leader. And here they were in Korea, a place so unlike Hungary it boggled the mind, though for Jozsi, this was not such a shock; his childhood daydreams had been of travel to foreign lands, making his current locale a bizarre version of a dream come true. Not Laci. He'd expected to live and die in the Hungarian countryside near Gyor, the city of his birth, not far from the Austrian border. Sometimes he awoke confused and uneasy, so far from home it made his stomach hurt. But then Jozsi, the Budapest city slicker, would insult Laci's ignorance, and Laci would relax. They had each other; at least he was not wandering alone.

They swatted at bugs. "I'm beginning to miss the boat," Laci said, which was ironic because although they had glided over a sea so calm it felt like they were still on land, he'd had to spend much of the journey from the States to Japan dashing off for private tête-à-têtes with the toilet. Tall and lanky to begin with, his frame held little meat after their stretch on the stately gray battleship. Dining on the American Army's fine canned food since then had done little to improve his heft.

"I am missing the money we made on the boat," Jozsi said, reminding Laci of their blackjack exploits during the voyage.

Years earlier, in Hungary, before the communists, before the Revolution, Jozsi had spent time in the company of Oscar, a notorious card shark Jozsi had met in Budapest. On the boat to Japan, Jozsi had recalled Oscar's bag of tricks and given Laci a crash course in card sharking. After several discrete dry runs, they'd laid out a tarp on the deck floor and sat playing hands for fun. They were so good at the fun part that within short order, several guys wandered over asking to join the game. A casual half hour passed, and then Jozsi blinked twice at Laci who, interpreting the sign, said, "Hey, let's play for nickels and dimes. It'll make the game more interesting." Jozsi did the dealing, and soon piles of nickels and dimes accrued among the soldiers, just as the Hungarian duo had planned. By and by, one of the more successful said, "How about we bump up the bet?" Jozsi smiled, "Let the good times roll," and set the minimum at a dollar. Later that night, they replayed the afternoon's activities, although Laci was unusually restrained.

"What? You're not happy we made almost $100? You are feeling foolish guilt?"

Laci looked almost bashful. "You never said I was doing good."

Jozsi took him by the shoulders. "Lad, I don't want your head getting too big. Maybe you could screw the penny out of an old lady in downtown Gyor, but you are in no way ready to meet up with the likes of an Oscar."

"Where did I screw up? We made money." Laci was genuinely puzzled.

"But we could've made more. When I'm the dealer, don't look at me like I'm your father confessor. Look at me like you're the shark coming after all my money. The others will start betting on your side." He patted Laci on the back. "I'm just trying to get you ready for our return to Budapest!"

Laci took heed and by the time the ship anchored in bustling Yokohama, they were each close to $500 richer than when they'd left the United States. The port city, a major base for arriving American supplies and soldiers, was wide open to receive their loot. The two wandered away from the port toward the city proper, their eyes widening at Japanese wearing flat hats and strange footwear, peddlers pulling wagons loaded with straw baskets and brooms. They stared uncomprehendingly at billboard hieroglyphics, store windows filled with merchandise, and foods that seemed recognizable, and yet at the same time somehow alien. Jozsi suddenly had a memory of himself as a child, sitting rapt while his uncle Peter, a herpetologist, regaled the family with his adventures in all parts of the world. He pictured Peter sitting at the family table, handing around a spear, or mask, or reptile skin from some far-off land. Jozsi had no idea then how he would manage to see the world; he just knew that somehow, he would, and that he would bring back his own trophies to hand around the table, his own stories to widen the eyes of small boys hanging by his elbow. And now he had stories. Did he ever.

Eventually, Jozsi spotted a bar where they soon met two lovely young Japanese women willing to introduce them to the local delicacies, teach them how to use chopsticks and best of all, drink sake, though Laci scoffed at the cups that came with the bottle. "What's in those tiny cups won't even get my tongue drunk," he complained. Their escorts giggled. He was puzzled, too, by the bedrooms the girls led them to, separated only by thin waxy paper, equipped with mattresses laid flat on the floor. Jozsi called out in Hungarian, "Now you know how the gypsies lived in your town." Laci, drunk and happy, just laughed. The next day they paid and left the girls, thanking them profusely for their generous efforts to keep American Army forces in good spirits.

On their way back to the ship, they noticed a few soldiers buying cigarettes from local boys who were standing on the street beside small wicker baskets filled with hand-rolled smokes. They got in line. In Hungary, it had been years since the dire deprivations of World War Two, but people still sold all manner of goods on the street, including their bodies, so these street transactions didn't seem odd. That the cigarettes cost a hefty sum was a shock, until their first few drags, when they found themselves doubled over at the foot of the ship's plank, laughing their asses off at nothing in particular, momentarily unable to board. Once they'd stumbled back onto the ship, they discovered most of the other soldiers in similarly goofy states. The officers, knowing what lay ahead in desolate North Korea, figured they'd let the poor bastards have some fun. They ignored the general hilarity and meandering haze of high-grade marijuana making its way across the deck as the pulled anchor and churned toward their next destination, the port city Incheon, South Korea. Which had brought them one giant step closer to the very swamp they now inhabited.

But back in Yokohama, as they'd left sake-sipping civilization to head toward Incheon and from there to the unappealing barracks of war, glumness had descended. Most of the military — the Americans, British, United Nations and Koreans — were lined up 15 or so miles south of the 38th Parallel. Incheon, less than 100 miles from there, was where soldiers disembarked and received their predictably dismal assignments.

A private in Incheon had loaded their personal and combat gear onto the jeep and driven north to the 38th Parallel, to Camp Kaiser, which he succinctly described as a shithole. The camp was tucked between the tallest rock cliffs Jozsi had ever seen. The cliffs greedily held onto both the heat and the cold — extreme versions of each inevitably charged down their rigid edges and shot into the camp. The Hungarians were assigned to the NATO Intelligence Unit. Jozsi had been trained to replace an outgoing sergeant in the communications section until a new permanent replacement arrived, poor soul. Laci, with an aiming-eye any eagle might covet, was put on guard duty and border patrol to ensure no North Koreans infiltrated the South.

omrades settled into a routine: every three months sent
patrol, followed by three months back at camp, with
ks for R&R. The pleasures of a two-week R&R, often
..y ended abruptly when they ran out of funds before the
.. weeks were up. If they couldn't round up a decent card game, or
come up with some other kind of scam, they'd end up hanging around
the Army base waiting to catch the next flight back to Korea.

Their most successful score had come on a day spent loitering by
the American Post Exchange, seeking to spend their last R&R money on
a few more of those funny cigarettes. Two very polite Japanese men had
asked if they wanted to make a few extra bucks: if Jozsi and Laci would
enter the Exchange and purchase a $300 golf set with the pushcart, the
men would tip $15. Jozsi had asked what made that particular golf set
so special. After they'd enlightened him — it cost triple the amount in
Japan — he'd agreed to give them a helping hand. One of the men had
handed Jozsi $300 in cash, as well as the tip.

"No," Jozsi had demurred, "you keep the tip till we bring out the
cart." He'd suggested the men wait in their truck to avoid being spotted
by any undercover police lurking about, hoping to nab soldiers doing
exactly what he was about to do. The Japanese men had returned to their
truck as Jozsi and Laci hurried in the Exchange front door, and even
more quickly out the back one. They'd grabbed a taxi, and without delay
set about donating to the Red-Light District every last penny they'd
stolen. Later, on their way to Camp Shithole, as they'd taken to calling
Camp Kaiser, Laci commended Jozsi on his patriotism in not letting the
good old American taxpayers be defrauded by sleazy Japanese looking
for a deal, and for being so good a Samaritan as to leave the men with
their $15 tip. They wondered how long before the men had stopped
waiting for the golf cart to roll through the Exchange doors.

~~~

Jozsi rotated his neck, stiff from hours of waiting for the sun to
mosey across the sky and vanish, which was essential for them to be
able to leave the swamp. Laci checked the telescopic sight on his high-
powered rifle for the millionth time and cursed under his breath.

"What's wrong?" Without thinking, Jozsi's hand went to his .45
Colt pistol.

"We are here, isn't that enough, *haverom*?" The Hungarian phrase for special friend felt grounding in this alien place.

"This is a tit job after all the training we went through. No poisonous snakes, no alligators. The swamp stinks, I'll say that," Jozsi sniffed and shuddered, "but as soon as we get back, I will, out of my good heart, treat you to a cavalry dinner in Hong Kong."

"Please, no," Laci winced. "I'm still having indigestion from that one in Rome." There they'd dined like kings and then fled, racing away like the cavalry, hence the name. Although it had seemed their waiter must have been in training for the Olympics — he'd given chase like it was his own mother being cheated, they'd had to run like the devil to lose him.

"You're developing nerves of lace," Jozsi sneered. Laci flicked swamp water his way, and they continued waiting for the sun to inch its way across the sky.

The minute the sun put its blistering face to bed they clambered out of the swamp, faces smudged like Indians in the Arizona desert. Jozsi looked down, scanning his colorful body, "I look like a tasty summer vegetable dish at an Italian feast." They'd crept through high grass to the designated crossing point, smoothly dispatching interference from two lethargic border guards, a task Laci managed with not even a trace of anxiety. Two shots. Two thuds. No remorse. Death comes to us all, Jozsi thought, shrugging. He'd seen, escaped, caused enough of it to consider death a familiar, so to speak, like a neighbor he didn't much like, but did not fear. Still, he reached in a pocket to touch the small whistle he always carried, his lucky charm.

From the crossing point they'd proceeded, crouching and crawling across rocky terrain, until they'd found a suitable cave high on a rise. Moonlight helped Laci's sharpshooter eye spot a small triangular opening, large enough for them, knees bent, to duck inside. In their first months, Jozsi had disparaged caves as lodging, but he'd since come to embrace them, dank and fetid though they be. At least the wind couldn't blast you cold to the bone; nor could an enemy bayonet swiftly pierce your being. The big disadvantage was that, if discovered, you were trapped, plain and simple. You might take a few men down before being smoked out of the cavern, but the odds were against your living long enough to ever enter another. This cave had the benefit of being angled toward the sun so that it warmed the first few feet inside the entrance, which made that area less ripe to the nose than others they'd hunkered in. They plunked their gear on large stones and clambered back out, binoculars in hand, to study their target area.

Not far from the entrance stood a substantial clump of rocks that they crouched behind for a view down the rise to the officers' quarters. They'd been assured that it was in that building that their quarry, an officer code-named Kimchi, resided. A meadow stretched out, pancake flat, for perhaps a half-mile, encircled by mountains. The camp, crowded with structures, had obviously been in existence for quite some time. Officers were housed in small, single-story barracks. Further on, rows of tents lined one side of a rutted dirt road. On the other side stood several hulking Quonset huts. It was still warm enough for the soldiers to sleep in tents, but once the monsoons came, they'd be moving into the Quonsets. The Hungarians could tell that tanks crunching across the land had been the sole engineers of this sorry excuse for a main road. Tanks shaved dirt, leaving in their wake a wide path, rugged and graceless. They watched jeeps jitter and bounce through the camp. At the meadow's furthest end, a trail led up into the mountains, but it was not a trail they had any interest in exploring on this mission. A mad dash down the hill to grab Kimchi, and then a return straight back up was the only feasible hope for escape. Any other move meant they'd end up dead or even worse: regretting they weren't.

The two men watched the guard change every two hours well into the night, making sure they hadn't been misinformed about the camp's rhythm. Then they slipped back inside the cave to sleep, if possible, before carrying out their assignment. On less sensitive missions, there would be a tank or personnel carrier nearby — those big square iron machines that Jozsi thought of as hippos with wheels. The back door dropped down, morphing into a ramp. Those carriers held sleeping gear and basic cooking equipment to warm C-rations, if it was safe enough to start a small fire. Sleeping bags were what you missed most on this kind of mission because travelling light was vital: C-rations in your backpack, weapons, ammunition, nothing else. If you had a chance to sleep, you lay down, no cover but what you wore, no padding but the ground.

Jozsi flopped on the damp cave floor, thoughts ricocheting around his skull. He wished for a sleeping bag, and then for a whore to climb into the sleeping bag with him, as sometimes happened on less secretive excursions. After all pleasurable activities had subsided and zippers had been zipped, the couple of convenience would spoon warmly through the night. But this was not such a night. First of all, it was hot and buggy, even inside the cave. Sadly, Korean mosquitoes were just as kamikaze as their Hungarian counterparts, though that didn't make him feel any closer to the land of the Hun. For a moment, he had an intense longing to be at his mother's table, a steaming bowl of goulash spreading across a fluffy bed of noodles. A bed would be nice too. Wait...make that Erika's table for the goulash, and then some time relaxing over a few glasses of *Tokay*, and later a happy tumble into her bed where he would express his gratitude for the delicious meal.

Jozsi sighed the sigh of a man melancholy and far from home. He was in no way close to falling asleep. He turned toward Laci and saw him twitchily dozing. A maroon sky brightened to the east, the temperature already up to uncomfortable and sticky, heading straight toward unbearably hot. He stunk of himself; Laci stunk of civilization. No wonder the mosquitoes loved them, they were the best banquet around.

Jozsi poked Laci. It was mean to wake him up, but he didn't care.

"I told you not to wash before we left camp. You smell like a French whore, and now the bugs are in love with both of us."

Laci cracked an eyelid and whispered, "Tell me, Jozsi, where is the big car, the diamond rings…where are the girls with big tits?" It was a running gag. A million times, Jozsi had promised, "Stick with me and…" a list of appealing items would follow: beautiful women, fancy cars, glittering jewelry, wads of cash, champagne and feasting. The good life.

"It's all waiting for us to bring this peanut-balled officer back so he can spill his guts," Jozsi sighed. He was referring to their mission: the capture and safe transport of a North Korean intelligence officer the Central Intelligence Defense had a yen to interrogate back at U.S. Headquarters. The CID was what the Army called the organization that in the civilian world was known as the Central Intelligence Agency. A meaningless distinction if you got caught — either way, you were on your own, all CI-people disavowing you whether their group ended in D or A. And their missions were always extremely dangerous. Usually they wanted the target brought back alive for interrogation, but if the "extraction" wasn't going well, then "termination," as they phrased death, was an acceptable alternative. They only enlisted fearless, even criminal, types for these ventures. Going so far as to offer Mob hit men serving hard time in jail, or other inmates with useful talents, the chance to help Uncle Sam for five years as a tradeoff for reduced sentences. It was a good deal…if they survived.

It was Sandor — Jozsi and Laci's CIA handler — who'd persuaded them that joining the Army was their best shot at a new life in the United States of America. Five years in and they'd be guaranteed American citizenship. When they were first stationed in South Korea, it had been Sandor who'd recommended the pair to the CID agents there. Jozsi had shrugged 'So what?' when a young CID officer with a hairy cheek mole had promised each a brand-new stripe if they could wrangle a target agent safely back across the border. The officer had given them a hard sell: the country needed their help; it was important work that would preserve American freedom. And after all, citizens are expected to lay down their lives when called upon. He'd waved the flag all over the place, but Jozsi had told Hairy Mole, "Keep your stripe. After I do my five years in your army, all I want is out. And we're not citizens yet, so forgive me if I don't give a shit about laying down my life for you."

Motioning Laci to follow him out the door with a nod of the head, the Hungarians had walked away, the officer howling, "I'm not through talking!" Jozsi had spat back over his shoulder, "Well, we are," and marched Laci straight over to the 24-hour club so they could toast to the beginning of another day. The Major's offer had put Jozsi in a mood, and it wasn't one that called for breakfast, despite the early hour.

It was one thing for them to cross the border. They'd done that many times, planting relay stations so that the intelligence community (a phrase Jozsi found ironically amusing) could transmit and receive messages from agents already stationed inside North Korea. Weather conditions were extreme, veering from 120 on a hot summer day to minus 40 in the winter, and beating so harshly on the equipment it needed replacing every six months. Jozsi and Laci had already logged many hours wading through swamps, slinking their way to one location or another.

When they were lucky enough to spend time in a tank or carrier, Jozsi would feel like a baby reluctant to leave the womb, especially during monsoon season, with rain funneling down at five inches an hour. The same held true in the depths of winter, when the wind charged across the land at a relentless 40 miles an hour. If you were outside and started a campfire to withstand the chill, you best have your affairs in order — sharpshooters would hone in like vultures on dead meat. The winters were brutally cold, though surprisingly there wasn't all that much snow. With snow, you get moisture in the air, Jozsi observed, it's a friendlier cold. In Korea, everything was inexorably and bitterly cold — the ground frozen, the rice paddies solid, the very air smacking you like a slab of ice.

Sometimes women working in the paddies would drag blocks of ice five feet thick into caves and cover them with rice and straw for on-site refrigeration. Once in a while, the two men would find themselves in the middle of nowhere and a paddy worker would approach. "Hey GI, want a beer?" (It might not be cold, but a beer was a beer.) On those days, Jozsi could have kissed them. And sometimes he did. Through sign and body language the soldiers would cajole their way into securing company for the night. It was so cold they wanted women, any women — grandmothers, hideously unattractive, didn't matter. A woman zipped into your sleeping bag was heaven-sent warmth.

Now and then, the Army trekked out with hot food, soup and potatoes; on an especially good day, shredded beef. But fresh meals were rare, and mostly they dined on field rations. Jozsi would have killed for a glass of *palinka*, a plate of spicy stuffed peppers, slice of salami, or forkful of sugary sweet apple strudel, anything that reminded him of home.

Wherever they went, their job was to install and booby-trap the equipment in case some curious North Korean soldier found the object intriguing enough to pick up and investigate. The booby traps would badly maim if not outright kill anyone within a twenty-foot radius, and so far, they'd managed to avoid self-immolation or any unexpected head-on meeting with armed and irate North Korean soldiers. Jozsi planned on keeping it that way.

After turning down the officer's "Bullshit deal," in Jozsi's words, they'd entered the humble confines of the always-open club, nodding hello to the bartender. Laci was too worried to toast to anything, though he did manage to polish off a full drink in one long swallow. "These guys are going to throw our ass in jail for disobeying. Even our special angel Sandor won't be able to get us out."

Jozsi had assured him, "If this was such an easy job, they'd do it themselves. They need us more than we need them." And as expected, a private had soon arrived at the club with an invitation from the major to

---

return for further conversation. An invitation they were not feeling quite rebellious enough to refuse.

Back in the conference room, they'd discovered Hairy Mole gone and two new officers seated side-by-side near the far end of the table, serious and calm. Jozsi and Laci had been seated opposite the officers, the major at the head. No one said a word. In Hungarian, Jozsi had muttered, "They think we'll talk if they stay silent. They don't know the Hungarian will." He'd rhythmically tapped a pointer finger on the table, waiting for words to be spoken.

Finally, one of the officers, a captain, had said, "We have a proposition for you, if you care to listen." He hemmed and hawed, but the basic proposition remained the same: do this for the good of the country. They'd held out no sparkly treats as enticement. Jozsi, saying he felt a thirst coming on, rose. "Unless you've got a big fat reward in mind, find other soldiers for your mission. If we ever get captured alive, you guys will deny us like Judas…and we'll even get screwed out of the thirteen pieces of silver." The major, sensing little improvement in the negotiations, had agreed they should again part company.

Laci had sobered up enough to protest as they made their way to the club. "But I want a new stripe on my shoulder! And you know we can't really say no. We're not in Budapest where you know the ropes and have six aces in your deck of cards."

Jozsi had ordered another round of drinks and explained his reasoning. "Our ace is how much they want us for this job. It's like chess: you have to think many steps ahead."

Laci had frowned. "I hate chess. Stupid little pieces on a board."

They'd drank and argued the merits of chess until, as expected, the same private had returned to again lead them out of the club for further negotiations.

On their third visit to the conference table, the major had looked on icily while the captain struggled to seal the deal. He told them that if they successfully captured this particular North Korean Intelligence officer, they'd be sent from Korea to Vietnam. The Vietnamese Army needed training on old communications equipment inherited from Korea.

This was a reward? Jozsi had been unimpressed and made that obvious with a sneer, a shrug, and a headshake no. The captain had held up his palm and continued. Also, after two weeks in Vietnam, they'd get two weeks of R&R in Hong Kong, all expenses paid, *and* a new stripe.

By the end of the captain's spiel, Laci'd been grinning as though he'd just inherited a gold mine. Jozsi had mulled the offer over for a minute, then shaken his head no. "Not good enough. Find someone else to do your dirty work." He'd risen and walked out.

Laci had followed him back to the club, yelling, "You are the biggest asshole the city of Budapest ever produced on the face of this earth." Which, for Laci, was a long sentence.

Jozsi had settled in at a dark corner table where the noontime sun couldn't ruin a good drinking ambience. "Laci, you're a country bumpkin who never saw electricity till you were old enough for your tiny wiener to salute. Shut up and buy me a drink!" Jozsi's street smarts always intimidated Laci. He'd pulled out money for the round while maintaining a blustery protest. Jozsi, eager to settle into a peaceful, pleasant drunken haze, had shushed his less sophisticated friend. "Let me explain, since your vision does not go beyond the tip of your almost-red nose. We have a few more years of service, and that's a fact. Perhaps you enjoy playing cowboys and Indians, but I'm sick of it. We manage to survive and get back to the States after this, I want to be assigned somewhere I don't have to crawl through slime or freeze my ass off on icy tundra. I'm holding out for more." They'd settled into a frosty silence, each lost in thoughts of being somewhere else, especially somewhere else without the other. When the private, who served as the captain's jeep driver, once again appeared, Jozsi had offered him a drink.

"Can't now, but after I get off duty, that's another story. I don't know what's going on, but I'll happily drink to your nerve. I heard the officers saying something about how 'the fucking Hungarians have us by the balls.'"

At this, Jozsi had clapped once, "Maybe now we have enough ante to get us a deal worthy of such fine men as we happen to be."

Drunk but determined, they'd managed to reenter the conference room without too much weaving or bumping into doorjambs or table edges. A new officer had joined the others at the conference table. Captain Lamp, according to the major loosely shepherding this Hungarians-for-Hire effort, was the son of a very well-respected Hungarian family in New Jersey. Jozsi had snapped his fingers dismissively. "I know a million Hungarians!" He'd turned to the major. "I thought we were making a deal with you guys, not a Hungarian prince."

Captain Lamp, dumbstruck by the audacity of this non-commissioned nobody, firmly closed his lips and let the major sally forth with a new offer: train the Vietnamese, get a lot more money for two weeks R&R in Hong Kong, and when back on the mainland, be assigned cushy lifeguard jobs at an army post. Jozsi had narrowed his eyes, brain whirring, and suggested a caveat: place them *in charge* of the lifeguards. Laci's eyes grew wide at Jozsi's nerve, but closed in admiration and gratitude once the major had agreed. Finally, they had a deal.

"Stick with me," Jozsi said for the hundredth time, when their copy of the contract had been handed over. "We will have women with breasts falling out of their bikini tops in no time."

Laci had put an arm around Jozsi for a manly hug. "I didn't know Budapest grew men with such big balls, but I am glad to know this one!"

~~~

After a couple of weeks of preparation and briefing, and what had felt like thousands of hours spent looking at photographs of their quarry, they'd been deemed mission ready. Two CID officers had sat close to our heroes, like priests at an Irish wake, Jozsi thought, pinching Laci to make sure they weren't dead. Laci's twitch let him know blood still flowed. The officers had asked the two to flip through the photo file of the North Korean intelligence officer one more time — they wanted to completely ensure the two would recognize and deliver the right man to the CID. Jozsi finally had said, "Hey, we can find the place blindfolded, and after all this time studying him, we can tell you the exact size of his balls. We're set."

The officers had then offered them a choice of cyanide pills, or stickpins for their lapels. This guaranteed that should they be captured, they could choose to bypass interrogation, and whatever torturous means might be used to extract a confession as to their being CID spies. In short, they had a way out. Either swallow the pill or bite the tip of the pin, and all their misery, along with their lives, would be over within seconds. Laci had stuck the magic death pin in his lapel and Jozsi, amused, had watched as Laci practiced bending his neck to see if he could reach the tip of the pin.

Jozsi had shaken his head pityingly. "You, my brother, are no swan."

The officers had exchanged a weary glance, saluted the dangerous duo with zero respect, and with their eyes, urged them toward the door.

The Hungarians had gone to collect their gear, packing as many extra rounds of ammunition as they could manage to carry, and the next day they'd bid adieu to Camp Shithole and made their way to the high grass at the border.

2

Jozsi

Not far from the cave entrance, Jozsi buried his head in his jacket, determined to sleep. His mind kept wandering to places he did not want to linger. Tied to a chair, for example, blood dripping from his mouth, his face stinging from the hard slap of a North Korean palm. Or splayed on a cold cell floor, the air dank and heavy on his beaten body, ears invaded by the sound of Laci screaming from a nearby cell. This was not good for morale. He struggled to get his semi-conscious mind away from present circumstances. A slight breeze found its way into the cave and he willed his mind to float back in time, all the way to the swimming hole that as a child was a hub for he and his friends.

His parents' land ran down to a small pond formed by the *Rakos River*, which flowed a few hundred yards from their home in a suburb just outside of Budapest. The river was wide and lazy at that stretch, teeming with fresh-water lobster, bordered by umbrella-like acacia trees, sturdy cedars, and willow trees perfect for hiding under in games of *bujni*. Ferenc, his best friend and classmate, lived two houses away. His parents' land also ended at the pond, which became the center of their youthful activities; summer days began and ended by the water. The pond sat at the base of a low-ranging, grassy bank, and between it and the house was an open space generous enough for games of soccer, triple cartwheel attempts, and all manner of racing about. Jozsi and Ferenc were constants, but other children congregated as well, especially Zsigmond, who'd moved to their area in grade school and glommed onto kind-hearted Ferenc.

The boys spent most of their time outside, feeding on raspberries and blueberries and grapes, and then plums and pears and apples as Hungary's bounteous trees bloomed through the warmer season. They learned in school how fortunate they were to live on Hungary's flat land, surrounded by the Carpathian Mountains. Czechoslovakians, Yugoslavians, Russians, all wanted to get their hands on the huge Hungarian valley where you could grow anything you wanted. That's why, Jozsi's father explained, so many Hungarians were farmers, it came naturally.

In their neighborhood, most houses were built in a railroad straight style, with three or four bedrooms, an attic, a cellar, and smokehouse out back. Houses of the more well-to-do were brick-walled with red clay roofs. Those with less poured mud wall frames a foot-and-a-half wide, adding horse manure to bind the mud. They'd coat the walls with even heavier mud that dried hard as slab, and then paint them white. Jozsi was grateful for the sturdy brick of his own home. Inside, each room had a small potbelly stove. Some homes had fewer but bigger bedrooms, with stoves in the middle heating both sides of the room. Often, living and dining room were all part of one long open space, which ended in a kitchen.

They'd led good lives until the war came. The boys tore around their neighborhood on wild bike races, and dunked each other in the pond. Each afternoon at *ebed*, when the stores closed from noon to two, the boys would linger by the pond, hoping Jancsi the grocer's son would join them for their version of childhood's story-time, *meseidő*. He was a few years older and a Hungarian Scout Troop member of longstanding, with knowledge to share. Jancsi would seat himself on the highest bank, sharing stories of things he'd learned about animals as big as houses, landscapes bereft of plant life, rivers filled with crocodiles.

One day Jozsi asked, "Jansci, how do people get to these far-away places?" He was hoping he wouldn't have to go to school for years and years to become a herpetologist like his uncle in order to see the world. Jancsi searched the ground till he found a dried leaf shaped like a boat and gently dropped it into the *Rakos*. The boys watched the leaf float downstream. Jancsi explained that it would drift toward the Danube, and from there join a larger sea, and eventually find its way to an even larger ocean where the waves were higher than any tree the kids had ever seen. Jozsi liked to imagine himself at the peak of one of those waves; seeing and at the same time being carried toward places far away. The war and its deprivations only increased those visions. Bread lines and food shortages, malnutrition and sometimes death from starvation, metal and fuel scarcities, anxious adults saying no, we can't do or have or hope for this, that, or the other, weighed on the children.

Jansci tried to encourage his young friends to be resourceful rather than resentful. There were no soccer balls to be found, so he showed the boys how to make them out of their mother's discarded, run-filled silk stockings. They stuffed the silk, turned it in, turned it around, stuffed it on the other side, knotted it, turned it again, stuffed it on the other side, turned, knotted, and eventually they'd create a cloth ball big enough to kick around. By the summer of 1943, the boys were expert at making those soccer balls and generally learning to make do with what they had. Manufacturing had come to a halt, and wartime scarcity squeezed the country. But for young Jozsi, it was still a good summer and he carried on happily until the day his father, Matyas, along with a number of other men in their town of *Rakoskeresteur*, received telegrams demanding they prepare to report for military duty at the local police station. Two days later, army trucks would pick them up at the same spot.

Matyas' law degree had availed him of a decently paying job in one of the Hungarian Central Office's legal departments. He'd tucked away his swashbuckling past beneath a neatly pressed brown suit. The only visible evidence of eight years spent in the Hungarian Cavalry during the First World War was his head, very bald and shiny. He'd served as an officer in the *Red Devils* Brigade, had "sat" a horse all of those eight years, galloped for miles and miles, getting as far as Russia and the shores of the Black Sea. Few of the *Red Devils* had ever seen the ocean. When given time to rest themselves and their horses, they'd dove in, treading water while they talked, then collapsed on the shore to dry. No matter what they did, their pates baked under the hot sun. Some sunburned so badly they lost all of their hair and it never grew back. His father had hated Russia then and ever after.

Given Matyas's former service, age, and position in the government's legal offices, the telegram had come as an upsetting shock to his wife and daughters, though an exciting one to Jozsi. He was the seventh and youngest child, nine at the time, who looked up to his father. Matyas's new mission filled him with innocent pride. On the appointed day, he, Ferenc and Zsigmond accompanied their fathers to the police station, waving and cheering as they watched the morose men head far down the road and out of sight. Their fathers were brave and brilliant, they would smash the enemy and return with stories of glory. That was what the boys thought as they turned to summer adventures. Everyone older and wiser indulged this naiveté.

Now and then throughout the summer, silvery Allied planes flew above, gliding toward the city to bomb German military bases and war factories. The boys would stop in their tracks no matter what, staring at smoke trails till the planes were out of sight, much as they'd watched their fathers disappear down the road, although they'd been heading in the opposite direction. At the moment, all the war meant to these boys was planes up in the air, no fear of fatherly discipline down on the ground, and melancholy mothers huddling together in their few spare moments to share news and worry; all such discussion trailing off in nods and sighs whenever children appeared.

Late one muggy afternoon toward summer's end, as the trio made their way toward the house from their headquarters by the pond, Jozsi heard a cheery commotion floating through open windows. Without being fully aware that somewhere in that cacophony he'd recognized his father's bass tones, he started to run. Suddenly Matyas strode into view, arms wide. At the sight of Jozsi lifted up in his father's arms, the other boys raced off toward their own homes. Within a short time, neighbors gathered to celebrate, uncorking wine and bottles of their local homemade brandy, *palinka*. It was time to toast his return. The news that Matyas did not have to go back to the Russian front compelled a great many toasts.

Eventually, Ferenc and Zsigmond found their way back to Jozsi, who was hanging by his father's elbow. Their faces held no big grins; their fathers' must be on a different train, they said. Matyas ruffled the hair on their heads. He didn't have the heart to share the truth — his age had gotten him released early; the two younger fathers were likely not coming back anytime soon, if ever. Let the boys enjoy the festivities thinking their fathers might appear on the next train, if next train there even were. In truth, both men were at that moment on a train steaming in an easterly direction toward the Russian front, where several miserable months in the future the Russians would capture and kill Ferenc's father. Later still, Zsigmond's would return a shell of a man, eventually to shoot himself in the woods behind their house.

When September came and the boys returned to school, Ferenc and Zsigmond remained convinced their fathers were still slaying the enemy and would return, heroes of the battlefront. The first day of class, Father Richter greeted the students in the backyard adjoining the church and the school — Sister Terezia on his right, Brother Francis on his left, a large metal Cross mounted atop the wall behind them. Jozsi whispered to Ferenc, "The Holy Trinity, back again." Father Richter's flaccid cheeks jiggled as he gave his traditional first day speech: attendance at morning mass required, doors locked at 7 AM sharp; boys late or absent must serve two altar boy duties; errant girls must spend Saturday afternoons washing all of the church seats. It should come as no surprise that Jozsi and Ferenc were expert altar boys. They each lived close to the church, a mere few hundred yards away, yet found themselves on the wrong side of the locked door again and again, thwarted by their nemesis, Brother Francis, the official locker of said door. Unfriendly and burly, the boys called him "The Enforcer," though of course never to his face. When Brother Francis welcomed the students, it was with a smile so chilly even a polar bear would have shivered, Jozsi said. Before sending them to their classrooms, the Brother announced that any boys caught smoking in the outhouse would have to spend two Saturdays cleaning the outhouse barrels with their bare hands. Bare hands? He's outdone himself, Jozsi thought, and sighed. Catholic school was back in session.

Happily, Jozsi was assigned a seat next to Ferenc and behind Erika, the only child of a beloved local doctor, and the smartest girl in the class. Her long blond hair hung in thick plaits, and Jozsi's new pastime became finding opportunities to tug on a braid when the nuns weren't looking. Erika refused to be a tattle-tail, so she put up with his antics, but also, she did enjoy his quick wit and confident way. She did, however, pull her braids forward now and then, just to frustrate him. Zsigmond, seated next to Erika, would watch her every move hoping he might catch her eye — he too was smitten.

One afternoon early in the school year, Sister Terezia, quietly distributing boxes of fresh chalk to each classroom, spotted Jozsi in action. She came from behind, yanked his ear and hissing, sent him to Brother Francis. The good brother promptly pointed him toward the basement, specifically in the direction of its smelly coal bins. Francis followed behind, carefully removing his clerical jacket, hanging it on a nail, slowly removing his shirt, carefully draping it over the jacket. By now Jozsi was humiliated and, in all honesty, more than a little scared. First: Erika had seen him being led away by the ear. Second: he was facing a muscular, half-naked priest. Rubbing at his eyes, irritated by the coal dust, he slowly inched backward. Brother Francis inched forward muttering, "No one can see us…I'm going to kick the shit out of you. Don't think about saying anything about it to anyone, ever." Then he chuckled, which made Jozsi feel even more uneasy. They each kept moving in an odd, subdued, pas de deux.

The priest sneered, "Go ahead, try to kick me, believe me, I won't complain." By now Jozsi's heels were pressed against a coal bin and his fear broke loose and galloped right straight into instinct…to survive. Afraid Brother Francis was losing his mind — being God's servant was a lot of pressure, he'd heard a priest could crack — he reached back, scooped up a fistful of coal dust, and heaved it in the man of God's face. He made one wild kick and ran, leaving his oppressor shocked, blinded, bellowing. Brother Francis doubled over, clutching his groin. Jozsi raced past Sister Terezia's office, wiping his coal-dusty hands hard on his pants, smoothing his hair pat as he returned to his seat, eyes glued to desktop, expression blank as he could manage. Eventually, after no door opened, no summons came, nothing more happened, Jozsi resumed breathing normally.

Brother Francis, true to his word, kept silent, and the two maintained a respectful, polite façade for the rest of the school year. For Jozsi, though, the incident lingered as a remarkable memory. It was the first time he had felt fear smother reason and instinct fire up, propelling him to act. He did not brag, he never told a soul, not even Ferenc. He held inside this knowledge he didn't quite understand: that whether it seemed wise or not, when physical danger appeared, his nature would be to fight to save himself, he would not be able to help it. What he didn't yet grasp was that he would come to treasure those moments when conscious thoughts scattered like startled pigeons, and a forceful wind took control. He'd feel his mind skimming across thought, triggered into direct action. That awareness would come years later. For now, he looked at himself anew, and with just a slight degree of awe.

~~~

It was a memorable year in other ways. Air raids occurred more frequently, and the local children shared sightings or word of planes shot from the sky in the vicinity of the German air base. They learned to recognize the white puffs made when ground troops fired artillery at Allied planes as they soared past on their way to bomb factories the

Germans had seized on the far side of Budapest. The B-24 bombers flew at 10,000 feet, leaving a smoke stream trailing behind. Everyone could hear them approach, propellers whirring, engines revving, often as many as two-dozen at a time chugging in tandem across the sky.

Sometimes there'd be a guard plane armed with machine guns riding alongside to chase off approaching German *Stukas* eager for an air fight. The B-24s, big and inflexible, loaded down with bombs, lumbered through the air like gigantic bumblebees. The smaller, lighter guard planes sprinted after the *Stukas*, giving the B-24s time to unload onto their targets. Occasionally a plane would get shot down, though often closer to the factories and far from their neighborhood. The children heard about most things by eavesdropping from hidden spots as adults chewed over the news of the day.

But sometimes planes crashed in their area, and you could hear and see the explosion. Occasionally, a downed plane would land without blowing up. The plane's controls might be shot out, but the pilots could still manage an emergency landing. Now and then the pilot would still be inside when the plane crashed. If the plane were descending badly, or likely to explode on impact, the pilots would lay the plane flat until they could jump out — American pilots were lucky enough to have parachutes. Downed planes could fracture into all manner of shapes and forms. The wings might separate, the tail fall off, the plane break roughly in half. Regardless of how a plane came down, crash sites always reeked of fuel. If fire broke out, the nauseating stench of burning fuel and metal, the viscious smoke, the dangerous flames, kept civilians at bay. But if there were no fire, the locals raced to downed planes, hoping to strip them of valuable materials before German soldiers showed up. Sometimes they rescued the Allied pilots. They'd stash them in their barns to protect the pilots from the Germans, who, if they got their hands on them, would torture the men mercilessly until they revealed crucial information about the position of troops, or unbroken, died.

The townspeople had no particular love of the Americans, they simply wanted the fighting to stop. They hoped the Allies could make that happen, so any act that might disrupt the German war machine, however minor, was worth the effort. And salvage from planes might bring in a few *pengo* notes. Metal and unbroken windshield glass could be sold or used. If someone found a parachute, it was an especially good day: they'd race home with the goods and make the women happy. Expensive silk parachutes could be cut up and made into shirts and underwear — warm and light, and the only new apparel anyone was likely to receive for a long time to come.

One spring afternoon as Jozsi, Ferenc and Zsigmond wandered through town, they noticed a crowd gathered around a farmer's wagon. Elbowing close, they saw the body of an American pilot laid out near the wagon. The spitting mad farmer was bellowing curse words they'd never heard before. This was not an everyday occurrence. The boys stared at the dead pilot, blood pooling around his body. As altar boys, they'd seen many dead bodies; they'd each endured the task of helping the undertaker prepare bodies for burial. But a dead pilot at the feet of an irate farmer practically in their front yard was worth full attention.

"He burned my wheat," the farmer shouted. "Never again he'll ruin my field." The farmer had clearly impaled the American with the same pitchfork he was now repeatedly jabbing into the dirt road.

Within minutes, German military police appeared and tossed the body in a truck. One German officer, speaking flawless Hungarian, harangued the farmer. "If you ever bring another dead pilot into town, *your* body will lay next to his." The farmer dropped the pitchfork, raising his hands in puzzlement. The officer brusquely shouted, "How can we interrogate a dead soldier?" The farmer retrieved his pitchfork and seething, climbed into his truck. The boys, recognizing the farmer, sidled out of the crowd and raced toward his field hoping to collect souvenirs, but the German police had already surrounded the plane and the boys trudged home disappointed.

But the fighting was escalating, so they were not disappointed for long. Days later, air raid sirens blared as the trio sprawled in Jozsi's yard following a rowdy game of chase. A dogfight broke out when German fighter planes tried to chase a pack of American bombers away from an airport the Germans had commandeered. At the sound of bullets hitting metal, followed by an ear-splitting metallic screech, the boys were up and running past the house. Not far off they could see two parachutes billowing, and the pilot attempting an emergency landing. Jozsi's grandmother shouted after, "Keep away, you *idióták*," but they were already heading down the road, following a dark smoky trail.

They found the wreck in a field near a marsh. Two soldiers,

parachutes flung aside, wildly slapped themselves, trying to extinguish sparks and flames from their uniforms. "Roll them," Jozsi yelled, not stopping to think that they themselves could get hurt. Ferenc and Zsigmond each ran to a man, while Jozsi used his jacket to help smother the flames. Then Jozsi ran around the broken-off wing, and climbed up into the plane just in time to offer his small boy's hand to a dazed soldier clumsily attempting to clamber out. Jozsi glanced over to see one of the pilots, propped up on an elbow, gasping for breath. The pilot raised his right hand forming an "o" with his thumb and index finger, moving it back and forth many times. It took Jozsi a moment to decipher the signal. "Okay." An American phrase he'd heard his sister Susan use. It meant all kinds of things to Americans: yes, all right, everything's fine, good to go. He did not think everything seemed at all okay, but maybe the pilot was just happy to be alive.

From the ground, Ferenc waved for Jozsi to jump down so they could find a place to hide the fighters. Zsigmond scrambled up next to Jozsi, saying no, they should search for souvenirs quick before the Germans arrived. In his mind, Jozsi vacillated: maybe search first, then help pilots. The parachutes on the ground were treasure enough, he thought, picturing his grandmother's face, beaming at all that material, a world of clothes hiding in the silk. But, there could be more. Snapping into action, he directed Zsigmond onto the plane to find the storage bin for unopened parachutes. Then tugging Ferenc by the arm, Jozsi raced to the open parachutes, dragging them a short distance away, toward the brushy area near the reed marsh. They did their best to fold and then camouflage the material with leaves and grass. Within seconds Zsigmond was at their side with unopened parachutes to hide. They were still tending these treasures, when from a not too great distance they heard the rumble of trucks. The boys froze, staring at each other, Jozsi silently mouthing "Germans." The Americans heard the trucks too, and looked anxiously at the boys. For a moment, no one moved, no one breathed. Then Jozsi raised his hand and with urgent gestures motioned the men toward them. Zsigmond looked at him like he was crazy, but for Jozsi there was now only one choice of action: hide the men.

The soldiers trailed their rescuers into the marsh. The boys knew secret roads in and out of the marsh, as well as the types of critters living there. They led the Americans to an old ravine; deep enough to conceal them from the German patrol they figured was speeding toward the crash site. As they huddled in silence and suspense, one of the pilots reached inside his leather flight jacket and pulled out three small chocolate bars. Jozsi's mouth watered. It had been awhile since he'd seen any kind of chocolate, much less an entire bar, much less three. The pilot put his finger to his lips as he handed them out. The boys nodded, yes, this would be their secret. Using sign language, Jozsi let the other boys know they were going to sneak back to the plane to grab the parachutes as soon as the Germans left. He indicated that the Americans should stay put, he'd be back with help.

The boys scooted toward the edge of the marsh, as low to the ground as small alligators, keeping an eye on the Germans still searching the crash site. A sudden blare of sirens startled them rigid. The Germans, raising their heads like geese at the call of their leader, left off searching, mounted their trucks and sped down the road toward town.

The boys retrieved the hidden parachutes and full of adrenaline from their adventure sprinted home. Jozsi excitedly told his father what had happened and led him to the ravine. They found crumpled reeds, but no pilots, no soldiers. Matyas called out in Hungarian and German that they were here to help. No response. Heading back out of the swamp as dusk fell, Jozsi spied twisted reeds forming an "O" and a "K." His heart skipped and he felt, for a second, as though he were already standing on top of a huge wave headed toward distant shores.

That night Jozsi lay awake wondering what had happened to the downed men, hoping they'd found their way to the orchard with its hanging market of fruit. In the morning, Jozsi found his grandmother joyfully ordering family members to stand for measurement as she organized the transformation of the pure silk parachutes into clothing for her loved ones. She hugged Jozsi, telling him how smart and good he was to rescue something of use to the whole family. So unlike his cousin Gyuri whose recent raid on a downed plane had led to the seizing of only one jacket, which just happened to be a perfect fit for Gyuri. Jozsi had been impressed by that jacket, though, and figured the next time, with the family set for underwear and undershirts, he could be exactly like Gyuri. He didn't share a word of that with his grandmother.

Pleased with himself, Jozsi didn't much mind his mother disrupting a plan-free Saturday to send him off to the family orchard to pick a barrowful of plums. The orchard was close to two miles away and he wanted company, so he pushed the wheelbarrow to Ferenc's to see if he'd want to tag along. No surprise, Zsigmond was there too. His parents lived in one of the humbler mud houses close to the edge of town. No one knew much about the family, and Zsigmond was a little vague as to why they had left Budapest in the first place, and what his father had done for work there. All they knew for sure was that Zsigmond's hair and complexion were darker than theirs. Matyas said his family was probably of Bulgarian or Yugoslavian background. Zsigmond's father had been working for Ferenc's father on the family farm before being called to serve, and Zsigmond had often been found hanging around their house. That didn't change when his father left.

Jozsi liked Zsigmond well enough, although at first, he'd been annoyed that his best friend had acquired a shadow. At least he was a cooperative shadow, easily swayed by any adventure Jozsi suggested, including searching for more downed planes in cornfields they'd pass on the way to the plum orchard. Ferenc, glad to escape his mother and her endless list of chores, grabbed the wheelbarrow as though it were essential that he be the one to push it. Also, he had big news to share. Ferenc had an uncle, Thomas, lame but able to get around. He'd heard about the stranded soldiers from Matyas, tracked them through the woods, and hidden them in his hayloft. It was not the first time he'd done this. An unnamed man would pay him and then lead the men through underground means to safety. Ferenc claimed he'd seen many pilots in the hayloft over the past months, but that Thomas had sworn him to secrecy. Since the boys had just hidden pilots in the ravine, Ferenc felt they had a right to know; plus, he'd been dying to tell them for weeks. The boys decided that given their new expertise, this was a business they should eventually go into; they'd already come to think the war would go on forever.

Now, as they passed cornfields lining both sides of the road, Zsigmond pointed out a plane, flashy in the sunlight, in a field not far from the road. With unspoken agreement, they left the wheelbarrow by the side of the road, and although there was no one in sight, snuck bent-backed up to the plane, an undamaged fighter plane, adorned with Swastikas and poised for takeoff at the head of a small cleared runway. Mysterious that there were no guards or pilots to be seen, and wonderful.

Ferenc crowed, "You were right, we *did* find something."

Jozsi had to admit it might be one of the best things they'd ever found. Unable to resist climbing into the cockpit, he crowed, "The Germans forgot it!" and pretended he was a pilot in dramatic maneuvers, imitating the sounds of *Stuka* divers in a dogfight, replicating sounds of the very gunfire they'd grown used to cringing from on the ground. His eyes scanned the cockpit, registering a series of buttons dotting the dashboard, and one big button on a handle right next to the seat. Without stopping to think, not even for one second, he pushed all of the buttons, and the world, as he knew it, went kerflooey. The front of the plane spit out a hailstorm of bullets, cracking and cutting into everything in sight. By some miracle, his two friends were standing behind a wing when Jozsi went reckless. Shocked, they dropped flat to the ground, hands over their heads and ears. Jozsi's hand sprang off the big button, and then followed a great silence. His ears felt like someone had poured mud into them. He was shaking. Within seconds, they were surrounded by German troops with machine guns pointed hard fast at the boys. Jozsi's head looked little and vulnerable in the cockpit window. He raised his shoulders and held his hands up with an expression of, "Uh-oh, what did I do?"

The soldiers yelled at the boys while shoving them into a truck, glaring as though they were criminals rather than terrified kids. Two of them, guns still at the ready, climbed in back with the boys. The truck fired up and drove to a hanger a few miles further down the road.

Ferenc whispered to Jozsi, "Your mother is going to be mad if you don't bring the plums home. Or the wheelbarrow."

"We will be lucky if we even *get* home," Jozsi whispered back. One soldier jerked his gun, shushing them. Ferenc paled, his lips clamped shut. Zsigmond stared open-mouthed at the machine guns, as though he wanted to lick them.

The three were told to stand in front of a building and wait for a summons from the commanding officer. An hour passed. They each imagined facing a firing squad. They each pushed the thought aside. They dared not speak. Finally, a German guard grunted a few harsh words and lined them up in front of the commanding officer's desk. The office was humble, with a temporary feel. Hitler's portrait hung on the wall. Propped on the desk was a small framed photograph of a woman. Jozsi motioned in sign language the equivalent of: "Look, what a beautiful woman. This is your wife?" The officer nodded yes, but did not smile or speak. Ferenc and Zsigmond shot horrified glances his way, as if to say, "We are about to die and you are admiring our killer's *wife?*" Jozsi didn't notice. He concentrated on envisioning his mother smacking him with a broom for having lost the wheelbarrow. He pictured their kitchen, his grandmother peeling carrots with her favorite paring knife. These thoughts of normal life calmed his nerves and to look at him, you'd never have known he was as terrified as the others. His piercing blue eyes focused on the line where the far wall met the floor, his face held an oddly commanding expression.

The officer, studying a sheaf of papers on his desk, tormented them with silence a while longer. The nerve of the boy with the blue eyes impressed him; he wished his own son had half that boy's balls. Finally, he inhaled deeply, stood, and in Hungarian screamed at them for being communist infiltrators and spies working for the Russians. Jozsi was as scared as he'd been while shooting up the field, though apparently not quite as scared as Zsigmond, whose pants were instantly pee-stained. Jozsi didn't dare raise his eyes until he heard the clunk of metal smacking against the desk. He peered up just enough to see a service revolver. The officer paused until he'd seen all three boys eye the gun. More calmly, he said, "Gentlemen, I have eight rounds in this pistol. You can attack me, try to kill me if you dare, but let me assure you, I'll use all eight rounds before I give up, and I guarantee at least one of you will die before I do."

Jozsi gulped. Voice shaking, he said, "No, sir, we meant no harm," and tumbling out of his mouth came words about his mother, the plums, the unexpected finding of the plane, a young boy's foolish curiosity, a fear of being killed by his mother, until finally he ran out of words.

The officer muttered something about punishing the inept guards who'd left the plane and then, face softening, reached into a drawer and pulled out three hefty German bars of chocolate, even larger than the ones the pilots had shared. As he handed them out, he suggested the boys stay out of corn fields from then on, and sharply commanded the guards who'd brought them in to collect the wheelbarrow, chauffeur the boys to the orchard and fill the wheelbarrow chock full. The boys watched, eating their chocolate bars, still shaken and amazed by everything that had happened since Jozsi pushed all those buttons on the plane. After that Jozsi still hated the Germans, though with a touch of moderation. He'd learned something that was so confusing it made him uneasy: even enemies can be human.

Jozsi was just settling into his summer routine when, arriving home for supper one evening, his sisters' subdued manner and sly glances around the table let him know something was afoot. After a prayer had been said, the girls gestured for him to help himself first. He was now certain he must be in trouble and they were just taking pity. All he could think was that his father had found out that he and Ferenc had urinated on the old science teacher's tulips the day before. This could be bad. Jozsi picked at his food. His father was tolerant of boyish antics, but disrespecting elders fell on the wrong side of the tolerance line. Jozsi hadn't even had to pee that bad, it was Ferenc who'd insisted on watering the tulips. After supper, his father turned to his young son, "We want you to know that we all love you." Jozsi nodded yes, but found his mind wandering to the Bible story about Jozsef's brothers selling him to merchants in the desert. With a serious, but still loving expression, Jozsi's father continued, "You know, there are more and more bombers, things will likely get worse in the weeks to come. To keep you safe, we think it would be best to send you away for the summer. You'll be in the country, with the Toths." Ah, it was a something for-his-own-good, not a punishment, though there certainly had been times in the past when one could have been mistaken for the other.

Although Jozsi had been to the Toth farm many times, the thought of leaving his friends for the whole summer was not a happy one. And oddly, he felt reluctant to leave his five sisters and older brother, most still living at home, all bossing him around and annoying as could be. Still, he was used to them. On the other hand, he'd never stayed at the Toths for such a long stretch, and he liked doing new things. Mr. and Mrs. Toth were very fond of him, and if he were lucky, perhaps the voluptuous Rebeka would show him her breasts. She'd hinted she might the last time he'd visited, but sadly, this had not come to pass. Jozsi figured she must be sixteen by now and probably her breasts grown even larger. He started to cheer up.

And there was Bandi. During World War One, Mr. Toth had served as Matyas's assistant in the Hungarian Cavalry. Toth was what everyone called him, what his first name was few knew. He'd cared for Matyas's horses all through the war and still had Bandi, Matyas' favorite horse of all. The Toth farm was a working farm, chores a part of the daily routine. When Jozsi visited, he was given the enjoyable task of caring for Bandi, who was by then quite old but still game for wandering the fields and forest. Jozsi couldn't exactly do much with him, no galloping, no jumping over tree limbs. But he could sit on his back and pretend to be a soldier or cowboy. The horse appreciated that Jozsi was generous with carrots and a good swatter of pesky flies and was happy to roam wherever Jozsi wanted.

Matyas decided to bring Jozsi to the farm the following Saturday, so he and the boys had much to pack in before then. The others' obvious jealousy over his leaving town, without his family, and for the whole summer, transformed any doubts about this exile. He was lucky. Now he couldn't wait to go away and then come back. Maybe he would sit on the highest bank, like Jancsi did, and tell tales of his adventures out among the cows, horses, pigs, and rows of vegetables; the many rows where he might happen upon Rebeka, bent low, looking for potatoes or onions. His summer plans grew more appealing by the hour.

Stirred by Jozsi's mention of Rebeka and her ripe hanging fruit, the boys raced with extra vigor up the stream, their daily ritual to see who could reach the bridge first. Ferenc had the highest score. Jozsi, panting as he struggled to pass him, noticed the water turning red behind his friend and called for him to stop. The boys gathered around as Ferenc plopped down on the riverbank. Indeed, a piece of glass had cut deep into his heel. Ferenc's face went white at the sight of so much blood, and he looked a little woozy. The other boys, most of them the sons of local farmers, weren't fazed by blood as long as it wasn't theirs — they'd seen plenty on the farm. But no one had any useful ideas for staunching its flow. Jozsi pulled off his shirt, tying it as tightly around the heel as he could. He helped Ferenc up, serving as a human crutch as they hobbled up to the road. Aware that all of the local doctors were gone, serving at the front, Jozsi guided them toward the veterinarian's office. It was lunch hour; the road was peaceful, devoid of traffic. They moved slowly, it seemed to take forever to get there.

Doctor Gazsi was often out of his office, treating large animals at various farms, but fortunately for Ferenc, he happened to have come home for lunch. They sat in his waiting area, alongside a woman they recognized but did not know, and a parrot that must once have belonged to a foul-mouthed soldier, judging from the commands and curses it periodically squawked. The woman blushed and carefully studied her feet.

When Doctor Gazsi appeared, he went straight to the boys, perhaps because there was now a good bit of blood dripping onto his floor. He tsked and mumbled while he examined the foot. Finally, he looked up at Ferenc. "You know, I treat animals as a rule, not humans?"

Jozsi, whose humor was wryer than that of his peers, leaned in to assure Doctor Gazsi that Ferenc would not know the difference. Ferenc gave him the hairy eyeball, but was too relieved at the presence of an adult with clean hands and a medicinal scent to do more. Medical supplies were scarce, so Doctor Gazsi handed Jozsi a pair of scissors and sent him out to find a long, strong horsehair to use for sewing up the gashed heel. Jozsi trotted down the road to the tavern where he knew the local farmers usually brought their wagons during lunchtime. Wanting to have a good supply, he cut off enough hairs to sew up the heels of a score of wounded soldiers. Doctor Gazsi, amused, thanked him for his thoroughness and offered to share the wealth. "Maybe you can make a blanket." Jozsi was certain the doctor was making fun of him, but he didn't care. He just wanted to get his wounded friend home in one piece, hopefully without Ferenc's mother noticing. Lately she blamed Jozsi every time the boys got in trouble. As they approached the house, they spotted Ferenc's mother out back, walking toward the smoke house. Jozsi quietly settled Ferenc on a chair in the empty kitchen and fled.

~~~

His day of departure finally arrived, and Jozsi was up like a shot soon after dawn. He ran to catch Ferenc early in his daily chores, out in the rabbit hut feeding their bunnies. Jozsi wanted to say a proper good-bye to his friend, out of view of his sisters who the last couple of days looked on the verge of tears every time they laid eyes on him. He also wanted to avoid Ferenc's mother, who was reported to have spat out something about "that unruly hooligan," as she fussed over the injured foot. The boys gave each other a quick hug, stood back like grown men, and exchanged their first serious handshake. That goodbye went much better than the one with his sisters. They fluttered around him, wiping their eyes as he picked up his suitcase and walked out of the house looking, and suddenly feeling, forlorn as an abandoned child. The way they carried on made him wonder if they knew something he didn't.

At least he and his father were headed to the train station and not the town square. He had gotten used to seeing men standing in front of the police station in the square, waiting to be picked up by army trucks that bounced and joggled them all the way to the Russian front. He knew he was too young for that to happen, so he wondered why exactly the girls were so sad.

Before Jozsi had time to ponder further, Matyas caught up with him and grabbed his free hand. Relieved at the touch, Jozsi forced himself to let go after a few steps in case anyone was watching. He did not want to look like a small boy who needed minding. But as they started into the woods toward the train station, entering the trail they'd follow for nearly a mile, a trail that wandered through the marsh created by the *Rakos* River, his father again took his hand, and this time Jozsi held on tight.

The train clanged into the station and they lined up along with other passengers toting suitcases and backpacks, and took their turn climbing up the metal stairs. Matyas explained that the trip might take longer than usual because of air raids. Two hours could stretch to five, even ten, but not to worry, eventually they'd get there. Jozsi had only a vague idea where Russia was, and knew nothing of what the battlefront parameters might be, but the thought that they might pass through battlefields perked him up, and he was quick to grab a window seat in case he had a chance to see action.

The train pulled out, and Matyas opened his suitcase to surprise Jozsi with his favorite raspberry drink; he'd taken the time to make it fresh that morning. Jozsi leaned against his dad, feeling content and loved. Once they arrived, the Toths would swarm around Matyas, and the day after that, his father would be back on the train, on his way home. Jozsi would enjoy having him all to himself for now.

The train ran smoothly for a time, but then screeched to a jerking halt. An agitated conductor burst into the compartment shouting and pointing out the window, "Air raid, air raid. Take cover in the field!" Within seconds, the passengers scrambled down the stairs, suitcases abandoned, as all raced to the cornfields and flung themselves on the ground. All but Matyas who stood like a statue watching the planes fly overhead. Jozsi tugged on his pants leg, but Matyas, seeming almost in a trance, pointed at the lines of vapor trailing the American planes. He spoke calmly. "They must be heading to Budapest to bomb the war factories." Jozsi was not worried. Though their house was a brief bus ride from Budapest, the war factories were nowhere near their side of the city, and his father had assured him the bombers wouldn't waste ammunition on a civilian train. So Jozsi lay flat on his back, unafraid but excited, content to imagine bullets whizzing by their train windows in the hours to come. Matyas eventually sat next to him, silently staring into the distance, his eyes as piercing and blue as his son's; his stoic expression that of a man weathered by the knowledge of the immense variety of brutal things human beings can do to each other.

3

Kimchi and Torte

Jozsi shook himself free of his daydreams. Homesickness for family, for childhood must be the reason his mind kept bringing him to the past. These yearnings for his former life surfaced now and then, unbidden, despite having come of age wanting to present his backside to Hungary as quickly as possible. The Russians and their stifling, mind-numbing soul-killing brand of communism had taken his natural interest in the world and burnished it into a crusade. He'd rather crawl in a coffin and die than live under their thumb. He'd rather wake up on a cave floor, with muscles tight and aching. Yes, he'd rather be right here.

Now he was wide awake, but the day was still quiet and dark. He sat up, reaching into his pocket to take out a small canvas waterproof pouch. It held a cyanide pill the size of an aspirin. He unscrewed the top and looked in, but it was still too dark to see. He gently shook the pouch and felt the slight weight of it shift. He appreciated that his fate could quite possibly be up to him. The officers had been very clear: get caught, you will be interrogated. You don't want to suffer, there's no shame in that. You don't want to betray your comrades, a solution exists. Pop the pill and within seconds you're gone. Seconds, they'd promised, without offering any details. Normally curious, he'd avoided finding out what came next. Was it your heart? Foam bubbling out of the corners of your mouth? Searing pain as all systems failed? Seconds was the promise, he left it at that. Anyway, he had no intention of swallowing the pill, no fear of being captured, no time for that kind of mishap: he hadn't come this far from Hungary to die. He hadn't hiked and sweated and spent sleep-deprived nights on cave floors, only to cash it in here, in this insane, wretched country. No. Korea was just another stop along the way.

Laci, on the other hand, had no big plans beyond inhaling the next meal, fondling the closest available piece of ass, and finding a target at which to aim. The man loved to shoot. As if reading Jozsi's mind, Laci rolled over, half-asleep, and reached for his rifle. Jozsi only had a .45 Colt automatic pistol, but was packing enough rounds of ammunition to scare the shit right out of any border patrol. He'd cede Laci one advantage: he had the aim. Even without the rifle's high-power telescopic sight, Laci could blow the head off a fly at 100 yards. But Jozsi had the brains. No question. He screwed the top back on his death kit and idly fingered the pouch, then tucked it in his pocket. He rose to a crawl position, inched his way forward, flattened, and lay with chin on hands, so he could comfortably peer out from the cave they were, for the moment, calling home.

Finally, the sun began to rise behind the ridge where they hid, allowing them extra protection. They couldn't be seen from the base below or the officers' quarters. The only object between them and those quarters was an outhouse which, assuming the North Korean Army was as devoted to rank as any other, they figured was officers only.

"We better hope Agent Kimchi has to dump a load and soon." Jozsi turned to Laci, who he'd heard rustling behind him.

Laci sat up, rubbing his face hard with his palms. He sighed. "I hope he gets the runs."

"No," Jozsi insisted, "That would be a mess. Hope for a good solid turd."

They readied their backpacks, in optimistic faith they wouldn't have to stay another night; an optimism based on the very track record that had made the CID so determined to employ these particular two men.

"How many border guards have we sent to their makers so far?" Laci asked, poking and probing every inch of his rifle with a gun-cleaning patch.

"You won't get far in this world keeping track of those numbers." Jozsi handed Laci his Colt for cleaning, just to give him something more to do. "Not in the next one either," he added, smiling grimly. Though he was good at it, Jozsi in no way enjoyed killing. His cold steel resolve made it possible, but nightmares alerted him to his soul's rebellion.

During their months in Korea, they'd crossed the border several times. Shot more than a few guards. Swooped up a respectable number of agents. They'd planted relay stations all over the mountains so the intelligence community could transmit messages to agents in the field. Due to the intense weather extremes, a large number of relay stations had to be checked on a rotational basis, repairs and replacements a regular occurrence. The two men were used to quickly scoping out their surroundings to determine the wherefores of the task at hand, and they'd gotten quicker and better at booby-trapping the camouflaged transmitters. At first, it was exciting, but once they'd gotten the hang of the process, it became tedious. Their main satisfaction lay in knowing that should any North Korean soldiers spot the equipment and pick it up for further investigation, *ka-boom* — anyone within a twenty-foot radius stood a solid chance of dying. But not them, they'd be long gone. They never met any of the turncoat North Korean agents, nor did they care to; what happened to the money they left for those helping the Americans was no concern of theirs.

The sun inched higher. It was nearly six in the morning and according to their knowledge of the human body, the officers would soon begin taking turns trudging to and from the outhouse. They were ready for Kimchi, his picture flashed before their eyes hundreds of times before they'd left the camp.

"I started seeing that asshole's face on the bodies of bunnies," Laci said. An American soldier had given him a copy of *Playboy* that he treasured.

"He better not be bound up," Jozsi said fretfully.

"Bound?"

Jozsi sighed, and with an exasperated look imitated the sounds of constipation.

"Ah," Laci nodded, and they again fell into watchful silence. After a time, the officers' back door opened, a man's head poked out, peered around, disappeared inside. The door closed behind him. A few more times, the door opened, men came out, or not, none of them wearing the right face. They waited.

Jozsi checked the sun's position. "They could be searching for us soon. They'll be expecting to hear from the guard station, those two border guards, and as you may remember, they no longer draw breath. As soon as they send anyone out there, we'll be about as safe as truffles at a pig farm."

The back door again opened, they glanced at the man striding toward the outhouse and at each other, both nodding a single time. At long last…Kimchi. Jozsi grinned, "Finally. Our all-expenses-paid ticket to Hong Kong is close at hand." He felt the shift that always occurred just before instinct took over and plunged him into action. Such a strange feeling. He didn't call it up, it just came. One minute he'd feel like himself, the next a more primitive being — visceral, feral and fearless.

They lowered down and scrabbled over the hard ground, moving fast but carefully, till they were hunched behind the outhouse, listening hard, trying to hear him do his business. Finished, with pants down was ideal. Hoping it was just the right moment, in one motion, Jozsi sprang forward and ripped the door open. Kimchi was mid-rise, pulling up his pants. Jozsi shoved him back on the seat and held the .45 to his temple as Laci crammed in, whipped a roll of tape from his pocket and taped the agent's mouth. As they checked to see if anyone else was coming toward the outhouse, the agent lunged forward, but Laci grabbed him by his nuts.

"You want die?" he squeezed. They'd been told the agent spoke some English. Apparently, he did, and he definitely understood the language of hand. He moaned, inhaled sharply, cooperated fully. Anything to ease the pain — Laci had huge, strong farmer's hands. "I know how to milk the cows," he'd say when they saw a particularly well-endowed woman, flexing his hands for emphasis.

They hustled Kimchi up past the cave. Without exchanging a word, they began hiking the route they'd been given by agents who'd left food, water, and medication in another cave located on a very high ridge a couple of hours hike away. After they'd settled the wary North Korean in the back of that cave, they fed him, hoping it would calm him down. They'd assured Kimchi they weren't going to kill him, but doling out some food, crap as it was, served as persuasive reinforcement. They left him tied like a bull calf, and hunkered down by the opening of the cave to watch for any search patrols on the move.

Jozsi spoke softly, so his words wouldn't reach the back of the cave. "I hope to hell they gave us accurate information about the dogs." They'd been told the North Koreans currently had most of their tracking dogs, sharp-nosed German Shepherds, spread along the border. From their vantage point the men could see several trails, and thus far no activity disturbed the peaceful vista. There were rice paddies in the far distance, and rice paddies meant bodies coming to tend them, but they were far enough away so it shouldn't be a problem unless some paddy worker happened to be packing a serious pair of binoculars.

Laci, glancing back, wondered in a whisper if the North Korean agent they'd pinched believed in his own cause. Wasn't it better to be a patriot for your country? A nobler activity than spying, stealing, even killing just to benefit your stateless situation and your own self? Jozsi realized that somewhere inside that farm boy heart, his comrade-in-arms wanted to believe in something and still felt a stinging guilt for having abandoned their homeland.

Jozsi shrugged, "We do it for ourselves because that's all we have. We lost our country, my friend. We'd have been executed if we'd stayed. What good is that cause?"

~~~

In 1956, they'd met in an apartment in Gyor. The Russians had just smashed the Revolution, and Jozsi was on the run from the Russians, who had repressed his homeland for so many years.

Sandor, Jozsi's rail-thin CIA contact, had provided him with an address in Gyor, and a man's name, and a password to say to the man… if, that is, Jozsi could manage to get out of Budapest in one piece. Laci Botlo was the man in the apartment, in hiding having fled the farm he'd inherited from his father. The Botlo farm was only an hour from the city limits, but for Laci, that was a world away. He missed his fields and ravines, the Hungarian Grey cattle with their long majestic horns. He missed the routine of chores, the smell of the barn, the sound of ducks flapping across the small pond.

Laci's father, an outspoken anti-communist, had always predicted no good would come of the blasted commies, as he called them. He'd had the good fortune to die in his sleep at a ripe old age, a couple of years before the Russians invaded with their tanks and brutality. At some point leading up to the Hungarian Revolution, his youngest son Laci had come to the attention of certain underground agents looking for a brawny, brave farmer located near the Austrian border. One willing to hide agents in his barn, feed them, and smuggle them to or from the border in the back of his wagon. One willing to kill if need be. Laci had thrown himself into this new line of work, knowing his father would have proudly cheered him on. Eventually Sandor had dealings with Laci as well as with Jozsi, and matchmaker that he was, envisioned the two as having the makings of a good team. They were both on "lists," which meant they had to make a run for it, so it made sense to connect them. He'd aimed Jozsi in Laci's direction figuring their odds were better together than alone.

Since the morning that Laci had answered Jozsi's knock at his door, the two had been nearly inseparable. After hearing the given password of "rodnas" (Sandor backward), Laci threw wide the door and warmly welcomed his visitor. Like Jozsi, he was in his early twenties, large-boned, with an easy smile, bushy brows, and huge hands, which he clasped around both of Jozsi's in greeting, pulling him inside at the same time, letting go only to grab Jozsi's bag and quickly close the door behind them.

"I've been waiting for you all morning," Laci said, "I was starting to wonder. What kept you?"

"As a rule, I shoot ten Russians before breakfast, but the last one kept me waiting!"

Laci grinned, "Don't let it happen again." They shook hands again and gave each other a warm hug, as though twins separated at birth. He told Jozsi they had better get the hell out of there before the newly appointed police came looking for him.

"What happened to the old police?"

Laci lightly punched his arm, "That's *exactly* why they're looking for me!" He scanned the apartment one final time, "The bastards had it coming. AVO secret police informants," he spat, grabbing his bag and a long metal rod, and beckoning Jozsi to follow. As they clattered down the stairs, he announced there was a special reserved car waiting, but that Jozsi should not ask questions or say a word. A silver Russian *Gaz Pobeda* sat in a sunny spot on the other side of the street. Laci popped the locked driver's side door with the rod, unlocked the passenger door, and set about hotwiring the ignition. He was a little clumsy and slow; within moments, a middle-aged man in a suit, attaché case in hand, came running out of a building screaming that Laci was a thief. All Jozsi could think to do was jump out of the car, stick his .38 against the man's head, and ask for his car keys...and while he was at it, his apartment keys as well. Laci took the keys, thanking the man and promising he'd mail them back. As they pulled away from the curb, the man pleaded, "Take care of my car! I've only had it a week." Laci called out the window, "Promise we'll change the oil every five thousand miles," and stepped on the gas. Soon they were on the main road, speeding out of town.

"It's good to have a Russian car, no?" Laci nodded, pleased with himself.

"Unless we get caught," Jozsi replied.

"That's the first time I ever broke into a car," he grinned. "Not too bad."

"You know, Laci, in Budapest we don't have the luxury of negotiating with the owner. If you can't hotwire a car in two seconds, you better stay on the farm because you're likely to be shot."

"You want to go with them?" Laci nodded toward a young couple pulling a small wagon piled high with suitcases. "Maybe they'll let you ride up top." Jozsi saw his point and withheld further observations as they headed west toward the border.

A steady stream of people walked the same road, many with young children, or elderly parents, or both, some pushing baby carriages filled with babies or belongings, they couldn't always tell. As the men drove, more and more Hungarians appeared, all fleeing the dire circumstances in their occupied country. The line of bodies stretched out of sight on either side of the road. People walked in pairs, carrying wicker baskets or round metal washtubs between them, overflowing with clothing or kitchen goods or bedding. Men carted duffle bags like giant stuffed sausages on their shoulders. Suitcases and hatboxes and satchels and knapsacks were wheeled in barrows or carried or dragged. Some people had nothing but the clothes on their back.

Jozsi noticed a small girl, maybe eight, hair covered by a red, white and green scarf — the Hungarian flag's colors: red for strength, white for faithfulness, green for hope. Although now the colors meant something different: red for the blood spilled for the fatherland, white for freedom, green for the land. The girl clutched a doll to her chest. A slightly taller boy trudged next to her, hugging a metal milk container. Jozsi noticed a grandmotherly figure that could have been his own *nagyanya* Alida, a white string bag holding clothes in one hand, a walking stick in the other propelling her forward. So many faces tugged at his heart. They passed a man much like his father, striding purposefully, posture perfect, chiseled jaw set to the future whatever it might be, his wife and children struggling to keep up. Jozsi could have wept, but he swallowed his tears, they'd only slow him down, and like all the others moving with this particular tide, he couldn't afford to indulge in emotion.

Young or old, the refugees flowed forward, glancing at their fine, shiny ride as it passed. The kids noticed only the clean newness of the vehicle; the anxious adults hoped it wasn't the AVO coming after them. Prison, torture, death were real options should they be caught up in the Russian net. But even if they'd been guaranteed a safe return to their homes, promised they could live free, it was crystal clear that a life under Russian rule would not be free. They moved on, toward what they did not know.

Laci veered off the main road when he spotted three large oaks just past a small market Sandor had told him to look for. From there, they were to locate a dirt road that followed along a brook. They were seeking a farmer Sandor knew of who might be able to take them over the border with little difficulty. Jozsi said Sandor had mentioned the man and the farmhouse to him as well, and added that he'd cautioned Jozsi to keep a watchful eye on the guy. Laci replied, "You know, this is what I don't like about Sandor, he only tells me part of the story." Jozsi assured him, "This is why I'm here."

They spied the brook, and drove about a half mile down the dirt road when they spotted a white stucco house with a gray thatched roof fitting Sandor's description. The owner came to the kitchen door with a shotgun tucked loosely under his arm. He looked like a typical Hungarian farmer: stubby, with a thick mustache, big belly pressing against his overalls. "What do you want?" he shouted from the doorway.

Laci shouted back, "Rodnas sent us," and walking toward the farmer, said more quietly, "You can help us cross the border?"

"If you have enough money, many things can be arranged. Come!" He headed toward the large barn, half-turning to keep them in view as they followed — this was not a time when a person turned their back on anyone except perhaps their own mother. Perhaps not even her. The AVH had secret policed the country into a state of paranoia and fear, turning citizen against citizen, ripping communities and families apart.

The barn held several mostly empty stalls, though a horse and two cows occupied a few. In the back corner stood a small round table, circled by a couple of chairs and an upended wine crate meant to serve as a seat. The farmer took the chair against the far wall and leaned back, saying, "You have firearms? I won't risk taking you across if you're holding weapons." Exchanging a glance, the two assured him no, they were not violent people; they were in fact desperate to get away from violence.

"We had no time to find guns," Jozsi said earnestly. The farmer simply said, "I check." He told Laci to move away while he patted Jozsi, keeping an eye on Laci the whole time. Then he checked Laci. Finally, he sat and reached to the side, lifted the lid of a box, pulled out a bottle of *palinka* and took a swig. He didn't offer to share.

"So, we do business," he said, wiping his mouth. Jozsi served as negotiator. Within minutes, the farmer agreed to accept ten thousand *forints* up front, and ten thousand more when they made it across the Austrian border. Sandor had managed to provide each refugee with a thick envelope packed with *forints*. Jozsi excused himself to run to the car for the money, and handed him the first installment, the second to Laci. They shook hands with the farmer, Laci looking longingly back at the bottle of *palinka* as they left the barn.

The evening was gray and foggy. The farmer had them park the stolen car under a huge willow tree behind the barn. They grabbed what little baggage they'd brought and headed where he pointed, toward a path into the woods. He trailed behind, until Jozsi rearranged the order, putting the farmer between them. No sense giving him an easy opportunity to slaughter them both from behind. The farmer understood this without explanation. Many things were left unsaid in those times.

In the distance, they heard machine gun fire. The farmer told them Russian guards were set up along the border, blocking roads, shooting escapees. They reached a dry riverbed and continued on for another half hour until they came to a river too wide and deep to wade across. By then, the fog had dissipated and they could make out the border police tower, its searchlight sweeping back and forth.

The farmer stopped, "Here you are. Just cross the bridge and you're in Austria." He held out his hand for the remaining ten thousand *forints*.

Jozsi shook his head. "You get paid when we are safely *in* Austria. Until then, nothing more."

The farmer raised and aimed his shotgun at him, and calmly said, "You boys pay now." Laci reached into his pocket and started counting the money. "Don't bother," the farmer said sharply. "Just hand that big fat stack over to Uncle Miska." He aimed the gun at Laci, while trying to keep an eye on Jozsi, who had inched closer during the count. Miska held out his open palm, and in doing so, allowed the shotgun nozzle to drift. Laci fumbled, letting *forints* fall to the ground, and in the second the farmer's eyes followed the *forints*, Jozsi reached behind his back for the .38 tucked in his waistband. He'd left it in the car with the *forints*. By the time that Uncle Miska had raised his eyes from the ground, Jozsi was holding the .38 a centimeter from the man's right ear.

Miska nervously licked his lips. Laci grabbed Miska's shotgun and told him to empty his pockets. There were a lot of pockets in those overalls and it took some doing, but eventually a wad of *forints* and several pieces of jewelry changed hands. Laci pocketed the haul while the farmer glared.

"Afraid to leave your loot home?" Jozsi asked, pleased by this unexpected plunder. He pressed the .38 into Miska's back. "Let's go. Now. Austria!" And with a lot of swearing, Uncle Miska led them back into the ravine. Laci protested; they were switching direction, why?

"Times are hard," Miska said, by way of explanation.

Jozsi snapped, "Where are you leading us? If you want to live, don't screw around."

Miska's words tumbled over each other as he confessed he had been planning to send them straight to the Russian guards. Why not? The Russian Army paid him by the head. A man has to eat. He yammered on… Of course, sometimes he did help people across, but this was a very bad stretch, he was truly desperate. He could no longer afford to have a barn full of animals; didn't they notice the empty stalls, stalls that were once full of livestock. He could barely feed the few animals remaining. And of course, he too needed food. Yes, a man needed to eat. And yes, now he was leading them across the border, absolutely, yes, yes. Finally, he ran out of breath and fell silent.

"Fucking Sandor," Laci muttered.

Jozsi shrugged, "He warned us to be careful."

"Fucking Sandor," Laci spat.

By this time, it was close to eight, and though the fog had evaporated, the sky was heavy with clouds, the night so dark they could barely see where their boots were landing. After a time, Miska, huffing and puffing with exertion and nerves, guided them to a deserted bridge. They walked over the river, the only sound water slapping bridge supports, and moved on into Austria. They hoped.

Soon headlights appeared in the distance, bouncing crazily along a bumpy road and heading in their direction. Laci, nervous, suggested they lay in the brush till the lights moved away.

The farmer scoffed. "Don't bother. That's the Austrian border patrol. That's what you want."

Jozsi, surprisingly polite given his irritation said, "Do forgive my not taking your word on that." But before they could hide, the headlights veered off in a different direction. They trekked further, and coming around a curve, saw a mass of lights far in the distance. Jozsi decided on a leap of faith. "We've had enough of you," he swung Miska around by the arm and shoved him in the opposite direction. "If I ever see you again, I'll blow your head off." The farmer lumbered away, muttering expletives as the fleeing Hungarians trotted toward the lights.

Many yards later, Laci tossed the farmer's shotgun away. "Enough of that. Too big to hide, too heavy to carry." And then a little wistfully, "That little gun of yours came in handy twice today. Someday, I would like to own one myself."

Jozsi reached behind his back and handed the .38 to his new friend. "Now you do." Laci thanked him and tucked it behind his own back, a big smile on his face.

On their way toward the lights, wind broke up the solid bank of clouds and a half moon appeared, blinking between the fast-moving cloud clumps. As they walked, they inventoried the treasures extracted from Uncle Miska. A hundred thousand *forints* to divide, and a variety of tasty rings, necklaces, and earrings which they agreed to sell as soon as they reached Vienna. They paused to stash their loot in various places in their clothes and boots, which was a good thing, because not ten minutes later, an Austrian patrol jeep's headlights lit on them when it turned onto the road. Questioned as to what direction they'd come from and where they'd crossed the bridge, the two answered as best they could in their school-taught German. One of the guards asked if they had weapons. Laci handed over the .38 service revolver. To his shock, the guard immediately handcuffed and arrested him for having flouted the Geneva Convention rule against "entering armed into a neutral country."

They piled into the jeep. "At least we don't have to walk anymore," Jozsi sighed, relaxing as best a person could in a bouncing jeep.

"Have you ever heard of that law before?" Laci asked. Jozsi nodded yes. First shock, then anger registered on Laci's face. "Son of a bitch. Why didn't you just throw it away?"

Jozsi reached over to pat his knee. "We might have needed it." Laci sighed. Jozsi assured him, "Before they execute you, I will bring you some very aged *palinka*." They continued on, the jeep bouncing less as they turned onto a bigger road, Laci grumbling the whole way into the city.

Once in Eisenstadt, emigration officers handled their papers, glancing at them. At the center, scores of Hungarian refugees and their belongings were spread out across the floor of a large hall, waiting to be processed and moved on to make room for new arrivals. Laci was taken off to jail where he ended up having more room to breathe than Jozsi, who was ushered into the packed hall.

Meanwhile, Jozsi lobbied for a phone and after a long wait, was able to call Sandor. He left a message with an underling: they'd reached Eisenstadt, he'd try to get Laci out of jail and would stay in the vicinity of the town hall hoping for Sandor or someone he sent to appear. Jozsi then used his powers of persuasion to convince the Austrian guards that after what their country had been through at the hands of the communists, no Hungarian refugee would give up a gun until absolutely certain he was in neutral Austrian hands. The police finally agreed to let Laci go. They needed the room: there were many more Hungarians lined up outside the station waiting to be booked for the same reason. The money that changed hands was no doubt helpful in Laci's release.

Outside, Jozsi told Laci how lucky he was to have met someone like himself, and that he hoped someday Laci would be able to offer the same kind of help to him.

Laci sputtered, "Bullshit! You gave me the gun, you knew it would get me in trouble. You let the police handcuff me, throw me in jail and now you come around big hero. What do you want me to do? Kiss your ass?"

"It would be a good place to start," Jozsi laughed.

~~~

Late the following morning the two sat on a bench in a small park next to the town hall. The sunshine was welcome, as was having nothing to do and no particular place to go. Suddenly from behind the bench, a slight cough. They swiveled their heads. Sandor Nagy — skinny, nearly six feet tall, dirty blond hair, blue-gray eyes — stood behind them. His small mouth was pulled into a polite tight smile. He wore a white shirt, dark brown fighter jacket and brown pants.

"You two getting along?" he asked, raising his hand like an orchestra conductor motioning them up off the bench. They rose, though Laci lingered for a beat, still miffed. But by mid-afternoon, they were in better moods, and on their way to Vienna. Sandor explained they first had to stop and check into a refugee center on the way to pick up official papers, after which they could move about the city as they pleased. He drove them to Klosterneuburg and both registered, receiving temporary resident permits. Following that, on to Vienna, where he checked them into a nice hotel. He handed them each a hundred dollars for spending money and told them he had other matters to attend to, but would return as soon as possible.

Left to their own devices, they headed to the local bank and exchanged what was left of their Hungarian currency for dollars. It turned out that they were among the last allowed to do so; the Austrian banks, afraid the Hungarian currency would collapse, soon ceased providing such fiscal convenience. The two pocketed nearly five hundred dollars apiece, a lot of money— the average worker earned about fifty dollars a month. Laci was beside himself with joy. After that, they found a jewelry store. The owner offered them two hundred dollars for the jewelry they'd stolen off Uncle Miska. Jozsi borrowed a page from Miska and drowned the man in words, telling him he couldn't possibly accept that paltry a sum. The jewels had been in the family for generations, and he didn't want to sell, and he wouldn't even think of it, but he was desperate for money for his mother who was ill and needed medicine. The jeweler rolled his eyes, added another hundred dollars to the offer and they shook hands on the deal.

Outside the shop, Laci gave Jozsi a funny look, "Why didn't I think to do that?"

"Maybe you never had a mother." Jozsi grinned.

They had money to burn and time on their hands and they were in Vienna. They wandered the streets for hours, admiring the majestic buildings and boulevards, enjoying the sense of abundance and happiness and warmth that seemed to pour off the Austrian people. Their years of life in the bleak, repressive world that Hungary had become under the Russians had stifled all but the most resilient feelings of joy and hope in these two young men. Here, suddenly, they felt giddy with both.

The sensation of not having to look over their shoulders gave them a strange sense of emotional vertigo. Both were so used to speculating as to what nearby person might be watching or eavesdropping, they couldn't entirely shake the feeling of living in a glass cage. It had been so long since they'd been able to trust any but their closest family and friends. And even then, you never knew for certain what private pressure someone might be under, what guilty secret the authorities could use to turn a person into a spy. To be able to speak frankly to each other, to be able to speak freely anywhere they stood, was almost too alien to absorb. They saw others walking the streets with similarly dazed smiles. Hungarian refugees were streaming over the border, and everywhere in Vienna it felt that they were being welcomed and warmly invited into a place where they stood a chance at a new beginning.

"Freedom," Jozsi said, standing in front of a café window admiring a shelf display of *strudel*, nut-covered *beugel*, puffy *golastschen*, tortes of various fruits, and other confections he could only guess at. Laci insisted he must immediately have a marzipan torte and an espresso. They rested their feet in the café, imagining what might happen next now that they were in the West. Fortified, they ambled from there to a convent that served as a refugee camp, hoping to find friends or relatives among the exiles.

The old convent had been seized for use as a military barracks by the occupying Russians following the Second World War. The building had been abused and then abandoned once Austria became neutral and the Russians departed. Recently turned into a refuge by the Austrian government, its walls needed painting, windows repairing, but the three hundred or so Hungarian refugees temporarily housed there were too grateful to care about amenities. Simply being in Austria was the best amenity in the world.

Neither Jozsi nor Laci recognized anyone at the center, and as it was by then late in the day, the two repaired to a nearby barroom and used their very basic German to make new friends. Word quickly spread that there were refugees at the bar and soon the two were drowning in bought drinks. The crowd on hand saluted the people of Hungary for their courage and bravery in standing up to and defeating the biggest army in the East, if only for a few days.

The men behaved in similar fashion in the days that followed. They splurged on good food and expensive wine and decided they could get used to this lifestyle, except for one thing: eventually their money would run out. Jozsi scoffed when Laci worried about spending so much.

"We are living like never before! Let's enjoy it. If I know Sandor, we'll hear from him before we have time to spend all this money. *Bizal bennem*."

"Trust you?" Laci replied, "Eh," he answered his own question, "What choice do I have?"

More days passed and still no word from Sandor. To alleviate Laci's anxiety, Jozsi talked the American Embassy into forking over another hundred dollars for their allowance. He blamed their financial straits on Sandor, who had told them to wait for his return because he had a job for them to do, only some of which was true. As they left the embassy, Laci mentioned he wasn't used to Jozsi's shell game ways, but was very impressed with his style.

Jozsi assured him, "City folks learn to think on their feet. I hope you're making mental notes for the future." Laci laughed at Jozsi's braggadocio, but stopped when, serious for a rare moment, Jozsi said, "We're alone in the West, we need to stick together." And for a moment they held each other's gaze. "So, partners going forward?" Laci nodded in assent. "Even though at the moment, our future is as clear as a fogged-up bathroom mirror." Laci nodded harder.

For the next two weeks, they enjoyed the best lifestyle money could buy. One evening, as they were wining and dining a couple of amenable young Austrian women in their hotel suite, there was a knock at the door. Sandor. They invited him to join the party. The women said they had a friend who would be happy to appear, but Sandor was all business, standing there in a brown suit, white shirt, his close-set eyes flickering everywhere, taking in the room, the girls, the state of inebriation. At their rowdy insistence, he entered the suite for a shot of *palinka*, and even managed a relaxed sigh as one of the girls, following Jozsi's directions, rubbed his neck and shoulders. But after a few minutes, he shrugged her off, and said he'd return the following morning, and with his eyes, indicated the girls should be gone by then. "You boys be ready to talk."

In the morning, over breakfast in the suite, followed by a toast from the last bottle of *palinka* on hand, Sandor capped the bottle and started talking. He thanked them for their work in Hungary, adding he was relieved they'd been able to make it across the border. But now he needed their help more than ever. Under the table, Jozsi kicked Laci. See, here it comes.

Laci leaned forward, his demeanor calm and solemn. Sandor continued, "The flood of refugees means we face new problems. The CIA believes there are spies coming out in that flood, and we would like you to track them and their contacts."

"How in hell can you expect us to trail a shitload of spies in Vienna?" Jozsi asked, irritable, and to be truthful, a bit hung over. Sandor assured them that all of the suspects were about to be transferred to Italy from Klosterneuburg. "On what basis?" Jozsi demanded. Laci's mouth fell open at his audacity, but Sandor replied, his tone level.

"The Austrian government asked the Italians to take some refugees, make room for new ones in Austria. The numbers are still huge, you know, and the Italians want to help. This is where you two enter the picture." Laci rubbed his hands in anticipation. Jozsi listened, face deadpan. "Five buses will carry refugees from Klosterneuburg to Italy in just a few days. At the camp, it's been announced that space is needed for new refugees, so no one dares protest. The assignments will be given out; no one has a choice. If anyone tries to sneak off, we'll know they're bad news. I want you to head back there tomorrow, your names will be on the list." Sandor paused to let the news sink in. "You agree?"

The two looked at each other, nodding yes without saying a word. "I knew we could count on you," Sandor said, rising. "Once you get to Italy a man named Bruno will contact you. Follow his instructions."

Jozsi interrupted, "What about you?"

"I will see you in Italy, *subito*," he used the Italian for soon. At the door, he shook their hands, and before turning to leave, said, *ciao*, and this time surprised them with a genuine smile.

"I guess we're going to Italy," Jozsi said to his new best friend. And they launched a plan for a final evening in Vienna, involving wine, women and the song they could make with the ability of those ingredients to fuel joyful spirits.

~~~

Now, huddled in the North Korean cave, waiting for the sun to set so they could leave this dank cavern and head south under cover of darkness, Jozsi said, "You will feel better about everything once we get to Hong Kong and are drowning in booze and good time girls. You know, if you stick with me, we will be riding in big cars, fondling women with big tits and small morals, dining on fine food, keeping diamonds in our pockets to hand out like candy."

Laci looked back and spoke loudly enough for their captive to hear, "How's that sound to you, comrade?" Above the tape, Kimchi's nostrils flared, but his eyes remained expressionless.

The night was humid as they journeyed south; when they crossed the swamp, mosquitoes swarmed, searching for skin. Jozsi took the lead, Laci covered the rear, and Kimchi kept pace, without Jozsi having to tug on the rope connecting them at the waist. As they crossed the border, Laci, switching to Hungarian, said "Now that he knows he's out of that hell, he may try to escape first chance he gets."

"And ruin our trip to Hong Kong? Not going to happen. But he's no threat to us now, so I'll be a good guy and start trying to convert him." He stopped and pulled the tape off Kimchi's mouth.

After several deep breaths Kimchi spoke, in halting English. "You Hungarians! We get you. Many agent look!"

Regretting he'd pulled the tape, Jozsi yanked the rope hard and brought Kimchi to his knees. "Not to worry, comrade. If I were you, I'd concentrate on coming up with good shit to spill. If you don't talk, the CIA will shove you back over the border. They'll put out the word that you spilled your guts. They'll say you were sent back because you're no longer useful. Your buddies will toss you on the dung heap in no time." Jozsi pulled him upright, but left the tape off, and Kimchi managed to keep his mouth shut as they marched on.

By six in the morning, they'd turned their captive over to the Army's CID agents with much handshaking and congratulating. Captain Lamp had apparently recovered his equanimity and was back on the scene. It gave Jozsi immense pleasure when Laci turned to the good captain and asked for a receipt. Captain Lamp nearly went cross-eyed. Another agent asked what was going on.

Jozsi explained. "My sharpshooting buddy here wants a receipt so there's no way we can get screwed out of what we were promised."

Laci stood to the side nodding like a bobble-head china doll. The CID agent reminded them they'd already extracted a written contract from the Army, no need for further paperwork, they'd get their due. The tired two aimed themselves in the direction of hot showers, and once revived, convened at the club where they congratulated each other over enough drinks to burn through their adrenaline and ready them for their barracks and some welcome deep sleep.

4

Ura, Ulee and Attila the Hun

After a very long day and night spent celebrating the success of their expedition into North Korea — the extraction and delivery of one pint-sized agent — Jozsi decided to pocket the money for his two weeks all-expenses paid R&R in Hong Kong and instead rent a room in Seoul and roam the city. Doubtful he would ever return to Korea, he decided to explore and absorb a little about this land and its customs away from the military base and the treacherous border to the North. Laci, flabbergasted that he'd pass up wild nights in Hong Kong, mocked him as a killjoy. To which Jozsi replied to his friend, *"Baratom,* worry not. There are girls in Seoul who will be happy to share my bed, fun in my future is guaranteed."

After Laci blew him a mocking kiss on his way out the door, Jozsi packed a bag and caught a bus that took a little more than an hour to reach Seoul. Weary from trekking back and forth across the Korean border, and from the toll taken by the hours of carousing necessary to wind down from such a tense mission, Jozsi leaned his head against the window and tried to keep his eyes open, much as he'd done so many summers ago during the long train ride to the Toths.

He had a clear memory of his ten-year-old body nearly vibrating at the thought of seeing battle on the way to Ura, and as the hours crept by, literally propping eyelids open with fingers so as not to miss a thing. After the passengers had dramatically dashed to the cornfield and then straggled back to the train, Jozsi had been more than primed. But the rest of the journey had been relatively uneventful. Despite several more air raid warning delays, they hadn't needed to flee the train again, or seen bombers overhead, or even heard shots in the distance. The only troops spotted were a trainload of Italians heading to the Russian front. Matyas emitted a strange guttural sound. "What, Papa?" Jozsi reached to touch his arm. "If those men ever see their homeland again they will be lucky. I remember how it felt to leave my country, not knowing if I'd return." He sighed deeply, sadness dimming his usually bright blue eyes.

Mostly Jozsi was puzzled because the Italians looked pretty much like Hungarian and German soldiers, only clothed in different uniforms — he'd expected they'd be more exotic. At one point, their train was forced to wait on side rails while the Italian troop train steamed by on the main tracks. Jozsi decided he'd seen much more exciting action down the road from home, what with bombers streaming overhead, an occasional plane crash, and unpleasant soldiers disrupting daily life. He decided he'd had enough of being on the train, but there was no point in protesting, he'd only irritate his father.

By the time they reached Ura, they'd been on the train for six hours and Jozsi was about to jump out of his skin. He leapt off the train into the arms of Mr. Toth, waiting on the station platform. Toth gave Jozsi a big beer-smelly hug, shook his former comrade's hand, and tossed their luggage into the back of his wagon. He scratched his horse's muzzle and led his guests into the tavern where he'd definitely spent time while waiting for the train. The bartender called out a welcome to the newcomers. Every train station had a tavern; it was normal for arriving passengers to stop in for a drink. "It's like visiting a shrine," Matyas said, noticing his son frown. Jozsi was now in a hurry to get to the farm, and really, he was so very tired of sitting still.

His spirits rose when Toth asked what he wanted to drink. Soon the biggest raspberry soda he'd ever seen was in his hands. The three took a table on the back terrace, the men sipping *Hubertus* as they talked. Jozsi felt like a big boy, swigging his raspberry soda, listening to the men discuss the news of the day. Any lingering unease about leaving home for the whole summer ceased. He and his friends would have done the same old thing the whole time, and who knew what adventures he'd have in Ura. Already, one thing was different. Usually children heard only the odd fragment of news; their parents worked hard to share information, fears, or schemes away from young ears. Jozsi couldn't wait to get back and brag to the others about his improved knowledge of world politics, although in his version he would be a participant in the conversation, not just an eavesdropper. After the steins were empty, full, then again empty, Toth lifted Jozsi into the back of the wagon. In the front, he and Matyas spoke in low voices about the aggressive Russian presence in Hungary and how bad things were likely to get. The horse trotted briskly forward, and soon enough they'd reached the farm.

It was late afternoon when the horse whinnied to a stop. At the sound of creaking wagon wheels, Toth's wife Matild rang the big bell nailed to a wooden post outside the farmhouse front door. Within seconds, family members appeared from various directions and gathered in front of the gate.

There were hugs and kisses and many words about how much Jozsi and Matyas had been missed. Matyas slipped away for a moment, to visit the barn and give Bandi a sugar cube, always the first and last thing he did when visiting. Matyas was dear to this hard-working, happy group; in their eyes his cavalry years with Toth afforded him family status. Farm life was not for Matyas, but he envied their simple, clear world: grow up, work the land, get married, have children. Help each other and those in need, live an honest life, die in the house in which you were born. They aspired to be nowhere, do nothing else; they were already living in their promised land.

Toth had two sons: Tibor and Shanyi. Tibor and his wife Kati lived on the Toth farm; Shanyi, whose wife Magdi was the only child of her parents, lived with his in-laws and helped with their farm when he wasn't working at his father's. But everyone had put aside chores to welcome their friends. They, along with Rebeka, whose bust Jozsi liked to eyeball, wandered over to the veranda, a section of which served as the summer kitchen. A big harvest table had been moved close to a nearly ten-foot-high fence that supported an enormous mass of grape leaves, which would eventually produce a plentiful harvest from which they'd make wine and *palinka*. Two smaller tables had been added to each end, and all were soon laden with bowls and platters of food, and jugs and bottles of wine and beer and juice, enough for a small army. Within a short time, excited neighbors arrived by horseback and wagon; they greeted Matyas warmly, remembering him from past visits. Matyas was viewed as a living newspaper by the country people gathered; his government job in Budapest made him privy to information and rumor relevant to the future of Hungary, and though the farmers' lives were simple, they were not simple-minded. They were eager to hear the latest news from the city.

Restless, Jozsi excused himself while the adults absorbed the latest distressing reports. Lena, the little girl of the neighbor nearest the Toths, had stared at Jozsi during the meal and now trailed behind him. He wandered through the gate and down the walk, trying to get his bearings, it had been many months since he'd been there.

On the left were the mud farmhouse's living quarters and bedrooms. A separate building on the right held a large open kitchen. The sweet aroma from a cherry pie cooling on the rectangular wooden table engulfed the kitchen. Lena caught up to Jozsi and Matild paused at the door to tuck a stray piece of hair back under her bright blue kerchief before fetching the pie. She smiled at the sight of the two little ones, still as statues in front of the table. She correctly surmised that the little girl had developed an instant crush on their summer guest. Lena, almost eight, was sweet-faced, with an appealing smile, but Matild had already noticed Jozsi's eyes lingering on the profile of her robust seventeen-year-old. In Matild's opinion Rebeka was ripe for marriage, but her high-spirited daughter was still too happy flirting with all the local boys to pick just one. She knew Rebeka was going to be amused by having yet another suitor, even though he was too young to do anything about it. "I think you have a ladies' man on your hands," she told Matyas, handing their guest of honor the first slice of pie.

Matyas laughing, agreed. "It's good no young girls live right near us. It's already enough, the trouble he gets into with the boys."

At six o'clock, many of the guests excused themselves and hurried home to feed their animals. Jozsi, tired from the day's travels, stretched out on a wide wooden bench just outside the kitchen entrance and closed his eyes. Toth emerged from the cellar, an unopened wine bottle in hand, and led Matyas to the veranda where they talked into the night. Jozsi lay listening to snatches of conversation that floated toward him on the warm summer wind. Bosnia, Herzegovina, the Russian front. He knew as the contents of the bottle dropped lower and lower, they'd get around to rehashing their World War One days, reliving the invasion of Sarajevo, the assassination of Archduke Ferdinand. He fell asleep on the bench, imagining Rebeka lifting up her most colorful embroidered shirt so he could view her enormous gifts. He slept so deeply he completely missed the moment when Rebeka, bending close, gently placed a goodnight kiss on the top of his head. Nor did he awake when his father carefully lifted and carried him to bed, tucking him snugly under goose-feather filled bedding to protect him from the cooler night air.

~~~

In Korea, Jozsi's bus bounced its way across the Han River, and after a time, he switched to another that took him into the center of Seoul, where with little difficulty he managed to find and rent a serviceable room. After dropping off his luggage, and changing out of sweat-damp clothes, Jozsi set off to explore the nearby area. The summer rainy season ended in July, and the monsoon rains of September had yet to arrive. The city streets were hot, humid, and bustling: filled with people, cars, and bicycles, jam-packed with all manner of shops and restaurants, lively with the living of life, rather than the chaos of war.

But soon he registered something more — a fury simmering against South Korea's leader, Syngman Rhee, who was dictatorial and corrupt according to what Jozsi had heard whispered by U. S. Army members unhappily sworn to support Rhee's reign. On the streets, Korean students were obviously riled up. Young people everywhere huddled in uneasy clusters, talking intently for a few moments, dispersing, vanishing in the blink of an eye. Jozsi knew that Rhee was only able to hang onto the presidency with the help of police and plainclothesmen who violently squelched all protest. No wonder the young kept moving, it was dangerous to stand still for long. Although Jozsi understood little of what he overheard, the feeling on the streets reminded him of Budapest during the months and weeks leading up to the Revolution, so much so that he felt strangely at home.

His first full day in Seoul, he walked for hours until, succumbing to the humidity, he entered a museum, hoping to find a ceiling fan to sit under before exploring the building's contents. What they were, he didn't really care; he mostly wanted to cool off. The reception staff consisted of two middle-aged women who, excited to discover a westerner in their museum, insisted on assigning him an English-speaking guide. Jozsi wasn't expecting much, perhaps an aged and knowledgeable curator with bad teeth and no sex appeal. Instead he got Ulee: recently graduated from the University of Seoul, taller than most Koreans, with the face of a temple goddess. He nearly swooned as she gracefully moved to the reception desk, spoke with the women there, inclined her head in his direction, and then glided across the museum lobby toward the bench where he sat.

They strolled through the museum, Ulee providing insights and rich detail in perfect English while Jozsi plotted a way to prolong his time with her. As the tour wound down, he peppered her with questions. Finally, when he could stall no longer, he asked if she could recommend a good restaurant specializing in local cuisine. Yes, she could, and she tried to explain how to find the place. Jozsi played dumb, which wasn't hard since he'd only been there a day and had no idea exactly where he was or even how to get back to his room. Would she be so kind as to join him? Her hesitation bested by his pleading, slightly helpless expression, and the encouragement of the reception staff, meant that before long they were out the door and into a cab. Soon after, they sat sipping cocktails at the restaurant bar. To hell with Hong Kong, he thought, he'd made the right choice.

During supper, he asked about life in Seoul, politics in Korea, and her work at the museum. Between the cocktails, *Yakju* rice wine with supper, and *Sikhye*, which Ulee explained was a traditional dessert drink, she was relaxed enough to ask Jozsi about his background. When he said that he was from Hungary, her eyes lit up. She had done some research on Attila the Hun during her university days, something to do with the conquests of both the Huns and the Mongolians. Jozsi was by now concentrating on his conquest of Ulee and anything that made her eyes light up was just fine with him.

Jozsi told her that all Hungarian children learned about Attila in school. He remembered that he was about six when he'd first heard pieces of Attila's grand saga. The family had collected in the dining area of their very large kitchen one wintry Sunday afternoon, waiting for a snowstorm to end. Matyas entertained them with the tale of Attila and his downfall. His father would do this now and then — recount Attila's invasions and conquests, or relate tales of St. Stephen, the first king of Hungary, or most often, stories from World War One and his days in the Red Brigade. He would fall into a near trance, his blue eyes fixated on a distant point in another dimension, or so it seemed. It was mesmerizing to witness, even for the girls, who weren't crazy about war tales. Their mother gentled them, "Once a soldier..." she'd shrug. "He needs to talk about these things."

"Tell me about Attila," Ulee urged. "I want to hear it the way your father told." So Jozsi tried to marshal his memories, but before starting, ordered more drinks knowing Ulee could not possibly decline. She leaned forward, chin resting on palms. Jozsi brought his mind back to the family kitchen on that snowy afternoon, his head tilted slightly to the right. Like his father, his eyes seemed fixed on a different setting, far away.

"My father would begin with Ruga, the leader of the Huns. When he was getting old, because he had no son, he chose two of his nephews to lead the army. Bleda, the older one, led his troops north and east of the Carpathian Mountains. Bleda's younger brother Attila settled his troops in the Danu valley. So, time passes, and Attila's two sons are born. The first, Ellac, was eventually killed in battle. The second, Herceg, a small man, not a warrior in build, was very clever, a good thinker. Like us, my father would say. He is such a patriotic man, my father; he loves his country, he loves everything Hungarian." And for a moment, Jozsi wished he were sitting at a table with his father instead of with Ulee, a bottle of *palinka* before them, and a long tale on the way.

Jozsi told Ulee that however stale the story might feel to him now, it had been fascinating to hear as a boy, filled with battles and treasures and wild horseback riding across the plains. Of course, he had forgotten whole sections of the complicated saga, but he did remember certain pieces, one being the story about the invasion of Rome and the end of Attila's reign. "I remember my father talking about Honoria, the sister to the Roman Emperor, it was Valentinian III, I think." Ulee agreed, yes it was. Indeed, she really had studied Attila. Here was a woman of substance, more at least than most of the bar girls he met in his R&R excursions. He'd always been attracted to intelligent women who were well read and had a keen interest in history. He couldn't believe his luck in connecting with one here in Korea. Jozsi continued with renewed vigor.

"From Rome, Honoria sent Attila a red ruby ring, along with an offer to become his bride — I imagine the King of the Huns looked like a good catch. But Attila was no gentleman. He'd long wanted to invade Rome to expand his power and plunder their wealth. He pocketed her ruby ring and gathered his armies for the journey to Rome. He put Herceg, his smarter son, in charge of the Danu Valley. Not only that, he insisted Herceg find a bride for him to wed when he got back." Jozsi chuckled, remembering his mother, Erzsebet, tut-tutting that if Attila had taken the trouble to seek out a bride himself things might have gone better for him. Ulee said his mother sounded like a wise woman.

"Not really, she married my father and has had to hear this story at least 500 times." Ulee smiled. She had humor too he noted before continuing. "Okay, so Herceg did find what he thought was the ideal bride for his father, Ildiko; willow thin, but strong and beautiful, long flowing blonde hair, the perfect woman. She was a member of the Avar tribe, a peaceful people who settled in the Danu Valley long before the Huns arrived. They raised horses, that was their special gift, and somehow, they managed to co-exist with the crazy, belligerent Huns. I bet Herceg was looking for new horses when he spotted Ildiko — her father Zolt had many for sale. Herceg thought an Avar bride would be fine for his father. As the rumors went, Attila was half Avar and half Mongolian — he was more light-skinned than most other Huns, taller too; big head, no neck, dark hair, and a thin dark beard. A horseman like no other, but you know that, yes?" Ulee nodded. "All of the Huns could ride, shoot with a bow and arrow. Warriors. Even when they were having fun, they were fighting. My father made the mistake of telling us about their head-to-head contests. You tell a six-year-old about a game like that, look out. Of course, I had to tell my friends, and the headaches we got when we tried to play that game. You know?"

Ulee shook her head, "No, not about the contests."

"The men would get drunk and two would stand back-to-back. Each man walked ten steps, then turned around and bent halfway down. When they were at eye level with each other someone would shout 'Start!' and the two drunken Huns would run into each other, meeting head on, like goats butting. Sometimes a head would split and then, dead Hun. They'd say he wasn't a strong soldier." He laughed, taking a deep swallow from his drink. "We make good fighters because we are crazy and mostly drunk." Ulee smiled.

"A long brutal winter comes, times passes, and Herceg's uncle Bleda arrives to tell him his brother Attila has been killed in battle, and oh, by the way, where is all Attila's treasure? But Bleda was telling a lie, trying to get ahold of Attila's bounty. You see there was only so much loyalty in a power-hungry Hun family. I forget how Herceg got Bleda to leave without any treasure, but he did. Eventually the not-at-all dead Attila returned from Italy loaded down with even more riches. Turns out, he hadn't invaded Rome after all; the new treasure was a ransom from Pope Leo. The Pope had met Attila in the Po Valley and offered him gold and precious jewels if he would return to his own valley without sacking Rome. Jozsi paused, his mind wandering. "If only we'd had a Pope Leo to bribe the Russians to stay out of Hungary." Ulee patted his hand sympathetically. They stared into each other's eyes for a long moment. He found himself liking her more and more.

"Well, Attila sent soldiers to take care of his brother, Bleda," he drew a finger across his throat. "He split the treasure among the soldiers, the widows of soldiers they'd lost on the way, and himself, of course, adding the goods to a special secret chamber beneath his wooden palace. Then he set about getting married. He sent a trusted scout to get an eyeful of Ildiko, and hearing the scout's description, approved of the bride his son had chosen. He sent Herceg to tell Ildiko's father Zolt that he was about to become a father-in-law. Zolt had no interest in being Attila's father-in-law, and if you think Zolt was unhappy, just imagine Ildiko's state of mind! Here my mother always says, 'And who can blame her? Who would want to be the fifth wife of a barbarian?' And then my father says, 'Or to be his father-in-law.'"

"Your parents sound very nice." Ulee looked wistful.

"They are good people," Jozsi's throat tightened slightly. He was feeling a confusing mix of emotions: affection and lust for Ulee, tossed into a pool of nostalgic longing for his parents whose influence on him was still a guiding force. He wasn't overly sentimental, but there were moments when the weight of all he'd left behind tugged at his heart. He took another sip, pulled his mind back to the present moment and continued.

"Zolt tried to convince Attila to look elsewhere for a bride, but Attila was not about to change his mind. Since Zolt knew that Attila always, always, always got his way, he sought counsel from a wise old woman of the plains." He smiled as another ritual of the telling popped into his head. "My grandmother, *nagyanya* Alida, always says, 'If this were a play that would be my part.' My father always tells her that in real life that is her role. And that is true," Jozsi pictured his *nagyanya* at her sewing machine, surrounded by piles of clothes needing mending, yet always ready to make time for childish concerns or adult need for solace. "So, he tracked down this wise old woman and explained what a mess his daughter was in. She told Zolt to allow the wedding preparations to go ahead because she had a plan and would return to help Ildiko in her hour of need.

"Then the wise old woman walked along the riverbeds collecting Amanita, one of the deadliest mushrooms known to man. She gathered a good amount and dried the mushrooms in the sun for days, until they became so small and powdery a gust of wind could carry them away. She mixed the powder with a little flour and rolled the combination into pea-sized balls. She let those dry in the sun. My mother made certain to tell me that she wore gloves; if you touch them with your bare hands bad things happen to your body."

"You truly were that kind of boy?" Ulee asked.

"Oh, I wanted to go find some as soon as I heard about them. You know what they look like? Chunky stems, big red caps dotted with white growths, easy to spot. You can imagine the appeal. My poor mother, she had reason to worry about me, I was always looking for excitement." He sighed, thinking about how distraught his mother must have been after he fled Hungary and the whole world thought he was dead. If he could only reach back through time and space and put his arms around her, hug her with all the love and gratitude alive in his body at this very second. But he could not. Leaving, he'd had to veil his emotions so his family wouldn't register that when he called out, *"Viszlát,"* see you again, he was in truth fleeing them, their country, everything he knew, and that *Viszlát* was the prayer of hope he left with, along with the ache in his soul. But this was not the time to veer off into emotional turmoil. Ulee wanted Attila, he would give her Attila.

"After the tiny poison balls had dried in the sun, the old woman put them in a hollow walnut shell so they wouldn't get crushed, saying that she'd show up at Zolt's farm the day before the wedding. Only then would she tell the family how she planned to save the bride from the groom. Next, she sent word to Zolt to plan a big party after the wedding. Hungarians know how to celebrate," Jozsi grinned, downed what was left in his glass and clunked it hard on the table as he motioned to the waiter to bring another. He was back in his body now, fully present.

"The wedding was set for the night of a full moon. This was going to be a *big* party. Roasted pigs, barrels of *Tokay* wine, expensive Chinese silk draped over everything. There was feasting, and gifts of precious jewels and gold. I remember, I wasn't so interested in this part of the story, I liked the gory parts more."

Ulee wrinkled her brows, "Gory? At a wedding?"

"Well, it was an *Attila* wedding, and an important wedding ritual was for Attila and all of his council members to take turns cutting their wrists, holding them over a chalice and letting the blood drip, drip, drip. A way of pledging loyalty, I think it was. They handed the chalice to Attila, he took a sip, passed the chalice to the priest, he took a sip, and then the council members passed it one to the other, and finally the chalice came to Ildiko. She pretended to sip. My sister Susan always gagged at that part." Jozsi noticed that Ulee was looking a little green around the gills. He distracted her by describing Susan, his elder by a few years, and the most outspoken, wildest of the girls, also the one to whom he was closest. Erzsebet joked that Jozsi and Susan were twins who'd gotten confused and come out in separate years. They did have a connection, no words needed for one to know what the other was thinking. They had a similar quick wit, and like Matyas, intense blue eyes, a color somewhere between azure and cobalt. When they stared at you, you felt fully seen.

"Susan sounds like someone I would like," Ulee smiled, looking steadier, so Jozsi continued with the tale. "The party went on, and at some point, the old woman slipped the poisonous walnut shell into the pocket of a special bridal apron Ildiko wore. She gave Zolt more instructions and told him to take his family home, that she would stay close to Ildiko. She sat on a chair outside the bedroom chamber, immobile as a gargoyle. On the other side of the door, Attila ushered his bride into a changing room, where Ildiko nervously donned her wedding nightgown and slipped the walnut into a secret pocket sewn into its folds. She found Attila, splayed on the bed in his plushest purple robe, and said she wanted them to share an Avar wedding toast. No blood involved," Jozsi assured Ulee. "Ildiko asked Attila to stay where he was, she, his wife, was there to serve him, she would bring the chalice to him. In the Avar tradition, she was careful to explain, they each had their own. She poured wine into two chalices, and dropped poison pellets into his. Attila asked what made this custom special, and lucky for her, she could think on her feet. My father always insisted he was quoting her exact words: 'The red wine we will drink came from the plains. It represents our blood and we are willing to pour it again to protect our land for generations to come.'"

Abruptly, Jozsi stopped. Those words, 'to protect our land,' sliced into his heart with the sharp burn of a knife. Here he was, far from his land, protecting what? He had fled his land, yes, along with thousands of others, and if he hadn't, he'd most likely be dead. But there were moments when he felt torn between shame and pride at having escaped. Ulee studied his somber expression. The compassion in her eyes rescued him. He could not repair the past, the communist sickness invading his country, the death of spirit it triggered. But he could, he hoped, feel joy with Ulee on this day. He banished his internal discord — no point wasting time agitating over his actions when a sympathetic Ulee was so obviously warming to him.

"Attila and Ildiko toasted. Greedy Attila tipped his chalice and downed the wine in one long swallow. Soon, the chalice clattered onto the floor and Attila fell back, his head hitting a silken pillow." Jozsi performed Attila's final moments as he spoke. "In short order, he gasped, his chest rose, his chest fell, his eyes opened wide and then, just like that, his heart stopped. Ildiko ripped off her nightgown, threw on her clothes, and she and the old woman fled. All that romantic moonlight made it easy for them to move fast and get to the wagon Zolt had arranged for them. Herceg saw them flee. He sped to his father's room where he found Attila dead on his bed. He allowed the party to carry on, but gathered his most trusted soldiers together and had them do their own chalice ritual, swearing loyalty to him. The next morning, he convened the council, told them of Attila's death, and began the steps needed to commemorate the death according to traditional custom. Do you want to hear?" he asked. "It's a little gruesome."

"It's all right," Ulee answered, "Go on."

"Well, the custom was for Attila to be laid out in a grand tent. All of the tents were made of layers of dried goatskin, but Attila's was draped in different colors of silk. The soldiers rode around the tent for hours. They cut their hair and disfigured their faces horribly, slashing deep wounds."

"Why?"

"So that their most gallant warrior would not be mourned by men looking and acting like weepy old women. You seem to know enough about Hungarians," he added, dropping the tale for a moment, "to know that we are all a little mad." He circled his finger by his ear, she laughed. "After all the crazy mourning ritual was over, Herceg summoned soldiers, had them pick out one hundred strong slaves, and equipped them with axes and shovels. By this time, the full moon had waned, and in the pitch dark one night, he led the group north across the plains, toward the mountains, until they found a place where the river split in two. Herceg had the slaves dam up one side of the river and let all the water run into the other side. But he had them construct the dam in a way that it could be easily destroyed. Then he went home to bid his own farewell to his father, the greatest warrior the Huns had ever known.

"And then Herceg directed his soldiers to round up all the blacksmiths in the area. He had them forge a grand coffin for Attila, coffins, really. The slaves carried up riches from the treasure chamber hidden below Attila's wooden palace. They melted all the gold and the blacksmiths forged the gold into a coffin. They melted all the silver and the blacksmiths made another coffin large enough to hold the gold one. Then the blacksmiths forged an iron coffin big enough to hold the first two. Once Attila's body was laid inside the gold coffin, they surrounded his body with jewels, and Herceg placed the final precious valuable, Honoria's ruby ring, in a corner of the coffin. Herceg had the soldiers seal the lid of the gold coffin, which was then lowered into the silver coffin. That was sealed and placed inside the iron one. The final seal was then set.

"That night the coffins were loaded onto the very strongest wagon. As they headed toward the river, thunder rolled in from the northern mountains, a sign of big rains to come — in Hungary, the big rains usually come from the direction of the mountains. The procession arrived at the dammed part of the river during daylight, but the clouds hovered so dark and heavy it seemed like they were struggling through an endless night. Thunder, then lightening, and then at last the rains pummeled down so hard the soldiers and everybody else must've wished they'd built an ark, not a dam. Herceg ordered the slaves to place the coffin under the dam and stand beside it. After that, he had his most trusted soldiers raise their bows and aim at the slaves."

"No!" Ulee winced.

Jozsi raised his hands, palms up. "It was their way. Then Herceg told the soldiers to destroy the dam. The water, cresting already, flowed fast into the empty ravine. It covered the coffin and it covered most of the soldiers too, with lethally thick mud." He paused, imagining the scene through Ulee's eyes. "My father always said that for those soldiers, it was an honor to be buried with the greatest leader of them all." He shrugged, almost angrily. "Bullshit is what I say." Ulee flinched, but he didn't notice. "What point is it to die when there is life to be lived?" He reached across the table and clinked his glass against hers, nudging it toward her. "To Attila! The maddest Hun of all."

"But wait, why wasn't Herceg vengeful?" Ulee asked. "He didn't go after Ildiko and punish her?"

"No, he didn't. He was distressed, but I would bet he was relieved, too," Jozsi shrugged. "Now Herceg had power and since he wasn't much for fighting..." He shrugged, Ulee nodded. They sat in silence for a few minutes. She thanked him. He had shared some of Attila's story, but more, he had cracked a door into his life, and the idea of getting to know him better was appealing. This was unusual for Ulee, ordinarily she was cautious with her feelings.

She told Jozsi that the museum was going to have her curate an exhibit on Attila the Hun and Genghis Khan. Would he be willing to look at her notes on Attila and the Huns? She would appreciate his opinion, and she wanted to hear more about life in Hungary. Jozsi leaned back in his chair, smiling like a Cheshire cat. Yes, he would be happy to oblige. He hoped very much to start with a lesson on the Hungarian approach to love making, but those words appeared only in his head. He did reach across the small table and take her hand, saying how very glad he was to have met her. Ulee, blushing, left her hand in his. It would be a good night, he knew.

~~~

During Jozsi's two weeks in Seoul, they spent as much time together as they could. She went to the museum to work while he explored different parts of the city. He was particularly drawn to Yongsan, an area not far from the city center. He'd hop a bus to the U. S. Army Garrison at Yongsan, or take it further, to the shore of the Han River where he'd disembark and spend hours walking. The banks of the river were sparsely dotted with spindly trees; shade was scarce, but the unblocked views were rewarding.

He might pass small numbers of Korean men sitting, watching wooden fishing boats maneuver down the river, or encounter a man leading an ox pulling a large wooden wagon loaded to the gills with bags of rice down a dirt road. One day he came upon a group of thirty schoolboys and their teachers, the boys in identical navy blue jackets, large bright buttons sparking off the sunlight, as they stood silent before the teacher addressing them. He was speaking intensely, his hand pointing to the other side of the Han. Jozsi couldn't understand a word, but he enjoyed the sight of the boys shifting from foot to foot, trying to contain their restlessness, sneaking glances at the white stranger standing off to the side. He saw himself in the boys, thought how alike they were, little boys the world over, buttoned into school jackets, feet fidgeting to be free.

When he'd had his fill of the river, he'd head over to the Itaewon commercial district, one of the more ethnically diverse regions in Korea. Soldiers and other foreigners connected to the Army base gravitated towards its shopping centers and nightlife. A variety of stores, restaurants and bars flourished, some appealing to foreigners, some reflecting the soul of Korea. Small markets were his favorite places to linger, tables covered with fish, chili peppers, cabbage, clay jars filled with soy sauce and *kimchi*. He'd linger in stores festooned with *gats*, the traditional Korean hat — tall, cylindrical and wide brimmed, and colorful Korean robes whose brightness reminded him of Hungarian holiday clothing.

He loved the variety of material, of human life. American and European soldiers and civilians were everywhere, and where they were, so too were prostitutes trolling and smiling in modern, alluring outfits. But in another blink, he'd see Korean women in their brightly patterned garb, robes falling to their ankles, hair in braids or tightly pinned up. The men wore the customary outfit of short white shirt with loose sleeves, pants that ballooned slightly, shoes with a single strap crossing just below the ankle. He loved the mysterious sound of foreign accents and words, the energetic bartering, the spicy smells, the wonders of otherness.

On one of Ulee's days off, they spent an afternoon touring *Changdeokgung Palace* and the large park from which it seemed to have organically sprung, so purely did the Far Eastern palace architecture belong to its environment. "It is in harmony," Ulee said, and Jozsi had to agree. They wandered from one pagoda-roofed building to another, from the queen's consort residence to the king's office, eventually settling on an unoccupied bench where they rested, surrounded by the lushness of Jeongwon Garden. The grounds held a greater variety of trees and brush than Jozsi had seen elsewhere in Korea. They sat silent for a while, hand-in-hand, eyes resting on the buildings in the distance, the other visitors wandering as they had, the ducks paddling and dunking across a small pond near their bench.

"This could be Hungary," Jozsi said, holding his hands in front of Ulee to frame a section of the pond. "There was a little pond near a farm I was sent to one summer."

"Why were you sent there?" Ulee asked.

"There was so much bombing near Budapest, my parents wanted me away."

"I see." Ulee understood about bombing, about violence; she herself was literally a child of war. During one tender moment, as they held each other late into the night, she told him the story of her birth. During the Japanese invasion, a Japanese soldier had raped her mother. Ulee was the result of that attack. And because she looked, as she put it, "Not pure Korean," some had branded her the child of a whore. She'd grown used to it, and as she'd come to learn, she was one of thousands. She no longer felt the sting as deeply as when she'd been a child, but he could see the memories hurt. On the bench in *Jeongwon Garden*, she asked, "What was it like, living on a farm?"

He decided he would tell her. Jozsi had been guarded about sharing too much of his past, deciding he'd rather not dredge up some of the things he'd had to do in recent years. Those memories sank him in painful gloom and caused him to shut down, fall silent, stare into space as though in a vertical waking coma. He'd learned to trod carefully through the minefield of his memory. But since she was interested, he would share some parts, let that act knit them closer together before life, as it always seemed to do, pulled him away. They never spoke of the future, there was no need. Two weeks was what they had. Then he would return to the base and be sent to Vietnam, and she would remain in Seoul.

Jozsi arced his back against the bench, stretching his legs out, crossing his feet at the ankles. She leaned into him and he put his arm around her and sighed contentedly. He would begin with his first full day on the farm, from the moment he awoke, not on the bench he'd lay down on outside the kitchen entrance, but in a bedroom, under a blanket filled with goose feathers, the sweet smell of Hungarian lilac drifting through a cracked open window. From the other side of the structure came the faint sound of voices. He realized the family must have already gathered on the veranda for breakfast in the early morning sun. He rose and stretched and went to find a place at the table.

5

A Summer in Ura

As soon as Jozsi appeared, Toth's wife Matild bustled to set him a place next to Matyas, who would be leaving later that day. The Toth's kitchen helper Mari served him fried eggs, sausages, and homemade bread; toasted on top of the stove, slathered with fresh butter, and topped with homemade raspberry jam. This was not the food rationing he'd grown used to at home.

"I brought the eggs in from the coop myself, still warm from the hen," Mari added. Jozsi smiled weakly. He wasn't about to encourage her because, as drawn as he was to Rebeka's breasts, just that strongly was he repelled by Mari's; for some reason, she liked to press them against any part of him she could reach. Mari, an unmarried daughter of a neighbor family, was considered a little touched in the head. She usually reeked of garlic and had long chin hairs she played with but never pulled. Mrs. Toth had creaky arthritic knees, needed assistance and was glad to help out neighbors, even though that family would have been happier had Matild's help extended to offering up one of her sons as a husband for lonely Mari.

After breakfast, Matild, Toth, Jozsi and Matyas piled into the wagon and drove to church. The morning was sunny and peaceful, but as the horse clip-clopped toward town, the long moan of an air raid warning ramped up, followed by the thrum of planes. Moments later, an explosion. The tower of the Protestant church that sat high on a rise, they could just make it out in the distance, blown to bits. Toth and Matyas exchanged tense looks. Toth explained the tower was being used as an observation post — the Germans tracked Allied planes as they flew toward Budapest to bomb factories seized by the Germans. Observers in the church tower would send the Germans warning, giving them time to rally fighter planes to protect the factories. Toth halted the horse for a moment as they stared at the smoke spiraling high in the sky. All jovial banter ceased, and then they continued on, somber and anxious.

At the church, there was distress over the bombing but also

enthusiastic greetings from people who recognized Toth's visitors, many marveling at how much Jozsi had grown since his last visit. After Mass, word spread that a few men had been killed, followed by relief when they heard the dead were German soldiers who'd been in the tower. The locals didn't care for those or any other Germans and were hoping they'd be forced to move on to a different location from which to track Allied planes.

Lena found Jozsi in the crowd of mingling adults and invited him to visit with her after church. Her parents, glad for her exposure to such a bright boy from the big city, welcomed him with one of her mother's aromatic cherry strudels. This was a big treat; Lena's mother was legendary for her fine baking. Jozsi made sure to mention that at home his mother only served such fine pastries on holidays or at weddings. Of course, they immediately offered him another.

Eventually, he had to pry himself away from dessert and return to the Toths in time to take his father to the train station. He and Matyas climbed back into the wagon, Mr. Toth picked up the reins and back to town they went, Jozsi standing in the wagon bed, leaning against his father while Matyas told him all the things he should do to help the Toths during his visit. Jozsi nodded yes over and over, despite knowing exactly what his father was going to say — the same thing he said every time Jozsi visited. Whether it was for a week, or this, his longest visit ever, his father's instructions were always the same, easily summed up in one brief sentence: do what they say to do.

Waiting in the station tavern, the two men drank *palinka* while Jozsi sipped at another huge raspberry soda. Jozsi would later brag to his friends that the bartender had remembered him from the day before and started preparing his soda as soon as they'd walked in the door. Sitting at the bar with the two men was the first time he'd felt on a par with his father. Not that Matyas would have looked at it that way. He too remembered the moment, but with a pang, because it was the first time he'd be separated from his son for so much time and under such worrisome conditions.

A train whistle blew in the distance, and Jozsi ran out to see if it was the right train — you never knew, with rail schedules at the mercy of war. And indeed, it was a train carrying wounded soldiers back from the Russian front, Red Cross signs plastered on every car. The soldiers, some with visible head and arm bandages, gazed impassively out the windows, dejected and weary. Jozsi waved with one hand and saluted with the other, but only a few mustered enough energy to acknowledge his earnest greeting.

Matyas suggested they head back to the farm since when his train would arrive was anybody's guess and Toth had work to do. Jozsi waved to his father until the wagon rolled around a curve in the road and Matyas vanished from view. Toth patted Jozsi's knee comfortingly, sensing the boy needed a little time to adjust to his father's absence, and assured him he didn't have to remember *all* of his father's instructions.

"The main thing to remember, my boy, is this: if we take care of our animals, they'll take care of us. That's a lesson for life." Jozsi didn't really know what Toth meant, but nodded seriously as though he did. "You do whatever is needed to care for the animals, help Matild with odds and ends, and be good to old Bandi. Your father likes to know he's getting special attention."

Matya's ancient horse, gray with a dark streak running along his side, was too old to be useful. You could throw on a rope halter, hop on bareback, or just lead him around, but Toth rarely had time for that. So, one of Jozsi's jobs was to give the old horse a treat by taking him away from the farm so he could amble across the flat open land of the ravine. He'd graze along the riverbank while Jozsi played with any neighboring children who showed up at a swimming hole created by the river's flow. It had been only a few years since Jozsi had gotten big enough to handle Bandi on his own, and from the first, he'd sensed a special energy about the horse that made him feel almost protected. He'd seen with his own two eyes the bond his father and Bandi shared and felt that somehow the horse recognized him as being "of" Matyas, and thus special. He looked forward to their excursions, just he and the horse roaming the earth.

That night Jozsi lay awake, any loneliness quashed by the pleasure of being back in the country, living this different life. He loved the night sounds: the comforting chatter of crickets, an occasional tap from a June bug bumping against the window screen. No traffic, no buses, no army trucks. From his bed, he could see out the window to a world of stars. He thought of Uncle Peter, pointing to the Big Dipper and telling him that it looked exactly the same from wherever you might roam. It made him feel better to think that if anyone in his family happened to be looking up, they would be looking at the very same stars. Matyas had told him that a star is so far away that when it dies, its light is still visible for many years, traveling mysteriously through space and time.

"Someday," Jozsi said to Ulee, "I will tell my own child what my father told me." Ulee sighed. The bench where they sat was years and miles away from that sparkling Ura sky, but she knew that soon she would do the same — look up and imagine Jozsi somewhere else in the world, seeing the same stars; their time together would end, but its light would linger. She was not looking forward to saying goodbye to her new friend, not at all. Jozsi gave her a quizzical look, but guessing the source of her sigh and not wanting to disrupt the moment, returned to his story.

Jozsi's second morning in Ura, Mari roused him, saying the sun was already so high his belly would get sunburned if he didn't get out of bed — in his sleep, he'd shoved the blanket down to his belly button. Jozsi ran to the summer kitchen where Matild sat slicing almonds for a special pastry Mari was going to make, along with the week's bread, and biscuits for supper. After breakfast, Matild directed him to free the animals before the town shepherd arrived to herd them all to the town pasture. Jozsi knew the routine from past years and let the cows, pigs, geese and ducks loose in the yard. As the town shepherd approached with the animal mob he'd already gathered, Jozsi threw open the gate to the road and the Toth animals joined the herd. Heading to town pasture for the day was like going off to school, Jozsi thought. He waved to the shepherd as he closed the gate, and careful to follow Toth's directions, returned to Matild's side to see what other help she might need. She told him to feed the chickens and tend the fire in the outside oven. After that, he could take Bandi to the ravine to graze. He was free to swim or do anything else he felt like doing, as long as he was back at the farm by three.

Jozsi went behind the barn and fed the silly chickens, clucking along with them as they raced after corn he scattered far and wide. After watching their food frenzy, he headed back toward the house and the big outside oven, which had always fascinated him. Ten feet in diameter, made of clay and fieldstone, it stood a few yards from the summer kitchen, its surface covered with flat stones set so close to each other the thing looked to be cut from one huge, flat stone. The oven was topped by a small round chimney to vent smoke. The front opening was two feet wide and a foot high, enough space for many loaves to bake at one time, and be easily maneuvered out once cooked. The door had a smooth stone inside; its pitch aimed a couple of feet down. Jozsi was fascinated by the mechanics involved when Mari or Rebeka slid the bread through the door on a big flat wooden shovel.

They usually started the oven fire the night before, filling it with dry acacia wood that burned through the night. The fire heated the foot-thick cement bottom and it stayed hot long enough to bake bread the following morning. They also made the bread dough the night before, with yeast, and put it in a round basket to rise. In the morning, the dough would be poured onto the hot cement surface and left to cook for four hours. Sometimes shaped into many small loaves and placed inside the oven on a thin wooden plate to bake for the entire day, other times shaped into huge round breads close to two feet in diameter. The rounds would rise to nearly a half-a-foot and weigh ten pounds or more. Every Monday Mari would bake enough fresh bread to last through the week. Jozsi loved the bread, whichever shape emerged, and could hardly wait for it to come out of the oven so he could break off a crunchy edge to chew. During the worst of the war, they sometimes cooked enough bread to last a month because firewood was scarce and it might take many weeks to gather enough, especially in the wintertime. Rebeka told Jozsi he was lucky to miss their winter bread, so stale they'd have to dip it in soup or risk cracking teeth.

Jozsi swept the ashes from the oven into a wooden bucket and dumped them on the compost pile not far from the vegetable and herb garden. Then he walked across the yard to the small barn and into Bandi's stall. The horse whinnied a greeting, really a call for the sugar cube he knew Jozsi would bring. Jozsi breathed into Bandi's nose by way of hello, and held the cube on his open palm for the horse to lap up. Then he eased the bridle on, patting Bandi's long snout, talking to him about the day ahead. Bandi perked up the minute the bridle went on; he knew it meant a change of scene was in store. Jozsi led him outside, gently patting his haunches, and over to a tree stump set outside the barn. He stepped onto the stump and hoisted himself onto Bandi's bare back, raised the bridle reins, clucked, and the two of them headed for the old ravine.

The ride out to the ravine wasn't a long one, the Toths lived near the edge of their small town — eight hundred people, give or take. Jozsi waved as wagons passed. It was always hard to part from his family and friends, but already he was happy inhabiting this different realm, his special summer world that would last longer than usual because of the war. But he didn't want to think about that; it made him nervous to imagine bombs falling back in Budapest.

As soon as they left the acacia-lined street and walked out onto the field, all Jozsi could see were acres of flat land stretching before him. On a hot summery day, he might see a mirage; on a clear day, looking toward the north, he could see the Bukk Mountains far in the distance. The late morning sun was strong, but a breeze ruffled Bandi's thin mane, cooling the pair as they meandered toward the older part of the ravine. There, the grass came up to Bandi's knees and he didn't have to bend far to nibble its tasty tops. The breeze sent the grassland dipping and waving, welcoming them, or so it felt. As soon as Bandi began to munch, Jozsi hopped off and left him to graze. When the horse lay down for a good roll in the grass, Jozsi figured it was time to lead him over to the *Galga River* for a cooling dip. Bandi would wade in up to his belly and allow kids to climb onto him and roll off into the water. Jozsi could hear splashing in the distance and knew there'd be at least a few familiar faces to greet him.

A small crowd of boys and a couple of girls perched on the bank, taking turns cannonballing into the water, each vying to make the most dramatic splash. Everyone stopped to make a big fuss over Bandi and a bigger one over Jozsi. They looked to the sharp kid from the city for excitement, just as the adults did to Matyas for news. But first Jozsi had to cool off. He stripped down to his skivvies and backstroked circles around Bandi, who was gently being used as a platform by some of the smaller boys. After Bandi had cooled down, he slowly climbed up the side of the riverbank to resume grazing. Each summer Jozsi held his breath a little hoping they wouldn't have to push Bandi up the bank. Once again, the old horse made it up under his own steam, swishing his tail in triumph. The kids cheered him on and then quieted down, waiting for Jozsi to tell them everything he'd done since the summer before.

All eyes were on him, expectant, a little anxious. He suddenly had a flash of Jancsi, the grocer's son, and wished that he had half of Jancsi's self-assurance and knowledge. The kids' questions came faster than he could answer, and worse he didn't know the answers to many and wished he did. But he found his bearings as he told this wide-eyed audience about the downed plane and the chocolate-bearing pilots, although in the telling the plane had landed closer — nearly in his back yard in fact — a small exaggeration that elevated the drama and was one of the first times he consciously chose to enhance a fact to make for a better story. Aside, of course, from the many times he'd chosen to completely alter the facts to stay out of trouble. His parents often commented on his creative way with words.

He'd gotten as far as telling them about helping the pilots' escape from the Germans, when he realized he needed to head back to the farm for afternoon chores. The kids made Jozsi promise to return the next day and tell more stories. His insides felt aglow, as though a tiny lantern had been lit in his chest. He roused Bandi, who by then was having a siesta in the grass and not at all interested in moving. After a good bit of tugging on Joszi's part, the horse rose and they ambled back toward the farm. Jozsi couldn't believe how wonderful it felt to be the center of attention, and for a change, not for bad behavior. Just for talking! He would try to remember some of Jancsi's Boy Scout stories. He would relate stories Matyas had told him, stories from traveling Uncle Peter, and even from *nagyanya* Alida! He walked along telling Bandi all about the great stories he would share. He figured that by the time summer ended and he went home, he would be as good as Jancsi. He would be a storyteller.

This visit, after the farmhands milked the cows, Jozsi's job was to take the milk down to the collection center to record the amount and have their book stamped. At day's end, Lena's father brought his wagon by to pick up Jozsi and two large metal containers. Lena waved wildly to her friend as they pulled to a stop. Her father hoisted the heavy containers into the back of the wagon, then the three settled together on the wagon seat, and Jozsi entertained them with the tale of the downed airplane. He made some adjustments, streamlining it a little since he wanted to finish the whole saga before they got to the milk station. It seemed to work better the second time through; even Lena's father hung on his every word. Lena begged to be allowed to tag along with Jozsi when he went swimming so she could hear more stories.

Their route to the collection center brought them past the iron main gate of a barely visible vacant palace at the end of a long entry road. Lena's father said the owner had moved to Austria some time ago, hoping to avoid the war. All that was left was an old neighbor man as caretaker, and a lot of ghosts, or so the locals said. The children felt chills as they passed the gate, and even the horse pulling the wagon seemed to step up his pace. Jozsi decided he'd have to sneak in there, see if there were ghosts, see if he could find a story to tell. Suddenly every place he looked he saw a story.

Ulee interrupted him. Did he believe in ghosts now that he was a man? Did he know where Lena was? Was Bandi still alive? She grabbed his arm, surprising him with her intensity. His description of life on the farm sounded so idyllic she felt a little weepy. Her childhood had taken place in a far harsher world. No father, she and her mother scorned by many, never enough food, kindness or comfort. No horse to talk to and hug. No entire other family welcoming her as one of their own. She knew he'd suffered, seen terrible things, smelled death, fought and killed to stay alive, but did he realize how lucky he was to have had such a childhood, rich in people and experience? He was a fortunate son, she said, the gods had smiled on him in so many ways. Yes, he replied, and he knew they smiled on him still because look where he was right this minute, and with whom. They held each other in silence, Ulee sniffling. When her breathing relaxed, Jozsi gently smoothed her cheeks. "You want me to go on?"

"Yes, please," Ulee said. "More about the farm."

Jozsi had always loved thinking back to life at the Toths, and her interest elevated everything in his memory, even the mundane seemed to sparkle.

He explained that the daily routine didn't change much from day to day, but he took great pleasure in tending to his tasks. Each evening, he was impressed anew when the shepherd clucked and shooed the throng of animals back down the road from the town pasture. Jozsi would stand by the open gate saying nothing, and out of the mob of four-legged creatures, only the animals that lived at the Toths would venture into the yard. First the cows, and then the pigs, and then the geese and ducks would scurry and flap to catch up. Sometimes a duck would ride in on the back of one of the better-natured pigs. The rest of the animals walked on with the shepherd until they got to their own gates, where they would peel off from the others and head to their home barns, coops, and pens.

On sunny days, the kids would wait for Jozsi at the swimming hole, and since he'd convinced them that strudels were essential to good storytelling, they'd arrive equipped with treats for the teller. Some days the sun was so strong the heat shimmered off the land and he couldn't wait to throw himself in the water. But almost always there was at least enough of a breeze to help make the journey a pleasure for he and Bandi. Every day before slipping the halter on he'd give the old horse a sugar cube, whispering that it was from Matyas. He knew it meant a lot to his father that Bandi was well cared for — he paid the Toths to house and tend his old steed. Matyas told Jozsi they both owed their lives to Bandi: had he not been such a great horse, Matyas wouldn't have survived the war and Jozsi would never have been born. Jozsi took that very seriously; he'd grown to love the old horse almost as much as his father did.

When Lena was at the swimming hole, they'd leave together. He'd hoist her up on Bandi and walk alongside as they meandered across the ravine. He saved special stories to preview with her, especially stories from Uncle Peter's time on the Amazon studying snakes. She was afraid of snakes and he'd see if he could get her to shiver, even atop a horse where no snake could possibly reach her. She would talk about how much fun they'd have when he was older and came to live in Ura. They could take over the vacant palace, the owner in Austria would likely be happy to have people living in it. She'd natter on and he'd humor her, but even then, and as much as he loved being at the Toths, he knew he'd never want to live in Ura. Jozsi was going to see the world. Someday he'd decide to find a place on earth he'd want to settle and grow old on. But he didn't tell Lena any of this, he didn't want her to fall quiet and look sad.

The summer moved along in its rhythms, the days packed with activity; the nights sweet with dinners at the summer kitchen table, fireflies blinking, crickets singing, an occasional night owl hooting from deep in the woods at the edge of the farm. Jozsi spent his chore hours tending the outside oven, feeding the animals, hoeing and weeding the vegetable garden. A few times Toth took him out to the land he worked to grow corn and wheat to feed the animals, anything extra made available for sale. Toth hitched a horse up to a large wooden plow and let Jozsi squeeze in beside him to practice steering. But the work was demanding, and Jozsi still too small to be of much help, so he usually left him at the farm to be at Matild's beck and call, and Mari's too. Even Toth noticed she brightened when Jozsi appeared. He'd pinch Jozsi's arm teasingly when Mari was especially flirty.

Jozsi tried to avoid Mari whenever possible, and kept a sneaky eye out for Rebeka, always hoping for a glimpse of cleavage, or a moment's attention. She was in and out, her afternoons spent working at a market in town, tantalizing the local lads in her spare time. In the fall, as soon as the grapes were ready for harvest, she'd spend more time at the house, overseeing the wine and brandy production. Most families had a wine press on hand and a cellar room dedicated to storing the wine in big fat wooden barrels that would be turned on their sides to help the wine properly ferment. When the wine was ready, they'd open a plug in the bottom and drain the liquid into bottles. Rebeka loved the whole process and had taken it on as her special task.

One day when Rebeka was wearing an especially colorful, low-cut blouse Jozsi asked her to explain how *palinka* was made. He already knew, but pretended he didn't so he could have a few moments of her undivided attention. They went outside to the fence of grapes. His idea was to get her to bend down; he wasn't sure how that would happen, but he was certain he'd be able to come up with a plan.

"What, you are going to be your family's expert?" she asked. "Why do you want to know, a young boy like you?" But she patiently described how, after squeezing the grape for wine, you take the grape shells, add water, and cook the concoction very slowly in a two-chambered vessel. The steam rises and in the second chamber you put cold water, so the steam condenses. The *palinka* goes on the bottom and drips out, and you capture and bottle that. All the time she was talking, she watched Jozsi's eyes with amusement. She knew he was up to something. Finally, he asked her about the grape roots, how deep to plant them, how you could tell if the plant was healthy, how to weed around them. She squatted down and when he remained standing, looking down, she realized his goal. She tugged on his hand to pull him down level with her, and once he was squatting, she pushed him over and jumped up.

"You devil child," she laughed, but then extended her hand to help the blushing boy to his feet. From the summer porch, Matild, who'd been watching, clucked and called him to her side.

"Jozsi," Matild said, "go to the garden and pick beans. You leave Rebeka alone, she has sewing to do." Jozsi shrugged, picked up a wicker basket and went looking for beans, trying to figure out an excuse to linger by the sewing machine. But no one would believe he cared two cents about how to repair a torn blouse, so he gave up.

Everyday life continued until one day Jozsi saw a number of German troops moving from east to west near the ravine. He had been laying on his back, daydreaming while Bandi grazed, looking over now and then to make sure Jozsi didn't jump up and run to the river without him. Jozsi yanked out a handful of fine grass and held it toward Bandi, calling, "Come, *haverom*," to his special friend, when the horse's ears twitched. A second later Bandi's head tossed in alarm, and Jozsi sat up quickly at the sound of roaring vehicles. A column of German motorcycles with sidecars and trucks were rolling down a nearby road in the direction of town.

Squinting into the light, he could see that the soldiers kept looking back over their shoulders. Suddenly, he heard the deafening sound of airplanes overhead and machine gun fire and the whistle of falling bombs. Within seconds, right before his eyes, bodies and motorcycle parts were flying all over the road. Jozsi sprinted toward Bandi, who old as he was, spun and bucked like a young stallion. Bravely, or more accurately, in a state of panic, Jozsi dove into the middle of a spin, grabbed Bandi's reins and pulled him down the nearest bank. Bandi had no problem following Jozsi and lay next to him as if he had been through this before. Bandi was sweating and panting, so Jozsi rubbed his neck and withers to calm him, even as his own heart pounded wildly. Jozsi wasn't sure who was more scared. He half climbed on the horse as they lay in the ravine, their noses close to the dirt. Suddenly a bomb landed nearby with a thunderous boom. Dirt flew everywhere; clods pummeled them, cold sweat poured down his back. Jozsi shook his head clear of dirt and carefully brushed off the horse's eyes and muzzle.

After the air raid a shaken Jozsi whispered to Bandi as calmly as he could manage, trying to relax the horse, whose heart was beating at hummingbird speed. He babbled nervously that of course the bombing was entirely Bandi's fault, his big rump had given their position away.

What pilot could pass up a chance to aim at such a target? He must have been visible for miles. Jozsi waited for what felt like hours, afraid to put his head above the bank. Slowly, he lifted up enough to peer over the tall grass. He saw German soldiers moving their wounded and dead in silence, in an organized manner, like it was a monotonous exercise.

They didn't seem to notice Jozsi, and if they did, weren't concerned with a kid spectator. This was the first time Jozsi had seen so many dead bodies, body parts covering the field like bones in an exploded slaughter house. The survivors waited for help, yelping in pain. At that moment, Jozsi realized that this was the kind of thing his father and Toth had been talking about; this must have been what it felt like to endure the battles they'd survived. Now he understood something about why, even all these years later, they needed to talk about their Red Devil days whenever they got together. A way of pinching each other to make sure they were still alive.

After the Germans had cleared the area and it felt safe to move, the boy and horse wandered around the ravine, Jozsi searching for shrapnel to take back with him to the city. Though he was in a form of shock, he was already thinking about how he'd brag to Ferenc about having survived a horrible air attack in Ura. As he was walking, he spotted a hole on the side of the bank, not far from where the bomb had landed. He investigated and found some intriguing metal pieces lying around, but by this time he was late for chores. He guessed everyone would understand, they had to have heard the bombing from town, and probably were even worried. He hustled Bandi back toward the Toths. He'd return with a large bag and gather all that metal another day.

When Jozsi returned, he found all the farmhands and most of the family on the veranda discussing the air raid. They were relieved to see him safe. Toth, worried, was already out looking for him. While Jozsi described the bombing and Bandi's fear, Toth appeared and reassured him that Bandi had seen worse in his life. Toth was calm, now that he knew Jozsi was fine, but everyone else remained frazzled.

After supper Jozsi made the milk delivery to the center with Lena and her father. Normal routines had to be carried on with as best as possible, out of necessity and also a fierceness not to let the enemy affect them. Lena told him how scared she'd been; the bombers had flown over as she and her father were returning from the market. She asked Jozsi if he'd been scared, too. He assured her that he had not, that bombings were a common occurrence in the city. He very much wanted to sound grown up and brave. She moved close to him, "The next time the bombers come, I want to be next to you."

"I'll be brave and you won't be scared," Jozsi assured her. Her father smiled at such comforting gallantry. As they approached the ice cream place, Jozsi asked her father to stop so he could buy them a treat. He bought three vanilla ice cream cones, which made Lena very happy. Her father approved too, since it had been a tense day, was now a very hot evening, and he was partial to vanilla ice cream.

After supper, Jozsi even helped Mari clean up the kitchen. He'd been avoiding her more than usual because she'd recently managed to press her breasts against his back, which had felt good and bad at the same time. But the air raid had seriously upset Mari, her hands were shaking, and he felt sorry for her. He hoped he wasn't making a big mistake in being too kind and giving her the wrong idea.

That night, Jozsi lay jittery, unable to sleep. Flash images of body parts and chaos kept startling him awake. Finally, he went outside to sit on the veranda, thinking about all that shrapnel he'd seen lying around the ravine. The next morning, it was as though the bombing had never happened; he could hardly wait to get back out to the ravine and have another look around. All memories of the horror he'd witnessed had slipped from his mind into his unconscious being; for the moment, he was unaware of any lasting impact.

As soon as the shepherd led the animals away, Jozsi grabbed a big burlap bag, mounted Bandi, and headed straight toward the ravine. He slipped off the horse and let him roam, while he headed toward the hole and started loading all the shrapnel he could find into the bag. As Jozsi handled the pieces, he noticed they weren't like other shrapnel he'd seen — these were old and tarnished, and some held inscriptions. Approaching the hole, he saw something that looked a bit like the corner of a coffin. It seemed to have been pushed out of the ground by the explosion. He picked up all the shrapnel lying nearby and then camouflaged the area around the exposed whatever-it-was with mounds of dry brush and tumbleweeds. He didn't want anyone else discovering his secret find. After yesterday's drama, he didn't expect to find anyone at the swimming hole anyway, but he was in a hurry to study the contents of the burlap bag, so he brought Bandi straight home. He brushed the horse, filled his water bucket, threw hay in the stall, and gave him a carrot before pulling the stall door shut. He dragged the bag out behind the barn and laid out the pieces of shrapnel, putting to one side the ones with inscriptions. After looking everything over, he felt very pleased with himself. Now he had something truly special to show his friends back in Budapest.

Jozsi carefully examined the inscribed pieces, trying to decipher words. Since he'd had to learn Latin in Catholic school, he had no problem figuring out the first word: Rex. That meant king. The next piece had a number, "53," but the piece appeared torn from a larger section, and who knew if there'd been other numbers before the "53." The third piece had a "V" inscription on it. None of it made any sense to him.

The next morning, after rushing through his chores, Jozsi returned to the ravine searching for any shrapnel he might have missed. He'd been thorough and didn't spot any, but crawling on hands and knees he did find several pointed arrow tips poking out of the dirt. He tried to clean them off but they were iron and the rust made them flaky. He put those in the bag and again disguised the area. "No one can tell, right?" he said to Bandi. Bandi nuzzled his arm, looking for sugar or a carrot or at least a little forelock tug.

~~~

The summer passed without further drama, and suddenly it was the day his sisters Susan and Maria were set to arrive with Matyas for a quick visit before returning Jozsi to the city in time to begin fifth grade. Jozsi rode back to the ravine one more time, just to confirm that the hole was securely covered and would remain that way. He knew he was too young to do much of anything with his find, but some day he wouldn't be. He'd been tempted to further explore the coffin, if that's what it was, but realized that coping with his haul of shrapnel was enough treasure for the moment. Also, if it were a coffin, he didn't feel quite ready to tackle exploring it all alone.

Late morning, Toth and Jozsi headed toward the train station. While Toth tied up the horse, Jozsi walked into the tavern and asked for his favorite drink. Again, the bartender recognized him, even though it had been weeks since he'd been there. He handed across the bar a tall glass of raspberry drink with lots of soda water. They were pleasantly surprised when the train arrived on time, and Jozsi was gladder than he'd expected to be to see his sisters, especially Susan. They told him Matyas hadn't been able to come; he'd remained to work in the office, getting rid of important papers before the war came any closer to the city. Jozsi shook off his disappointment, he would see his father soon enough. His sisters enjoyed the wagon ride and told him how much Ferenc and Zsigmond had missed him all summer. The girls said Jozsi's friends drove them crazy, stopping by the house almost daily, asking when he would return. That made Jozsi's day, and he was ready to go home right then and there.

By the time that they got to the farm that afternoon, there were young men hanging around that Jozsi had never seen before. Word had spread, he had no idea how, and the men were waiting for his sisters, wearing their best clothes; some even had symbolic good luck red poppies pinned to their hats. They were all young men Rebeka had already rejected, but she kept that to herself. His sisters didn't even bother with supper that night. They spent the entire evening entertaining the boys on the veranda. Some of the young men had even brought candy wrapped in fancy wrappers. Jozsi lurked nearby and snatched pieces; the boys were too distracted to notice. Both young women were attractive, with faces like rosebuds, and they knew how to make a show of themselves. Matyas often said their perfume was strong enough for the American pilots to catch their scent twenty thousand feet in the air. There must have been at least ten boys around the Toth house, which annoyed their fathers, who were expecting their sons to get home and feed the livestock. Toth enjoyed every minute of it, thinking back to when his own sons had been helpless with lust.

Later in the evening Jozsi went to pack, soon realizing that he had so much shrapnel it couldn't possibly fit in his suitcase. Knowing how much Jozsi treasured his collection, Toth loaned him a footlocker and helped him carefully stack the shrapnel inside. Jokingly, Toth commented that he had an old plow in the backyard and if Jozsi wanted that too, he could have it. Everyone burst out laughing and Jozsi promised that he would return for it the following summer.

That night, they stayed up late into the evening, sitting out on the terrace in the pitch dark — a blackout had been issued throughout the country. The Germans believed that if everyone obeyed the blackout, the Americans wouldn't be able to spot them from their bombers. His sisters told him the humming noises they heard overhead might be the sound of American bombers heading toward the city.

Lena stayed with them till late, and Jozsi gave her two pieces of fancy candy as a goodbye present, and promised next summer to bring her a better gift from the city. She was shy and gave Jozsi an innocent look when she handed him her going-away present, a handkerchief she had carefully embroidered with his name. Jozsi was so impressed with her handiwork he kissed her hand, and even in the darkness everyone could see her cheeks redden. Jozsi walked her home and she told him that as long as she lived in this world, she would never forget that night since no boy had ever before kissed her.

In the morning, Jozsi went to brush Bandi one last time. The wagon was loaded up, and goodbyes said all around. The family and farmhands lined up in the courtyard to wish them a safe journey. At the end of the line stood Mari, who hugged Jozsi hard, burying his head between her huge breasts. God knows he hated that; he could smell garlic and had to work hard not to gag. Instead, to her delight, he stepped back and bowed with a flourish. He hoped God would notice his sacrifice.

The wagon started toward the train station and a couple of suitors from the night before appeared on their horses. Soon more appeared, and as they neared the train station, there were close to a dozen young gallants galloping and whirling around on their horses, showing off for Jozsi's sisters. Susan flirtatiously dropped her scarf to see what the boys would do. A few jumped off their horses to retrieve it, which of course started a fight. The scarf, still in one piece, somehow made it back to Susan.

Jozsi told Toth what a good time he'd had and how much he was looking forward to seeing them the next summer. Toth said they would meet again far sooner. "Four of the pigs you let out each morning belong to your father. Once the weather turns cold enough, we'll slaughter them and smoke them in halves. When they're ready, I'll put them on the wagon and bring them to your house. Of course, when I get there, I expect you'll give me the royal treatment." Jozsi promised he would. Toth put his hand on the boy's shoulder and said, "Jozsi, you better be a man of your word because I'll hold you to it."

The train showed up on time and the remaining young men jumped off their horses to help transfer the baggage, and have another chance to inhale the Budai girls' fine perfume. Jozsi gave Toth a hug and with glistening eyes, Toth told Jozsi, "If they don't treat you right in the city, you know there is a family waiting for you here." Jozsi knew he meant it. As the train pulled away, the young men galloped alongside, the same way legendary bandit Sándor Rózsa rode with his gang, hoofs pounding — though these men were cheering and waving, rather than yelling and shooting. Jozsi's sister Susan poured perfume on the scarf and opened the train window. She leaned out, teasing the boys to come along, shouting, "Faster…"

As the train sped up and the boys fell behind, she let the scarf blow free in the wind. The guys were after it like it was the treasure of all time. Jozsi pictured them wrestling over it for days to come. As Susan sat down, she was laughing so hard tears came out of her eyes. Maria told her that was a mean thing to do.

Susan told her younger sister, "This will keep their minds occupied for the winter." And then, tossing her head, added, "And by the way, Maria, that was your scarf I threw." Maria howled, "You wretch! I thought it looked like mine," but couldn't herself keep from laughing. Jozsi leaned back in his chair grinning, happy to be with his sisters and content with everything in his world.

6

Lessons

By the time Jozsi had told Ulee about the train ride from Ura back to Budapest, a ride so uneventful he'd slept through most of the journey, it was time for them to catch the bus from *Changdeokgung Palace* back to Seoul.

He devoted their bus ride, walk to a restaurant, entire meal, and walk back to her place to the story of his return to Budapest late that summer of 1944. Ulee had been seven at the time, and all she had were fleeting memories of Korea's final months under Japanese rule. Her mother's hands pressed tight over her eyes as they hurried away from soldiers beating a young man in front of a market. The small rag doll her mother had stitched together, her one and only toy. Adults stone-faced as the very air simmered with anxiety and suspense. Her mother, pale with fear, trying and failing to appear calm. And hunger. She remembered being hungry day and night.

For Jozsi, buffered by family, friends, and the vigor of being a ten-year-old with a yen for adventure, life had been different. He'd been excited to return to Budapest, see his friends, share his adventures, and make the most of the days before school began. Ulee wanted to know everything about what he found waiting when he returned to Budapest.

"All those planes flying over you that summer were heading for Budapest, yes?" she asked.

"I didn't worry too much," Jozsi said. "I don't remember why not. I probably figured they were only bombing the factories, far from my house and family."

He remembered that, as the train steamed toward Budapest, his sisters hadn't wanted to say much about things at home. "You'll see when you get there," was all Susan volunteered. He remembered that their parents had been waiting at the train station, the train surprisingly close to on time. And that as he bounded down the steps, to his surprise, his friend Ferenc was standing on the platform, dressed in his Sunday church clothes — clean white shirt and dark pants — although Mass was long over. Between the luggage and Jozsi's footlocker of shrapnel, there was no way they could manage to carry everything home. But Ferenc's aunt and uncle lived near the station and he ran to borrow their wheelbarrow. Meanwhile, the Budai parents and their daughters started toward home, carrying what they could.

As the boys took turns steering the wheelbarrow Jozsi noticed all manner of debris and wreckage on the sides of the road. He pointed here and there, puzzled. Ferenc explained. "While you were gone, they started bombing almost every day. Many nights we're sleeping in the cellar. Some families hid in bunkers away from their houses. Our parents are upset and yell about nothing. Just know this: you didn't miss much fun."

Jozsi couldn't quite take in all of this upsetting news. His head was still in Ura, when nighttime meant lying down on a comfortable bed, under an open window to enjoy the smell of fresh sweet air, the hoots and trills of owls and crickets, followed by peaceful sleep. Yes, there had been a horrible air strike, but for Jozsi that was now a great story. Yes, there had been blackouts, but for him they had been fun and given him a new appreciation for the moon. When the moon had been absent, or hidden by clouds, he'd pretended to be blind. He'd practiced finding his away around, imagining himself a sort of bat with legs. Now Ferenc was telling him that nighttime meant fear and discomfort, and morning brought more apprehension because who knew what had been demolished during the night. The boys walked in silence for a time as Jozsi tried to absorb this transformed landscape. The vista of wrecked buildings and torn up sidewalks was overwhelming. No wonder his sisters hadn't wanted to tell him much about what had gone on over the summer.

Jozsi now discovered that many of the places he remembered most sharply had been destroyed. In this part of town, the bombers had spared hospitals and churches, but little else. His mouth fell open when they passed the road to the old electric station, the building had been leveled. In fact, Jozsi realized all of the tallest buildings had been smashed and were now nothing more than gigantic piles of rubble. Not one building higher than ten feet was left standing. The wide road was transformed, as though a furious giant had destroyed everything in its way. But the further they got from the railroad station, the closer to their residential area, the more normal things appeared. Neither Jozsi nor Ferenc's house had been touched.

They wheeled the footlocker behind the Budai's chicken coop. Jozsi promised that the next day he'd dump everything out to show his friend. With that, Ferenc took off to return the wheelbarrow, leaving Jozsi disappointed that his air raid story and mountain of shrapnel might not make much of an impression after all. It seemed Ferenc's summer had been even more dramatic than his own. The rest of the day he plunged into being home. First his mother had to look him over, make sure her baby boy was still her baby boy. He indulged Erzsebet's flood of questions, wolfed down a big bowl of goulash, allowed her to hug and squeeze to her heart's content, and even give his hair a trim.

The next morning, Ferenc appeared bright and early and Jozsi led him to the footlocker. As they pawed through the metal, Jozsi described the day bombers had attacked the German troops while he and Bandi watched from the ravine, and how the following day he'd collected all of this shrapnel near the battlefield. Ferenc agreed it was an impressive amount, but cautioned Jozsi not to get too excited; shrapnel was no longer a collector's item, there was simply too much of it around. These days the valuable goods to salvage from downed planes were live ammunition, canned food, and as before, parachute material and leather jackets that belonged to dead pilots.

He decided to leave the contents from the footlocker out by the chicken coop, but paused over the inscribed pieces. Something about the mysterious inscriptions appealed to him; he felt like he was in the presence of a secret message, an invitation to a puzzle he needed to solve. He placed those pieces in a burlap bag, and after Ferenc left, hid them in the attic. They might not be worth much now, but as he was learning, things did change. Then he wandered down to touch base with the *Rakos River*, the swimming hole, the woods. Later he helped set the table for the big Sunday meal where he was able to share his summer adventures with the entire family. Just as they finished, Ferenc appeared at the door calling for Jozsi to grab his bicycle, it was time for adventure: a plane had been shot down a mile away. "*Óvatos!*" Erzsebet called from the door. "*Mindig,*" Jozsi yelled, as he mounted his two-wheeled steed. The call and response of "be careful," "always," was a ritual with them. Hearing it made Matyas smile. His son was truly home.

The boys peddled to the crash site where they found two downed planes — one a smashed wreck, its fuselage all over the field; the other in better shape and already occupied by a couple of farmers struggling to rip out and carry off its windows. Ferenc explained this was prized material. Celluloid. Jozsi had never even heard the word. It was amazing stuff, Ferenc said, that could keep bullets off, and if you held a match to it, it would burn for hours. Jozsi wasn't sure what was so appealing about any of that, but they stayed off the plane till the farmers had finished scavenging.

Once the farmers left, the boys poked their way through the plane, but there wasn't much of anything to take except for a couple of family pictures Jozsi found taped up in the cockpit. There were no bodies, so they figured the pilots had parachuted out before the crash. In each picture, a man in uniform posed with family. In one, the man appeared with his parents and a look-alike younger brother in front of a stoop on a city street. In the other a different man, his wife, and several kids of various ages, were framed in front of a car parked on a dirt driveway, a small farmhouse in the distance. Jozsi stood transfixed by the portraits. The uniformed men must be the pilots. Where were they now, he wondered. Their American families, a million miles away, had no idea what had happened. Having just returned to his own family, this struck Jozsi as very sad. He carefully, almost tenderly unpeeled the photographs. Handwriting on the back of each listed the names of the people shown, and the date the pictures had been taken. He carefully tucked them into his pants pocket. This became a new habit. By the time the war ended he had scores of photographs. He tucked them away in the same special place he kept the shrapnel with the mysterious inscriptions.

~~~

September came, and suddenly the house was wild with activity. Trunks were dragged out, summer clothes packed away, and winter clothes unfolded, inspected, aired out and draped everywhere. His mother pinned and cut new material, *nagyanya* Alida helmed the sewing machine making repairs and creating new apparel, and Susan and Maria took turns wielding the odd little ironing machine that worked like a tiny stove with a wooden handle. It was the size of a lunchbox with a hole in the bottom, and Jozsi was assigned to feed it with charcoal and swing it back and forth to keep the embers hot. The girls insisted on ironing their best clothes for the opening of the school year, and while they were at it, everyone else's clothes, whether everyone else wanted their clothes ironed or not.

Jozsi had no special clothes to worry about, or so he thought. But one day Erzsebet eyed his favorite pants, already so short two bony ankles showed beneath the cuffs, and shook her head no. The next thing he knew, his parents had him on the bus to the city where they forced him to stand and be fitted for a suit a young person would wear to a wedding or a funeral and nowhere else. Jozsi protested that for him it would be more like a funeral than a wedding since he'd have to wear it to school. He protested that he'd be the only boy in the schoolyard wearing a suit, the other boys and girls would have a good laugh at his expense, it was unfair. He suggested this was unnecessary in a time of war. It was time, his father insisted, war or no war. He was entering fifth grade, he needed a real suit. Jozsi didn't even tell Ferenc, he just quietly counted the days till the dreaded moment he'd have to face the jeering.

Jozsi woke early the first day of school, hoping that maybe an American pilot would mistake the school for a German fortress and bomb it, thus freeing him from his misery. By the time the school was rebuilt, he'd be off exploring the world, released from all nuns and brothers for the rest of time. But in reality, he was sitting at the breakfast table, and the only explosions taking place were from his excited sisters, bursting with anticipation at seeing their classmates again.

Erzsebet filled his backpack with sharp pencils, two notebooks, and held it up for him to step into. "It's orientation, Mama," Jozsi protested, "there's no classes today, I don't need pencils, I don't need a backpack." But she simply tugged on the front straps to adjust them so nothing would wrinkle his suit, and handed him off to his sisters.

"Don't let him get away," she laughed. Surrounded, he had no choice but to start walking the much too short distance to school. In Jozsi's mind he was a revolutionary leader walking toward his execution, about to have his head cut off on a public stand while wearing the best clothes the family could afford; a noble exit, a hero's demise.

At the schoolyard, his sisters immediately ditched him to seek out the friends they'd been yearning to see. Jozsi could barely bring himself to raise his eyes, but was relieved when he did: Ferenc and most of the other boys in his class were standing stiffly in equally formal attire. It must be a conspiracy, thought Jozsi, but he was quickly distracted by the sight of Erika, tidy as ever, hair braided, shoes polished, looking almost regal. The school bell clanged, startling everyone. "It's the archangels, it's the last day on earth," Jozsi yelled, and there was a lot of laughter that abruptly stopped.

High on the school steps stood Father Richter, flanked as usual by Brother Francis and Sister Terezia. Father Richter's expression was that of a ruler pleased at the sight of his subjects, while the sister clutched her rosaries like a drowning seaman with no life jacket, and Brother Francis shouted as though he were Julius Caesar convening the senators, "Come closer, gather students, and listen to what Father Richter has to say." As the crowd assembled and quieted down, the trio of adults scanned the yard, their eyes moving from face to face.

Jozsi leaned toward Ferenc and whispered, "I think they are looking for someone they can blame the war on."

Father Richter, smiling as he always did, welcomed them as he always did. He was glad to see them (he always was), but more so this year than ever before. They were fortunate to be attending this Catholic school, he pointed out, because it was the only school left standing for miles around.

Ferenc muttered to Jozsi, "Does he think we haven't noticed there's hardly *any* buildings still standing?"

Jozsi would have smirked, but the air raid sirens suddenly blared and after a whirlwind moment in which the students' eyes shot wide with fear, Brother Francis yelled that everyone should run home, but return the next day at the same time. Susan and Maria found Jozsi in the mob of kids and together they raced home, where Jozsi's mother shepherded them into the cellar. His father had been out in the field and Erzsebet trusted he'd taken shelter in one of the many bunkers constructed in the area. The air raid lasted five hours, but no bombs dropped. Finally, the siren ending the air raid sounded and Jozsi ran to find Ferenc so they could roam around seeking shot-down planes. The search for valuables was of necessity on the part of adults, for kids, it was just another part of the adventure of daily life.

As they wheeled along, they saw several military ambulances parked in front of what had been an orphanage before the war came to

Budapest; it had since been converted into a hospital. Approaching, they could see wounded men on stretchers being carried into the building. They saw that the men wore jackets, each marked with a six-point yellow star. By now both boys had seen a number of dead bodies, but they weren't used to being just a few feet from the mangled bodies of the living wounded, moaning until they lost even the strength to whimper. This level of suffering froze the boys and they stood stock still, watching the stretcher-bearers move back and forth. From inside and out, they heard the weak cries of wounded men begging for water.

"We can do something," Jozsi blurted. "Water." Ferenc nodded vigorously. Without another word, they pedaled to Ferenc's house — it was closest — dropped their bicycles, filled two buckets with water, grabbed a couple of cups from the kitchen and waddled back down the road, trying not to spill so much as a drop. Ferenc's mother would be mad about the cups but she wasn't there to stop them.

The boys struggled not to be sick to their stomachs as they moved from victim to victim. Jozsi concentrated on the faces, avoiding the wounds when he could, whispering, "You'll be all right," nodding acknowledgment when the injured managed any expression of gratitude. They ran back for more water, and then again. They were exhausted and shaken, but Jozsi reminded Ferenc this was much better than sitting in school.

That night, Matyas explained what had happened to those injured men. The wounded and dead were all Jews the Nazis had been using as laborers at the airport. There were two large hangers, one on either side of the airfield. The Germans had painted a huge swastika on the roof of the hanger where the Jewish labor force worked. Across from that, the German soldiers painted a Star of David on the roof of the hanger they themselves occupied. The American bombers had done just as the Nazis hoped and bombed the wrong building. Jozsi still had only a vague idea of what it meant to be Jewish, but he knew his family was very proud of him for helping the injured, especially Matyas. He squeezed Jozsi's hand saying, "Those people will never forget what you did for them as long as they live."

Jozsi's father had made him feel he'd done something extraordinary, and he liked the feeling. He'd store this memory as special, the way he'd stored the inscribed shrapnel and the pilot photographs. He didn't quite understand his urge to keep the photographs; he just knew he liked looking at them and wondering about the missing pilots and their families, as though his thoughts could somehow help the pilots find their way home.

The next morning, Jozsi made it to the church door on time, thanks to Susan and Maria dragging him along when they left for school. Sister Terezia put check marks next to their names as they entered the building. An elderly priest was saying a Mass at a side altar, and a handful of grandmothers were praying, perhaps for a better harvest, or for their sons to return from the Russian front alive. It occurred to Jozsi his grandmother was never there, though they lived only a few hundred yards from the church. That night he took her aside saying he had something very important to ask her. "*Nagyanya*, how come you're never at church with the other grandmothers?"

Her eyes welled with tears. "My Jozsi," she said, wiping at her cheeks, "when your grandfather went to fight in the war, I was in the church every morning, praying for him to come home alive." She stopped and blew her nose into a little handkerchief she kept in an apron pocket. "I prayed in church and at home, I prayed night and day. But my husband never came back. I don't even know where his body is. I was told he might have been buried with other soldiers somewhere in Russia." She sobbed for a moment, but caught herself, swallowed hard and said coldly, "God didn't answer my prayers and now I don't care if the church burns to the ground. But you keep that to yourself, you understand?"

He'd never seen her cry so he took everything she said very seriously. At the following morning's Mass, he could think of little else. He looked around at the statues and paintings of Jesus Christ and those of the saints whose names he could never remember, and all he could think of was his grandmother praying her heart out until her heart was empty. He asked himself if any of this made sense. To his grandmother, it no longer did. That was enough for him. From then on, he decided he would look at church attendance as a necessary evil, something to satisfy his parents, and at the school as something he had to live with until he could roam free. But he would no longer struggle with the fear of damnation or the rest of that mumbo jumbo the brothers and nuns spouted. If *nagyanya* Alida could stop believing, then so could he.

After Mass, the students lined up outside the church and marched over to the school. It suddenly occurred to Jozsi that they were now behaving exactly like the animals he'd let run through the Toth gate for the town shepherd to lead to pasture. Trained to believe, obedient out of habit. He would obey for now, but know inside that eventually he'd end up being the black sheep that wanders away from the flock.

In their first class with Sister Terezia, they sat on the hard classroom seats, hands tamely clasped behind their backs, as Sister called the roll alphabetically. Next, she asked the children to come forward with their bags of dried corn. Jozsi called it "the mean corn," because it was used as punishment for bad behavior. He'd more than once been directed to a corner of the classroom where he'd had to pour out a handful and kneel on it — a painful, dread discipline.

Zsigmond had no corn — either he'd forgotten or perhaps his parents had none, their family poorer than most. Either way, this was unacceptable and required punishment. Sister Terezia apologized to Erika for taking some of her corn, though of course, Erika had never once had to kneel on so much as a kernel, and poured out a small pile. She pointed at Zsigmond and then at the corn. As he trudged across the room she directed him to roll up his pants, kneel, and think about his omission. The class exchanged glances. This was unjust, even for someone as punitive as Sister Terezia who, ignoring Zsigmond, began carefully printing a series of numerals on the chalkboard in preparation for a mathematics lesson.

Jozsi couldn't keep his mind on the lesson; his eyes kept wandering over to Zsigmond, who was soon wiping tears from his eyes. Jozsi noticed blood coming from his knees as he shifted around to ease the discomfort, and he couldn't help himself, he raised his hand.

"Do you have to go to the bathroom already, young man?" the Sister asked with an edge.

"No, Sister. Zsigmond needs help, he's bleeding."

Sister Terezia inclined her head toward the corner and studied Zsigmond, head bowed in embarrassment as a small tear coursed down his cheek. "Enough," she said, and motioned for him to rise. She turned to Jozsi. "Since you are too busy to pay attention to the lesson, you may take his place until the end of class." She adopted the tone you'd use to reward someone. "Some bonus," Jozsi thought, as he rolled up his pants, and kneeled down. Fortunately for his knees, the class ended within a short time. Moments later the children were skittering down the hall and out into the schoolyard for recess.

Jozsi rubbed his sore knees and reflected that sticking his nose into other people's business didn't always work out so well. Ferenc and Zsigmond ran to his side cheering his bravery at standing up to Sister Terezia. Zsigmond doubted he'd have the courage to do something like that. Jozsi assured him that if Zsigmond ever saw someone suffering, he too would do the same thing. They shook hands, friends in a new way, and Ferenc, who had until then been Zsigmond's only real friend, was glad for that.

The week passed without any further torment at Sister Terezia's hands and the boys went wild on the weekend, burning off all manner of pent up energy racing around on their bikes, thrashing each other in the pond, and playing war in the woods.

When Monday came the air raid sirens blared before the students even had a chance to line up for the 7 AM Mass. The air raid was short-lived though, so Jozsi still had to attend Mass. Now that he'd had his irreligious epiphany, he resented any time in the pew. As they filed into church a scattering of leaflets fell from the sky; the Allied planes were passing low, dropping flyers all over town. Jozsi picked one up and excited, read the contents aloud. The flyer announced that the war would soon be over. It urged all patriotic Hungarian citizens to refuse to assist the German Army, and further, to sabotage the Germans any way they could in order to hasten the war's end. There was such a commotion among the students that Sister Terezia ducked inside and grabbing a big bell, rang and rang to get their attention and settle them down enough to enter the church in properly submissive fashion.

That night, Jozsi and his family stood at the window watching as American planes flew overhead, dropping parachutes that spilled bright flares across the city. They were dubbed *Stalin's Candles*. The flares created so much light over the city that they magically managed to turn night to day, or at least that's how everyone felt. The leaflets and the lights coming one right after the other felt like the beginning of something big. Anticipation flew from one body to another. "Did you see?" was the phrase on everyone's lips.

The following Monday began as usual: church, followed by Sister

Terezia leading them the few yards to the school. But instead of shooing them up the steps, she told them to stay in the schoolyard until Father Richter arrived. Soon enough, he appeared on the top step, the rest of the Holy Trinity flanking him as usual. But that was the only thing usual about his address.

Jozsi didn't know what to expect, but it wasn't what came next. Father Richter held his hands out to the assembled and said, "My dear students, I know how much you were all looking forward to this promising school year." In the distance, they could hear planes, but no sirens blared. Father Richter looked in the direction of the planes and waited a beat. "It is very difficult for me to tell you this, but day by day, the war is coming closer." He paused, breathing deeply. "For your safety, we will have to close the school until further notice."

The students' serious expressions fell away as the news sank in and they erupted in cheers and joyous leaping up and down. But Father Richter held his hand in the air, pope-like, and continued speaking, sobering the mood in an instant. "But do not fear, we are not abandoning you. The school may be closed for the moment, but you must continue to attend Mass every Sunday. Sister Terezia will keep attendance records until school opens again."

Excitedly chattering about the news, the students dispersed in a mad rush. The decision must have been made that very morning, since none of the parents were expecting their children to come racing through their doors. But beneath the excitement, the students registered that matters far weightier than sudden freedom from school's drudgery were at hand. They watched their parents closely for clues. And waited for something to happen.

7

The War

The chilly fall winds swept in from the North and seemed to stir up more than just the leaves swirling in the road. Suddenly Arrow Party members, the only police force in town, if not in the whole country, were patrolling the streets day and night. Unfortunately, their members were neither the finest nor the noblest members of the community. In Hungary, Arrow Party members who supported the Nazi Party were excused from military duty, as long as they helped the Gestapo. Most people saw them as cowards betraying their own people to avoid being sent to fight, and most likely die, in Russia. Even *nagyanya* Alida cursed them under her breath. What everyone feared was the looming siege of Budapest and how savage it might become.

One evening, the Budai family stood in front of the house watching distant explosions as Allies bombed the inner city some miles away. A jeep crammed with Arrow Party members came weaving down the street.

"Too much *palinka*," Alida muttered, tracking the jeep with narrowed eyes. The jeep slowed to a crawl and the man in the front passenger seat called out cheerfully, "Don't worry, this is only an exercise for the German army. You are safe."

Jozsi's father usually managed to control his disgust with those he considered cowards and traitors, but his nerves were fraying and he blurted, "If this is only an exercise, why is the city on fire?"

Erzsebet grabbed his arm to silence him, but Alida chimed in, "That's right!" shocking everyone. The jeep's brakes squealed as it came to a dead stop. Everyone in the family drew close, a single organism alerted to threat. Erzsebet squeezed Jozsi's hand for courage and control — she didn't want him imitating his father. The man in the passenger seat glared at Matyas for many seconds, then gave him an insulting Hungarian gesture — left fist slammed into the crook of the elbow of raised right arm. Icily he added, "Shut up or you'll be coming with us." Erzsebet dug her fingers deep into her son's hand, and Jozsi leaned into his mother. No one said a word. Abruptly, the jeep's driver gunned the engine and peeled away, shouting to all that the German army was winning the war.

But by October, even Arrow Party forces couldn't convince themselves the Germans were winning. In the Carpathian Mountains German and Russian tanks clashed like giant rhinos. The Rumanian people, allied with the Germans, could see their partnership crumbling under the weight of a relentless Russian advance. They stood back and did nothing to stop the onslaught. News that the Russians were smashing their way through the Carpathians made its way to the Budai home. Matyas summed up the events for Jozsi: "The Rumanians are busy turning their coats from German cloth to Russian. Rumanians don't believe in anything, they just cling to the strong till someone stronger comes along."

Jozsi didn't understand how you could abandon your brothers-in-arms — for him, that would be like deserting Ferenc — but Matyas was too preoccupied to untangle the boy's confusion. Rumanians deserting could mean only one thing: the German line was broken. In a matter of days or weeks the Russians would be able to chase the Germans away and take over Hungary, but this was hardly a cause for celebration. Most Hungarians, much as they detested what the Germans had created with their mad dog war, were even more afraid of the Russians. And because Hungarian soldiers were mixed in with the retreating Germans, when people looked in the faces of the young German soldiers, they didn't see Nazis; they saw scared young men swept up in a nightmare. Just as scared as their own sons.

Some days later, late for his afternoon chores, Jozsi peddled his bike as though the devil were on his tail. Turning onto his street, he spotted a wagon in front of their house. Toth's wagon. Salvation! Toth and Matyas were sitting on the veranda, toasting with *palinka*, laughing like they hadn't a care in the world. Toth jumped up at the sight of the boy and opened his arms wide for a big hug and a kiss on each.

"You're getting too big for me to pick up," he said with affection. At his feet was a package, a present from Lena — several cherry strudels and a note, which he handed to Jozsi. Lena had written carefully with pen and ink; her flowery handwriting spoke of how much she missed him, adding that the boys at her school could not hold a candle to her dear friend Jozsi. He shared the pastries with his family, but kept the contents of the note a secret. He'd show it to his friends, a token to brag about since none of them had a girl pining for them all the way from Ura.

As promised, Toth brought four pigs, gutted and smoked in halves, each half weighing close to 200 pounds. The pigs had been cut lengthwise, from head to tail, and smoked to last for eternity. Jozsi's mouth began to water. After the men had carried all the meat up to the attic, Toth brought in the sausages and fresh pork meat. Erzsebet felt relief. Food was scarcer and scarcer. It was too dangerous to go into the city, and the war had spread to the countryside, so you couldn't safely venture there either. Storing food was common practice, and this particular fall, if you had nothing to store, you were going to be in trouble. It was a good thing Matyas had thought ahead and paid Toth to raise extra pigs. Smoked pork could last for close to a year stored in the attic. They'd already hung grapes up there, filled bags with corn and flour, and metal containers with lard. Stored in the wine cellar were wooden barrels filled with wine and apple cider. Who knew what lay ahead; they'd readied themselves as best they could.

That night they feasted and talked late, discussing the war and how it had already changed their lives forever. By this time, much of their town had been without electricity for a few months. His mother was using the summer kitchen's wood-burning stove to cook their meals. And now that daylight hours were short, they were acutely aware of the lack of light. The glow from a single kerosene lantern lit their suppers; they climbed into bed early, exhausted from the stress and deprivation. Yes, they were fortunate enough to have good food, but Erzsebet had been rationing for some time, so no one ever ate enough to feel full.

Later, Jozsi lay on his bed thinking about how good it felt to know they missed him on the farm. He thought, too, about the treasure in the ravine. He planned to claim it just as soon as he could get back to Ura… and be big and old enough to manage the task. He finally drifted off to sleep, lulled by the list of items he imagined the coffin held: golden goblets, sapphires and rubies and emeralds, rings and chains and furs, and weapons and, and…

After breakfast, Toth hitched up his horses. Jozsi and Matyas gave him a couple of precious sugar cubes for Bandi. Jozsi rubbed the cubes in his hands so Bandi would recognize his smell, or so he hoped. They wished Toth a safe journey — there was no way of knowing what he might run into on his way home — and stood waving until he was out of sight.

Then Matyas called the family into the living room. He cautioned that the war would be fully on them before Christmas and that people would be desperate for food. What Toth had brought had to be kept a family secret or they'd end up needing to stand armed guard over their bounty. Jozsi was proud to be trusted enough to keep a secret, his father hadn't directed any particularly stern looks his way, and he swore to himself he wouldn't even tell Ferenc.

The sun set and rose again, and that day Jozsi and Ferenc journeyed to the playground. Warned their freedom to roam might soon be ending, they'd made a list of places they'd miss, vowing to visit each one. After a benign excursion to one of them, they'd stowed their bikes behind Jozsi's house and discovered what seemed like thousands of shoes piled against the cellar entrance. Matyas, who rarely joked, came outside and said, "You like? I got them for you boys. Hope they'll last the winter." Then he explained how they had come to be drowning in shoes. He'd heard word that one of Budapest's shoe factories had been bombed and ventured into the city to see if he could buy whatever shoes were left to use for fuel. Leather burned clean and hot, and he knew coal and wood would be scarce in the days ahead. The Allied forces were now bombing the railroads and there'd be no way to haul supplies in to withstand the winter. Jozsi was again amazed by his father's ability to plan ahead and imagine how life might be in the future. He knew that was a skill he needed to develop…someday. For now, he'd stick to trying to think five minutes ahead; it was all he could manage.

Jozsi's chore for the rest of the week was to carry and stow away all the shoes in the attic. "Make them tidy," Alida emphasized. Ferenc volunteered to help and was rewarded with a matching pair of brand new shoes that fit him perfectly, his first new pair in three years. He raced home to show his mother. Jozsi hoped this might stimulate some goodwill in his direction. He'd been trying to win over his friend's mother forever. She was one of a very few people who just did not like him. Ferenc said not to worry; she didn't much like anybody.

~~~

The arrival of the shoes was about the only good thing that happened for a long while. Yes, there was no school, but the effects of war pounded their days into misshapen lumps; their freedom was very far from carefree. Late one morning, after playing in the woods, Jozsi and Ferenc pedaled through town and noticed that Mrs. Gubo's general store was closed, a big yellow star painted on the door. Mrs. Gubo was short and round, hearty as a horse and Jozsi couldn't remember the store ever being closed. The boys wondered about the star, too, although without alarm, and then moved on.

Jozsi and Mrs. Gubo had their own special friendship. He'd often stop in to say hello. A little bell would jingle when he opened the door, and her round face would appear, a hair net holding thin white strands in a bun, a welcoming smile on her face. He'd wander the store, his pockets empty of coins, knowing she'd give him his favorite raspberry candy, money or no. Sometimes she'd have him sweep the store, most often, she'd simply hand the candy over, "*Élvez*," enjoy, and wave him on his way. Jozsi would rush home, candy tight in his fist. He'd settle into his secret spot under an eave in the attic and suck on the candy till it melted on his tongue. Then he'd hold the wrapper to his face, filling his nose with the sweet aroma.

Later that afternoon, knowing Ferenc's mother would have him submerged in chores, and with nothing better to do, Jozsi headed back toward the town center, hoping the store might be open, or that some other interesting event would occur along the way. Without school to endure, the days could feel long, though he'd never admit to that.

Up ahead he saw a number of townspeople walking in line toward the railway station. They were either carrying suitcases, or had large sacks slung over their shoulders. Approaching, he noticed they each had bright yellow stars sewn on the back of their coats. Catching up to the line, he saw that yellow stars were sewn on the fronts as well. Confusing. And why were all these people heading to the train station looked miserable. Where were they going? He pedaled slowly alongside the line, hoping to hear words that would explain the situation.

He recognized Mrs. Gubo's hair-netted bun, poking out from under a wide brim straw hat. She was struggling with her suitcase, using both hands to handle its heavy weight. Suddenly she stumbled. She stopped, wiped her brow, again hoisted the suitcase and tottered unsteadily forward. Jozsi laid his bike by the side of the road and ran to help.

"Oh, my dear," she said, "no, no you mustn't. Go home, go now." She was flustered and struggled to tug the suitcase from his hands. Jozsi thought she was embarrassed or just plain stubborn and held on. She looked around worried, but kept moving forward. They passed German soldiers standing on each side of the column of marchers, commanding people to walk faster, *"Lauf schneller,"* they shouted harshly.

At the station, the marchers huddled in clumps to wait for the train. Jozsi was afraid to open his mouth enough to ask what was going on. Tears trickled down Mrs. Gubo's cheeks as she stammered muted thanks, *"Köszönöm,"* then hissed, *"Elmenekül!"* urging him to make a run for it. She nudged him, but the second he took a step, a German soldier shoved him from behind and he fell to the ground.

The soldier pointed his bayonet at the boy's chest and ordered him back in line. Jozsi had one of those moments where he reacted without even a second's thought. *"Nem, nem, nem,"* he screamed at the soldier: no to the order, no to the people in line, to the yellow stars, to the luggage, to the war. Since Jozsi wasn't wearing a yellow star, the soldier wasn't quite sure what to do, but he kept pointing him toward the line. Finally, a Hungarian officer appeared to see about the ruckus. He grabbed Jozsi by the shoulders and swung him around. Lucky for Jozsi, it was Vilmos, a distant cousin to the Budai family. He spoke to the officer in German — Jozsi had always heard Vilmos was a bit of an idiot so was impressed that he could speak German. The soldier backed away and Vilmos roughly pulled Jozsi out of the line.

"Get the hell out of here before I kick your ass." He clapped twice. *"Megy!"* Go.

He went. Lucky for him, his bicycle was still by the side of the road.

As soon as his father returned from work, Jozsi told him what had happened. Matyas thought carefully before he spoke. "You are like Ganix," he said, a mysterious reference he said he'd explain to Jozsi when he was older. Matyas was proud of his son for helping Mrs. Gubo, but his blood ran cold when he imagined what might have happened if not for Vilmos. He explained that the Germans didn't like the Jews and were trying to force them out of the country, and that Mrs. Gubo was

Jewish. When Jozsi demanded to know why the Germans had the right to tell any Hungarian they had to leave, especially kind Mrs. Gubo, all Matyas could do was sigh.

"You have to be careful," he said, finally. "We all have to be careful." He hugged his son, and sent him to the kitchen to help Erzsebet. Matyas's head hurt from all the things he could not say. He knew Jozsi was too young to make sense of what he himself could not bear to accept.

~~~

During the weeks that followed, Jozsi, Ferenc and Zsigmond formed a small pack. Each day they trolled for downed planes. By this time, despairing German patrols had given up even trying to track down and interrogate downed pilots. The boys would quickly guide any pilots they found to Ferenc's uncle, who gave them each a small chocolate for anyone they brought his way.

Another source of pleasure came from Jozsi's 18-year-old sister Katalin, who was fortunate enough to have a job at a local candy factory that was still in operation. This brought in money as well as the occasional candy bar. She was dating Miklos, a boy from their town, who'd been spared army service because he was a weapons expert and worked in a nearby weapons factory. He had good standing with Jozsi. While wooing Katalin he'd slip the boy candy and chocolates purchased from the factory. Alida also thought him a worthy suitor because Miklos would bring her candy as well. Erzsebet and Matyas would have been more enthusiastic had he been Catholic, but he was Protestant and that was concerning. They hoped Katalin would tire of him, or that he'd be sent to fight when the factory was inevitably bombed. When the young couple announced that they intended to marry after the war, Erzsebet cried herself to sleep, murmuring, "How is she going to cook for Protestants?" Alida, hearing from her son that his wife was beside herself, took Erzsebet aside the next day.

"You must know," she said firmly, "there's no difference in the cooking, except for the salt."

"Salt?" Erzsebet asked, puzzled.

"Salt," Alida nodded sagely. "The Catholics put salt in while you're cooking. The Protestants add salt *after*."

"Hunh," Erzsebet answered, in a rare moment of opposition to her beloved mother-in-law, "you just like the boy because he bribes you with sweets."

Most of the time the Budais were too busy preparing for the Russian Army's impending occupation to fret about much else. They hid away immense amounts of the lard they'd need for cooking before the Russians could arrive and seize it. Erzsebet carved out fresh pork roast and chops from the Toth-raised pigs, then stored them inside 25-gallon barrels in melted fat. This insured the family would have a substantial stockpile for rainy days. Alida told Jozsi the meat could stay fresh for years since there was no air to age it.

"Thank you for the science lesson," he answered, "but I'm hungry for a chop right now!" She'd been right, though, because two years after the war, Jozsi and his family were able to enjoy small bits of fresh pork roast. She'd been happy then to again remind him of the wonders of lard. The government had forbidden anyone to hoard food while the whole country was starving, but not one of the Budais felt guilty.

By this time, Matyas had stopped going to his job and instead spent his days preparing the wine cellar for the family to sleep in at night and hide in during the day when necessary. Matyas' great-grandfather had constructed it close to a hundred years ago and to Jozsi it felt like an Egyptian tomb.

The wine cellar, close to a hundred feet long and forty feet wide, was beneath the house and driveway. Its walls were built close to six feet high, straight up, and made of a very thick stone the Hungarians called Aged Stone, which was really microscopic shell molded together and cut into 3-by 2-foot squares. On top, the stones were laid at angles, so the ceiling had a half-round, arch shape. The stone was so strong it could hold a house built directly on top. The microscopic shell had tiny empty spots of air and the millions of shells used in building the cellar kept the temperature stable. Matyas explained to Jozsi that the barrels of wine needed steady temperatures, otherwise the wine would spoil or start fermenting. Matyas had never been much for making wine and in happier times had leased their cellar to others for storing their barrels. But now everyone fortunate enough to have a cellar was readying it as a hiding place. The cellars were so sturdy no bomb could penetrate. Matyas assured the children that if necessary they could stay underground for the rest of the war. This did not cheer them up; they'd already spent too much time in the cellar during air raids.

On the right-hand side was a huge room where barrels were stowed. On the left, a 12-by-12-foot room. There they stored vegetables in benches hollowed out to hold a bed of dry yellow sand; the sand protected the fresh produce from rot-inducing humidity and moisture. At the end of summer, harvested vegetables were laid in the sand. Jozsi had run up and down the steps hundreds of times carrying baskets filled with carrots, potatoes, celery, and cabbage. Onions, corn, and grapes he'd take up to the attic where the dry air kept them fresh. The rafters were hung with bags for certain items, though the grapes were simply tacked to the roof for easy grabbing. Most houses had a smokehouse, and the Budais had always made good use of theirs. But Toth had saved them the trouble this time. The pigs he'd delivered hung in the attic where one of the elder children would be told to go cut a rib, or ham or loin. Everyone in the house old enough to handle a large knife knew how to butcher.

Matyas moved all of his barrels to one end of the large room. Then he had the family assembly-line bundles of straw down through the outside bulkhead door. They brought down their bedding — large sewn-together cloths filled with straw — to lay upon the straw padding. After each harvest, they'd empty and wash the cloths and put in fresh straw. By the end of the year, that straw was flat, and everyone complained of sore backs. At least they were starting out with hefty bedding, their sewn-together blankets stuffed with chicken feathers, thick and warm. You needed to dress warmly when you stayed in the cellar because there was no chimney, no way to have a fire. The stone held onto the cold and released it straight into their bones.

Since they were already used to sleeping several to a room, the lack of privacy came as no great hardship. They spent daylight hours upstairs, living as normally as possible. Each night they'd pile on warm layers and climb down through a trap door in the floor. Matyas would disguise the door with a throw rug and a reading chair, and then enter through the bulkhead, locking it tight behind him. Jozsi tired of the cellar's wine smell, but Alida said she didn't mind it, not one bit.

After several days of flurry, everything was set up. Many times, they'd had to rush to the cellar during nighttime air raids, dragging along for warmth whatever they could grab. Now, to find their bedding ready and waiting seemed a luxury. Jozsi liked the suspense of throwing open the bulkhead door each morning to find the rest of the house still standing. He came to savor his freedom to move around the house during daylight the way he'd once appreciated raspberry candy. War taught you odd things, he thought, but he was looking forward to the end of all its teachings. Despite the disruption to their daily life, and the necessity of sleeping in a fortress, for some reason Jozsi was never really afraid; it didn't occur to him that he could end up as just one more dead body.

~~~

By November the German police had completely vanished, and any planes shot down by the Allied forces were easy pickings for pillaging. Most often, the pilots and soldiers parachuted off before the planes crashed. People would scramble onto a wreck, grab whatever jackets and food were on hand, and then strip the gas tanks of their rubber linings. In the only kind of science lesson Jozsi was then getting, Matyas explained that the Americans lined their gas tanks with raw rubber in case bullets penetrated a tank. The tank would start leaking gasoline and the rubber would melt, but as soon as it came into contact with air it would harden, and that would seal the tank. The pilot might never even realize his gas tank had been shot. Once the raw rubber was dissolved in alcohol, it became useful for sealing bicycle tires, shoes, and household appliances. "We learn to make do," Matyas said, over and over. Jozsi felt great pride in his father's knowledge and ability to explain. If he grew up to be half that smart, he thought, he might be able to make something of himself.

During the following weeks, they watched the German army retreat toward Budapest to make its last stand against the advancing Russian army. The soldiers were spent; their uniforms dirty, torn, battle-worn, their boots a bare memory of what boots could be. The family stood outside the house, occasionally offering passing soldiers water and bread, though some of the soldiers didn't even lift their heads to look up, they simply trudged on, dead-eyed, marching toward the city. The sight of those downtrodden soldiers reminded Jozsi of Ura, and of lying in the ravine with Bandi, watching the soldiers pick up their dead and injured. He swore he would never be a soldier. Even though you got to carry a weapon, it didn't look like fun at all.

By December, the only men wearing uniforms around town were the Hungarian border patrol, who drove up and down the streets alongside the Gestapo, looking for deserters. Sometimes they'd find an exhausted, scrawny deserter huddling behind a barn, or corner one cowering in a cellar. The Gestapo soldiers were heartless. They'd drag their victims — blindfolded or not depending on whim or scarcity — to the center of the town square and shoot them like rabid dogs. Some victims, either resigned or emotionally gutted, went along easily, as though about to tend to a straightforward municipal transaction at the town hall. Others flailed and fought, inviting a hideous beating before being killed. Often, shots rang out several times a day. People avoided the town square if they could, although seeing dead bodies on the ground was no longer uncommon. Every man, woman, and child had seen a lifetime's worth.

Jozsi wondered how the Gestapo, how all the Germans, had come to the conclusion that they were so much better than others, better enough to have the right to shoot those with different views. Before he even understood exactly what he was feeling, a patriotic fire began burning in his heart and it never ebbed.

One night, just before Christmas, the Budais were lingering late at the supper table when they heard the sound of tanks. That wasn't unusual and no one reacted until a sudden loud knock at the door sent a chill through the room. Matyas opened the door to find his cousin Kazmer, standing tall in his Hungarian Army uniform. Within seconds the rest of the family surrounded him, hugging him all the way to the table. Before Kazmer had joined the army, he'd been a regular visitor to their home. His mother, a cousin of Erzsebet's, had died when Kazmer was 17, and her husband had died not long after, so he'd become an honorary member of the Budai family.

Before Kazmer could sit, Matyas poured him a glass of *palinka* and they toasted their health and good fortune. They might be in the midst of wartime, but they were alive and well and sitting together as they had on so many other nights. Kazmer quickly quieted the celebration. He was a captain in the Hungarian division, covering the retreating German Army, and he had news to share. He caught Matyas' eye, inclining his head toward Jozsi with a questioning look: too young to hear? Jozsi, on high alert, didn't miss anything. But his father's hand motioned him to sit back down, and the boy flushed, feeling very grown up at being allowed to stay for the discussion.

Kazmer had only a few minutes to spare, but he'd wanted to stop and warn them the Russians were only a few miles away. He said that Stalin was hell bent on taking control of Budapest in order to make a forceful impression at the February Yalta Conference. The Russians were coming full on and fast. Erzsebet jumped up and hurried to the kitchen while Kazmer talked.

"How soon will they be here?" Matyas asked, his eyes intense, voice steely hard.

Kazmer tossed back the *palinka*. "We set a Russian tank on fire at the crossroad. By the time it burns out, the Russians will be here." Jozsi thought: this is how you tell time in war, by how long it takes a tank to burn. Erzsebet returned with a sack of food for Kazmer, and as he moved toward the door, Matyas caught up to him with a full bottle of *palinka*.

"For you and the men in your command." They embraced and wished each other luck.

Kazmer winked at Jozsi, as if to say, "See you later," then jumped onto his tank. Within minutes, the group of tanks were roaring toward Budapest to make a last stand. They hoped to see Kazmer again. "There's no use for a dead hero," Matyas muttered.

It was time to disappear into the cellar, though everyone was too keyed up to want to hide. They readied the trap door, but stayed in the dark house, peering out from behind curtains windows and waiting. By the light of the moon no more than three hours later they spied a thin stream of soldiers advancing in the direction of the city.

"These are Rumanian soldiers," Matyas whispered, shaking his head in puzzlement, "not Russian."

The Rumanian company passed the house, and right behind came the Russian KGB. Kazmer had not mentioned anything about Rumanians. Early in the war, when Hitler was winning, the Rumanians had enthusiastically linked arms with the Germans against the Russians. The Germans had relied on the Rumanians to hold the front against the Russians, but now the tide had turned and with it the Rumanians. Okay, thought Matyas, the Rumanians allowed the Russians to stride through the Carpathian Mountains unobstructed. But to have the Rumanians lead the invasion seemed crazy. What idiots would count on them? He would soon learn that the Russians indeed looked at the Rumanians as a nation without honor, not to be trusted. They welcomed the Rumanians, yes, and then placed them at the head of all invasions. In any ambush, the Rumanians would fall by the hundreds, and if any tried to turn back, the KGB would shoot them on the spot. To the Russians, they were nothing more than cannon fodder. But in that moment, all Jozsi knew was that his father, who usually understood everything, was mystified. This made him even more nervous than the fact that a new and feared army seemed about to take over their town. Matyas's cool steely gaze was replaced by another expression, and it bordered on fearful.

The struggle for control of their town was over within days. The Russians set up a command post in the area from which to launch an invasion against the Germans, who still held the city of Budapest. In no time, the locals felt the pain of occupation by this new army. Russian soldiers quickly began looting the locals and raping women. The Budai girls were never left alone at home, nor did they travel alone. But still, one afternoon a drunken Russian soldier showed up at the house, swigging from a bottle of *palinka*, demanding a woman. The only two at home that day were Alida and Susan. While he shouted, Alida hid Susan under her bed in case he broke into the house. Alida, in her eighties, had a steely calm to match her son's. She was not afraid for herself; if he shot her dead, so be it. But she would not stand for anyone else being harmed.

When the soldier kicked open and stumbled through the front door, she shouted from upstairs, "Here is woman," and sat on her bed. The soldier followed the sound of her voice to the bedroom doorway where his eyes lit on Alida, blouse up, exposed breasts hanging to her waist like two enormous pods. He shook his head, spat *"Nyet,"* took another pull of *palinka*, clumsily made his way back downstairs and out the door, and stumbled off down the road.

There were many such incidents during the first months of the occupation. Almost every night they heard Russian voices on the street outside their house, frequently followed by pounding on the door. For Katalin's boyfriend Miklos, this was a bit of a positive, because suddenly Matyas and Erzsebet gained a new appreciation for his 6'2 height, powerful build and commanding voice. Matyas even fixed him a place in the cellar, many feet from Katalin, but still, the two were happy to be breathing the same air.

A few nights before Christmas, as they finished supper, another drunk Russian soldier starting banging on the door, demanding a woman, a *young* woman. Matyas ordered Jozsi to quickly move the women's plates from above to under the table, while he hustled his three daughters and wife through the trap door to the cellar. Alida demurred, she could not move fast enough. Quickly, the secret hole in the floor was covered and the males flopped into their seats and continued eating. The determined drunk kept pounding, and in fractured Hungarian let them know he'd heard there were many girls in this house and they must open the door. He only wanted one he added plaintively, the most beautiful one.

Miklos held his palm up to Matyas; he would handle this. He shouted at the soldier to hold on a minute as he pulled Jozsi up from his seat and hid him behind the couch. Then he strode to the front door, craning his neck to see if any other soldiers lurked nearby. He let the drunken Russian in, then closed and locked the door behind him, talking loudly so the soldier didn't hear the lock click.

"Just one," the soldier begged in Russian. He didn't look so tough now that he was inside — more young and dirty and weary than fierce.

"Come, Ivan," Miklos put an arm around him and led him into the dining room. "Sit here. I'll call in the girls and you can pick." The soldier smiled crookedly, so drunk he looked like the only activity he might manage would be to topple like a felled oak onto a woman before passing out cold. By the time the Russian had taken a step toward what he hoped was a night in nirvana, Miklos had bent down and grabbed a small sawed off shotgun he'd placed under his chair. He said, "The next time you'll have a young girl is when your maker grants you one." The Russian didn't have time to decipher the words. Miklos shot him in the chest, blood sprayed everywhere, and Alida screamed. Jozsi, huddled spot behind the couch, heard the soldier's gurgled effort to hold onto life.

"*Dosvidania*, comrade," Miklos said, bidding him a soldierly farewell. The body collapsed like an empty grain bag, falling to the floor where it lay motionless, legs askew. To Jozsi's surprise, Alida made the sign of the cross in the air above her plate.

Miklos stared down at the dead man and Matyas took command. "Jozsi, open the trap door and get your mother up. Tell the girls to look for an empty barrel down there, tell them to open the cellar door."

Erzsebet, the crown of her head emerging through the trap door, saw the body before her head had cleared the floor. "My god," she murmured, thinking of what might befall them if anyone found out, and clambered out to find an old blanket or sack to throw over the dead man. Then she directed Alida and the girls to grab buckets of water and rags and start scrubbing every inch of the dining room where blood had spattered. Susan was stoic and immediately went into action. Katalin, the most high-strung of the girls, was rattled, but managed to pull herself together enough to grab a rag and start scrubbing. Maria, the true beauty of the family, was terrified, shaking too much to be of any help. As the most beautiful, she knew the Russian would have gone after her; she couldn't stop imagining what might have happened. They let her be.

Meanwhile, Miklos and Matyas rushed to bring the empty barrel upstairs while Jozsi ran to the front door to act as lookout. They couldn't afford to be seen bringing a barrel into the house. They forced the body into the barrel and nailed it shut. By eleven that night, the two men had pushed the barrel down to the Rakos River and rolled it in. "I want to make sure this gets to the Danube by dawn," Miklos said, giving it one last kick with his huge boot. They stood in the dark, listening to waves jostling the barrel away.

Relieved they'd managed to dispose of the body, Matyas called for a celebration. Even Jozsi was given a glass, making this his first official manly shot of *palinka* from his father. After having heard someone shot at close range, Jozsi was grateful for the drink.

"You are a man now, my son," Matyas said, proud that Jozsi swallowed his first sip without gagging. *Palinka* was without doubt an acquired taste, but he'd tasted it before; his grandmother had been sneaking him secret sips for years. At Easter, most boys old enough to hold a glass were allowed a sip if they could stand the taste, but Matyas hadn't yet allowed Jozsi to indulge.

Alida was beside Jozsi and whispered into his ear, "You see, fathers love to be the first to officially offer the *palinka*." She winked at him and the world tilted right again; he felt calmer. Forever more, this moment tied together for Jozsi the insanity of life, the safety of home, the love of family, with the reality that at any moment a knock on the door could topple the entire world.

~~~

As Christmas day approached, at least they managed to find a small pine sapling to place on a bureau. There was no piling of presents, no baking of special holiday desserts. They didn't even have *szaloncukor*, a traditional Christmas candy — its brightly colored foil wrapping, tasseled at both ends, made it perfect to hang as Christmas tree decorations. Katalin managed to procure a small stash of bright foils from the candy factory, and the girls had a fine time wrapping bits of coal in the foils. Jozsi broke up the coal, while Alida cut the foil into small pieces. They were tiny replicas of *szaloncukor*, but better than nothing, and the colors were cheery. They hung them from string, creating a miniature version of Christmas trees of old.

They did manage to have a traditional Christmas Eve meal of baked fish, apple slices, oranges, grapes, prunes, and nuts. Matyas managing to provide all these special foods seemed a magical act for Jozsi. Alida nodded in agreement, not wanting to ruin the mystery. But she'd raised a smart boy, she thought, and if anyone in the city had goods that Matyas was determined to purchase, she knew he'd find exactly what he was looking for, and at the lowest price. Let Jozsi think he'd waved a magic wand. It was good to see the boy smile.

No one attended midnight Mass. The Russians were roaming the streets looking to steal watches and decent pairs of shoes from anyone fortunate enough to be wearing such items. Miklos said the loot was to bring back to their remote villages, they wanted to show off their treasures to the ignorant heathens who lived there. They especially liked bright, shiny watches, which was ironic, Miklos said, since they couldn't even tell time.

Christmas morning, there was a knock on the door, but instead of the Three Kings, they found a huddle of Russian soldiers, asking about a missing comrade. "And looking for food to steal," Alida muttered in Jozsi's ear. The family was very cooperative but said they hadn't seen any lone soldiers, just groups. The Russians looked around the house, and while they were at it, stripped all the candies off the tree, leaving with big smiles on their faces. It took only a few minutes before one of the soldiers returned and threw the candy at Alida, who happened to be near the door when he knocked.

"You need this to keep warm, old hag," he shouted, stomping off, spitting on the ground with every other step. The family laughed about that the rest of the day and re-hung the coal. They were relieved nothing more serious had happened.

~~~

Winter dragged on, unusually cold, as though the weather were at war with them too. Within the city, the battle for control raged; on the outskirts of Budapest the suffering was constant, though less explosive. In January, Hitler agreed to withdraw his troops from Pest, in order to concentrate on defending Buda. German troops mined and destroyed all eight bridges in order to cut off the Russian advance from the east and the fighting on Margaret Island was especially brutal. The island, in the middle of the Danube, was still attached to the city by a section of the Margaret Bridge that remained and was being used as a parachute drop zone.

As the war intensified, city folk began to abandon their homes and seek shelter with relatives elsewhere, hoping to return some day, if the war ever ended. Coal and wood were scarce no matter where you were, fuel invisible, the electricity out for months on end. Those lucky enough to have kerosene used lanterns sparingly, saving up tasks that required light for a flurry of activity, everyone simultaneously bustling to do what needed doing. The Budais were lucky to have small amounts of kerosene, thanks to Matyas' resourcefulness.

They burned a lot of shoes during that long winter, and when the temperature plunged, Matyas put coal in the stove, just to raise the heat to a more bearable level. Jozsi's friends were frequent visitors, desperate to take the chill off. Having shivered in their own homes the night before, the warmth would often cozy them so much they'd fall asleep wherever they happened to be sitting. Matyas never minded. "The more bodies in the room, the less air we need to heat." When he'd spot heartbreakingly worn shoes on a guest, he'd let them dig through the piles till they found two that fit, even if they were of different shapes.

Supper became a time of dreaming, of remembering sumptuous holiday meals, or delicacies they'd enjoyed from what felt like back in ancient time. Supper was often a soupy goulash, which, as the war wore on, became skimpier, more water than substance. Matyas had stockpiled potatoes; those at least gave the goulash a little heft, and reminded their teeth what it felt like to chew. But they rationed the stored pigs carefully and very rarely did they have meat of any kind. Bread was a staple as long as they could manage to hold onto their supply of flour, but even that needed to be replenished now and then, and sometimes they had to do without.

~~~

The Russian command was not far from Jozsi's house, and soldiers built fires in barrels to keep warm as they readied themselves for the next clash in the city. Guards kept the fires going and directed traffic for exhausted soldiers returning from the city and those well enough to embark on another skirmish. The wounded and dead were transported back in trucks, the dead dropped off at the same crossroads where Jozsi's uncle had set a Russian tank on fire just a few months earlier.

By late winter, the Russians had buried over five hundred soldiers in a series of mass graves. The Germans put up a desperate fight, knowing this was their last chance to stave off defeat. The Hungarians fought hard too, fearing the Russians would savage them if they took charge. Casualties mounted on both sides as the Russian Army fought to take the city, street by street, extending even into the sewers, with both sides using them for moving troops.

For days, injured and dead, soldiers and civilians, littered the boulevards of Budapest; there was no one to care for the wounded much less to bury the dead. People would do just about anything to feed their starving families. If a horse was killed on the street, people risked their lives to run into the middle of battle, hoping they could carve a piece of meat off the horse. It horrified Erzsebet that the horses weren't always quite dead when attacked by knife-wielding people. Matyas and Jozsi were relieved that Bandi was far from the city.

~~~

One afternoon Jozsi and Ferenc roamed near the crossroads, arriving just in time to see 50 or more soldiers being lowered into a mass grave. Their young lives had been so transformed by war that this was what passed for entertainment; 50 dead bodies at a glance left them unfazed. What made an impact was a Hungarian woman wearing an ill-fitting Russian uniform who stood at the edge of the grave, howling with grief, begging the soldiers to let her jump in. She screamed a man's name, repeatedly lunging forward to free herself from two soldiers, arms crooked through hers to hold her back. The boys wondered if she mourned her husband or her lover. How could a Hungarian love a Russian? And what was Zsigmond up to? He hadn't been around in a while. This was a normal conversation during the war. They'd completely forgotten what it was like to complain about homework, or classroom boredom.

The boys trudged toward home. These days they rarely rode their bikes far from their street lest someone steal their precious transportation. Walking took longer, but they had nothing in particular to do, other than chores, which even war did not erase. As they walked, they filled their pockets with live ammunition spotted along the sides of the road. It was amazing how many live bullets and hand grenades a person could find just walking down a road, enough to start a whole new war.

The tavern hall came in view just as the sun lowered enough to set a chill. A couple of wounded soldiers sat on wooden crates outside the hall, now converted into a primitive hospital. The boys noticed smoke coming from a barrel near the hall. They knew they were already late for supper and in trouble. A few more minutes' delay wouldn't change a thing.

"Let's warm up," Jozsi said, pointing toward the smoke. "We still have a long way to go." But when they got close to the barrel, they felt no warmth; the fire, embers now, was close to dying. There didn't seem to be a lot of wood immediately at hand to feed it back to life, but Jozsi had a bright idea. If he tossed ammunition into the barrel it might help flare things up. He told Ferenc to look for any kind of wood he could find. Ferenc raced away and came back with fallen branches and twigs and a piece that you could almost call a small log. He dumped all of it in the barrel. Jozsi emptied his pockets and threw ammunition into the fire. His coat had big pockets, so he carried the bulk of what they'd found. They stared into the barrel, afraid all they'd managed to do was smother what little blaze was left.

A few more soldiers limped out of the hall with canes and crutches. With no flames in sight, the boys ceded their spot and hurried away, not seeing any reason to interact with unhappy, injured Russians on this dark, chill evening. The soldiers went straight to the barrel and held their hands out for warmth, while another able-bodied soldier hacked away at a nearby fence with a hatchet, and still another carried out empty ammunition boxes and tossed them in. The boys hadn't gotten very far and kept turning back to see if the soldiers were having any better luck than they.

The fire finally flamed to life, they stopped for a moment to watch, as though their eyes could call its warmth straight into their veins. The Russians huddled around what now had to be a warm barrel and began singing their native songs. A few threw their arms around each other, others looked to be weeping, even sobbing. The boys whispered to each other, guessing at what they were witnessing. They'd never seen the brutal Russians cry.

"They are talking about how the war is taking them one by one, and they will never see their motherland again," speculated Jozsi. "That's what I would be crying about." He pictured never jumping into the Rakos River again, or seeing Toth's farm, or sitting in his special spot under an eave in the attic.

They resumed their journey home, bodies shivering, stomachs grumbling, feet weary. Suddenly, the cacophony of exploding ammunition. Within seconds the area sounded like New Year's Eve around the world. The boys, invisible in the darkness, outside the range of light thrown by the mad explosions, couldn't resist stopping to witness. They saw the soldiers begin to look around for the person responsible for turning their warming, melancholy sing-along into chaos. A few locals who ventured outside shrugged in ignorance. If anyone had noticed the two boys throwing things into the barrel, they weren't saying. The boys turned and ran home.

Jozsi made up an excuse when Matyas sternly questioned him as to why he was so late to the table. The next day, the Russian command announced a new rule: no civilians allowed on the streets from seven at night till seven in the morning. Jozsi was impressed with their ability to further screw up life and decide to ignore the command. He assured Ferenc that meeting any time they wanted to was legal since the rule clearly said "on the street." His parents were too preoccupied to make sure he was in before seven. Everyone was worn down by the war and the winter. Everyone knew someday each would end, but both ground along, pounding their spirits lower day by day.

8

Spring

Although the Russians had wrested control of Budapest from the Germans in February, sporadic fighting continued into the early days of April. The occupying troops conscripted able-bodied Hungarians to build pontoon bridges across the Danube. Once the spring thaw had come, bloated bodies piled up against the cobbled together pontoons and pylons. Depressing signs of carnage surfaced no matter in what direction you turned.

Easter arrived on the first of April that year; just a few days before the last of the German forces were overpowered and the soldiers finally left for good. Though the fighting wasn't quite over, there was no mistaking the sense of momentous change permeating the air. The Budai family embraced Easter with passion, but that year's celebration was especially poignant. Matyas sent Jozsi out to invite relatives and friends who'd suffered through the harsh winter months, all of them literally starving for a hearty meal. He brought out the best part of the ham from the last of their smoked pigs; it weighed nearly forty pounds. Erzsebet started cooking the day before and the family was near delirium from appetizing smells wafting through the house and yard.

Jozsi kept the kitchen stove warm with dry wood he'd scavenged, and managed to keep his hands from picking at any edible-looking pieces of the pig. Rolling around in his head was Father Richter's warning: if you ate meat before the Resurrection you could count on hell being your home for all eternity. The Father would always lean especially hard on that last word. It was annoying how Father Richter's words haunted him, especially since he considered himself a non-believer. Since late-morning Easter service was only a few hours away, he intended to wait for a taste of ham till their noon meal. But the slow torture of spending the early morning in and out of the kitchen was too much for him. When *nagyanya* Alida went outside for a moment, Jozsi reached into the boiling pot and sinfully pulled out a few chunky pieces floating on top. He figured he was young, hell was a long way off and he had time

---

to make up for this transgression, and anyway, he was a non-believer, at least mostly.

A Hungarian Easter tradition was for the single men in town to set out at seven in the morning and make the rounds, wishing all of their relatives and any unmarried girls they fancied a happy Easter. They carried vials of fragrant lilac water to sprinkle on the girls, which caused the streets to smell like spring. Young boys arriving at the door would be rewarded with colored eggs and a few coins, although during the war, there'd been no spare coins to be found. But somehow even in these hard times, the alcohol flowed. The younger boys often tried to keep up with the older ones and by ten in the morning could be spotted stumbling around town in a drunken stupor.

Ferenc and Jozsi started out early that morning, downing hard-boiled eggs and sipping wine. By nine they were flying high, but then so were many of the older boys, the ones old enough to be considered bachelors. After a horrific winter, they embraced this ritual with particular fervor. You could barely look down a street without seeing a young man lurching along, or veering off to throw up. The tradition was to spread happy Easter wishes until ten or eleven o'clock Mass, and then make your way home for the Easter meal.

The two boys made it to Jozsi's godmother's house, where Ferenc collapsed in the front yard with a big idiot smile on his face. Jozsi's godmother folded her arms and peered at Ferenc where he lay.

"He has no legs," she said. "Forget about him getting to church." She loaned them her wheelbarrow so Jozsi could roll his friend home, Ferenc hanging his head over the side, periodically vomiting. One very elderly man heading toward church cast a disgusted look, muttering that people were starving in the city while this stupid boy heaved eggs.

At Ferenc's house, Jozsi quickly tipped his dear friend on the ground in the front yard, hoping Ferenc's mother wouldn't catch sight. It was Easter; he didn't want to come anywhere close to being crucified. He turned to run, thinking he was safe.

From the kitchen window, Ferenc's mother called out, "What have you done? You dump his body like he's dead!"

Jozsi sprinted toward his house and of course, at Mass, Ferenc's mother scowled at him, nostrils pinched as though he smelled bad. Once settled in a pew, Jozsi relaxed. The church smelled of spring, the result of all the girls' hair having been dampened with lilac water. He soaked in the scent, at least when he wasn't dozing, the *palinka* having caught up with him. He'd startle awake at the robust singing of men in the congregation; their voices oiled by alcohol, they sang so loudly Jozsi thought the pictures of the saints might tumble off the walls.

Easter Mass ended and Jozsi raced home before the hordes they'd invited arrived for the meal. While the women bustled to get everything ready, the kids ran around in the sun, gathering spring flowers for the table and chasing butterflies, while the men gathered on the veranda to talk about the war. Matyas took in the air, too, haphazardly wandering around the back yard with his brother, Bela, Jozsi's favorite uncle. Jozsi didn't understand exactly what Bela did for a living, just that he was an engineer of metals who was always reaching into his pocket and holding forth some mysterious metallic object in his palm. The brothers were deep in conversation; he didn't dare disturb them. Instead he popped into the kitchen, hoping the women would feel sympathy and sneak him a piece of ham before he died of hunger; he was definitely emerging from his drunken stupor and ready for food. But the women were all too busy to even notice his hangdog expression.

Suddenly his father summoned him from the back yard, "Jozsi, come!"

"Uh-oh," he whispered, thinking Ferenc's mother was at that moment standing in the yard, propping up her disheveled son. He trudged down from the veranda, staring at his feet like a captured soldier on his way to the firing squad. Pausing to look back toward the veranda, he imagined the family gathered for a farewell wave before they watched him die like a hero. But at that moment, there was no one standing watch. "Someday there will be people writing about my death," he muttered, and continued his lonely death march. He was ready to die for whatever reason, there were many he could think of. No matter the cause, he envisioned Ferenc's mother smiling and applauding as shots rang out and he collapsed to the ground, his soul leaving his body to become one with the earth he had lived on for too short a time. He only wished for some ham, just a taste, before he died.

He was snapped out of this melodramatic scenario by the big smile his father wore, and the embrace that followed — it was the kind of hug you'd give a survivor after he'd emerged from years in the jungle.

"Good news, my boy," Matyas shook him excitedly. "We walked by the chicken coop and Bela noticed your pile of shrapnel. It's good, Jozsi, it's the purest silver he's ever seen." Bela stood to the side, with a smile a mile wide plastered on his face.

Jozi realized it was much better to be an alive hero than a dead scoundrel. He looked around for Ferenc's mother so he could give her the Hungarian gesture, which could definitely land him in hot water with his father. Lucky for him she was nowhere in sight. Bela wanted to know where Jozsi had found his treasures, but he kept that secret, saying vaguely, "In a ravine somewhere. I'd walked a long way, I'm not sure where I was." It didn't matter Bela said, no matter where it was from, no matter who took over the country now that the fighting had ceased, what Jozsi had found was worth a small fortune.

That Easter day Jozsi became the most celebrated person after he who had been resurrected. Matyas poured *palinka* into glasses like it was the last day of Pompeii. Jozsi lay in bed at night, his head spinning with visions of other valuables that might lay buried in the ravine, and images of the inscribed pieces hidden in the attic, and of wonderful old Bandi grazing in the tall grass, until finally he fell asleep.

A few days later, Matyas put all the metal from behind the chicken coop in two suitcases and brought them to the city. The silver weighed close to twenty pounds. He found buyers for everything within no time and spent the rest of the afternoon shopping. Arriving home with a pleased expression, he emptied the suitcases on the kitchen table, spilling out special delicacies and items they hadn't laid eyes on in many moons — chocolates, sugar, coffee, along with fancy soaps and other special items for Erzsebet, Alida, and the girls. They watched in disbelief as he unloaded one thing at a time from the suitcases. They looked at each other, dazzled. How could this be real? Things like this happened in books, not to them.

After everyone but Jozsi had received their gifts, Matyas turned to his son. "We wouldn't have any of this without the treasure you found and we thank you." He spread his arms wide as though about to embrace the boy, and said, "This is for you" just before quickly pulling out a small package from his jacket pocket.

In a flash, Jozsi ripped open the wrapping and found in his hand a shiny bullet shell made into a whistle, strung from a thin silver chain. He raced out of the house like a dog with his tail on fire, and tore down the street to Ferenc's, not caring one whit what kind of expression Ferenc's mother had on her face. Behind him the family laughed, in joy at his happiness, and then in joy at the sound of all the laughter. It had been a long time since such sounds had filled the house.

That night, having blown his new whistle at every living thing he came across, he slept with it under his pillow. In the morning, he rose early to slip up to the attic and gaze at the rest of his treasures, trying to figure out exactly what he had in front of him. The inscriptions mystified him, but staring provided no answers. He wrapped everything back up in an old grain bag and tucked it back in his secret hole under the rafters.

~~~

The Easter weekend marked the beginning of a new world. Within days, military operations ceased, the German forces collapsed, and while life did not return to anything like normal, the bombing, the daily destruction ended. The air grew warmer, the sun stronger, and the trees and bushes flowered with leaves and blooms — in celebration, Erzsebet said, of the end of the troubles.

Now that the fighting was truly over, Zsigmond was allowed to roam further from home and he rejoined Jozsi and Ferenc in their daily adventures down by the river and around the neighborhood. From the Budai house the family could often track Jozsi's whereabouts by the sound of his whistle. They smiled hearing its joyful trill.

The Rakos River split in two about a mile before their swimming hole and reunited a mile further along. The split made a small island and the boys decided to make that their kingdom. Jozsi took a page from things he'd overhead his father saying about business dealings. He suggested the boys come up with a little money toward researching the land rights before they claimed it as their own. The boys emptied their pockets. Jozsi marveled at how easy it had been for him to talk his friends into doing things; a skill he figured would come in handy no matter what he ended up doing in life.

With less to distract them, Jozsi's parents kept a closer eye on his whereabouts and behavior. Sometimes Jozsi thought Ferenc was lucky because his father was still away, probably captive in Russia, his mother went easy on him, directing all punitive looks at Jozsi. His own parents were back to their typical vigilance: everything had to happen at the right time and in the right place and there was no room for screwing up. Matyas's ten years as a cavalry officer in the Royal Hungarian Army's *Red Devils* brigade had instilled a ramrod sense of discipline he tried to impose on Jozsi. It did not take.

But Jozsi did love to hear about his father's exploits during the war; he was in awe of his courage and daring. The *Red Devils* were considered elite fighters who rode some of the wildest horses Hungary had ever produced. During his military career, Matyas had fought the communist uprising of the proletarians on the streets of Budapest. There was no tear gas for dispersing the crowd and no clubs were used. When the Cavalry rode in among the striking workers they wielded swords; they had no mercy for the communists and the death toll was high. Matyas was tough to begin with and his time in the *Red Devils* burnished that toughness to steel. And so, the *Red Devils* were the soldiers sent to battle the Serbians after Ferdinand, Franz Jozsef's brother, was assassinated in Sarajevo. Their reputation preceded them, and even the most daring demonstrators ran for cover; the *Red Devils* were not known for taking prisoners. Many times, Jozsi had heard his father say to Toth, who'd fought alongside him, "How could we have taken prisoners? We only had one saddle." They'd nod to each other and stare into the distance as they remembered these shared moments.

One summery afternoon, as he made his way back across the yard, Jozsi spotted his mother shelling peas on the veranda. He saw an opportunity to make up for his previous day's transgressions and perhaps score a few points in advance of future bad behavior. He sat down to give her a hand. Matyas had been especially out of sorts the day before, and even his mother had steered clear of her husband's dark expression.

"Mama," Jozsi asked, grabbing another handful of peas to shell, "what made you want to marry papa?"

She gave him a curious look — this was not the kind of question he'd normally ask — and sat silent for a time, the only sound the dull ping of peas on porcelain. Finally, she spoke. "We fell in love. Simple as that."

"But how?" Jozsi pictured his father galloping madly down the road, brandishing a saber, death in his eyes. Trying to imagine the scenario from his mother's point of view as a young woman, he determined the picture might not have seemed all that appealing.

"Well, your father carried himself a certain way. I'd see your father coming into town with his Red Devil jacket halfway covering his shoulders. All the girls in town would look and say they wanted to marry someone just like Matyas. I was no different than the rest. We weren't even 20 yet."

"But he married you and not the others."

"You are surprised," she laughed. "That is not very flattering, son. You will never find a bride if you can't do better than that."

Jozsi blushed and she gave him a quick hug. "You really want to know?" He nodded emphatically. So, she told him about the dance held at the local tavern one warm summer night.

All the young girls without dates stood outside, peering in the windows to watch girls fortunate enough to have escorts gliding blissfully across the floor. She'd spent many weekend nights just so, studying dance steps, observing behavior and clothes, making herself ready for the day she did have a date. A gypsy band played a string of romantic songs and the boys held the girls so tight Erzsebet couldn't understand how anyone could breathe. Just watching, she caught her own breath, the view was so romantic. Suddenly she heard whispers that Matyas from the *Red Devils* was approaching the tavern. He came striding down the path, handsome in his Hussar uniform. Her cheeks reddened at the memory.

"As he passed, he asked if I had a date for that night. I said no, I did not, and he said, 'Well, now you do.' I told him I wasn't properly dressed and the people inside wouldn't like that. He took my arm and said, 'If they don't like it, they can complain to me.'" She sighed. "We went inside and for the rest of the night, I didn't even notice there *were* other people in the tavern. From then on, we were dating, and we got married as soon as he was discharged from the cavalry."

They were long finished with peas, and Jozsi thanked her for telling him, and rose to carry the bowl inside.

Erzsebet grabbed his arm. "This is important. Don't tell your sisters a word about the way we met. I don't want them to get any ideas about running off with some soldier. I mean it," she said seriously, then winked and sent him on his way. Later he realized that everyone knew the story but him. His sisters had been pestering her for those details since they'd been little girls dreaming of princes and castles and lavish weddings.

~~~

As he described the end of the war to Ulee, Jozsi realized he hadn't thought about that conversation with his mother for a very long time. Love for his family was always in his heart, but the life he now led meant recollections often arose at odd moments — lying in a cave, or bouncing along on a long bus ride, or staring out at the horizon as a battleship cut through the waves. Ulee thanked him for his tales; the sharing made her feel so close to him, and to his family, though she knew they'd never meet.

Whenever he spoke about Hungary, his face registered a range of expressions easy to track: nostalgic yearning, conflict, relief, resignation. She knew he missed home and family, but also understood that he'd been eager to leave those confines. In some ways, he had the Communist Party to thank for that. But really, they had lit a fire under his already exploratory nature; he'd always seen himself setting out to discover the world. Flight from Hungary had ended up sending him places he'd never dreamed of going: into the American Army for one, and the alien world of Korea for another.

By this time, they had very few days to share before Jozsi's return to the military base. Ulee was deep into research for her upcoming exhibit on Attila and Genghis Khan, and each day after work she'd rush to meet him at her apartment. His wish would have been for her to rush through the door and dive into bed, but she was so focused on her project, she'd insist he dive into her research instead. She was as willful as his sister Susan.

"I have you, my expert Hungarian, for only a little more time," she'd murmur, massaging his shoulders as he bent his head toward a fresh pile of papers. He'd groan, in a worked-up state from having thought about her silky thighs much of the day. She'd massage deeper, murmuring, "Later...soon...but now, look." She wanted his opinion, affirmation, and insights about her research, at the same time she wanted to inhale his life — what she saw as her path to understanding something true and real about the Hungarian character. It became a tug of war, her hunger for knowledge versus his hunger for her. There was barely enough time to sleep between the research papers, the sex, the sharing of their lives.

One night, as he went through her notes, he found a description of how Attila had been laid to rest in a casket made of pure gold, placed inside a slightly larger silver coffin, and then inside an even larger iron coffin. Slaves dammed up a shallow riverbed and then lowered the coffin down into the bed. Attila and all the treasures held within the tomb were buried far from his home, and the slaves had been shot within moments of finishing their labors. It appeared this wasn't simply a legend handed down from Hungarian to Hungarian. Researchers had verified the tale was real. The next page revealed that Attila's coffin had been inscribed: *Rex hvnorvm 453*. He thought of the Rex and 53 he'd seen on one of the pieces he'd found in the ravine. Jozsi's face paled so dramatically it seemed he'd seen a ghost among her papers.

"What? Tell me what you found."

Jozsi smiled, shaking his head in disbelief. "Over dinner," was all he said, and lowering his head he continued reading.

That night, he took her to her favorite restaurant, and over cocktails revealed that not only did he think he knew where the coffin was, he believed he'd touched it with his very hands.

"You know about the summer I spent in Ura."

"Yes," she said. "You and the Toths and wandering with Bandi."

"That coffin must be what I found in the ravine after the bombing. It has to be." He repeated this several times because he couldn't quite believe it, but yes, it had to be. He relayed the long hours he'd spent sporadically digging around in Hungarian libraries, rooms where public records were stored, hoping he'd find some information about a wealthy landowner buried in that area whose coffin it might have been.

"I'd forget all about the metal stashed in the attic for months on end, but then something would remind me and I'd go digging. But nothing ever added up. Still I didn't want to show anyone else until I had some idea of what it was I'd found." He described everything he could remember about the metal pieces, the feel, the texture, how he'd run his fingers along the inscribed pieces, hoping the touch would communicate enough to spark a light bulb in his head. He'd carried it all in his memory for so long — the metal pieces still tucked under an attic rafter, the large clunky edge coffin tucked in the ravine he'd so carefully disguised.

Ulee was amazed that with all her work on Attila, she'd chanced to meet a Hungarian in Korea, and that her research had led him to perhaps solve a mystery that had baffled historians and scholars for years. It was too strange to be true, yet there it was: her Jozsi might have found Attila.

Late into the night they discussed what Jozsi should do next. But with the communists in power, there was no way he could return to Hungary to unearth his great find. Even if he could manage to sneak in, there was no way in hell he would reveal such treasure while communists ruled.

"I have to wait," he concluded. "Wait for the right time and circumstance to reveal the site. And when I do, I will send for you," he promised, embracing her. They both knew he wouldn't, but why ruin such a lovely moment with reality.

They passed their last couple of days in what felt like an endless embrace. She took off from work and they spent most of the time in her apartment, venturing out only for walks and to eat. They agreed that life was crueler than kind, but always surprising. And although they dreaded parting, they were grateful for having met. For Jozsi the time with Ulee was a respite from the harsh life of a fighter, and a reconnection to a place in his heart that had grown icy and still. Since leaving Hungary, women had been a happy indulgence, not a deep connection, but Ulee helped him remember what it was to love. For Ulee, the experience was a miracle. For much of her life, she'd focused on her studies and work, ignoring her heart; her mother's experience left her thinking there was no point in loving. But Jozsi showed her that a man could be so much more than brutal, and this gave her hope that somewhere in Seoul was a man just as fine as he. Still, as the moment to part approached, the thought pressed both hearts flat with melancholy. Between her tears and his stoic sighs, the hours of life they would share drew to a close.

9

A Red Rose in Budapest

The view from the bus returning him to Camp Kaiser passed unseen. Jozsi's mind was not in his body; instead it flitted from one memory of Ulee to another like a hummingbird seeking sustenance: by the window in her living room, gliding through the museum lobby, across the table at a restaurant, stretching herself awake in the gentle light of dawn. He could feel her hand in his, resting on his thigh, stroking his cheek. He could hear her cooing laugh, satisfied sigh, and the loving way his name slipped off her tongue.

The bus bounced along, but Jozsi felt not so much as one jolt. When his mind briefly settled in the present, he felt a terrible ache inside. Fleeing Hungary — abandoning all he'd known and loved — had sealed his heart shut, or so he'd thought. Not for him, wallowing in sentiment and nostalgia. He'd set out to be an adventurer, sailing from one willing body to another, a ladies' man with no investment, no attachment. Thanks for the good time, a hug, a kiss, and on to the next. With one exception, things had worked out that way. For a night, for a week, for months even. Lots of fun and everyone walks away smiling. He'd thought Ulee would be just that, a happy fling. He'd been wrong.

The bus rattled to a stop and Jozsi slouched off, too melancholy to lift his head. He dumped his bag at the foot of his lonely little bed and sat forlornly, elbows on knees, chin in hand. It took a while before he noticed a bag poking out from under Laci's bed. So, his comrade had returned. Blue as he felt, it seemed unfriendly to sit and mope when he could be moping while drinking and listening to Laci's Hong Kong exploits. It would take his mind off Ulee, who at this moment would, he guessed, be in the museum where they'd met. She'd seen him off at the bus and then headed to work because that's how she'd been raised. Things are hard and you hurt, but you stand up and cope. He respected that.

Just before parting, Ulee had told him it would take her a long time to forget him, the ghost of his presence would fill her daily life. But he would see her in his memory only, and he'd quickly forget her in the midst of all that was new to him. He had tried to comfort her, reminding her that every time he thought of Attila and the treasure, he'd think of her. But her expression told him that was not at all the right thing to say, more like a hefty pour of salt into the wound. He'd put his arms around her; she'd rested her head against his chest and sobbed. He shook the memory off and entered the 24-hour club where he was certain to find Laci.

"You are moping, *haverom*," Laci observed, moments after the first of many toasts. The night was young and they had no immediate particular tasks to accomplish — their flights to Inchon and then on to Saigon were scheduled for a few days later.

"It's nothing, I'm just tired," Jozsi answered, avoiding the truth because he didn't want to confide; mostly, he didn't want Laci making fun of him for being heartbroken. Instead, he encouraged his friend to walk him through his two weeks in Hong Kong, the many bar girls, the crazy nights and amazing food. Laci was now the big expert on Hong Kong and listed all the places they would have to visit on their next R&R. Finally, he wound down, having run out of stories. He observed a still morose Jozsi, the booze having done little to lift his spirits.

"What did you do in Seoul to make you so miserable?" Laci poked him in the chest.

Jozsi sighed. "Not since Erika," he said to himself more than to Laci.

"Erika?"

"In Hungary...I must have mentioned her."

Laci searched his memory. For all the time they'd spent together, they'd shared little of their lives before the day Jozsi had knocked on Laci's door. Finally, something clicked. "The one who was a good shot?"

"Yes, that one. But we knew each other long before she picked up a gun. We went to the same grade school." He pictured Erika sitting in front of him in class; long braids tidy but for a few stray hairs at the nape of her neck.

"So...a woman in Seoul got to you. Well, forget about her. When we get to Hong Kong there will be more ass than a toilet seat ever saw." But he could see that at the moment, nothing was going to cheer his friend. "What about this Erika, then?"

Jozsi smiled weakly. "What can I say? I always liked her smile, but she was just a skinny little kid back then. We didn't see much of each other during the worst of the war. School was cancelled, she didn't live close by, and I was busy running the streets with my friends Ferenc and Zsigmond. But when we were older, studying in Budapest, then I saw her again."

"You were lucky to go to university; big dumb farm boys like me didn't get to do that."

"And you're lucky to have me looking out for you. And I'm helping. Look! The innocent farm boy made his way back from Hong Kong in one piece. Proof you are learning from the master." With that Jozsi perked up enough to tell Laci about how he ended up in university, and how he and a grown Erika found themselves in the same place in Budapest. At least talking took his mind off Ulee.

~~~

By 1953, when Jozsi and his cohorts turned eighteen, the government had disbanded all private schools, and students either tested high enough to continue on to public universities, or were assigned to study agriculture or manual trades. The boys took the tests and were each assigned slots foreshadowing their future direction: Jozsi to study electronic engineering, Ferenc to learn metal casting, and Zsigmond to train as an administrator. They spent their last summer glued to each other and swore to meet monthly after relocating to Budapest.

Jozsi's test scores were so high the government paid his school and living expenses. The fact that the communists were footing the bill dimmed his pride, but he was practical and not about to turn up his nose at the benefits. Especially not the small apartment on Rákóczi street, in the heart of Budapest, provided him so he could devote time to studying, not waste it traveling to and from his parents' home. And, Matyas noted, because the communists saw no value in family ties, they had a secondary reason to pay for his isolation. Jozsi's first day of school, students assembled in the gymnastics room while a string of officials stressed how lucky they were to be granted all this assistance from the government. Followed, to be sure, by a subtle threat; the officials reminded students there were hundreds of others willing to take their place should they fail to do their best.

The boys from Rakoskeresteur had planned to meet monthly, but under the pressure of school and work, their plan immediately fell apart. Three days of classes, classwork, and three days of internship at a workplace devoured their time. In occasional free moments, Jozsi took advantage of his access to the Budapest libraries, scouring them for books on Ura, Attila and anything else that might relate to his treasures, hoping to find a revelation or two.

For their internships, Jozsi was assigned to a radio-manufacturing site, Ferenc to a smelting factory on the outskirts of the city, and Zsigmond to the Secret Police, the AVO. Officially called the AVH as of 1948, most people still referred to the dread suppressors as the AVO. Now that Zsigmond regularly entered 60 Andrássy Street, an address that sent chills down Hungarian spines, his two friends were less motivated to keep in close contact. Of course, Zsigmond had no say in where he'd been assigned, but the stigma of being attached to that building cast him in a new light. Known as The House of Loyalty, 60 Andrássy had been the headquarters of the Hungarian Nazis. Back then, the boys were too young to have heard the horrendous details of what went on inside its walls after the Soviets had taken over, first the building and then the entire block. But by the time the boys entered university, they were hearing stories of people brought inside the building who vanished forever, or of those released who were never the same. They'd even seen a few local men broken by their time inside. It was an address to avoid.

On weekends Jozsi returned home to visit and be doted on by his mother and grandmother. Matyas was always happy to see him, but he was increasingly bitter about the government and regularly railed against them. "The Russians are paying for you now, but there's no such thing as a free meal. They'll want something in return. You'll see, later on, they'll want to profit from your education and god knows what bad things they'll ask you to do."

"Papa, I'll take education however I can," he'd counter. Jozsi saw education as the suitcase he needed to fully pack in order to make his way in the world. He'd hated Catholic school, but that was a long time ago. Despite love for his family, and for the land he'd grown up exploring, and even for the grand buildings and wide boulevards in Budapest, his feet were restless for new ground. "And where is this ground?" Matyas would ask. Jozsi didn't know, but he was looking forward to finding out.

Meanwhile, he cautioned his father to be careful with his words. It was no secret the communist regime came down hard on any Hungarians who dared voice opposition to the government. As the years dragged on and the AVO recruited more and more spies, its network spread like veins through a body. Everybody was spying on everybody; you had to watch what you said, what you did, where you went, who you talked to. People turned each other in for money, or to avoid torture. People turned each other in on a whim. You couldn't trust your neighbors, it was said you couldn't even trust your own mother. To be overheard saying communism was bad was to put your life at risk. But it was worse than that, because all someone had to do was say they'd heard you utter those words and you might end up dead, or be sent to labor in Siberia where you'd *wish* for death.

Matyas was a stubborn man who felt he'd served his country well and deserved to speak his mind. He'd mutter that the Russians were poisoning his countrymen with their vicious ways, turning citizens against each other, making spies of everyone, destroying the bonds of family, friend and neighbor. He was not alone in his rancor. Increasingly intellectuals and young students shared rebellious thoughts in schools and side-street coffee houses. And gradually their whispers of opposition spread to workers and out into the countryside. The communists tried to seduce as many as they could to their side while smothering all sparks of thought and spirit, reasoning that if they starved the Hungarian spirit of lifeblood they could control the population. Fear was their main cudgel.

"They turn us into soulless serfs," Matyas would lament, pounding the table in rage and frustration.

"I know, Papa," Jozsi would answer, "but it will change. It *must* change."

~~~

After school, as a break from the pressure of school and work, Jozsi began visiting the American Cultural Center to watch movies they'd screen. The Hungarian government forbade the showing of any American movies in public, so the movies allowed were mostly Russian propaganda films, or very dull Hungarian fare. Not so at the Cultural Center. There he'd find old American cowboy movies starring Gene Autry and Roy Rogers, and war films like *Destination Tokyo*, and even the occasional French film.

The Center was in a building connected to the American Embassy — a large hall, filled with moveable chairs, a small stage, a screen, and a small kitchen area containing simple refreshments. At the Center Jozsi found other restless, curious students he felt comfortable with, and one day he walked in and found one of them standing deep in conversation with a tall, blond woman, whose back was to the front door. She turned when Jozsi's acquaintance nodded hello. It took him a moment to place her, so entirely out of context was this face that for some reason seemed familiar. But the second the woman smiled, he knew. Erika. She recognized him straight away, and made a downward yanking motion with her hand, echoing the way he used to pull her braids in class.

Erika was in Budapest studying biology. Like Jozsi, she'd received a full scholarship. He teased her that she'd end up a doctor just like her father, living in the same house, in the same town for the rest of her life. She said she saw nothing wrong with that; their town was a fine place to live. They took to meeting after class and walking together to the Center, and soon she was inviting him to the apartment she shared with two other girls. They were always happy to see Jozsi because he often brought food, compliments of a cousin who was a food distribution manager in the district. Rations were tight, fights would break out, and shopping could be a perilous activity. But Jozsi's cousin would sneak him in the store before it opened and give him first pick.

One day as they walked toward the Center, Erika mentioned she had run into Zsigmond, who'd asked her out on a date. He'd tracked her down somehow, appearing in front of her classroom door one afternoon.

Jozsi looked surprised and a little uncomfortable, but they were just friends and he had no claim on her, so he simply wished her luck. "Zsigmond is a nice guy. He had such a crush on you in school he could hardly breathe when you were around. You don't remember? He'll probably take you to a good meal; he can afford it with his connections. You know what he's doing?"

"I know where he works," she frowned. "I don't like it, but he asked nicely and I don't want to be rude. It's only supper."

"I doubt he's looking at it that way," Jozsi said. He was feeling a little jealous, but he couldn't see her falling for Zsigmond, and anyway, he had his own Saturday afternoon meeting to attend. One of the Embassy employees had asked Jozsi if he'd give the newly arrived director of the Cultural Center a tour around the city.

"The man's parents are Hungarian, but he grew up in America. They want a real Hungarian to show him the city," Jozsi explained to Erika.

That Saturday, the retiring director introduced Jozsi to a tall lean man with dirty blond hair. His large blue-grey eyes made an immediate impression —they were alert, almost sparkling. His name was Sandor Nagy and he was from Akron, Ohio. Jozsi had no idea where that was.

"Jozsi, I want you to take Sandor all over the city so he gets to know it from a Hungarian point of view. And show him the best restaurant in the city. Knowing Sandor, he'll pick up the tab." With that, he shook hands with each and walked out of the room.

Jozsi led them toward the majestic Chain Bridge, the first permanent bridge to cross the Danube, linking Buda to Pest. Sandor had heard about the bridge and was eager to see it. As they walked, Sandor told Jozsi how his parents had come to America in the early twenties, settling in Akron for no other reason than that a relative lived there. The relative happened to have a job at the Goodyear plant making zeppelins and thought he could get Sandor's father hired on. Zeppelins, Jozsi thought, now there's an interesting reason to pull up stakes. Eager to hear about life somewhere else, he was happy that Sandor, who'd been raised in Akron's small Hungarian neighborhood, spoke the language fluently and didn't mind answering all his questions about what life was like in Ohio. Jozsi decided Ohio was not for him, so he thanked Sandor for saving him the trip.

The two talked easily, walking and walking, stopping in cafés, Sandor paying for everything, each time saying, "Compliments of the firm." Jozsi assumed he was referring to the Cultural Center, but the phrase echoed later that night when he remembered a certain moment. They'd been walking along the banks of the Danube at twilight, and Jozsi had suggested they call it a night because he still had classwork to do. He'd pointed toward a side street as a good route for their walk back. It just happened to be the street Erika's favorite restaurant was on. He wanted to see if he could spot her there with Zsigmond, but Sandor didn't need to know that.

"But it's shorter if we take that one," Sandor answered, pointing toward the next street. In an instant, it occurred to Jozsi that Sandor seemed about as ignorant of the city as Jozsi's mother was of the church near their house.

"Ah, you remember the way we came in," Jozsi smiled, and Sandor nodded yes. He is a very good liar, thought Jozsi. But he liked the man anyway and, at least as far he could tell, Sandor wasn't working for the communists.

The following Monday, Jozsi caught up with Erika after classes and invited her to take a walk by the river and tell him about her dinner with Zsigmond. He'd told himself he wasn't worried, but his stomach had been troubled all weekend and he'd finally admitted to himself he was interested in being more than her friend. They claimed an empty bench and she described how after an expensive meal, Zsigmond had surprised her by bringing her to the Hungarian State Opera House. All he had to do was flash his official card and they were ushered in by the ticket agent — normally it would take weeks to get such tickets. Jozsi's stomach sank. But Erika surprised him. It had been a fine evening, but she did not want Zsigmond to think of her as anything more than an acquaintance. Not even a friend, Jozsi crowed to himself. But her expression was unusually serious. Had Zsigmond tried to grab her for a one-night stand? He couldn't imagine that; Zsigmond would be too in awe to be aggressive with Erika.

They sat silent, watching riverboats ferry fresh vegetables from the countryside north toward the city. Jozsi peeked sideways. Her long eyelashes moved up and down as she blinked away tears. "What's wrong?" he asked.

"It's my father, Jozsi."

He reached for her hand. "Your father?" Jozsi could see him in his mind's eye, a large handsome man with a goatee, always in a suit jacket or a doctor's coat. Erika had his same shape eyes and nose.

"Six months ago, men came to take him away..." Another long silence. She took a deep breath, forcing herself to continue. "They brought him to Andrássy Street. I thought maybe Zsigmond would tell me something; that's the real reason I agreed to go out with him. I didn't dare ask, but I hoped. But he said nothing."

Jozsi was sick at this news. His biggest fear was that if his father kept talking against the government he'd end up on Andrássy Street. But he remembered Dr. Simon as circumspect, never revealing his political thoughts to anyone, entirely focused on his work as a heart specialist at Budapest's Rokus Hospital. Erika told him that one day the then head of the secret service, a rotund, ill-tempered general, had been brought to the hospital in the midst of a severe heart attack. The general was turning blue and almost certainly beyond help, but the police insisted Dr. Simon save him. He tried to revive this hopeless case but the general's heart had no will to beat on and he soon stopped breathing. In the emergency room, the police wasted no time taking her father into custody. He had not been seen since. Her mother had been told he'd been conspiring with the enemy, had in fact allowed the general to die, and that his fate would be determined by the people's court. When? No one would say.

All Zsigmond revealed to Erika was that he'd been promoted from intern to official worker, and was about to become an officer.

"He bragged about being in the AVO?" Jozsi was incredulous. How could his boyhood friend be proud of such a job? Endure it, perhaps, but brag? Had he turned into an AVO puppet? Jozsi reached over to wipe the tears from her face, and then they walked hand-in-hand back to his apartment, shared a simple, quiet supper, and entwined in his bed, became a couple. She never asked about his meeting with the new head of the Cultural Center and he didn't bring it up.

~~~

During the next few weeks, Sandor and Jozsi spent many evenings together and Sandor seemed fascinated by Jozsi's work, peppering him with questions on what he was learning and what he was observing around him. Each time they met he asked increasingly pointed, specific questions.

Jozsi excelled in his classes; the school assigned him work as an assistant engineer for the brilliant Dr. Geller, whose research on military communication equipment was enthusiastically sponsored by the Russian Army. Matyas struggled between pride and rage over this, not wanting any child of his to be in any way useful to the Communist Party. But his pragmatic son saw no other route to an escape from a life of drudgery under communist rule. Jozsi insisted he'd make up for it by figuring out a way to screw the communists with the very training they'd supplied him.

One evening, seated at a café's outside table, Joszi and Sandor drank espresso and rum, commenting on one attractive girl or another strolling past. Emboldened by the combination of caffeine and alcohol snaking through his veins, Jozsi took a deep breath and asked a question that had been poking at him for days. "You keep wanting to know about what I see and do at work, even ask me about confidential matters. Either you want me dragged off to Andrássy Street or you want me to spy against the Russians."

"Or both," Sandor laughed darkly, raising his glass in a toast. "No, truly, you're a good companion, I don't want you to disappear."

Jozsi smiled weakly. Any mention of Andrássy Street stole a little oxygen from his lungs. "And never letting me pay for the drinks, the food, for anything; always, 'It's on the firm.' What is that?"

Sandor beamed, "Lucky for you, is what. I know the Russians don't give you a generous stipend. And let's eat, by the way, to celebrate our partnership."

"I'll eat, but doesn't being partners mean *sharing* knowledge? Two-way street?"

Sandor smiled enigmatically, but all he said was, "No. Not partners, then, but let's eat anyway," then waved to a waitress through the café window.

"Have I agreed?" Jozsi asked. "I didn't hear myself say yes. Let me think." The waitress took their orders for borscht, and the two men sat silent while Jozsi pretended to mull over undertaking what he was thrilled to be offered: a chance to stick it to the communists. By the time their food arrived, Jozsi had tired of making Sandor wait and nodded his assent. They spent the rest of the evening voices low, discussing ways to subvert the communists and prevent their Russian allies from absorbing Hungary as another state under the rule of Mother Russia as they'd done with other small nations.

Jozsi knew his father would have loved to be sitting in on this conversation with Sandor. In his heart, he felt that if put in his place, Matyas would have agreed to the same thing. He wished he could share the news. He knew his father would worry, of course, but also that he would be immensely proud.

The two parted with the understanding that they'd meet and exchange information while watching Roy Rogers' movies or whatever other silly diversion was being shown at the Cultural Center. Late that night, unbeknownst to Jozsi, a coded message was sent from the American Embassy to Langley, Virginia: "Contact made with 8152."

Some days later, Jozsi walked home from the Center after watching Gene Autry in *The Sagebrush Troubadour*, his mind preoccupied by dreams of throwing wrenches into all sorts of communist plans. Dreaming big was a favorite pastime. Suddenly, a couple of brawny men grabbed him by his arms. One whispered in his ear, "You are under arrest. Don't make a scene." They handcuffed him, shoved him into a Russian-made *pobjeda,* and since the only people who drove that kind of car were from the Secret Police, Jozsi knew exactly where he was headed. A tremor of pure fear shot through his insides.

In the car, the driver announced they were taking him to AVO headquarters for questioning. Jozsi said nothing, there was no point in asking why. As they drew near to 60 Andrássy, Jozsi's teeth clenched. He'd had occasion to walk by the stone columns, curved archway, the huge chiseled wooden doors, but like everyone else with any sense, he'd steered clear of the place as much as he could. To an innocent eye, those doors looked as though they likely opened into a building full of rooms, shelved floor to ceiling with books; a place of knowledge, not terror. He inhaled deeply as the car came to a stop.

The two men roughly pulled him inside, down a hallway, around a corner, and another and another, and up a flight of stairs. Good, he thought, the basement was where he'd heard the torture cells were. At least he was going up. But who knew anything for certain? They brought him into a small office containing only a plain pine table and two straightback wooden chairs. They pushed him down on one and left. He heard a key fit into the keyhole and the unhappy sound of tumblers clicking to lock. The two officers walked back the way they'd come.

A long time passed during which Jozsi imagined a range of unhappy scenarios. Perhaps his father had been arrested, a neighbor or eavesdropping stranger having turned him in for uttering harsh words about the communist regime. No, he decided; were that true he'd already be in a dark cell in the basement, and his father alongside. While he waited, he heard no screaming, a small comfort. Occasionally the smack of boot heels on wood as someone strode down the hall. Voices in the distance. A name called, a sharp command.

At last, after a little fumbling, the door unlocked, opened, and to Jozsi's surprise, there stood Zsigmond, greeting him with the warmth of a dear friend, long absent. He ordered a police officer behind him to remove the handcuffs, and invited Jozsi to follow him to his office for a coffee. Jozsi was stunned to see his old friend ordering anyone around in this terrifying building. Clearly, he'd climbed up the ranks in leaps and bounds. Despite the setting, Jozsi was glad and relieved to see his old friend. Unless Zsigmond had turned into a monster and a damn good actor, he figured nothing terrible was about to happen. But to test the waters, he told Zsigmond how impressed he was with his authority as they walked to Zsigmond's office. He could see his friend was strutting like a peacock at the praise.

They settled in, sipping coffee, talking about the good old days, as though at a café. Zsigmond asked after Ferenc, but made no mention of his night out with Erika. He apologized for being too busy to make any of their monthly planned get-togethers at the tavern, complaining that he had practically no free time from his job and hadn't seen his own family in months.

Finally, Jozsi leapt into a pause in the conversation. "Zsigmond, it is good to see you, but we both know I wasn't handcuffed and brought here to talk about the good old days. I need an explanation." He tried but failed not to sound fretful. He resolved to get a grip on his fear; he did not want to appear weak.

Zsigmond fidgeted with papers on his desk and cleared his throat. Jozsi remembered him doing that in school whenever he felt uncomfortable. He waited patiently for Zsigmond to finish his ritual. After several small coughs and some snurfling sounds, he said that the secret police, noticing how frequently Jozsi stopped by the American Cultural Center, had expressed concern. Jozsi did his best to react with casual surprise. "Really? I'd think they'd have more important things to do than keep an eye on who's watching Roy Rogers' movies. We all need a little entertainment, a little relaxation. You should come some time, those movies are funny." Remembering a young, insecure Zsigmond helped Jozsi relax; he felt himself in the zone of cool rage where he felt better able to calculate his reactions — he knew he was smarter and quicker on his feet than Zsigmond, and that knowledge buoyed him.

"Maybe better for you to relax watching Russian movies," Zsigmond's mouth registered a quick tight smile.

Jozsi nodded, thinking about the tedium of Russian propaganda films. Even Hungarian films were dull, except for the Hungarian classic *Dollar Papa*, which tells the story of a Hungarian who goes to America and returns to his native village almost broke, but still able to tip the coachman, leading everyone to hound him thinking he's rich. They'd seen it together when they were teenagers; every Hungarian had seen that movie. But all Jozsi said was, "Are there any charges against me?"

Zsigmond's expression grew shifty. "I was curious about why you're taking books out of the library about the Hungarian plains. You spent so many summers in Ura, you should know all there is to know about the place."

And I took a shit today, Jozsi thought, but maybe you already know that too. "Well..." He reached for his coffee, stalling. "I'm thinking of writing a book about the history of the area. Something to inspire the young to stay there, to live the kind of life I knew growing up. Everybody in the younger generation is leaving the country for the city, all those dreams of a better life. He forced a small laugh. "Someday I might want to return and live there and I don't want to be all alone."

Zsigmond looked like he wasn't buying this line of bullshit, and Jozsi realized he'd been doing more than just passively watching. He sent his mind into overdrive as Zsigmond pressed on. "So why all those books about ancient times? Why bother about 1453?"

Jozsi bluffed Zsigmond with a swift putdown — his weakness in history back in school, disinterest in it — followed by a stream of words about wanting to fully understand the reason people settled there to begin with. He talked so fast Zsigmond leaned against his chair back, daunted, and changed the subject back to the Cultural Center.

"You should know all these visits aren't doing anything for your reputation. You could have a good future in Socialist Hungary but your connection to the Americans might count against you. You have to think of your career. These kinds of activities matter." Zsigmond explained he was handling this matter himself, as a friend, in order to save Jozsi's future, and that he would be wise to tell him what went on inside the Cultural Center, and who spoke with him, and about what. He opened a manila file folder and spread out pictures of Jozsi and Sandor walking together in the city, sitting at various outdoor cafés, leaning on a railing by the Danube. He confided that Sandor was considered to be a CIA agent, and as soon as the AVO could prove it, Sandor would be arrested, tried and executed promptly. "He is dangerous to you, my friend."

Jozsi acted shocked, pretending to have no idea what the initials CIA meant. Zsigmond somewhat pompously explained what the CIA stood for, went on to rail against capitalism, and rattled off a litany of Lenin's teachings, posturing as though they were his own conclusions. Jozsi didn't know Zsigmond had it in him to memorize so many words, but was glad for the time it gave him to sit silent. Eventually, Zsigmond ran out of steam.

Jozsi clung to a casual tone. "He's a nice enough guy, Hungarian background, you know, and he likes learning about what it was like to grow up here, so he likes talking to me. And I like funny movies and now this puts my career in jeopardy? When Hungary starts playing amusing cowboy movies, I'll stop going to the Cultural Center. It's a release, is all, a place to laugh. You haven't forgotten how to laugh, have you?"

Zsigmond stood, exasperated by his seeming lack of impact, and ushered Jozsi to the door. "I am warning you, my friend. You should pay attention." They shook hands and Zsigmond said, "You are free to go." But he did not smile in parting and neither did Jozsi. It depressed him that this man he'd known most of his life had turned into an AVO hack willing to obey authority no matter how odious the task.

Jozsi stayed away from the Cultural Center for a few days, and when next he saw Sandor there, he warned him that the AVO was onto him.

"Well," Sandor said, unruffled, "it was only a matter of time." He suggested other arrangements for meeting. They could meet at the Szecheny heated pool. Or on the Buda side of the river, under the Liberty Statue dedicated to Russians who'd lost their lives liberating Hungary from the Nazi's during the Second World War. Sandor had a wry sense of humor. They agreed to a dropoff place for information so that if either got picked up they wouldn't be carrying anything confidential or incriminating. Some days Jozsi dropped his information in a subway trashcan, wrapped in dirty underwear to insure no beggar would pick it up. Some days a used condom served as the disguise. Nasty work, but the cause was worth it.

A red rose in the lapel signified a warning that one of them suspected he was being followed and to meet two days later, same time, same place. "Red for the Reds, only fitting," Jozsi quipped. Most of those assigned by the AVO to lurk around the Cultural Center, or follow men like Sandor, were young students and their prey quickly figured out ways to elude them. Soon Jozsi learned that the factory Dr. Geller was affiliated with had been given a contract to make the most advanced communication systems for the Russian Army. The news motivated him to take his spying seriously. Jozsi was now officially drawn in. And Sandor was the perfect coach.

10

Into the Blue

Sandor was so pleased with all of Jozsi's efforts that he arranged a special late evening dinner to celebrate, surprising Jozsi by inviting Erika to join. Sandor had observed their special friendship at the Cultural Center. "She provides good cover," he explained. "If anyone spots us it'll look like I'm having a friendly meal with regular visitors to the center. Even if they're suspicious of you and me, with Erika here, they won't think we're up to much." The men let Erika choose. "Any place, any price?" she asked, unusually playful. She chose a restaurant on the Buda side, far from the American Embassy. Jozsi had never set foot in *The Golden Bull* — the price of an average dinner equaled a factory worker's monthly wage, an interning student couldn't even afford a bowl of soup there. Erika knew a hostess, which was how they managed to finesse a table on short notice.

Erika directed the men to wear their finest clothes, "So you don't look worse than our waiter." Once inside, Jozsi saw she had a point: the sharply creased black pants, crisp white shirts, and fine cotton bow ties worn by the waiters were a little intimidating. A hostess led the three to a table on the terrace. They gazed across water reflecting the bright lights from the Pest side of the Danube. The setting felt magical. The river seemed to be flowing directly beneath their feet and the sun was seconds from dropping down behind the mountains of Buda. Gypsies serenaded the diners with Hungarian music, at just the right volume to float conversation without drowning it. Tourist boats motored downstream from the upper Danube, and small fishing boats put-putted toward their docks and moorings to tie up for the night. A tour boat returning from Visegrad, one of the oldest forts on the upper Danube, deposited a group of young boys and girls dressed in dark blue pants and skirts, white shirts with red ties around the neck, modeled after the Russian Young Pioneer's uniform.

"Would you want your children brought up like that," Sandor asked, pointing toward the cluster of kids making their way down the boat ramp.

"That would be up to Erika," Jozsi said, speaking before his brain fully appreciated the serious implication of what he was saying. Her cheeks flushed and she grabbed her water glass with both hands, staring intently into it. After a beat, still using both hands, she took a sip, then smiled to herself.

Sandor ended the awkward silence with a grin. "In America, we have a saying: 'It takes two to tango.'"

"My hope for the future is to tango in America," Jozsi answered, and was saved from further awkwardness by their elegant waiter, who appeared with the wine list.

During the lull before their food arrived, they got right to work. Jozsi shared further news of the technologies being tested in the communications field. Erika now knew who Sandor really worked for and had vowed to keep it secret. In a country filled with spies, their trust in her meant a great deal; she knew Jozsi had sworn to Sandor on his parents' lives that she would never betray them. As Jozsi rattled off the information he'd memorized for Sandor, Erika scanned the restaurant for anyone who seemed to be glancing too frequently in their direction. Sandor scribbled notes like a seasoned secretary, never dropping his eyes, looking around sleepily, as though he were only half paying attention to Jozsi, his pencil scratching madly across the paper he held on his lap as Jozsi spoke.

Following an after-dinner *palinka*, Sandor bid them goodnight. Erika and Jozsi splurged on a taxi back to his apartment. As they crossed the durable Margaret Bridge, Jozsi felt overcome with sadness. He saw one fact quite clearly: he would not be able to stay in his native country much longer. Each day his longing to escape the soul-strangling web of spies and lies the Russians had let loose on Hungary grew, and his disgust at the veiling of intelligence, opinion, and hope deepened. The constriction constant fear placed around a heart hungry for life had grown too tight. He was weary of feeling uneasy all the time, as though something behind might strike a blow he'd never see coming. His forced visit to 60 Andrássy Street amplified what before had been a whisper: you are not safe here. At least feeling unsafe someplace new would be different. Here, in his country, his home, the invaders had the upper hand. Someplace else, he could be an explorer, not a victim. Wrapping his hand around Erika's wrist he felt her pulse beating strong. They turned to exchange a glance as the taxi moved off the bridge, but neither spoke. He liked that about being with Erika, it was easy to be together without words. He had a feeling that she had already sensed the coming wind that would carry him away; and that she cared enough for him to be sad at the thought of his absence.

~~~

The image of being carried off by the wind was a constant in his head. During the late winter, he'd joined a glider's club. He'd always wanted to fly, what little boy doesn't? And this was a step in that direction. Even more important, it was an exciting distraction from the hard work of school, the drudgery of life under communist rule, and the challenge of doing whatever he could to bring an end to the poisoned Hungarian regime. At the club, there was no discussion of politics or loyalty amongst the members, just talk of ridge lifts and thermals and birds. Up in the air, far above the ground, Jozsi's mind calmed; he felt peaceful. He liked being alone, aloft, looking down on the city as he felt his way through the sky. When he couldn't fall asleep he indulged in the comforting image of floating on air...right straight out of the country.

As spring approached, the fantasy of gliding his way to the west became concrete. Jozsi began to plan his escape. He read everything he could find about other attempts to flee, studying the plans of those who'd tried and failed, not wanting to make their same mistakes when his turn came. The Cultural Center was a good source for such news; through the grapevine Sandor often heard about the failures and successes and, Jozsi suspected, was more than likely involved in some of the attempts.

Between school, work, his sporadic research into the source of his secret treasures, the identity of the body in the coffin only he knew about, and three nights a week of glider classes, he barely had time to keep up with Sandor's needs, much less be with Erika. At the club, he studied aerodynamics and sat blindfolded in a classroom-built glider, pretending to fly while other students tilted the glider this way and that. During these listing sessions, he developed a feel for the angle of the wings without needing to look at the instruments. When the teacher called him the Charles Lindbergh of the class, Jozsi imagined himself triumphantly gliding into LaGuardia Airport, although truly, he'd settle for Orly, or *any* airport as long as it was on the far side of the Hungarian border.

Because of his busy schedule their dinner at *The Golden Bull* had been a special occasion. But since that night, Erika had been subtly cooler to him. He sprung for opera tickets to see the ever-popular operetta, *The Czárdás Queen*. She was pleased, but not overly so. He feared her feelings were cooling as his desire to leave increased. Not a good feeling. Not fair of him to expect otherwise, he realized, but still. After a few weeks of this subtle shift, he brought her to his apartment to try to get to the bottom of things. He lived in a small bedroom-kitchen combination. The apartment had ceilings ten feet tall, large paintings hung on the walls, the artwork looked to be from before the First World War. What at one time must have been the large home of a wealthy family was now broken up into small apartments. He was lucky to have the space, a bed, a table and four chairs all to himself.

Jozsi fussed at the kitchen's small counter top, fixing espresso with Puerto Rican rum, compliments of Sandor. He hoped the rum would warm and loosen her tongue; he wasn't enjoying the chilly treatment. Eventually, the rum and some gentle probing did the trick. She held the pebble in her shoe out to him: all of the time he spent learning to pilot a glider, and doing things for and with Sandor, made her feel like an outsider in his life; his comment about doing the tango in America had been the final straw.

"While you are doing the tango in America, where am I? Every night, I hear those words in my head and I cry," which she proceeded to demonstrate. He was surprised. He'd often spoken to her about wanting to leave the country "as it is now." It wasn't for him to put words in her mouth; he didn't assume she felt the same about fleeing. But, she countered, his family went back generations, as did hers, and she knew *they* would never leave. How could he?

"I cannot live this way forever," Jozsi said, meaning every word. "I'll die here; I can't stand this prison. Whatever exists on the other side of the Iron Curtain, it has to be better than this. I can't work like a dog just to survive from day to day, with no joy or freedom." He spoke so passionately she cried all the harder, finally curling up on the couch, a shuddering mound of sobs and whimpers. During the exhausted calm that followed, they fell into bed, whispering late into the night of their lives, their connection, their dreams for the country. He confessed his plan for the summer: to take the risk and attempt to glide his way to

Austria. He needed to qualify for a cross-country flying permit and be fortunate enough to catch a west wind strong enough to carry him as far as the border. If all went well, he'd be free.

This fully confirmed her fears, but she held the tears at bay. "Would you take me with you if you could?" He put his arms around her and nestled her head under his chin. He loved her, but he was young and hungry for new experiences. Making your way in an unfamiliar world was hard enough for one person, he wasn't about to commit to trying it with two. He did not want to hurt her, though. If things had been different in Hungary, he'd have been planning to build a life with her.

"I would take you and all the people who want to leave this country."

"But Jozsi," she sighed, "I don't want to leave, I want our country back, I want it to be itself again."

He got out of bed, fetched his wallet and pulled out a picture he'd taken of her by the Danube, her blond hair loose and lovely in a breeze, a smile on her face, the mountains of Pest in the distance.

"That was the day we saw those two swans with their babies trolling near the vegetable boat," she said, happy at the memory. "I remember so well. We had a little bag of berries and a canteen of water, and we walked for hours."

"You'll be with me one way or another," Jozsi said soothingly, slipping the photograph back in its permanent home. "I'm not going anywhere just yet. Let's have what we have; we can't know what comes next," he whispered, slipping into bed. And given all the change and disruption that war had wrought across Europe through most of her life, Erika saw the wisdom in cherishing the lived moment and not worrying so much about the future. It didn't hurt that Jozsi massaged her tense shoulders until she drifted off to sleep. By morning's light, she'd regained her composure and they were again close, the chill gone, at least, he thought, for now.

~~~

"You are something else," Laci shook his head in awe. "Always the girls want to marry you. Me, they say, 'Let's have some fun and then get out of here so I can find a good, reliable man.' Remember in Italy? You could have been lord of the manor!"

"The villa, you mean?" Jozsi laughed.

"But tell me about the gliding!" Laci didn't want Jozsi to digress. In all their time together, Jozsi had never opened up much about his own life in Hungary. There had been too much else going on, and no one talked about the people they'd left behind, it was safer for everybody that way. "You were good at it, eh?"

~~~

Jozsi had been good at it. By the summer of 1955, he was a confident solo flier. His instructor Bela promised that by late summer he'd be able to fly cross-country, and perhaps even become an instructor. But for glider events there were more qualified cross-country pilots than the club had glider planes, so it wasn't just skill he needed, but luck as well. There were six openings for that summer's cross-country flight and over 50 applicants. The Russians made a big stink about maintaining secure airspace; even if there had there been more planes available they'd likely have forbidden a larger number of flights.

Jozsi's spirits flagged as he realized his chances of gliding out of Hungary that year faced an obstacle course he had little chance of overcoming. He rallied himself the Sunday afternoon the news was to be announced, ready to cheer for whomever won a spot. Sandor was always reminding him that patience was a large part of the mix in achieving any goal. The head instructor emerged from the hanger office holding a single sheet of paper. He stood looking his students over as though he were a general assessing the troops before battle. At last, he spoke.

Jozsi almost ran to kiss him when his was the first name out of Bela's mouth. His head got so big he couldn't fit the rest of the names into his ears and had no idea who else had been chosen. He was wild with excitement, with only a month to get ready for his flight. His mind reeled with visions of striding down Viennese boulevards, gulping freedom's air, speaking his mind. He slept little, each morning leaping out of bed and into the day as though propelled by a bolt of lightning.

He practically danced into his next appointment with Sandor at a remote tavern where they sometimes met. The tavern owner treated him to a free *Hubertus* simply because he looked so happy. Sandor told Jozsi to scale it back or he'd be screaming in an Andrássy Street cell before he knew what hit him. Jozsi begged Sandor to help him defect by finding out exactly where, between Budapest and Austria, the Russian radar was located. He was only authorized to fly as far as the city of Gyor; the Austrian border was due west, exactly 75 miles further.

Sandor used the word 'harebrained' over and over while trying to talk him out of his gliding scheme. "Patience, Jozsi, you must have patience. I can help get you out of here, but not yet." He confessed that Jozsi was too good an accomplice to lose, told him his information was important for a larger cause, and that he needed to keep his personal desires in perspective.

"Fuck the larger cause," Jozsi sputtered, trying to keep his voice low. "I want out *now!*" Sandor ticked off all that he would do to improve Jozsi's life if he stayed: more dinners at *The Golden Bull*, a better stocked bar in his apartment, help with a plan for escape a little further down the road. "No," Jozsi said over and over, "Not enough. No." He'd been thinking about this for too long, there was no stopping him.

"I don't want to hear you've been shot out of the sky," Sandor pleaded. Too dangerous, too reckless, he emphasized. Jozsi would not budge.

"I'm going," he stated. "You can help me or not, but I'm going. You have your job to do, but this is my life."

Sandor caved. At their next meeting, he brought information about the radar station locations and advice: "Once you're in Austria, head for the American Embassy. They will take care of you. But I will also try to line someone up to find you at the border."

"I knew I could depend on you," Jozsi said. "No hard feelings?"

"None," Sandor said, and it felt to Jozsi that he meant it. "If we see each other again, we are friends." They toasted with *palinka* and Jozsi even dared to hug his CIA mentor before dashing out the door.

By the time Jozsi had followed a zigzag route back to his apartment — always alert to the chance he was being followed — his mood had darkened. The enormity of what he was about to undertake began to weigh. He sat at his little round wooden table, staring out the window, thinking about his family, his friends, the Toths, the world of people he'd grown up knowing. Chances were slim that he'd ever see any of them again, certainly not as long as the communists governed. He thought about Erika and how close they were. He thought about being on his own, truly on his own, in a land of strangers. He thought about bleeding to death in a field. About vanishing into the bowels of 60 Andrássy, never to be seen again. Or being sent to an internment camp — the AVO's favorite method of disposing of people they didn't have enough evidence to arrest. No, he thought, if they catch me escaping they'll shoot. He sat late into the night, sipping plain rum, no espresso, thinking complicated sad thoughts. But at the end of the bottle, he again pictured himself in beautiful Vienna and his heart lifted.

The following day he took the next big step and broke the news to Erika. "You love me?" he asked.

"You know I do," she answered.

"Then be happy to think of me breathing in freedom. Who knows what comes next, but whatever does, you will always be with me," he patted the pants pocket where he kept his wallet, with her photograph tucked inside.

Erika had spent a lot of time thinking about his departure and had made peace with it as best she could. When sadness hit, she'd recite a little list. The AVO were on his tail. It was only a matter of time before he would again be taken to Andrássy Street. She didn't want him to disappear like her father. She didn't want to hear he'd been sent to work in the Siberian mines. It was best for him to escape. And whether the secret police constantly shadowing Jozsi was a result of the political situation or simply an outcome of Zsigmond's jealousy she did not know, but Zsigmond kept popping up in her life, "keeping in touch," he said. She wasn't really afraid of Zsigmond, believing she could handle him, with or without Jozsi. What she did know was that it hurt to see Jozsi leave the country that he cared for so deeply. But she also knew that harm would likely befall him should he stay, and that would hurt so much more.

They spent the evening before his scheduled flight at *The Golden Bull*, arriving early and sitting at the same table they'd occupied the first time, ordering the same fine meal.

"This is history repeating itself," Erika said, trying to be cheerful so his last memories of her would be good ones. She could dive into a deep well of glumness once he'd left.

He raised a glass. "To meeting again, perhaps in America, in New York City, or someplace we've never even thought of." They clinked glasses and he reached over to wipe away the tears she hadn't realized were sliding down her cheeks.

"To meeting again," she said, managing a smile.

They made it an early night, walking back to his apartment across the Margaret Bridge, pausing to enjoy the warm breeze, and the view of lights sprinkled through the hills on either side. Returning fishermen tooted horns as they passed under the bridge, signaling that they'd had a good day on the water and the catch was ample.

Jozsi put his arm around Erika and said, "What a beautiful country this would be if the Russians would let us live as we want." She leaned into his shoulder as cars and buses sped by. Later, they sat on the balcony drinking, watching Hungarians head home after a hard day of work. There wasn't much left to say, so they didn't say anything.

They rose early, in the still dark city, to catch the bus that would take them to the airport. Jozsi scanned the sky, trying to get a sense of the wind and coming weather; his escape depended entirely on its conditions.

The bus picked them up and the younger students on board all wished Jozsi luck, they knew this day was his chance to earn a cross-country flying award. Erika escaped back into sleep during the hour it took to get to the airport. Jozsi tried but failed to drift off, his head filled with thoughts of his parents. He and Erika had visited them the weekend before and kept a tortured silence about his plans. When leaving, he'd hugged his parents a little longer than usual, turned back for a perhaps final look at the two, standing firm in front of the place he knew best. He'd said under his breath, "I'll see you again in better times," but that hadn't calmed the shaky feeling in his stomach.

Bela, the instructor, was already in the control room, and as Jozsi entered he held his hand toward the sun-filled window with a ta-da flourish. "My boy, you have the best weather God could give you to get to Gyor. Their air controller says it's perfect by them, too." Jozsi thought: I need all the luck I can get, and circumspectly tried to wheedle information about what the weather was like further west in case a storm loomed. "All clear to Austria!" Bela crowed.

Erika stood by the side of the hanger, holding back tears, forcing her face into an expression approximating normal anxiety, with no hint of heartbreak. It wasn't easy. She waited for him to say goodbye at the hanger, realizing she couldn't hold calm in front of the others. He trotted over, his heart beating hard, full of so many different emotions he felt it might burst. They held each other close, kissing deeply. Then pulled slightly apart, hands pressing hard into each other's upper arms. Jozsi leaned in and whispered he'd be back as soon as he could manage, Erika whispered that until then she'd be missing him every minute of every day. Another quick, tender kiss and he rushed to the glider before her expression crumbled and the tears flowed.

His single-passenger glider was hooked to a cable attached to a small plane. A group of new recruits held the tip of the glider's wings, ready for takeoff. The flag came down. Erika's hands flew up to cover her mouth. The single-engine plane started down the runway, pulling the glider while the recruits ran alongside holding up the wings until suddenly the glider was airborne. Jozsi waved, thanking them with a thumbs-up, mimicking pilots in American war movies he'd seen at the Cultural Center. As the glider gained altitude, he turned to see the airport slowly diminish in size. Erika was just a spot, and soon, so too was the hanger.

At 5,000 feet, the pilot signaled for Jozsi to disconnect the glider, and he reached down and pulled the release cable, severing his final connection to Hungary but for the national colors painted on the glider's wings. The glider flew by instruments. The ground radar station couldn't pick him up without a radio, couldn't tell if he went off course. The airplane dipped and turned back toward the base and Jozsi was alone in the heavens, heading west into a pure blue sky.

Though he'd poured over the map, he was having trouble identifying the towns below, but he knew he was heading in the right direction. After a couple of hours, he estimated the Austrian border was perhaps thirty minutes away. He could only hope that Sandor had been able to alert people near the border, people who would be on the lookout for him, people who would give him some money and help make proper arrangements for his future. He hoped this was true.

Since he was already way off course and in the off-limits zone, Jozsi flew lower than normal, hoping to avoid Russian radar. If spotted, the Russian air force would swoop down on him like hawks on a sparrow. Even though the glider contained virtually no trackable metal, his tension mounted as he neared the border and saw below Russian military bases and their installations. Abruptly the wind died down; Jozsi lost the air current and began losing altitude. "Please God, just fifteen more minutes, just a big gust, please…" He could see smoke rising from the Austrian farmhouses in the distance; he knew the glider was on the right track even as he entered the path of low clouds moving in from nearby mountains. Visibility lessened and within moments he was flying blind. So much for perfect weather, he thought wryly, to keep panic at bay. As the glider gently continued to lose altitude, he dipped below the clouds seeking a soft hayfield he could land in, praying it would be on the Austrian side of the border.

He spotted a green pasture seconds before noticing several jeeps filled with border patrolling bodies, racing toward that same pasture. Euphoric as the glider bounced onto the grass, he pounded the dashboard excitedly, shouting, "I did it, I did it!" He saw the jeeps haphazardly parked behind him, soldiers jumping out and running toward the glider to welcome him when he opened the cockpit. Tears ran down his cheeks; he was feeling so much gratitude at landing, and so much emotion at being free of Hungary.

Jozsi jumped down from the plane, blinking away tears of relief and joy. To his horror, he saw red stars on the soldiers' uniforms. He blinked some more. "Holy shit," he thought, "where *am* I?" Hearing the soldiers talk, he quickly realized he'd landed in the Republic of Czechoslovakia, very close to, though on the wrong side of, the Austrian border. A soldier stepped forward — the border patrol recognized the national colors on the glider in an instant and had a Hungarian-speaker on hand. Jozsi thought fast, talked faster, telling the truth where he could. First cross country flight. Sudden storm. Totally lost. Ah yes, the translator agreed, an unusually sudden storm, especially for this time of year. It had just missed them.

After he'd been questioned and found believable, the translating soldier announced with a grin that Jozsi was indeed a lucky man: he'd missed the Austrian border by only 300 yards. Jozsi wanted to throttle the man till he turned blue, but he remembered that you never kill the messenger. Plus, he was outnumbered.

The translating soldier and a crony drove Jozsi back to Hungary, back to the glider club, where everyone on hand sympathized with his troubles and celebrated his safe return. He offered the weakest smile imaginable and no excitement about his adventure; people figured he was exhausted from the journey. Next stop, the police station for a detailed report as to why he was so far off-course, suspicions of an escape plot obvious in their questions. At least he wasn't taken to Andrássy Street. He was relieved Sandor had persuaded him not to carry anything on his person — no map, no ID, no money, no nothing. Nothing except for the bullet shell whistle his father had given him many years earlier. He'd long since taken it off the chain, but always carried it on his person for luck.

"I will do my best to have people waiting for you," Sandor had promised. Jozsi figured those people must have gotten tired of waiting and gone on with their free lives in Austria. At first, he felt sick, dispirited, broken. But he was never one to wallow and soon shifted to a more positive position: he was alive and not in a jail cell, he would find another way.

Zsigmond had gotten wind of Jozsi's misadventure and appeared at his investigation hearing, although he asked no questions. At the end of the hearing, Jozsi, to his great relief, was free to go. Zsigmond was waiting for him at the gate and suggested they raise a glass at a nearby tavern. Jozsi knew it as a stool-pigeon hangout — a place the local police received information from weak-willed losers and guys who would turn their own mothers in for a shot of *palinka*. Of course, Zsigmond received a warm welcome from the barkeep and several of the customers.

They sat near the door, Jozsi carefully eying everyone who came and went, thinking there was no one in that shithole he could trust. They toasted *Egészségedre,* "To your health," when the waiter delivered their *Hubertus*. Then Zsigmond launched into a patronizing lecture about how, although they were friends, he couldn't keep covering Jozsi's ass forever. Jozsi assured him there was no cause for concern, while ordering another round and scrutinizing his manner. The old Zsigmond would have cautioned while at the same time wheedling for Jozsi's approval, wanting to preen at his new power. This was a new Zsigmond: guzzling, waving his hands like a potentate, pointing his index finger at Jozsi's face, leaning forward to jab it into his chest, saying, "You better watch your ass, my friend — all the small talk and reminiscing about old times is gone by the wayside. If you don't keep your ass straight, you'll find yourself at 60 Andrássy Street and I won't be able to help you." Jozsi thought: and you won't want to.

Perhaps it was the force of Zsigmond's jealousy about Erika, combined with an ego fed by his new power, but something about the man caused a slight chill in Jozsi. He'd never before been afraid that Zsigmond would let something truly bad befall him; he no longer felt that way. He wondered if he were being paranoid. He knew Ferenc hadn't seen Zsigmond in a long time, but then, Ferenc wouldn't trigger the same reaction in Zsigmond; Ferenc wasn't up to anything dangerous, wasn't trying to escape his own country, and was not the object of Erika's affection. Ferenc might notice no change at all.

At home, after his return, Erika cried with him in frustration that he hadn't escaped, but couldn't hide her joy at having him by her side. He reviewed the flight, trying to figure out exactly what had gone wrong, imagining himself gliding, turning a different way, dropping low sooner, anything that might have gained him those crucial extra 300 yards. Erika hugged him hard and went to bed. But Jozsi grabbed a bottle of Sandor's pricey whiskey and sat on the terrace watching the city gradually settle into darkness, lights going out one by one as he absorbed the sad fact that he was still in Hungary.

In the morning, he asked Erika if she'd noticed a change in Zsigmond of late. No, she said, with her he was the same as always, fawning from a distance, not too aggressive, and rarely mentioning Jozsi except to suggest that for her own safety she should steer clear of him. Of course, he'd been saying that since she'd first run into Jozsi at the Cultural Center.

Still, Jozsi didn't have to literally witness Zsigmond studying his daily surveillance report to know that's exactly what he was doing. So, it was always the same. After school, after work, he saw Erika — sometimes they ate at a restaurant, they stayed at one or the other's apartment, but never did they go to the Cultural Center. Jozsi knew he had to stay away from Sandor — he was afraid that another visit to 60 Andrássy would lead to a slow, painful death. Erika volunteered to become their main contact. He hated to put her in the middle of things, but she insisted. Neither thought that Zsigmond would ever allow Erika to be hurt, his adoration of her was too longstanding; it turned him into an eight-year-old boy in a man's body. For the moment, they all trusted his obsession with Erika would be enough to keep her safe.

11

The Answer to a Question

The Budais celebrated the Christmas season of 1955 with as much of their usual joy and largesse as they could manage. Each morning when they awoke, Matyas and Erzsebet would exchange a look, take a deep breath, rise, and force themselves to feel strong and hopeful. They invited family and friends to join them Christmas Day, including Erika and her mother — most everyone anticipated that Jozsi and Erika would announce their engagement any minute. When Jozsi stood to propose a toast, the room quieted. Instead, he toasted to their survival and to the love and support of good friends and family. It was a big disappointment for the assembled, but the next day Jozsi and Erika laughed over the crowd's letdown, Erika less loudly than Jozsi. Hid within a small cocoon in her heart lived the hope that he would give up his dreams of flight and cleave to her from now till the end of their lives. But her mind, as riled as his at what had befallen their country, knew better. He had to leave or the situation in Hungary had to change and she didn't see the latter happening any time soon.

Jozsi continued excelling at school. The director of his division knew he was working on highly confidential communications systems and was proud that one of his students had been selected for the task. He pretty much gave Jozsi free reign, allowing him to come and go as he pleased; all Jozsi had to do was whisper that he was needed at the factory. At the factory, he would tell Dr. Geller he had catch up on classwork and the good doctor would intone: "Knowledge is power: use it when you need it," as he waved him on his way. Jozsi's increased ability to freely bounce between school and factory emboldened him to resume sporadic contact with Sandor. He'd race to wherever they'd agree to meet thinking: I *am* using power! Meanwhile Zsigmond's goons were going mad trying to nail down his schedule.

One afternoon, while waiting for Sandor on the street, Jozsi observed obviously weary proletarians trudging past. He knew their thoughts: if they could manage to make it through another month, and another after that, some day things would change. It wouldn't be soon enough for Joszi though; he wanted the better life now, right now, not later. He was tired of waiting, tired of hearing how if you worked hard enough each and every day you would get to the Promised Land. This was not his idea of living.

More to his liking was Sandor sitting across the table, stuffed billfold in pocket, paying for everything Jozsi put in his mouth. This windy day Sandor, slightly breathless, hair mussed from his rush to their meeting, shook his head across the table. "How in the hell do you manage to get away in the middle of the day to park your ass on this terrace? Even I have trouble freeing up time to meet you."

Jozsi leaned over to put his arm around Sandor. "My friend, knowledge is power." And when the bill came, he grinned merrily as Sandor motioned for the check. They agreed to meet a week later at a different location. As they parted, Jozsi turned back cheerfully, "One more thing, Sandor. Make sure you bring the money." Sandor smiled, nodded, and looked down to where he was surreptitiously giving Jozsi the American middle finger. Jozsi caught the gesture and returned it before turning, with an insolent flip of his head, and striding off. He was feeling his oats, Sandor thought, fretting that his ego might get him in trouble. He'd grown fond of his young protégée. But neither fondness nor fretfulness were encouraged in CIA training; agents needed to keep a clear head.

For New Year's Eve Erika suggested they have a small party at Jozsi's apartment. They invited Ferenc and his girlfriend Beatrix to spend the night. Erika took the day off from work to prepare, telling Jozsi to make himself scarce until early evening.

He met Sandor at an out-of-the-way tavern where they talked about the usual madness and the populace's increasing outrage at the regime. There was a feeling on the streets that the New Year would not end the way it had begun, that things simply could not continue on in this way. Sandor sympathized with Jozsi's failure to glide his way to freedom and promised there would be other opportunities to escape. He assured Jozsi that all his activities to help the CIA were important, that all actions supporting subterranean shifts in the country would eventually lead to change.

Sandor handed Jozsi a package, "For your celebration tonight," and regretted he could not take Jozsi up on his offer to join in their festivities. "You know how happy that would make the AVO, me going to your apartment. They'd rush you straight to Andrássy Street. Better to let them stand watch in the cold."

In the package was a bottle of Chivas Regal; a fine scotch Jozsi had heard of but never tasted. Jozsi inclined the bottle toward him in a toast of gratitude, "To better days." They double-kissed cheeks, like friends, and Sandor promised that one day they would ring in the New Year together. So much for keeping clear boundaries, he thought. Jozsi had charmed him; there were no two ways about it.

Jozsi returned home to delicious smells emanating from his apartment. He inhaled deeply and his mouth literally watered as a whiff of veal paprikash wafted from the kitchen. Few Hungarians had been able to afford to make that classic Hungarian dish of late. Ferenc and Beatrix arrived with bags filled with apple and cherry strudel and clinking bottles of wine. Erika wore a white shirt, red skirt, and green sweater, making her the embodiment of the Hungarian national colors. She had laid the table with a green cotton tablecloth and white linen napkins, and arranged winterberry branches in a vase to add a touch of red to the table. Their supper was delicious and joyful, filled with toasts and laughter, reminiscences of New Year's long past, and hopes for the future.

After supper, Jozsi opened the Chivas and they sipped as the conversation moved to more serious matters: the future of Hungary and the possibility of a full-blown uprising. They agreed a revolt had to occur. Nothing less would force Russia to accept that the Hungarians had no need of Russian "protection" from the West.

As the level of Chivas in the bottle fell, their intensity rose. Jozsi went to the window, pulling aside the curtain just enough to see the street without being spotted from below. He reached into a pocket and held his lucky bullet shell whistle. "One of Zsigmond's louts is lurking just across." Ferenc had not seen Zsigmond in many months and still could not quite accept the change that had come over him. "We were friends," he said mournfully to Beatrix. "In childhood, inseparable. For him to turn on Jozsi, no, it is unbelievable. And it's my fault," he drunkenly slapped the flat of his hand repeatedly against his chest. "I brought him into the fold, I befriended him first. You," he pointed to Jozsi, "you would never have been his friend without me; you are smarter than that." He shook his head, Beatrix patted his knee. To pull him out of his misery, Jozsi suggested they should bring their spy some food and a shot of *palinka*. "Yes!" Ferenc practically shouted. "Let us be the better men, let us feed the evil enemy." He really was quite drunk.

Erika stepped in to put a stop to this nonsense. "Let's not irritate them, all right? This is our night to celebrate safely. They make it hard enough on us as it is." And with that, they agreed to ignore the spy and again turned to passionate talk of revolution and how best to encourage that.

~~~

After the holidays, in frustration at Jozsi's ability to dodge his trackers, the AVO started bringing Erika to headquarters. The first time she'd been terrified, and so had Jozsi. Fortunately, she'd already stopped being any kind of go-between with Sandor, so she had nothing in particular to hide, and Zsigmond always managed to be there and get her quickly released. Soon she grew calloused, suspecting he was having her brought in just so he could have her released, be the big hero. "This keeps happening because you are spending time with Jozsi," he told her. "You are lucky you know me. I can't stop them from bringing you in, but so far, I can get you released. They look at me a little sideways, but they know I am loyal to the Party."

After several of these "accidental" meetings, he braved asking her to accompany him to a special dinner at the parliament. "It will look better for you, being seen at an event with me." Excitedly he informed her that the famous Russian KGB officer Andropov would be speaking. As though she cared, she thought, amazed that he was still trying to woo her, given her relationship with Jozsi. To torture him, and give her time to consult with Jozsi, she said she'd think it over.

Still desperate to hear any news of her father, she was tempted to go, hoping Zsigmond might relax enough to let something slip. Jozsi reluctantly agreed that it was worth a try — after all she might glean other useful information while with that bunch. The thought of Zsigmond touching even so much as her arm made his chest tight, but he tried to rise above that; after all, she was the one who would have to endure Zsigmond's foul company.

She could barely swallow a bite the night of the dinner, so sickened was she by the special welcome the Hungarians gave Andropov. They'd dressed in clean crisp uniforms; medals hung from their jackets, some of which they'd no doubt ripped from the bodies of deceased fellow countrymen. The AVO officers catered to Andropov, she later told Jozsi, "like he was Caesar in Egypt." A few times during the evening she'd tried to turn the conversation to her missing father, but Zsigmond would shake his head and change the subject, or derail the conversation by waving to someone across the room. She learned nothing of use to either Jozsi or Sandor. It had been a mistake to come, she felt, especially when they reached the door to her apartment and Zsigmond made it clear he was more than open to being invited in, eager for a goodnight kiss, and hoping for another date, in that order. Finally, he insinuated that he might be willing to make an effort to locate her father if she were willing to discuss the circumstances at his Szondy Street apartment.

Erika's stomach twisted in rage and without thinking she snapped, "Don't you ever try this again just to get me in bed," and slammed the door in his face. That he could break the door down and drag her away crossed her mind as she stood shaking, though more with fury than with fear. A few long moments later she heard him turn and stride off, boots thumping angrily against the wooden floor all the way down the hall.

When she recounted the evening's events Jozsi was furious — at his former friend, and at himself for not talking her out of going in the first place. At his next meeting with Sandor, in a run down, sleazy tavern on the outskirts of the city, he was clearly in a foul mood.

"What the hell is eating you?" Sandor asked, puzzled by Jozsi's sullen mood.

Since the miserable night of the Andropov dinner, Jozsi had been mulling over the limits of what he could ask of Sandor and in that moment decided to go for broke. "We meet next Friday, yes? By then I'm asking that you find out what happened to Erika's father after he entered 60 Andrássy Street. I have to know. If he's still alive, I have to know where he is."

Sandor raised both hands in a plea of disbelief. "I have little access to that hellhole, there is no way I can find this out in a week."

"Life is a bitch and we all have our share of troubles," Jozsi shot back. "There will be no more information for you until we hear what happened to Dr. Simon." From Sandor's expression, he knew he had enough leverage to be taken seriously.

"I'll have to lean on all my goons," Sandor sighed.

"Whatever it takes," Jozsi snapped. "Or as plain as the ass on a goat, I'm done helping you. Without me and my information, your people will find a *new* you, and you'll be back in Akron harvesting hay for the rest of your life."

"Calm down, Jozsi," Sandor ventured, "you need to be careful. Blind rage won't do you any good." Easy for him to say, Sandor realized; he'd had the anger trigger mostly trained right out of him and rarely exploded. He felt sorry for his young friend, upset, frustrated by history and politics, hounded by the AVO, his head and heart turbulent with thwarted dreams. They agreed to meet the following week and Sandor left Jozsi, his rage spent, sagging at the table…a balloon with no air.

That night Sandor activated the few agents he felt might be able to ferret out the necessary information, while Jozsi went home and fell into a deep dreamless sleep.

The following Thursday after work, Jozsi stopped at *The Thirsty Horse* tavern on Kalman Square to have a few beers with friends, a weekly ritual that provided him the chance to pop into the men's room and reach behind a ceramic urinal to find messages from Sandor. "*Hat elnyom,*" was scrawled on a small piece of paper — Hungarian for six and quench. Jozsi promptly flushed it down the toilet and rejoined his friends. Six was for the sixth day of the week and Elnyom was the name of a railway tavern at a station on the route from Jozsi's hometown to Budapest. An aunt of his lived across the road from the station.

He'd told Erika of the ultimatum he'd given Sandor. She could barely speak she'd been so moved, and was even more affected when he promised to bring her along for the meeting. They planned to leave early and stop at his aunt's house for a visit, enabling them to spy on the tavern door for a good stretch and make sure none of Zsigmond's minions were for any reason watching the tavern.

They sat on the veranda while Aunt Julianna ferried out pastries and small glasses of wine. Workers shuffled out of the tavern to head home after the one or two drinks they could manage to afford. Erika watched Jozsi watch the workers. "This is what you want to get away from."

"Yes," he answered, "but I want to come back and free them too. I want to come back and see them enjoy an easier life, the life they're supposed to have. Hard work, yes, but also the ability to enjoy the fruits of their labors. They can barely afford one drink after work, and you know that none of them can ever afford to eat there." It drove him crazy to see his great nation bending down to a country like Russia. The Allies had helped save Russian asses and now Russia was playing god with Hungary, his once wealthy nation, brought low by war.

They entered the dingy tavern. Some customers looked like they'd been there so long their bodies had melded into their stools. Sandor sat at the far end of the bar, eating raw pickled fish and drinking a glass of *unicum*. Jozsi and Erika took a table in a corner, a sticky table. Jozsi restrained himself from making a fuss with the waiter, not wanting to draw attention. Instead, he mildly asked for two glasses of wine and a double of whatever was in the glass for the man at the end of the bar.

After both men had carefully perused the tavern for any possible AVO presence, Sandor took his last bite of fish, finished his first drink, picked up his new one, and moved toward them. He placed the drink hard on the table, thanking Jozsi loudly, then leaned close to his ear and without looking at Erika said "She wasn't part of the deal."

Jozsi raised his wine glass, "To your health." They all drank, though Sandor's lips were grimace-tight, his sip so small he didn't need to swallow. "Sit," Jozsi said, unapologetically.

"I don't take this kind of shit from anyone," Sandor murmured placidly. As cool a customer as he was, Sandor did not relish the thought of Erika hearing what he was about to share. He looked at Erika, then at Jozsi. "Can she handle rough information?"

"What do you mean?" Erika asked, her stomach sinking. Any small hope she had that her father was still alive vanished. She took a big drink of wine to steady her nerves.

"What I mean is..." He paused, still addressing Jozsi, refusing to look at her, as though they'd never met. "Can she handle an ugly description, can she handle news that..." he trailed off, frowning.

"Sandor," she jabbed angrily at his arm, "it's *my* father, look at *me*." He turned to face her. Coldly she said, "After what my mother and I have been through, knowing cannot hurt more than not knowing."

Sandor's expression said: don't be so sure of that. But he said

171

nothing, merely stared at a spot slightly to the side of her face. Jozsi reached for her hand. Sandor downed the rest of his drink and began to share what he'd learned. Dr. Simon had been interrogated at great length. Why had the communist general, the head of the secret service, died on his operating table? What were the reasons? Why had other communist officials died on his table? It didn't matter that Dr. Simon didn't think any had, and that the communist general was basically dead on arrival. They wanted to know if the doctor was an agent for the Americans. They wanted to know if he had conspired with other agents against the Hungarian government. They wanted to know if he knew other doctors who were, who had, who did this, that and the other. Or nurses. Or orderlies. The torture that followed these questions went on and on and on. He described the torture in as much detail as he knew, blow-by-blow. Then he described the way Erika's father had died: slowly, and in excruciating pain. He felt slightly sick to his stomach, wishing to be anywhere but here saying the things he was saying. But she'd insisted on hearing; he was only doing what she'd asked.

Jozsi was going to interrupt but he'd been the one to make Sandor do this so he kept silent, flinching slightly when Erika's fingers dug deep into his palm. Sandor finished and the three sat stone-faced for a good while. Rising, Sandor said to Erika as gently as he could, "Your father's remains were disposed of in the Danube two weeks after they took him to Andrássy Street." Erika looked ill and excused herself to hurry to the bathroom. Sandor put on his coat, but before leaving looked at Jozsi, his eyes widening ever so slightly in warning, and nearly whispered, "You should know one more thing…the final interrogator was Zsigmond. I'm very sorry about all of it," he said sadly. Then turned and walked out of the tavern. Even more devastating. Jozsi decided not to tell Erika that detail just yet.

For the next few days, Jozsi held Sandor's story up, examining it this way and that, as though it were a kaleidoscope whose versatility intrigued. Knowing that the CIA had many reasons to turn Jozsi against his former friend, he had certain reservations about Sandor's story. It might be true, it might be that someone told Sandor it was true, it might be that Sandor made the whole thing up. Deciding he had to know for certain, he shared his quandary with Ferenc.

"Zsigmond brags when he drinks," Jozsi mused. "He hasn't seen you in a long time. If I give you money to get him drunk..."

Ferenc nodded. "I haven't seen him in a few months. I'm small potatoes, too small for him to bother with these days. But if I can get him to meet me, he'll be more than happy to rub my face in his success."

The two friends decided the old railroad tavern would be the perfect place. It was not far from an area they'd played in as children, and their favorite waiter, Oszkar, was a quiet rebel who would be happy to put a stake through the heart of anyone supporting the communists, the Hungarian regime, the AVO, anyone who had anything to do with ruining his country. They arranged for Oszkar to put tea in Ferenc's beer bottles instead of *Hubertus*. He even promised to set out a clean tablecloth. Jozsi promised him a big tip if all went well.

After much effort, Ferenc managed to reach Zsigmond and convince him to meet his old friend at the tavern. It had been too long since they'd reminisced.

"What about Jozsi?" Zsigmond asked.

"Ach, he's too busy and too big a snob. Let's just make it you and me."

"I too am busy," Zsigmond said, "but I will make time for you. It has been a long time, and I have good news to share." I'll bet you do, thought Ferenc.

They set a date for the following Saturday, and Ferenc arrived a little late, allowing Zsigmond to get a head start. Indeed, when Ferenc arrived, Zsigmond was already at the bar, a glass in his hand. He put it down to give Ferenc a big hug. Kind-hearted Ferenc felt two things simultaneously: sentimental at an old friend's hug and suspicious that the old friend was looking for a soft spot on his back to stab.

They took a table in the back, Oszkar indeed laying out a clean tablecloth — in these times a rare occurrence, one that impressed Zsigmond. Ferenc, with a flourish, ordered two *Hubertus*, telling Oszkar to keep them coming. For a while they talked about the old days, Ferenc saying, "Let's drink to that," at the mention of almost anything. The swimming hole, Brother Francis tripping on his way up the stone stairs, the day they walked backwards all the way to town.

Eventually Zsigmond started bragging about his own rise in the AVO and increased power, how all he had to do was snap his fingers and he could have anything he wanted. "I mention a name," he snapped his fingers, "the person is brought to my office." He snapped twice. "And then they disappear." That the person would be tortured or executed went without saying.

Somewhere amid the torrent of boasts, Ferenc dropped a toxic little pill into the water. "I bet Jozsi is jealous of how well you're doing."

Zsigmond's face skewed ugly. He spat out the name. "Jozsi. He's been looking down on us since we were boys. Always thinking he's the smartest." He leaned back in his chair and belched. "I will have Erika eating out of my hand whether he likes it or not." He slammed both hands hard on the table. "Jozsi can't stop me, he has no power…It's only a matter of time before he gets in so much trouble even I can't save him. I would, too, you know," he thumped his heart. "For old times, and because I am the better man. I have already saved his hide more than once."

Ferenc, seeing the red-eyes and blurred movements of extreme drunkenness, wheedled, "Remarkable, all this power. I had no idea you'd risen so high, so fast."

Zsigmond leaned back, closed his eyes, and for a moment Ferenc thought he'd waited too long, that the new King of Budapest was falling asleep. But then Zsigmond's eyes shot open. His head wobbled for a second, but he got his bearings, and elbow on the table, wagged a finger at Ferenc. "You have to promise me that whatever I tell you goes no further. It must stay among friends."

Ferenc, pleased at the opportunity to give an honest answer, assured him it would stay among friends. "Absolutely."

"When my superiors told me to go after Erika's father, I held them off at first. His daughter is my old classmate, I told them; let me make certain he is what you say he is. So, I looked into it and yes, he had turned against the socialist dreams of our country. When I was ready to accept that he was a turncoat, they gave him to me to interrogate. The weasel tried to use the past to gain my sympathy. At first I wasn't too hard on him, but he wouldn't bend, he wouldn't tell the truth, he wouldn't *admit* to anything. And I know a liar when I see one."

A little chill went up Ferenc's spine, but he managed to keep his expression one of open admiration.

Zsigmond was on a roll. "I'm telling you, he was a turncoat and for this he had to die. He deserved a slow painful death."

"What did you do?" Ferenc almost whispered.

Zsigmond looked around to make sure no one was paying attention. Oszkar was, but feigned otherwise. Zsigmond leaned forward and spoke low to Ferenc, whose face whitened, his hands digging into his knees, his heart sinking at the proof that his childhood friend had become, there was no other word for it, a monster.

As they walked back to town, they crossed the Rakos River Bridge and Ferenc thought about exactly how sloshed Zsigmond was, and how easy it would be to choke him and throw his lifeless corpse into the river. By sunrise he would be a bloated log floating in the Danube. He did nothing of the sort, but imagining it made him feel slightly less ill. Instead, Ferenc escorted him to the local police station and half-dragged him in the door to let the local goons take care of him. They were used to it.

Jozsi was both amazed and dismayed that what Ferenc told him matched what Sandor had related, the unvarnished truth — a rare occurrence when dealing with the CIA. He had the sad task of confirming Sandor's story to Erika, who had managed to continue holding on to some minute hope that it was fiction and that her father was alive, toiling miserably in a Russian salt mine. He'd hoped she wouldn't mention Zsigmond, but at one moment she did, wondering if he'd been involved. Jozsi still couldn't bear to tell her the full truth, but neither could he bear to tell a full lie. "Zsigmond knew he was there," he said, still not revealing that Zsigmond had been the one to finally destroy her father. She shook her head in disbelief. "He did not save him," she wept. "He could have, and he didn't." She laid her head on her hands and sobbed for a long time. When Jozsi next saw her eyes, they were red and filled with rage.

After the private funeral arrangement Jozsi made with their old church, Father Richter presiding, Erika went home to spend the night with her mother, and Jozsi went home to sit on his little balcony and think about the exact right punishment for a person like Zsigmond. Finally, he could no longer stand the darkness of his thoughts and escaped into sleep.

12

A Change in the Air

The long grim winter finally ended, spring came, flowers bloomed throughout the city, and all over Hungary, but especially in Budapest, farmers, workers, students and intellectuals lifted their heads and waited for change. Although no one could put their finger on exactly why they felt something would happen soon, or what that something might be, a sense of event permeated the air. People could feel an agitated pulse throbbing in the streets of Budapest; a fiery energy charging from person to person, unstoppable, like a virus gone rogue.

Three years earlier, following a similar wave of unrest after Stalin's death, Khrushchev had replaced Hungary's dictatorial Chairman Prime Minister Mátyás Rákosi with a less brutal politician, Imre Nagy. Nagy promised "A New Course," in socialism, implying that a higher standard of living and greater access to material goods would inevitably come to pass. Rákosi and the Soviets had never encouraged such a path. Rákosi had held powerful positions in Hungary for years, over time purging non-communist officials and intellectuals from government. He'd called himself "Stalin's best Hungarian disciple," although he had managed to displease the Soviet Politburo by not enthusiastically enough embracing their "collective leadership" ethos.

Although the Politburo replaced him with Nagy, Rákosi retained his position as General Secretary of the party and had done whatever he could to interfere with Nagy's efforts to lessen oppression. In March of 1955, the Central Committee of the Hungarian Worker's Party condemned Nagy for "rightist deviation." Nagy was also blamed by Hungarian newspapers for failing to fix the county's economic woes. Eventually the Politburo decided Nagy's "New Course" was altogether too risky; within two years he was removed and Rákosi returned to power, which did nothing to calm the waters.

Rákosi's use of the AVO to hunt out and frequently slaughter opponents had been a constant source of citizen rage, some of which could be traced back to 1948 when the communists had forced the Social Democrats to merge into the Hungarian Workers Party. Rákosi had promptly ceased pretending any form of democratic government existed and Hungary had then officially become a communist state. Since the push for communism never sprang from the people themselves, but was a totalitarian system imposed and supported by the Soviets, Rákosi had plenty of reasons to use the AVO. He'd even invented a term to describe his approach to destroying the opposition person by person: "salami tactics."

Then, shockingly, at the 20th Congress of the Soviet Party in February of 1956, its First Secretary, Nikita Khrushchev, had denounced Stalin's "cult of personality" in a secret speech. Of course, word of such an astonishing statement had leaked and spread, fueling sparks of hope across Eastern Europe. Intellectuals, writers and students rallied in protests, which frequently became violent. Quickly the Communist Youth League created a discussion forum, hoping to siphon off and better control at least a degree of the venting. They imaginatively named this forum after the beloved Hungarian national poet Petőfi, a move that backfired when the Petőfi Circle, as it became known, morphed into a hotbed of dissent solidifying opposition to the regime — circles popped up everywhere. Their demands centered on Rákosi's removal, the "de-

Stalinization" of Hungary, and the return of Imre Nagy.

Jozsi followed the developments, but kept his distance from Petőfi circles — he did not want to jeopardize his work for Sandor. But he was as distressed as those in the "Circles" when the Soviets summoned Rákosi to Russia, replacing him with the equally loathed deputy party leader Ernö Gerö, whose reputation for brutality was cemented during the Spanish Civil War, when he became known as the Butcher of Barcelona. Gerö arrived in Hungary and quickly released a few hundred political prisoners and promised reforms. But nothing he said or did swayed the intellectuals and the young, many of whom were from working-class backgrounds and acutely aware of the suffering caused by Soviet rule. In the factories, agitated workers held animated discussions about the need for change. There was talk of boycotts, motivated by pure rage at the way Russia was siphoning off Hungary's lifeblood to benefit itself: money, materials, harvest, equipment that should have stayed in Hungary, to help the people of Hungary, was being sent to assist Mother Russia. Enough was enough.

The AVO couldn't keep up with the quantity of information informants passed along, all of it seeming to signal the existence of a massive conspiracy. But there was no known leader or group of people the AVO could point at to arrest, no way for them to smother the flames, derail the train, put a finger in the dike. The secret police were edgy to be sure, and with good reason. People working in factories, and students and professors in universities, were talking more and more openly about *doing* something to reclaim their country. People, in cafés, walking by the river, sitting on buses, were whispering to each other, out in the open, where they could be seen though not easily overheard. Frustration with government suppression of small business, resentment at a person's inability to earn enough to feed themselves let alone a family, allowed anger and disgust to take root in a person's guts and once rooted, sprout into action. People were stealing from any government-run business they came in contact with; it didn't make them proud, but anything that helped a person get by became morally acceptable. One did not set high standards in this climate.

Jozsi and Erika looked forward to their summer break from school — a month's vacation, followed by assignments to countryside towns where university students worked with locals to help increase their skills and improve their standard of living. "Communist standard of living," Jozsi shrugged. "Why bother?" But he enjoyed the time away from the tension of life in Budapest, along with the demands of school and work and Sandor.

Jozsi asked his supervisor Dr. Geller for a favor: to use his influence and get Erika assigned as a doctor-in-training in the same town where Jozsi would be serving as engineer and manager of a small radio station. Jozsi wanted her far from Budapest, out of Zsigmond's reach, and, if possible, by his side. Erika was still struggling over the death of her father, haunted by where her mind went whenever she thought about the two weeks of torture he'd endured before dying. They also planned a trip to Ura where Jozsi promised her nourishing respite with the Toths. Once they knew that Dr. Geller had managed to pull the right strings, they looked forward to spending the summer together in Bekes.

Jozsi was looking forward to the simplicity of life in Bekes. There was one radio station — a room, really, in the town hall — and each peasant's home was hard-wired to that station. The communists saw no irony in the fact that many of the homes in Bekes had no electricity whatsoever. Each household had a radio, and each day the communists controlled what was broadcast into it. Each radio had a speaker and a single control knob that moved from off to on. There was, however, a choice of stations: you could listen to the Kossuth station, named after the famous Hungarian general who led the Hungarian uprising against the Germans in 1848; or you could listen to the Petofi station — the poet had died in the same revolution. Either way, Jozsi thought, a constant reminder that uprisings led to death; a way to underscore for the workers the value of keeping their heads down and focused on tasks as they labored to benefit the state. Oh, lucky peasants, fortunate beneficiaries of a radio and its wealth of communist propaganda, ever so kindly provided from town hall. What cares could they have — huddled around kerosene lamps, their only source of light, exhaustedly eating a meager meal — when they had the voice of the state to keep them company? He would have to keep his tongue in check in Bekes, but still, he hoped the smallness of the town and lack of distraction — there really was nothing much to do — would result in many weeks of peaceful coexistence with Erika.

But before that, they were off to the Toths, where Erika would finally get to meet this family whose life and land she'd heard so much about. Jozsi promised he'd take her to the ravine, to show her that such a place really existed. For a time, she'd maintained a skeptical distance from his efforts to research the story of the coffin, even going so far as to gently suggest that he was perhaps a bit delusional. Soon after they began sleeping together she'd asked him directly about the mystery that so compelled him.

"Jozsi," she'd taken his hand as they sat at his small dining table, looking into his eyes with sympathy and concern, "when we were young, we used to make up stories and we lived in that world for a long time. Sometimes we get so attached to these stories we think they're real and we don't accept that maybe they're not real. You understand what I mean?"

Jozsi had bristled. "I am not making this up. Someday I will show you the metals I found in Ura. I saw the coffin there; it is as real as I am, sitting here across from you." But seeing her genuine concern, he'd shaken off his irritation and jumped up from the table to tickle her, whispering in her ear, "I am the Lord of Ura, I have come to haunt you." Eventually his obsession became a running joke between them. He'd even convinced her to join him at the library, poring through records from the mid-fifteenth century, noting down the names of counts and landlords. Whosoever coffin it was had been well off. He warned her he'd be bringing a trove of research materials to Bekes.

"Is this your idea of entertainment?" she'd shaken her head. "Between that and the garbage coming from the radio it's going to be a long summer..."

On the train to Ura they passed their old town and the railway tavern where Zsigmond had revealed to Ferenc the true depths of his toxic new persona. She shuddered as they passed; Jozsi held tight to her hand, saying nothing. A while later their train pulled over to allow right-of-passage to a special convoy on its way to Russia. Jozsi asked the conductor what the train was carrying.

"Restitution goods," the conductor answered, his expression signaling that he did not approve. That phrase was shorthand for Hungarian goods being sent to Russia as restitution for the Soviet Union so generously liberating their country from German occupation.

"*Szemetek!*" Jozsi said, loudly enough that other passengers heard.

Some began repeating the word loudly. Bastards. The panicky conductor quickly shushed them all.

Erika reprimanded Jozsi. "If Zsigmond were here, if he even *heard* about this, you know where you'd end up? No stupid risks, Jozsi. Isn't that what Sandor always says? And this business on the train, this is stupid." She pursed her lips and turned to look out the window. His lack of control frightened her sometimes; she didn't want to lose him to the goons. What he did for Sandor was risky enough, but at least it had the potential to achieve something concrete. Riling up passengers on a train would accomplish nothing.

By the time that they reached Ura, Erika had recovered her good spirits and was excited about meeting the family. Mr. Toth was waiting at the station for the traditional drink in the tavern. At the farm, the Toths lined up at the gate to offer a big welcome, embracing Erika with warmth. She felt safe; these were not people who would turn you in. Mrs. Toth showed Erika where she'd sleep and told Jozsi he'd be sleeping in his old room. "Now, if you were married," she joked, "I wouldn't have to go to all this trouble." The young couple smiled. "Any plans?" she asked with wink.

"You'll be the first to know," Jozsi hugged her, and thankfully just then Mari hollered from the kitchen that supper was ready and the subject of marriage did not come up again.

After breakfast the following morning, Toth took them around back to look at the few remaining animals. The state had seized most of his flock and farmland, leaving the family barely enough to support them. There were no farmhands on the property and only two horses, a mule and a cow, but Toth considered himself one of the lucky ones. "At least I have something of my own to work with," he shrugged, though Jozsi could see the loss had taken its toll. Toth looked diminished, as though pints of blood had been siphoned from his veins.

Toth explained that everyone's farmland had been appropriated as part of the collective farm. Of course, the farmers were welcome to work on the collective and at year's end receive a portion of the profit, based on some amorphous point system.

"Miniscule point system," Jozsi added.

"Yes," Toth agreed, "a bad deal all around. I was fortunate the first time," he added, referring back to radical land reform the Soviets had bulldozed through in 1945 — confiscating all land holdings over 57 hectares and redistributing to the poorest peasants. Of course, portions that size simply were not large enough for people to be self-sufficient, a detail the Soviets ignored.

Further on, Toth showed them the spot he and Matyas had buried Bandi the summer before. They stood reminiscing about the fine old horse for a time, and Jozsi, in a rare display of sentiment, kneeled to kiss the ground.

The morning sky was cloudless, the warm air tempered by a gentle breeze: perfect weather to walk to the ravine and swimming hole, and to the spot where the coffin lay hidden. He and Erika carried apples and slices of fresh baked bread, and walked slowly down the road and out onto the field that led to the ravine. Red poppies, yellow buttercups, and violet-hued wild geranium speckled the meadow, like dots an artist had painted to contrast against the rich green of the field. Butterflies circled when they paused to admire the view and the flowers. Erika was in seventh heaven walking through a field more peaceful than any she'd ever seen. Soon she was skipping through the tall grass, carefree as when he'd first met her, a school girl with long braids and a warm smile.

It took Jozsi longer than he expected to find the covered hole, which by now was thoroughly disguised by all the branches he'd placed, and years and years of fresh growth. Erika sat on a fallen log watching; he ignored her skeptical expression, kept digging and finally found the coffin's edge. He brought her close to see and touch it, taking pleasure in her expression as it shifted from disbelief to amazement.

"This *is* very old," she stroked the edge, brushing away dirt to get a clearer look. "I'm sorry I doubted you."

"Doubt? You thought I was nuts."

"Only a little," she laughed, rising to make room for him to again carefully erase any signs of activity.

At the River Golga they stood arm-in-arm and Jozsi told her about the boys and girls who used to shout "Watch me!" as they jumped from the highest banks they could find. It all looked so much smaller than his last visit, but still idyllic.

They took the long way back to the farm so Jozsi could show her the vacant palace he and Lena had been spooked by so many years earlier. Lena was married now, the Toths reported, but still asked after Jozsi, and would be coming over to say hello that evening.

The following morning, they headed back to Budapest, Jozsi's spirits restored by seeing his second family. As they placed their suitcases in the wagon, Mrs. Toth put her arm around Erika and leaned close to her ear, "Don't wait too long to marry this dear boy," she whispered before standing back to wave them on their way.

"Sorry," Jozsi murmured. But Erika didn't mind. Their elders saw no reason for war, occupation or hardship to stand in the way of starting a family, and though Erika would never press Jozsi for a proposal, she appreciated the occasional reminder of normal behavior. If only they could be normal, she thought wistfully, and reached for his hand as the wagon lurched forward.

~~~

Their summer in Bekes passed peacefully. Jozsi poured over his books and reference materials for information that might shed light on the coffin, and Erika studied her medical books. The remote, almost medieval village had no library, and offered little in the way of entertainment beyond the villagers' company. They were fortunate their lodgings had electricity, enabling them to read late into the night.

At six each morning, Jozsi turned on the radio station and followed a very specific sheet of directions. He was to start each day with the National Anthem. This was followed by pre-recorded propaganda statements about the great Socialist country of Hungary that, with the help of the United Soviet Socialist Republic, was able to bring them this broadcast. He talked to himself as the bullshit recordings played, iterating his alternate view of the Hungarian government, though for the benefit of his ears only. This passed the time and helped sharpen his arguments. The station shut down each night at 7, allowing all residents the peace and quiet that was crucial for the restful sleep necessary so that they might rise the next morning refreshed and ready to slave away on behalf of the corrupt regime. At least that was his version of life in Bekes.

On Friday nights, the town hall meeting room opened. On one side, Jozsi taught kids to play chess, on the other, Erika alternately instructed groups of girls and boys about health and hygiene and other matters more discreet. They agreed that the most important thing they could teach the kids was to think for themselves and to question, but they had to be subtle about this effort.

The day before their return to Budapest, the town held a small celebration honoring the couple. Townspeople showed up bearing strudel and salami as going away gifts, all youngsters outfitted in their pioneer uniforms. The mayor gave a heartfelt speech thanking them for their work and for having given so much to the young people. Jozsi and Erika thanked the townspeople, and then Jozsi launched into a speech encouraging the young to expand their minds beyond the town, to look into new ways of thinking and doing," until Erika stepped hard on his foot. Although they knew from subtle comments that many of the townspeople had lost any faith they'd ever had in communism, there was no reason to court trouble from any true believers that might be in the crowd. There were always a few true believers — if not in the cause, then in ratting out others to benefit their own standing.

~~~

Back in Budapest, their energy restored, the two hurried to connect with friends for updates on the political situation in the city, and to get ready for school. The stirrings they'd seen in the spring had gained momentum throughout the summer; demonstrations and appeals to free Hungary from the Soviet occupation ratcheted up as the new school year began. Nightly meetings about reform led to bleary-eyed students in class. The pace of protest increased as the weather cooled, and by mid-October the city air practically sparked with excitement emanating from those agitating for change. Whether you were an intellectual or a blue-collar worker, the concerns were the same: give us freedom to breathe, to think, to study, labor, live, love. The hands of communism were strangling too many throats, leading desperation to fuel fearlessness, and the like-minded to find each other and hold fast.

At the Technological University of Budapest, professors and students drafted demands for what they wanted from the government. Throughout the city, institutions of learning became hothouses for clarifying and refining their demands, and for organizing. For students, studying seemed an act too paltry to indulge; for teachers, expounding on course material too inconsequential to matter. Every moment was fraught with the import of making a difference in their political world. Erika, the more politically active, went into high gear. Jozsi paid attention, noting whatever might prove useful to Sandor.

It was known that Party Leader Ernő Gerő would be away from the city on October 23rd. Groups of anti-government students planned to hold a peaceful public protest outside the Parliament building that morning, to show support for the recently squelched Polish uprising and to fire up revolt in Hungary. A few days earlier, university students had formed an independent political organization, compiled a list of sixteen key demands for changes in national policy, and began distributing them. The flyers, like invasive weeds, appeared everywhere overnight, as did word of the protest.

The students marched, carrying Hungarian flags on their shoulders, but with a shocking subtraction: the Russian red star and hammer, the symbols of communism, had been cut out of the flags. Something about seeing that hole in the flag took hold: onlookers cut the symbols from their own flags, cheered on the marchers, poured into the streets to join in protest. The crowds grew, the sense of outrage intensified, the feeling of power expanded, and by late afternoon hundreds of people were marching in support of the student delegation, and all of them were heading toward the radio station. It was there the students intended to broadcast the sixteen points over the airwaves to the entire country.

Erika raced through the crowds to Jozsi's apartment, shouting up at his open window, continuing to yell as she took the stairs two at a time. Demonstrators were just a few streets away, they needed to join the crowd. He grabbed a jacket and met her at the door, where, with tears in her eyes she shook him by the shoulders. "It's happening. This is what we've been waiting for." Jozsi was stunned. Much as he hated what the communists had done to Hungary, much as he wanted the Russians gone, much as he was willing to help Sandor undermine their power, he wasn't sure he was ready for full out revolution. Still, he scrambled down the stairs behind her, running right into Zsigmond, who stood leaning against his car in front of the building.

"What's your hurry?" Zsigmond smiled, oddly relaxed given the clamor of raging marchers in the near distance. He made a frame with his fingers, pretending to click. "There will be photographs of the leaders. There will be interrogations. There will be…" he paused, seeking just the right word… "difficulties for participants. You lovebirds are better off staying clear of the mobs. Just a little advice from an old friend." Erika ignored him, her face impassive as marble, but Jozsi, unable to restrain himself, shoved his left fist into the elbow crook of his raised right arm. "I could arrest you for such disrespect," Zsigmond shouted as they strode away in the direction of the crowds. Even through the hubbub they could hear his car door slam.

Within seconds, flyers were shoved in their hands: *Sixteen Points,* demanding everything from free elections, to freedom of expression, to dissolution of the secret police and removal of all Soviet troops, to a return to the old Hungarian flag — the latter already being enacted on the streets with scissors. Each demand guaranteed to infuriate the Hungarian communists in charge, as well as the puppet masters pulling the strings from Russia.

Flyers littered the streets, plastered walls and windows. Strangers grabbed each other's hands, workers and teachers, students and angry old men, all moving as one, shouting "Freedom at last!" and "To the radio station!" There were no police in sight and soon students began to heave rocks through communist bookstore windows as they marched past. The sight of hundreds of flags waving, holes cut in the middle of each and every one, the communist emblem excised from the Hungarian standard, caused eyes to tear up. A pure symbol of what they were marching for: the end of Soviet control.

Demonstrators roamed the city — some to the Petőfi Statue, built to honor Hungary's revolutionary poet, some to the Bem Statue that honored Poland's great and fearless general. By mid-afternoon 50,000 people had gathered at the Bem, where a member of the Hungarian Writers Union read aloud a proclamation of independence, to which the students added their 16-point resolution. Hordes moved on to demonstrate outside of the Hungarian Parliament. By six in the evening close to 200,000 had assembled, awaiting an 8 o'clock speech by Prime Minister Gerő.

Meanwhile, other students converged on the radio station, where they found the AVO manning hastily assembled barricades. Crowds called for Imre Nagy's return and shouted "Freedom!" Their flags flapped in the breeze, the hole-cut centers proclaiming a wordless call for revolution. The AVO, restless behind the barricades, began to fear the growing mob would be difficult to disperse. Some AVO hoped Gerő's voice of force and authority would convince the marchers they'd been heard and could now go home, others eagerly anticipated bashing protestors in the head. The adrenaline outside Radio Budapest could have set off a bomb.

At the first sounds of static from the loudspeakers, the crowd in front of the Hungarian Parliament quieted to hear Gerö's words. Gerö immediately dismissed the demands of the Writer's Union, of the students, of the people. When he described the assembled as a "reactionary mob," he lit a fuse.

One group of protestors decided to begin implementing the 16-point demands on their own. They raced to *Városliget Park* to attack the giant statue of Stalin that had been erected there in honor of his 70th birthday. Others veered off to join the crowd at the Radio Budapest building. Jozsi and Erika were at the radio station, shouting with the crowd, "Russians, go home!" as Gerö finished his speech.

As the crowd surged forward, attempting to force its way into the building, the AVO acted. Tear gas bombs flew from the radio station's upper windows. Suddenly the AVO opened fire, instantly killing or wounding a number of civilians. In shock and rage, a full-scale riot broke out. Many Hungarian soldiers, horrified by the cold-blooded secret police, began siding with their fellow citizens against the AVO. Chaos followed. Police cars went up in flames, weapons were seized and handed to eager citizens, and any communist symbol in sight was ripped down and vandalized.

Moments later, people began to hear the sound of tanks grinding their way toward the station, coming to reinforce the secret police. Jozsi and Erika had become separated, and he shadowed a tank hoping to follow it inside the gates. By this time, marchers were brandishing small arms they'd gotten from certain policemen who'd decided to side with their own people rather than with the imposed government. Soldiers revolted by the thought of harming compatriots began handing students their own arms, and further, directing them to a nearby army base where they could obtain more weapons.

As soon as the tanks rolled inside the gates, the drivers turned the behemoths to face the approaching demonstrators. Jozsi and five others hunkered behind a tank, not sure what to do next. Suddenly the hatch opened and the tank commander clambered down. He yelled commands up to a solder poking his head out of the open hatch, then hurried toward the radio station. As he moved behind the tank, the men grabbed him, and before he had a chance to call for help, a broken neck silenced him for good.

The AVO fired wildly at the demonstrators; randomly-hit bodies' fell in front of the radio station. After killing the commander, Jozsi and the others crawled under the tank to figure out what next. One of the older men had snatched a service revolver from the dead commander. He pointed up, and without a word climbed to the top of the tank and banged on the hatch. The others heard the hatch creak open, followed by a quick series of pistol shots. The brave elder scrambled back under the tank, panting. "I did my job. Now who can drive a tank?" They looked at each other, no one moved.

The shooting from the streets grew fierce. Workers from the arms manufacturing Chepel Plant arrived with a truckload of guns and ammunition for the demonstrators. Jozsi and his allies remained pinned under the tank, listening to bullets ricochet around them. From where they hid, they could tell the Chepel workers were passing out rifles and bullets to anyone with an outstretched hand. Jozsi did not know it, but Erika was one of those reaching out, and soon she held a rifle in one hand, a clip of bullets in the other. Most students had been taught how to use a rifle in school, and though this was nothing like target range practice, anyone eager for real action was soon armed.

During a lull in the shooting, Erika dashed from one wounded person to another, offering whatever comfort she could. She felt a surge of hope when a few ambulances pulled up near the radio station; perhaps some of the wounded could be saved. To everyone's shock, the first ambulance passed by the bloody bodies lying on the ground and headed for the main entrance. Suspicious students aimed rifles at the men inside it, demanding they emerge and stand in front of the vehicle. A little wisp of a student bravely threw open the back doors and found boxes of ammunition stacked all the way to the roof. He shouted, "It's full of bullets!"

The surrounding crowd closed in on the men, dragging them out of the ambulance, ripping their white hospital uniforms off. Erika arrived just in time to see that under their uniforms they wore AVO attire. As she watched, the men struggled to writhe away from the frenzied students. Years of rage boiled up in her gut. Her doctor father murdered and these heartless bastards showing up in an ambulance was too much. She pictured her father's face, she pointed her gun in the direction of the ambulance and commanded the students to let the men go. They did. The men struggled to scramble under the ambulance as Erika approached. Without remorse, she aimed and shot, again and again, until she'd emptied the clip. The small crowd gathered around the ambulance first fell into shocked silence, then erupted in cheers before turning to attack the other two ambulances.

When it was apparent the police had momentarily run out of ammunition, the armed demonstrators began running to the building entrance. Jozsi and his comrades left their tank hideout to join the fray. He grabbed a Russian-made machine gun from a student struggling to manage two of them, and was among the first wave to enter the building. The remaining police offered little to no resistance, instead hiding in closets or crawling under desks. None of the students had an interest in keeping the secret police alive long enough to stand trial. Jozsi had never shot at a human being before, but his brain went to that place where instinct fired up and took him beyond judgement or reason to a place of pure action. It felt as though a cold steel door closed against the part of his soul that valued human life, even his own. He became not reckless but primeval.

The students raced up and down stairs, searching, diving under desks, checking closets. Once they'd established there were no secret police still drawing breath in the building, Jozsi ran back outside to look for Erika. Passing the ambulances, he saw police lying dead, their bodies shredded by the bullets of an enraged nation. He searched the whole area, looking for Erika among the wounded and prone. Others spread out from the building, shouting for doctors. The wounded with any strength left screamed in pain, begging for help. Jozsi searched and scanned, no Erika. He stood still, letting relief wash over him. If she wasn't here, she must still be alive.

A truck driving toward Hero's Square slowed to collect more passengers, and Jozsi climbed onto the truck bed. They drove down streets littered with bodies, both in and out of uniform. Blood stained the sidewalks, broken glass from smashed windows sparkled in the streetlights, and everywhere there were flyers floating down to rest on bodies, only to rise again with the breeze of passing vehicles. Voices yelling, gunshots ringing out, all seemed surreal. Finally, they reached

Dozsa Gyergy Square, named for the peasant leader who'd led a failed revolution hundreds of years earlier. Legend had it that Gyergy's body had been set on fire, his followers forced to eat his flesh. "A fitting place to fight for freedom," Jozsi said to a young boy jostling against him as the truck circumvented a body in the street.

Hero's Square, the largest, most impressive square in the city, had been built in 1896 to commemorate the 1,000th anniversary of the Hungarians arrival in the Carpathian Basin. Matyas had brought Jozsi there when he was a young boy and he remembered his first sighting of the gigantic Archangel Gabriel statue. It stood atop a sky-high center pillar, holding the holy crown and the double cross of Christianity. On a stand below ranged the seven chieftains who led the Magyar tribes to Hungary. Later, Matyas would test Jozsi on their names and brave deeds.

Jozsi kept his eyes fixed on the Archangel as they drew near the square, his heart pounding when the truck lurched to a stop. Men were bravely climbing an enormous statue of Stalin, some tying ropes around its thick neck; the ropes attached to a large truck parked at the foot of the statue. Welders aimed torches at Stalin's legs, sparks flying as they worked to sever the body of the hated Russian leader from his boots. Hundreds of people stood watching. Finally, the welders gave the men in the truck a sign — it was time to topple the statue. The welders waved the onlookers off, clearing a big space where they expected the statue to fall. No one wanted Stalin capable of inflicting any further damage.

Once the area had emptied, the truck's engine revved, and then the truck inched forward. The bronze statue gradually began to lean, the crowd hushed in anticipation. Slowly, slowly it tilted…at the halfway point gravity spoke and in a flash, it crashed. The crowd, cheers ramping up in volume the further it leaned, went wild as Stalin smashed to the ground. Dust flew, and people began attacking the statue with picks and metal saws and blowtorches; like buzzards on carrion they tore at it, wanting to destroy, wanting souvenirs as proof. Something had changed. Finally.

Jozsi stood on the truck, watching, feeling reverence for the seed of freedom he knew had lived in the hearts of Hungarians since the dawn of time. His eyes scanned the crowd, on the lookout for Erika. After observing the frenzy, Jozsi began trudging from *Hero's Square* to his apartment, thinking of what the destruction of Stalin's statue symbolized. Though it was after one in the morning, he could make only slow progress, moving against a tide of bodies. Snatches of excited voices penetrated. People recounting the fighting on this street, or that building. He heard two men talking about a fierce woman, dubbing her "The Beast of Budapest," and a woman weeping that her son was missing and she feared him dead. Word of the statue had spread; scores of delirious protestors streamed toward the square to see for themselves the unbelievable sight of gigantic Stalin on the ground. Shouts of "Death to the Russians!" rang out, especially from the young. They had been waiting much of their lives for this moment. Those older held back; the knowledge that things don't always turn out the way you expect restrained any elation. They'd seen too much, suffered too long to completely give themselves over to wild joy that oppression was truly at an end. And as both young and old soon would discover, before the end of that day Gerö had asked the Soviet Union for a military intervention to suppress the uprising. Whatever elation existed was soon tempered by anxiety about what such intervention might mean.

Jozsi continued elbowing his way home, passing small groups violently dragging secret police out to the streets and beating them... to death, he assumed. He did not stay to watch. A light shone from his apartment window. Erika! Or perhaps he'd left it on when he ran down to the street. He couldn't remember. He was by now too exhausted to run up the stairs. Hesitant, afraid he wouldn't find her, he moved in slow motion. In the apartment, he laid the machine gun on the kitchen table, and holding his breath moved to the bedroom door. Cracking it open he saw Erika, fully clothed, flat on her back, a gun beside her where he usually lay. Her beautiful long blond hair was bloody and matted; she seemed to be asleep. He gasped with relief. Startled, her eyes flew open. She raised her arms and he fell into them, kissing and hugging her, their bodies sticky with sweat, blood and dirt. And then her tears flowed. Erika sobbed in a strange mixture of sadness, happiness, confusion and relief. Jozsi watched her face register all these emotions as the tears fell.

When she could finally gather enough breath for words she said, "I've killed so many policemen and I felt nothing; in the moment of shooting, nothing at all." She shivered with horror at her own capacity for slaughter. Jozsi comforted her, assuring her that he too had killed without remorse. "The sons of bitches deserved it. They deserved it," he repeated over and over, until exhausted, they collapsed into dreamless sleep.

The next morning, they washed up, forced food into their mouths, picked up their guns, and headed back out to the streets where they heard guns sporadically firing from all over the city. Erika pointed in the direction of Szondy Street — the majority of AVO officers lived there in apartments reserved for them. "Let's find that bastard, she snapped. "I have unfinished business." Jozsi did not need to ask which bastard.

Erika wore a long dark coat; her hair splaying over it gave the appearance of an extra cushion for the machine gun holster strapped around her shoulder. Somewhere along the way, she'd replaced the rifle with a machine gun, she couldn't even remember where. Passing a group of revolutionaries, rifles slung from their shoulders as they looked over a clump of dead secret police, they were enthusiastically greeted — the camaraderie of the oppressed, Jozsi thought. He heard whispers of "The Beast of Budapest," but at that moment, he still had no idea who that could be.

As they approached Szondy Street, volleys of shots rang out, and turning a corner, they found a dozen revolutionaries pinned down by gunfire. Jozsi whispered, "Maybe they're looking for him too," and grabbing her by the arm, pulled her down to join a group huddled behind an overturned car. Erika stared fixedly at Zsigmond's building, not saying a word. When there was a lull in the gunfire, she leapt up and rushed toward the main entrance before a surprised Jozsi could even attempt to hold her back. The man next to him let out a low whistle of amazement, and exchanged an awed look with Jozsi. Jozsi could barely breathe. As soon as Erika got to the entrance, a barrage of gunfire shot from windows above. Several times she darted out, firing up at the windows, giving others behind the car time and cover to dash to the entrance. Jozsi knew she was brave but this was something more, this was heroic.

The police trapped in the building appeared to be running out of ammunition, the return fire became more and more sporadic, and finally ceased altogether. Looks were exchanged, heads angled in various directions, agreement reached without a word as to who would search where. Jozsi stayed close to Erika, though he doubted she even registered his presence. Occasionally a shot, a plea for mercy, a moan, or the thud of a falling body, reached their ears. Finally, they found Zsigmond's apartment, empty, clearly abandoned in haste. She sat on a wooden chair, rubbing her forehead with both hands, the machine gun resting against her knee, then looked at Jozsi with an expression so haunted he had to look away. He knew she was thinking of her father. Pulling her up off the chair he said, "We'll find him, but if we don't someone else will." She nodded, and they left, hoping to find Zsigmond, or news of his whereabouts, in the inner part of the city. Where the energy came from Jozsi did not know, but they strode on, registering that overnight an astounding number of red stars had vanished from buildings and signs. The five-pointed stars, long a symbol of the Communist Party and the Red Army, were pointedly absent, as was any human being resembling a Russian soldier.

Jozsi and Erika spent many hours searching for Zsigmond, but he'd managed to vanish. Wherever they walked, broken glass from exploded Molotov Cocktails crunched beneath their boots. More horrifying, many of the AVO, shot like dogs, had been hung from street lampposts. Those were captured alive strung up by piano wire, along with Russian soldiers who'd tried to crush the uprising. Piano wire sometimes served as a vertical guillotine, the wire cutting into the neck severely enough to decapitate, especially those who struggled hard. By no means had the revolutionaries caught everyone — some had escaped into the bowels of the city, scurrying through the sewers, hoping the Russian Army would come to their rescue. And indeed, many miles away, the Russians were planning their invasion strategy. But in the liberating days immediately following the uprising, elation and hope filled the heart of many Hungarians.

By October 27th, four days after the Revolution began, Radio Free Europe was broadcasting encouragement to the Hungarian people: telling them to continue fighting vigorously, saying that America supported liberation, claiming this would have a powerful influence on the U. N. Security Council. Help was on the way was the message. That the help would come from the Americans went without saying, although as things turned out, it went without doing as well. The American government instead suddenly turned its full attention to the Suez Canal crisis, abruptly dropping Hungary from its place high on the priority list. There was more at stake for Western interests in settling the troubles at the Suez Canal. After all, "helping" Hungary would have involved sending aid to the landlocked country, which was not easily accessible by sea or sky — not without a major battle, not without warfare. Apparently, Korea had exhausted the United States' appetite for war. But in that heady moment, the Hungarians believed what they heard on Radio Free Europe and were counting on eventual support from the West.

As the street fighting came to an end, people wandered the city searching for missing relatives or friends, or simply driven to see the effects of all that had happened. History was being made; everyone knew it and wanted to witness. Even days after the uprising, dead AVO and Russian soldiers remained hanging upside down on Rakosi Street, among them the son of Andropov, the most feared KGB Director of the Soviet Union. As people passed, they spat at the bodies with passion and satisfaction. People also set about collecting the bodies of dead Hungarians for burial in mass graves throughout the city. Jozsi and Erika walked through *Soldiers' Square* and saw at least a hundred bodies, dusted with chlorine, ready to be laid to rest in one such grave. Children were allowed out of their apartments to play on burned out Russian tanks while adults stripped the tanks of whatever they could grab for souvenirs of this historic time. No one doubted the Russians planned to retaliate, but many believed the Western Allies would do or say enough to discourage the Russians before they could act.

Hope had been suppressed for so long that when it sprang to life, its power was immense, blinding, a thing of wonder. People felt resurrected after years of being petrified by oppression. Popular demand returned Imre Nagy to leadership, and with it came optimism about a return to something like normal living. People again felt they could participate in the life and growth of the nation; they desperately wanted to improve everything they could see, touch, or influence, and in every way.

During this blooming, while imaginations raced with thoughts of how the country could transform, the Russians began assembling their armored divisions in the Rakos Valley. They idled there, outside of the city, waiting to see if the Western Allies dared interfere, if they cared enough to come to the rescue of the Hungarian people. In the meantime, the Hungarian people kept on dreaming their dreams of freedom.

13

Taking Flight

Hungarian hopes for autonomy began evaporating under the atom-crushing weight of reality. In the brief calm that followed the Revolution, the Hungarian people began to grasp the full impact of decisions made by the president of Egypt upon their own situation. He had nationalized the Suez Canal, which at first glance would seem to have had no particular effect on a country an ocean away. But it did. The Western world panicked over the threat of an interrupted oil flow and as for the Hungarian struggle, well... As Jozsi said, "American promises are all bullshit now. They talk about our fight for freedom, they talk about sending help, but the only thing they *care* about is money." People holding out hope told him he was too cynical, while Radio Free Europe voices jabbered on, encouraging listeners to expect a tangible manifestation of Western concern any hour now.

Jozsi would have given anything to be proven wrong, but he could not overcome his distrust of authority, at home and abroad. Everywhere he looked he saw the individual smashed by one government or another, misled, abused, deserted. But Erika continued to hope for the best. She had not picked up a rifle for nothing, she had not shot into human guts and heads and hearts just to have her dreams of liberty crushed by Soviet tanks. She had lost her father; she was determined not to lose the fight for her country's survival. "We can't win with only rifles," Jozsi declared again and again. "The Russian Army will crush us like grapes in a press while the Western world frets about oil flow, profits, investments in South Arabia. If the American president is going to step in anywhere in the world, you can bet your life he will be sending troops to South Arabia. Pleasing his senators is more important than taking a moral and humanitarian stand." He would pound the table in frustration. "They don't care about our freedom, they don't care about our lives. More Hungarians will die and they will turn their heads and look the other way."

His assessment was, in fact, correct. The Suez crisis completely commandeered Western attention; the struggle for control of a manmade body of water connecting the Mediterranean and Red Seas was deemed far more crucial than that of beleaguered Hungarian freedom fighters. On October 31, British and French forces bombed the Canal. The Russians watched and waited to see what exactly the West would do to help the Hungarians, and finally determined they would do nothing, as Jozsi had asserted all along. On November 4th, the Russians took action, sending 150,000 soldiers and 2,500 tanks rampaging into Hungary.

Erika cried and railed. Jozsi set his brain to figuring out what to do next. Sandor arranged a quick meeting and informed Jozsi that American Embassy workers had been recalled to Austria and ordered to flee Budapest within 24 hours. The Russians were approaching the city from the East; the Americans didn't want to lose any of their own citizens.

"Right, because then they might have to do something," Jozsi said, through clenched teeth. He was so furious he wanted to punch Sandor just because he came from America.

Sandor absorbed the anger, understood the rage. He urged Jozsi to consider fleeing to the West, saying, "You cannot fight if you are dead. They'll be looking for you; they know you're connected to people from the American Cultural Center. Sandor gave him a name and address in Gyor. "You can pass through Gyor on the way to Austria and meet up with this man, Laci. He's worked with us, he's solid. I think you'd make a damn good team."

Jozsi kept the note, but hoped he'd never have to depend on Sandor again. As much as he wanted out of Hungary, as often as he'd imagined the adventures and freedom awaiting him on the western side of the border, some part of his heart had a hard time imagining actually *being* somewhere else. And he was too angry to stop fighting.

Jozsi and Erika fought side-by-side as the Russian forces invaded. But within days, the Russians suppressed most of the street fighters, who either died or fled; their guns no match for the powerfully equipped, well-trained Russian army. By the time the most ferocious violence had subsided, 700 Soviet troops had met their maker, along with 2,500 Hungarians. Looking up to register the clouds of a hard storm gathering, Hungarians envisioned years of Soviet Occupation. A great many chose to flee.

On November 6, exhausted and resigned after endless hours of discussion and nights of agitated sleep, Jozsi and Erika went to say goodbye to his parents and her mother — they both assumed they'd have to flee to avoid torture or death once the Revolution was fully squelched.

Jozsi told his parents he'd been involved in enough fighting to be a target for the communists; most likely to be killed or left to rot in jail for the rest of his life. He'd never told them that Zsigmond had been stalking both he and Erika and saw no reason to share that now, it would only alarm them. That Jozsi and Erika knew Zsigmond had survived pained them both and had been a sticking point in their decision to flee — Erika wanted him dead, preferably at her own hand. But regardless of Zsigmond, the threat to their safety was real, and Matyas and Erzsebet were already worried enough. Local police seeking Jozsi had visited the house earlier that day. Jozsi told his parents they were going to escape to Austria, but that he'd return as soon as he safely could. Erika wept, watching the Budais' emotional goodbye. Erzsebet held Jozsi's face in her hands for the longest time, murmuring, "My boy, my boy," soaking in his presence; it would have to sustain her over the long absence ahead.

Matyas emptied his wallet. "Take it my son, you'll need this."

Jozsi knew how little money his parents had and folded his father's hands over the wad of bills. "For years, I've been saving money in case I needed to escape, I'm all set." Which was, he decided, a forgivable lie.

Matyas carefully put the money back in his wallet. "I knew your heart was headed west from the time your glider landed in Czechoslovakia, but to see you go..." He pressed his hand against his chest as though it needed to hold his heart in place. They hugged without exchanging another word; the love between them felt so loud there was no need. With a nod, tears held at bay, lips pressed tight, they parted.

In his apartment, filthy, disgusted, exhausted, a machine gun lying at her feet, Erika had said she would leave with Jozsi for a new life in the West. But ever since, internally, she'd been wavering. How could she leave her ailing mother alone? But how could she carry on without Jozsi? She managed to say a tearful goodbye to her mother, and her mother bravely did not ask her to stay. Once back at Jozsi's apartment Erika put her head in her hands and sobbed. The sight of her mother's frail body had broken her will to flee.

Jozsi had observed the stricken expression on Mrs. Simon's face as she held back tears and comforted her weeping daughter. He took

Erika's hands in his own. "It's too hard a decision, I know, and I can't tell you what to do," he said. "Who knows what will happen on the other side of the border, or if we'll even get that far." They made tender love, and drifted into fitful sleep.

Jozsi woke to find her standing at the window. She turned and her expression telegraphed her decision. They ate breakfast with barely a word exchanged, they could hardly look each other in the eye for fear of an emotional collapse. He packed his bag, and the two of them walked across the *Margaret Bridge* as they had done so many times in the past. On the far side of the bridge, Erika held him and whispered in his ear, "This is as far as I go." She reached into a small carrying sack and handed him a .38 handgun, saying, "I won't be needing this as much as you will." He thanked her, tucked the gun behind his back, and kissed her long and hard, one final time.

They walked in opposite directions, Erika biting down on her lip so hard she drew blood, random thoughts batting around her head. How was she to take care of her mother? She'd better dye and cut her hair — the secret police were already looking for the Beast of Budapest. Was anything worth the pain and killings of the last week? How could she avoid falling prey to Zsigmond? The one thing she did not think about was turning to look behind, afraid she'd lose control and run after her beloved.

Jozsi did turn to look, pausing long enough to watch her thin, strong body make its way back across the bridge. Her long blonde hair was pinned up, though some wisps fluttered in the breeze. As thick fists of fog rolled in off the water she vanished into the mist like the princess in a fairy tale his mother used to read aloud when he was a child. He turned to the west and moved forward. A sentence from one of the tedious History of Communism classes he'd been forced to endure came to mind. China's leader, Mao, had said, "The thousand-mile march must begin with the first step." "There are many first steps," Jozsi said aloud, and moved forward. By the time that he stepped off the bridge, the fog was thickly drifting over a number of dead civilians and Russian soldiers. There are many kinds of final steps, he thought, scanning the faces.

He bent low, carefully making his way among the bodies, searching for a dead person who somewhat resembled him. He figured a change in identity could be good insurance if he got captured by the Russian Army. Or not. Hard to say. Even if he made it across the border, it was vital that his eventual pursuers think him dead for as long as possible. And in this moment, a new identity felt right — a new identity for a new beginning. After pocketing the ID of a man close in size — his face destroyed by a heavy caliber bullet — Jozsi headed toward the Vienna Highway, hoping to catch a ride to Gyor.

Soon a car carrying three young men pulled over. They had stolen it from the police and were heading to Austria. They urged him to skip Gyor and come with them before the Russians closed the borders. His gut told him he'd be better off connecting with Sandor's contact, so he faked needing to check on a dying relative before leaving Hungary. Another forgivable lie, he thought. Impressed by his family loyalty, they kindly drove him for free, "Compliments of the AVO."

He hopped out in the center of Gyor and asked directions to the address provided by Sandor. The non-descript apartment building was only a few blocks from where he'd gotten out of the stolen car. Within minutes, he was knocking on a door two flights up. A young man near his age opened the door after Jozsi had given the password, "Rodnas." Before he could utter another word the man said, "Hello Jozsi, I'm Laci. I've been waiting for you. I was wondering what held you up. Sandor told me you'd show up one of these days."

By this time in the recounting, Jozsi and Laci, still in the 24-hour club where Laci had been trying to help his friend forget Ulee, were three sheets to the wind.

"I remember," Laci said, "That's *exactly* what I said! And then we hugged like old friends. And then I said we had to get going before the new police department came looking for me."

Jozsi picked up the thread, "And I said, 'What happened to the old police department?'"

Laci was laughing so hard he could barely manage to repeat his reply: "That's exactly why they're looking for me!"

The two collapsed, breathless with laughter, and decided to call it a night. They would be leaving for Saigon in forty-eight hours and needed every moment of that time to sober up.

~~~

Two weeks later, after their stint in Saigon, where they'd done their best to train a select group of Vietnamese soldiers on the outdated, shabby communications equipment the Army had shipped there from Korea, the two sped to Hong Kong for R&R. In between wining and dining beautiful women, swilling cocktails, eating like condemned men, and generally being lazy good-for-nothings, it was Laci's turn to fill in a little of his own story for Jozsi. Laci wasn't one to dwell on the past, but on their final afternoon in Hong Kong, relaxing in a hot tub, Jozsi managed to learn a few details.

"So, your father hated Russians or communists or both?" Jozsi asked, splashing water at Laci to distract him from what looked to be a sex-filled daydream, judging by the sly half-smile on his friend's face.

Laci swiped at the beads of water. "He couldn't stand the communists. Hated them even more than the Germans, I think. When the CIA came nosing around, he jumped to help any way he could. Running spies, carrying messages, hiding people, he lived to poke sticks in the eyes of the *korcs*," he said, using the phrase his father always used against anyone he loathed.

"It paid well, too," Jozsi pointed out, though Laci claimed his father would have done it for free. After his father died, it had been only natural that Laci take over the family farm, and the business — operating an underground spy-running operation. When Laci was a little boy the local spies and their enemies, the border guards, all knew him; the border guards would even pass him candy bars as a treat. Years later, after his father's death, Laci would fix up some of those same guards with prostitutes; it encouraged them to look the other way while Sandor ran his spies across the border. Just before the Revolution, Sandor warned Laci that he was on a list of people to be investigated and likely interrogated. Sandor suggested Laci's best bet was to escape. And he'd mentioned a good running partner, a city slicker from Budapest, and directed him to the Gyor apartment that actually was rented to a CIA contact.

As they leaned back in the hot tub, Laci thanked Jozsi for helping him learn how to live it up, and hoped he'd absorbed some of Jozsi's negotiating skills as well. Laci still considered himself to be a bit of a country bumpkin, though not nearly as large a bumpkin as he was deemed by Jozsi.

"You are very lucky you ran into me," was all Jozsi had to say, too relaxed to even mention big cars or diamonds. Jozsi closed his eyes, giving in to the effects of the warm water as it eased sore muscles and unwound all tension. Eventually he hoisted his pruned body out of the water, Laci climbing out right after, afraid he'd fall asleep and drown if left to his own devices. Besides, by now, Jozsi was like a guide light for Laci, the two so used to moving in tandem they'd forgotten what it was like not to have the other near.

Jozsi stretched out on his bed and nestled his head against the pillow he still didn't take for granted, and his mind wandered back to the time they'd reconnected with Sandor at that bench in Austria. Sandor had presented a plan: the two would go to Italy. Jozsi remembered being with Laci in Austria, standing at the bulletin board in the Klosterneuburg refugee center, searching the tacked-up pages listing names of those authorized to temporarily relocate to Italy. Jozsi had turned to Laci, "My parents must think I'm dead by now," assuming that by then the corpse, whose ID he'd switched with his own, had been found and shrouded.

The two had been assigned to different vehicles; there were five small buses for the 125 refugees, all ages and size, from babies to the elderly. Jozsi quickly grabbed a window seat, and watched the bodies lining up, wondering which ones were spies, which escaped criminals, which innocent refugees. Only the babies were trustworthy. He was plotting a way to get word to his parents that he was in fact alive when an older man — in his sixties by the look of his thinning gray hair, weathered skin, and mottled hands — sat beside him.

"Janos," he introduced himself, reaching out a hand. "I am a poet." Jozsi half-truthfully introduced himself as an electronics engineering student from Budapest. Sandor had taught him to always stay as close to the truth as possible. The bus driver announced in German that due to an early blizzard their journey across the Alps would be slow. And after noting the refugees' looks of complete bafflement, Jozsi took it upon himself to be their unofficial translator, and standing near the driver, repeated all the news they needed to hear. By the time he again sat, Janos was writing in a small notebook. Jozsi studied a list of all passenger names on the buses, to see if he recognized any. At one point, Janos paused in his writing, crossing out, and writing more, to say, "How the hell am I going to manage starting over? Hungarian, it's the only language I know. My country, my home." He shook his head sadly. Jozsi didn't know what to say, so he simply nodded.

They bounced along across the Alps. At every rest stop, the escort counted all heads to make sure no one slipped away. By morning they were in Italy. As they passed through towns, people greeted them, offering food and wine wherever they stopped. Posted signs read *"Viva la rivoluzione!"* The bus driver told them Italian radio announcers were following their route, urging the local citizenry to welcome the refugees to Italy. No one could quite put into words how wonderfully astonishing it was to have people wave instead of shoot. The refugees on the bus chattered cheerfully, the snow abated, and finally, just at dusk, they reached Lido di Jesolo, and their hotel, which was, amazing to all, right on the beach.

Normally, the Italian Red Cross ran the hotel as a summer place, a respite for inner city children, but in late November it was deserted. The building consisted of six large rooms, with two on every floor. Each room held 36 beds, 18 on either side. Families were kept together by partitions, and smaller partitions afforded a degree of privacy to occupants doubling up. Jozsi and Laci shared an area on the first floor, both wanting to be as close to the waterfront as possible. A large dining room and kitchen were in the basement and on the side of the hotel, other staff were housed in a separate building connected by a passageway.

Jozsi and Laci were assigned to serve as liaisons between the refugees and the Italian staff. They'd each had enough Catholic school Latin to pick up pigeon Italian in a short time. The staff consisted of female Red Cross volunteers from upper-class families. The camp director, Countess Angela Ricci, was in her early fifties and a well-packed two hundred pounds. "A *countess*," Laci, impressed, whispered to Jozsi when they were introduced. The other countesses came from the Venice area, excited to be helping the refugees. For their work, they earned recognition from the Red Cross and a feather in their status cap. The oceanfront location was an enjoyable bonus for their good deeds.

The first morning, Angela welcomed the refugees with the help of a Hungarian-born priest. She assigned one countess, Adelina, to help Jozsi learn the language, and another, Maria, to help Laci.

After the day's work, Jozsi and Adelina would take long walks on the beach and tell each other about their very different lives. Jozsi, who knew next to nothing about the Italian people and their customs, absorbed all he could from her. The first few days they walked side-by-side, but soon, as they padded along the shore, their hands would entwine. One November night, warm for that time of year, they'd walked far from the hotel. In the dimming light, Adelina tripped over a piece of driftwood and landed on the sand. Jozsi reached down to help her up, and when he bent, she pulled him down, slipped her arms around his neck, and gave him a kiss so passionate the clothes practically jumped off their bodies. Much time passed, and when they walked back hand-in-hand, it was as lovers, although they tried to keep that a secret. Of course, anyone with eyes could see the glow of romance shimmering around their bodies any time they were in the same vicinity.

~~~

The two Hungarians spent their days translating as best they could for the rest of the refugees. They did everything from arranging doctor's visits to filling out visa applications to doing laundry. Food was a constant problem. Italy, still recovering from WWII, had little to spare, so the two were on the lookout for any kind of special deals they could find. There was always pasta, usually spaghetti, although Jozsi grew to hate the feel of what he began to think of as gluey string.

One of their jobs was to read through all of the outgoing mail, note the contents and addresses, and search for coded messages, subtext, or questionable information. To their surprise, most of the news was simply descriptive of the camp, filled with worries about those left behind, and nervous excitement as to when and where they'd be shipped next. Soon their workload doubled as responses poured in, all of which had to be read by the two Hungarian spycatchers. As far as they could tell, there was not even one spy in the group. As Laci put it, "It turns out, we are the spies!"

Just before Christmas, a man from Radio Free Europe came to see if anyone wanted to send a message back to Hungary. They were each allowed a few words, which would be read for broadcast every hour after the news. This was the chance Jozsi had been waiting for. He composed a brief message, heart pounding. "Dodi from Rakoskeresztur is alive and well in Italy." Dodi was a nickname known only to his relatives. Even if everyone thought he was dead, he knew his parents would still hold out hope, knowing how clever and resourceful he was. And he knew they faithfully listened to Radio Free Europe. He felt confident he'd just about whispered the good news right into their ears.

This thought cheered him through what quickly became a melancholy atmosphere around the hotel. Christmas made the refugees profoundly homesick, so he and Laci arranged for a gypsy band from another nearby refugee camp to play at the hotel. Tears flowed as the fiddle and lute music danced through their ears, sashaying straight to their hearts. By the end of the evening, the music had given the Italian hotel the feeling of a festive Christmas-festooned market square in Budapest and the refugees were in better spirits.

Adelina invited Jozsi to join her family in Venice for the holidays, and Laci was agreeable to staying and covering their hotel duties, especially since Maria was on duty through the holidays as well. "I can improve my Italian," he grinned.

"How do you say grope in Italian?" Jozsi asked, grabbing at Laci's chest.

Adelina's parents arrived from Venice to pick them up and were soon treating Jozsi like a war hero, so captivated were they by his stories about the horrors of the Revolution. Their beautiful stone house, with floor to ceiling arched windows, felt like a castle, and Jozsi happily settled into his room, on the third floor with a balcony overlooking the canal. Adelina's room was next door; they could have held hands across their balconies, but they were never apart long enough to need to. Her parents seemed to be sizing Jozsi up for marriage. There was no pretense about the two already being lovers.

His first holidays away from his country were made bearable by the romantic haze through which he saw Venice and himself. He tried imagining life as an honorary count, the breathtaking Adelina on his arm, the canals of Venice to explore, and the…the…he ran out of things to imagine. Italy was beautiful, Adelina was too, and smart and kind, and her family seemed ready to give him the keys to the castle. But he knew it was not for him. He would suffocate here with the family, the position; the days flowing into each other, punctuated by wine and laughter and warmth, but too predictable for someone with his nature. Maybe if he were older it could be a life he'd want. He did not intend to string Adelina along, so he made no promises, although he knew the visit had been designed to entice him, and that in the future, she might very much regret having gone to all that trouble. But in the moment, they awoke in each other's arms, strolled arm-in-arm through the city, stepped in and out of gondolas like characters in a romance novel, and sat in cafés, nibbling biscotti, sipping espresso, making eyes at each other. After what Jozsi had been through, he felt no guilt at reveling in the pure hedonism of this holiday.

One evening, as a surprise, Adelina's parents took them to the *Ristorante Budapest*. Count Lombardi knew the owner and was proud to show off his houseguest. The owner greeted them with open arms, made a huge fuss over Jozsi, saying in Hungarian, "God brought you here," which Jozsi chose not to refute knowing that his saying, "No, Sandor brought me here," would not impress a soul.

After dinner, a trio of gypsies played Hungary's most romantic tunes, though he believed only a Hungarian could fully connect to the music. Suddenly, all Jozsi could think of was Erika. The places they'd sat listening to these same notes flooded into his head and for a moment he felt almost dizzy. The violinist seemed to read his mind, and began playing so emotionally that Jozsi had to hold his breath so as not to break down in tears. He could not cry in front of these people, he could not let that happen. The violinist, having moved the entire room to attentive stillness, gave Jozsi a sympathetic smile and a wink and helped him by switching to the more cheerful Hungarian *Chardash*.

The holiday at an end, Adelina and Jozsi headed back to Jesolo in one of her father's cars. Her family was most impressed, she said, and hoped to see more of him in the future. Uh-oh, thought Jozsi, sensing she would soon be tiptoeing up to the subject of marriage. Instead, she threw him for a loop by asking about the covert operation in which he and Laci were involved.

"You know?" he sputtered.

She giggled, "You think you are so clever? Countess Ricci told us as soon as we arrived that you and Laci were the only refugees who could be completely trusted."

Jozsi shook his head thinking of all the scamming the two men had done to get out of Hungary. To be called honest almost made him uncomfortable. He assured her there was no one to worry about; the refugees were all honorable, though displaced, people. He hoped he was right, and so far, he'd seen no evidence to the contrary. He really believed there was no reason for her to worry; even bad Hungarians would pose no threat to their Italian helpers.

Laci spotted them arriving and took Jozsi off to fill him in on the holidays at the hotel. The news was grim. Two suicide attempts: one successful, one not so; the survivor in intensive care at the hospital.

Jozsi was shocked. He hadn't imagined anyone's emotions would be distraught enough to try to take their own lives; after all, they'd already survived so much horror. Jozsi immediately went to the hospital to visit the recovering Paul who, his voice thready and weak, told him how ashamed he was at having left his wife and children behind. The day he left, they'd had a big argument about fleeing with the kids. His wife had refused, and he'd bolted to join other Hungarians heading to the West. He'd been exhausted, he said, after days of fighting, unable to think straight. He could not believe he'd deserted his family and truly felt he deserved to die.

Jozsi comforted him as best he could, cursing Sandor for not having better prepared him for occurrences like this. Jozsi returned from the hospital to find an ambulance in front of the hotel, a covered body on a stretcher being rolled toward the ambulance, Adelina weeping by the door. Janos, the poet, sitting in a chair in the dining room, had died. Cardiac arrest. "His heart broke," Adelina sobbed, while Jozsi tucked her head against his chest and patted her like a colicky baby.

At the somber funeral a few days later, one of the women refugees, who, truth be told, had developed a crush on the poet, lost control and shouted, her hands raised, waving back and forth as though trying to get the attention of a waiter in the sky, "What will happen to us? Are we to die in this hell hole like Janos?" Laci looked over at Jozsi with a "She's all yours," expression. This was not his idea of fun work, but in looking at her, Jozsi thought of his mother. He knew how he'd want someone to treat Erzsebet, so he murmured soothing Hungarian words in her ear until she calmed.

~~~

By the end of February, the sponsors of a number of refugees had helped get them out of the camp and on the road to Canada, Australia, and America. The remaining refugees were anxious, especially as they began hearing from or about other countrymen who'd fled Hungary and were already settling in various countries.

Jozsi and Laci had officially determined there were no possible crime suspects or possible agents for the communist regime at the hotel, and they began wondering when they themselves would be moving on, and to where. Meanwhile, Adelina kept dropping subtle hints that she was ready for marriage and that her parents approved of him, which made Jozsi even more anxious to move on, fond as he was of her.

One evening, as the two sat drinking at a local tavern, Laci wondered about the shrinking head count. "How much longer before Sandor shows up to tell us we're no longer needed? I want to know."

Jozsi agreed he had a point, and after a few more drinks, screwed up his nerve, saying, "Watch me. This is the way we do it in the big city." At the pay phone he dialed an emergency number Sandor had provided. A woman answered, but within seconds Sandor was on the line wanting to know what was going on. Jozsi, snapped, "Get your ass over here and you can find out," and hung up on him.

First Laci's mouth fell open in shock, then in uproarious laughter. "You're something else. But I'm learning from you all the time, and someday I might even let you call me friend. And now the next round is on me!"

They discussed what to say if Sandor showed. "Don't trust that bastard," Laci drunkenly repeated as they walked back to the hotel. The next afternoon, they were called away from their respective tasks — Jozsi helping a soon-to-depart baker with his visa, Laci helping Maria hang wash — to meet Sandor at the tavern.

He frowned at the sight of them. "This better be good. You two hauled my ass out of an important meeting yesterday, and I need to get back to Rome."

Jozsi clapped him on the shoulder. "We don't give a shit how busy you are," which was not at all what he'd planned on saying, but he was anxious and that made him even more annoyed. "The head count is shrinking by the day and we're wondering if we should apply to be bricklayers in the downtown Jesolo employment office. Exactly what is the plan?"

Sandor was exasperated. "You have the patience of a flea. Calm down and I'll be back with answers in a week. You've already held me up, making me leave Rome because you're in a goddamned snit." He bought them several rounds and as Jozsi's tantrum subsided, Sandor was able to share the latest news from Hungary, and they even managed to have a few laughs.

As they parted, Jozsi called over his shoulder, "A week from today, brother, same time, same place."

Laci glanced back to see Sandor's galled expression and the American middle-finger salute aimed in their direction. "You must have balls the size of an elephant to talk to Sandor like that," Laci said as they walked back to the hotel.

"I was so scared my ass was sucking wind, but he already has us by the balls, we have nothing to lose *but* our balls. On second thought, that means you have nothing to lose!" And in the middle of the road, they wrestled each other to the ground; giddy with relief that Sandor had promised to return with a plan.

After they'd dusted themselves off, Laci said, "Adelina looks at you like a messiah, you know. Everywhere you go, she's digging holes for you to put down roots."

Jozsi put his arm around Laci and started to speak, but Laci cut him short. "I don't want to hear anything about diamond rings and big cars."

"We need Sandor more than he needs us, but we've done good work for him and I bet he'll want to set us up for more. Don't worry. We'll be out of here before you can get Maria pregnant, I promise. Once we're on the road again, you'll get more ass than the toilet seat, "*Légy türelmes*," he urged. Be patient.

The following week, Sandor sent word they should meet him at *Greco's Taverna*, which was one of the seedier spots in the area, greasy, with a smell so ripe it could overpower mosquitoes. They sat with glasses of cheap wine, an edgy Jozsi jumping on Laci every time he opened his mouth.

"Shut up. I'm trying to think about how to get us out of this rat hole," he gestured to the restaurant, but meant the whole town. "If you have a problem with that, get the hell out of here because I'm getting sick of carrying you!"

"I'm just making conversation, you fuck," Laci snapped back.

For once, Jozsi apologized. "I'm trying to figure the angles is all." He motioned to the waiter, who brought with him a bottle of the same bad wine they'd barely drunk.

"Bring something decent," he said, "and don't mix in any of the cheap stuff, I'll just send it back." The waiter's eyes widened in surprise that this foreigner had a clue about wine.

Laci shook his head, "I know...big city boy, you of the big cars and diamond rings and good wine."

Just then Sandor arrived, pausing before entering to make certain no one was following him. "We're not in Hungary any more, you can relax," Jozsi called out in Hungarian. "And no one would follow you to this shit hole anyway."

Sandor shrugged, "You never know." And then they got down to business, Sandor explaining that Eisenhower had screwed the Hungarians by not helping the Freedom Fighters, but that he was trying to rectify his mistake through the person of one Senator Lodge.

"I don't care about all the details," Jozsi said, "Just tell us what we need to know."

Sandor ignored him and continued detailing the Senate bill that would allow recruitment of Eastern Bloc citizens to serve under the U.S. Army Special Forces. "Mostly they want to develop potential spies that could be easily reintegrated back into their own home country." Sandor paused, sipping from his glass. "I've got two options for you," he flattened his palms against the table, then flipped the left hand face up, saying, "Number one, we provide you with new identification and send you back into Hungary. You live in a new area, receive monthly pay, and perhaps have to do some sort of shitty job in an office while secretly working for the firm." He turned over the right hand. "Or, you can sign up for five years in the U. S. Army, join the Special Forces, and receive the best training money can buy. If you keep your ass out of trouble and manage to stay alive, after those five years, you can apply for citizenship."

Jozsi grimaced. "We were hoping that after all we've done, we might get a free passport to the good old U. S. of A."

"I'm sorry," Sandor said, looking like he meant it. "At this point, you have to be sponsored by relatives in America to get in the door. Neither of you have anyone to sponsor you. I looked into it. Basically, you're shit out of luck unless you take one of these options. To sweeten your decision making, here's a little gift," and he slipped an envelope filled with lira across the table.

"We'll think it over and meet you again in a week," Jozsi rose from his chair. "But somewhere else. Pick better next time." Laci jumped up to follow him out the door as Sandor called out, "You two are sticking me with the bill again!"

Jozsi turned with a flourishing bow, "Si, Signore," and bowed his way backwards out the door. That night they treated their girlfriends to a night out at a classy restaurant. Adelina wondered where the money for this extravagance came from.

"Uncle Sam sent it from America," Jozsi assured her. Adelina, tipsy as could be, just giggled. Later that night, Jozsi explained that he and Laci would have to go to Rome in the near future to do some covert operations, and they had no idea when they'd be able to return.

Adelina, yearning in her eyes, said, "But if we are married, no more covert operations. We will be in Venice, my father will help you find good work, and someday you can go home to see your family in Hungary."

There was no way for him to explain that, as much as he cared for her, life had to hold more than Venice, so he simply said, "There are things I am contracted to do. I have no choice."

The next few nights, they bundled up against the chill March air and walked the beach together. One night she broke down, sobbing, "I know you love me, and I you, but you are going to leave me anyway. You are looking for a rainbow somewhere in the distance…"

His mind slipped back to his boyhood when he used to imagine himself riding the crest of a wave to other lands. And in that moment, his decision, already clear, became firm: he would join the army and go forward in life, not remain here or try going back to Hungary.

Adelina continued. "I hope someday you will come back to me. I will wait a long time."

"Oh, love, look at how things are in this world. It's not wise to wait," he sighed and held her close.

The next day he and Laci conferred and agreed to join the U. S. Army. Jozsi sent word to Sandor that they would sign up and hope for citizenship.

~~~

Just before Easter, Sandor had arrived with two train tickets, five hundred dollars to tide them over for a bit, and an address in Rome where they would stay. He promised he'd contact them soon after they arrived.

Jozsi's last night was a hard one. Leaving two women he cared for deeply in less than six months tore into his very being. He felt weak, as though a vampire had been at his neck. He decided he'd had enough of being in love for a while. He'd be better off making love, not falling in it. No serious relationships, he swore. Laci agreed. "Falling in love is for fools, we have to stay free," he declared. And then they trotted off to find Maria and Adelina for one final night of passion.

14

When in Rome

The following morning, Adelina and Maria drove them to the railway station. After extended and tearful embraces, the young women watched their Hungarian paramours climb aboard the train. They stood on the platform, arms around each other, waving and weeping as it screeched and lurched away from the platform.

The men sat in their compartment and opened presents from the girls: two bottles of champagne. Corks popped, they guzzled the lukewarm champagne and toasted, "To spring in Rome." They spent the long train ride wandering back and forth from the dining car to their compartment, entertained by a knowledgeable waiter who explained the historical significance of various sites as the train cut through the landscape. The waiter had become extremely friendly at the sight of U. S. dollars. Those had been supplied by Sandor once they'd agreed to join the Army; along with train tickets to Rome, and instructions to wait for an escort to fetch them from the station.

Jozsi peppered the waiter with questions, saying to Laci, "This is a much better way to learn history and geography than sitting in a schoolroom." Laci shrugged, claiming his interests would continue to center on guns and adventure, women, wine and food. At noon the following day, after several hours of rattling across Italy, the train pulled into the *Roma Termini* railway station. After so many calm months living by the beach, the chaos of the city overwhelmed. The station buzzed like a disturbed beehive, with Sicilians struggling to be understood by Northern Italians and vice versa, and travelers, beggars and thieves jockeying for floor space. Jozsi and Laci stood near the main ticket windows as Sandor had instructed, watching the pandemonium, waiting for their escort to appear.

After a time, a young man, black hair slicked back, hand-rolled cigarette between his fingers, tapped Jozsi on the shoulder and in Italian asked if he was waiting for someone, and told yes, said "Rodnas?" Their escort had been told to bring them to a safe house in Via Valambrosa, outside of Rome. He shared that it was on one of the Seven Hills of Rome, adding they were fortunate to have access to such a grand view.

Upon arrival, a butler whisked their suitcases away, while their escort introduced them to the director of the safe house, a robust, stern, raven-haired woman in her late forties named Maria.

"Another Maria," Jozsi rolled his eyes at Laci, with a hubba hubba expression.

"Too much spaghetti," Laci whispered, outlining her hefty waist and hips with his hands.

They were directed to a wooden bench in the front hall and she stood facing them, papers in hand. She haltingly read the English words from the top page.

"Number one: you are guests of the United States of America and you must obey all the rules while in residence. Number two: at no time disclose the address of the safe house to anyone, while in residence or at any time thereafter. Number three: you cannot entertain guests, even if you think that he or she is a contributor to your mission."

Laci's face fell. Jozsi shrugged and offered to paraphrase the sheet to speed things along. She gratefully handed it over, and Jozsi said, "Four, if we get in trouble, we've got some phone numbers."

Maria handed over two note pad pages, sealed in protective plastic.

Jozsi continued, "If we get involved in a criminal case, they'll deny knowing us, we're screwed." Maria frowned. Jozsi held his hand up apologetically, "We're on our own as far as defending ourselves. All right, number six: they don't keep logs of our departures and arrivals, but at the end of the day we have to report in full on anyone we've had contact with, including whores and homosexuals. No worries, there," he reassured Maria, "I mean, about the homosexuals." Maria let slip a small smile. She liked these boys; they had an easy way and lively eyes. Some of the other residents were far more unsettling.

Laci raised his hand in her direction. "What about masturbating in my own bed?"

Maria shook her head, "Full report," she said in English. "For our records." They couldn't tell if she meant it as a joke.

Jozsi rattled the paper to refocus their attention. "Finally, number seven: all meetings and contacts outside the safe house must be reported upon arrival at the office. I don't see how that's different from number six, but never mind. And if we have language difficulties there's a 24-hour secretary service 'for our needs.'" He underscored the last three words.

Laci said, "Needs? All needs."

"*Silenzio*," Jozsi said.

Maria took the page. "Have good stay. You need help, I help." She shook their hands and ushered them toward their rooms. As they climbed the stairs, Laci whispered, "Remind me not to even think about sleeping with her. She'd keep records of every second of pleasure."

"Really? Laci, how much could she record about a magic two seconds?"

They spent the rest of the day getting acquainted with the layout, stretching their legs in the garden, enjoying the view and the swimming pool, the whole area festooned with begonias, bougainvillea, jasmine, crocus, and dahlias.

They dined on the ground floor terrace while the sun set in the west, and watched the city of Rome light up as the sky darkened. The butler, whom Laci referred to as "our new *amico* Filippo," plunked a bottle of scotch on the table, indicating it was for them to keep.

Their feet propped against the terrace railing, the two savored the evening air. "I like this style of living," Laci said. "If this was the style Sandor provided in Budapest, I'm sorry I missed out on that."

"Laci," Jozsi replied, "I've told you before, this is a cruel world and what's good enough for me may not be good enough for you."

Ever humble, Laci assured him that this kind of life was plenty good enough for him and that whatever happened in the future, he was glad for Jozsi's company and all the benefits he reaped from their friendship.

"Sandor was right," Jozsi said, "We make a good team. You do what I say and you get to enjoy…" he opened his arms toward the bottle of scotch, then spread them wide to include the entire view.

In the morning, they awoke to a clear blue sky, the breeze gently brushed them with the promise of spring. Jozsi stood on the balcony their rooms shared, gazing at Rome, feeling a conqueror's satisfaction. Laci emerged groggily from his room, shirtless, his hair standing straight up.

Jozsi turned to him. "My friend, I've told you before and I'm telling you again, if you stick with me, you'll wear big diamond rings and drive around in big cars with beautiful girls."

Laci rubbed his eyes. "And where are the girls?"

"No girls. Sandor thinks you're really after guys and the CIA forbids shit like that." The two were giddy from the general upheaval in their lives and months of work at the hotel. Here they were allowed plentiful food, and booze, and time to catch their breath. They spent the first few days by the pool, waiting for Sandor to get in touch.

On the third day, he appeared in unusually good spirits, with two bottles of Hungarian wine in hand. They ate on the terrace. Jozsi, expansive after enthusiastically downing a couple glasses of *Tokay*, cheered by the familiar taste on his tongue, raised his glass toward Rome, shouting, "Look at this city! Attila the Hun tried to conquer it a thousand years ago and failed because the Romans bought him off. And here we are with no money and no army, yet Rome is under our feet begging us to take their virgins and spare their city from destruction." Laci applauded and yelled variations of "Give us your virgins or we'll burn Rome to the ground."

Appearing at the door, Maria said, "Start burning. There are no virgins in Rome." The three, taken aback by her unexpected humor and rudimentary understanding of Hungarian, invited her to join them for a drink. And in a somewhat jumbled potpourri of languages, she relayed entertaining stories about past guests at the safe house in rapid fire Italian, which Sandor translated into Hungarian and English. Their heads were spinning by the time she took her leave.

"What brought her to the door," Laci wondered.

"She's after your body," Jozsi said. "Has been since we walked in." He sounded so serious Laci looked convinced, and nervous.

Sandor took pity. "It was the shouting, you idiots. They could hear you all the way to the Coliseum. So much for a low profile." He made ready to leave, provided them with a new number where they could leave word for him in case of an emergency. "I'll be in touch as soon as there's something to report, but I won't be around for a few weeks; I have to take care of matters elsewhere. Anything else I can do for you two love birds before I head off?"

"Please take Maria with you and dump her ass in the Tiber River on your way to the airport. I'm not going to sleep well, thinking she's coming for me," he joked.

Jozsi shrugged, "At least she's amusing."

That night the two sat late on their balcony, again enjoying the view as the lights of Rome sparkled on in a spate, and much later, extinguished one by one. They were silent, each spurred by the combination of Sandor and *Tokay* to thoughts of home. Laci's mind went to the smells of the farm, the animals, images of his father, pitchfork in hand, bandy legs in sturdy boots and heavy pants, walking out to the barn. Jozsi drifted to thoughts of his parents, and with pangs to Erika. He hoped she was still alive, he hoped Zsigmond didn't have his hands on her. When those thoughts stabbed too deeply he thought about Adelina, how pleasurable it was to touch her soft skin, and how sad she looked at the train station. He had to stop falling in love. He was in no way ready to settle down in one place, and the tears in his heart from all this leave-taking did him no good. Still, as he drifted off to sleep that night, his arm went around his pillow, hugging it close; there was no denying his head might yearn for freedom without ties, but his heart was still calling out for connection.

A happy week spent exploring Rome passed, and then one evening, as they returned from an afternoon of loitering by the *Trevi Fountain*, Maria approached and handed them an envelope. Sandor. His letter explained that the bill Henry Lodge was trying to move through the American Senate had run into roadblocks. This was not good news. The bill, allowing well-screened Hungarian freedom fighters to join the U.S. Army in exchange for citizenship, was what Jozsi and Laci had been banking on. But Sandor told them not to despair, it was just a delay, and he expected its passage within a month or two. Till then, they'd have to cool their heels.

"American expression," Jozsi said to erase Laci's confusion. "It means wait."

To inspire patience, he'd sent a check for five hundred American dollars to cover expenses. Maria would arrange to cash it, he wrote, in exchange for a kiss from Laci.

"He did not write that," Laci, indignant, snapped.

"Yes, he did, but it is a joke, I think…maybe." Jozsi was enjoying watching his friend squirm at the thought of having to make nice with Maria.

Despite Sandor's suggestion that they lay low and not mix with the locals, the two couldn't just sit at the safe house or sightsee all day every day, so they went searching for a Hungarian Restaurant to bless with their dollars. And there, Jozsi ran into Alex, an older acquaintance from Budapest who'd been an electrical engineering instructor at the university. They hugged like brothers, whooping happily at this surprise encounter, and settled in at the bar. Jozsi told Laci, "Not only did I know him from the university, he was the one who taught me how to cut up clothes-hanger wire to sell at the farmer's market." Alex, Jozsi discovered, was an excellent engineer and teacher, but his strongest talent lay in an innate ability to fast talk and scam his way through the world. "It is much more fun than teaching," he'd explained.

Laci was lost. "Why would anyone buy hanger wire?"

Alex said, "You are not from Budapest, I take it."

"Gyor was my home."

"Ah," Alex said, "then let me explain." And he described how they'd spread the word that flints for cigarette lighters would no longer be available. The Russians feared that Hungarians could make bombs using them — and the cut hanger wire looked very much like flint. They'd told some smalltown farmers they had the very last shipment of flints and that farmers would be wise to buy as many as possible, take them back to their towns and sell them for double what they'd paid. The two scoundrels even offered a discount if they bought in bulk. Alex told Laci they'd made good money that day, and would have made more but they'd run out of clothes hangers to cut up. He'd been impressed by how fast a study Jozsi turned out to be, quick on his feet with clever banter to draw in and distract customers.

"They were stupid like monkeys — learn hard and forget fast," Jozsi added.

"You probably fucked over friends of mine," Laci grumbled.

Jozsi ignored that and went on to remind Alex of the scenario he'd painted back then. "You said, 'With your brains and my money, someday we'll make it big.' You treated me to a fine supper, but somehow never got around to handing over my share of the money. I wrote it off as the price of my education." Alex grinned like a Cheshire cat.

As the sun went down and their stomachs woke up, Alex called for a cab and offered to treat them to dinner. "We'll have the best cavalry dinner you can find in Rome."

"What the hell is a cavalry dinner?" Jozsi asked.

Alex smirked, "Trust me. I know you enjoy fine dining; we're going to have a classy meal."

The cab arrived and Alex asked Jozsi to pay for it, since he would be picking up the dinner tab. As they entered the *Osteria Azzuro*, looking a little more disheveled than the rest of the clientele, Alex instructed them. "We don't have a reservation, so when the waiter shows up, stick some money in his pocket and act like you're a rich kid taking your father out for dinner." As they entered, Laci did as Alex asked and within no time, they were seated at one of the better tables in the house.

With drinks in hand, Laci toasted to "Alex, the smartest Hungarian I've met in Rome."

Jozsi joked, "You better check to make certain you still have your wallet," and the three toasted each other several times.

Alex leaned close to Laci, "My friend, I'm going to let you in on a secret."

"Yes," Laci said eagerly, looking interested and gullible, Jozsi thought.

"The secret is, if you hang around me, you'll soon be wearing big diamond rings and driving around in fast cars."

Laci laughed and said, "What about the beautiful girls?"

Alex told him, "That's Jozsi's department. I'm too old and wrinkled."

They ordered food, Alex urging them to have whatever they wanted. The restaurant atmosphere was straight out of *Casablanca*, a movie Jozsi had once seen at the cultural center in Budapest.

They ate like kings, drank glass after glass of wine, and at the waiter's suggestion, sipped *Galliano* as an after-dinner drink.

"Did you enjoy your meal?" Alex asked, motioning to the waiter for another round of *Galliano*. "Friends and countrymen, it is now time for me to explain the cavalry part of this gustatory adventure." He motioned for them to lean in close. "When the bill comes, I will give it to Jozsi, and you will say 'thank you' without looking at it. We'll keep talking amongst ourselves like we are discussing world politics. I'll go outside as if I'm getting the car. I need a head start." He patted his slightly gimpy right leg. "After that you two charge out of here like the famous Italian cavalry officer Garibaldi. Run like hell, and we'll meet at the good Hungarian restaurant five streets away."

Laci looked like he was ready to throw up his expensive meal, but Jozsi felt charged up and secure, like he was with a big brother who would make sure all would be well. Somehow, with Alex, things usually turned out fine, sometimes just barely, but still…

They followed the plan and reconvened at the Hungarian restaurant, where a clearly rattled Laci paid for their drinks in advance.

"You're pretty nervous for a big-time smuggler," Jozsi teased.

"I'm nervous enough going into a fancy restaurant, much less running out of one." He shook himself. "Especially without a gun in hand. Especially when we *could* have paid."

Alex turned to Jozsi, "Are you sure he's even *from* Hungary?"

Laci, annoyed with them both, stalked off to the bathroom to throw cold water on his face, smooth his hair, and avoid punching either one of his countrymen.

Later, back on the balcony, Jozsi mentioned that while Laci was in the bathroom, Alex had mentioned an idea he had for making some fast cash. Jozsi urged Laci to consider the plan, "As long as we're hanging around with nothing in particular to do."

"I suppose he wants us to join the Italian light cavalry brigade," Laci answered, but now that he'd recovered from the dinner adventure, he seemed open to considering anything that might fill his pockets.

"Not quite. Before I explain, one thing: never tell Alex where we're staying. Don't give him the phone number here. We'll arrange to meet him, and if he needs us sooner, he's shit out of luck. For our own protection, you understand?" Laci nodded and Jozsi proceeded to explain the plan. The Italian government was taking bids on design proposals to run power lines in from the north in order to satisfy the future electrical needs of Rome. Alex was a certified electrical engineer with a European work permit and could apply for a permit to survey the land from Rome to Milan.

"What does he need us for?" Laci asked.

"Money to purchase surveying equipment and to act like his crew. He can get the permit next week. The proposal is due at the end of the year, months and months from now. We'll be long gone."

Laci asked, "What's to stop Alex from taking the money and disappearing, leaving us broke in Rome." Or we get caught and end up as dead soldiers buried in an unmarked grave somewhere."

"Don't get carried away," Jozsi smiled.

"I just don't want to hear one more fucking word about diamond rings, you understand."

"Hold on," Jozsi said, "all this good shit will come to an end sooner or later, but listen to the beauty of this scheme. We go out to the countryside and select the best vineyards between here and Milan. When the owners notice our surveying equipment they'll be on us like flies on horseshit. We'll show them our permit; tell them about our plan to run power lines. We'll describe how big bulldozers are going to come and cut through their vineyards. That'll scare the shit out of them, and then all we have to do is hold out our palms."

"I don't see where the money comes in."

"That's because you were born under a rock, *haverom*," he paused and sighed with great exaggeration, enjoying busting his friend's balls. "Pay attention because there's going be a test on this later. The farmers will offer to bribe us to change the direction of the power line. We'll agree and give them a written commitment from our 'company' and it'll all appear entirely legal."

Laci nodded. There was no discussion of how wrong it was to steal from the farmers, though Laci shuddered, imagining he could feel his father's disapproval from beyond the grave. But much had happened since his father died, and he knew if he brought any moral questions up to Jozsi he'd be mercilessly ribbed.

Jozsi felt no such compunction. Everything he'd gone through to survive Hungary's communist regime had skewed his moral compass. He knew the difference between right and wrong, but as long as he wasn't killing good people, he couldn't get too worked up about a little thievery here and there. The Italian farmers would not go under or perish because of their little escapade. Thus, it was only so wrong. If all his wrong doings caught up with him, so be it, he'd pay the cost. Believing in neither heaven nor hell, he had nothing to fear.

Joszi was a little distracted as well, having just had an engaging conversation with Zitta, a lithe doe-eyed young woman with a slightly goofy smile, who helped Maria run the safe house. She claimed to have come from Milan, though in Jozsi's mind, she was likely just a spy amongst spies. The safe house held about thirty people at any one time. Refugees from various war zones, agents from the States, an international den of men, many of them up to what most people would call no good. Zitta told Jozsi, "You shouldn't mix with any of the others. They are killers, most of them, nothing more."

He did not know what to believe, but he and Laci chose to opt out of eating in the dining room, instead taking advantage of the safe house's luxurious custom of providing room service.

When they met up with Alex a few days later, he arrived, permit in one hand, the other held out, "For money to purchase equipment," he explained. But Jozsi was nobody's fool. "I'll handle the expenses this time around," he announced, as Laci nodded agreement in the background.

Alex chuckled. "I don't like that idea at all, my young student, but it shows you have learned well." Then more seriously, "I will get a third of the profit one way or another."

"Agreed," Jozsi said, and meant it. No point trying to steal from the master, since he knew he'd only live to regret such a foolish, cocky act. Using Alex's driver's license, they rented a car and headed north. He drove as Jozsi spread a map across his knees, and Laci, in the back, turned his head from one window to another, like a small boy on his first car ride.

"How are you figuring out where to go?" Jozsi asked, having no idea where good vineyards lay.

"Ach," Alex answered, feigning exasperation at Jozsi's denseness. "It's as plain as the ass on a goat. All we have to do is look at any menu in any decent restaurant and we'll find where the most expensive wines come from. Look in my satchel," he directed. Jozsi did, pulling out several menus from restaurants he didn't even know existed. "I do my research," Alex said, and Jozsi filed that away: another lesson learned.

Within a week, they'd made a staggering amount of money, close to ten thousand dollars, and felt like they'd hit the jackpot at the roulette table.

"This is the life," Laci crowed, after their second score. "Drive around, eat well, meet nice farmers who invite you in for a good meal and hand over wads of cash." Apparently, the wads of cash obscured all doubts he'd earlier felt about the rightness of their endeavor. Every few days, they headed back to the safe house to check in and make sure Sandor wasn't looking for them. Each time Zitta smiled her goofy smile at the sight of him, Jozsi felt his heart lift just a bit. Uh-oh, he thought, and then set to flirting with her as though she were the last woman on earth.

One morning during breakfast on the balcony, Laci announced he was thinking of staying in Italy to work with Alex. Screw Sandor, the Army and U.S. citizenship. Jozsi had been worried Laci might get carried away by Alex's sparkle and tried to clear the stars from his eyes. He spoke seriously of Alex's past, and the many reasons he'd had to flee Hungary, most of them having nothing to do with the Revolution. "I hate to say it, but he is living on borrowed time," Jozsi said. "Sooner or later he'll screw up. He's not as savvy here as he was in Hungary — the language, the customs are not second nature. One of these days the police are going to catch up with him. If you stay, you'll end up fleeing to God knows where, or spending 20 years in some shithole jail."

The talk brought Laci's head right down out of the clouds. "My father used to try to help me think things through, but you make more sense than anyone else in my life ever has."

Jozsi hid his relief. He didn't want to see Laci get mangled by Alex's ways. "I'm not much for emotional bullshit, and the last thing I want is for you to cry on my shoulder and tell me I remind you of your father."

Laci slapped him lightly on the face. "You don't remind me all *that* much of my father."

~~~

The spring passed quickly and pleasantly. The men engaged in a couple of other moneymaking ventures during the days, and spent nights enjoying Rome's nightlife, Zitta at Jozsi's side many of those nights. Laci had yet to find a steady girlfriend and played the field, all the time avoiding being alone with Maria who truly did seem to have taken a fancy to him. It was Maria who tipped them off that the police were looking for three Hungarians. She knew nothing of Alex, but she was no fool and had noticed their frequent absences and lack of reported contacts. "You talk to nobody all day?" she'd say skeptically. She hadn't bought their "tour" of wine country, either.

Fortunately, just as they decided they'd had enough of Rome and perhaps of Italy, Zitta walked in holding a telegram; no goofy smile on her face and tears in her eyes. "Bad news from your parents?" Jozsi asked, concerned.

"No. Bad news for me from America," she said, handing him the telegram. It was from Sandor. The Lodge Act had finally passed and the two men were told to get ready to leave for Germany within ten days.

Jozsi read it, controlling his excitement at the news, promising Zitta they'd live it up every night they had left. He wiped tears from her cheeks, "Let's make hay," he whispered in her ear, using an Americanism Sandor had shared. She caught his drift without exactly understanding the phrase, and rallied so as to enjoy him while he was still in Rome. If wartime had taught her nothing else, it had taught her to seize the moment. He promised he'd return as soon as he could, and in moments of shared passion, even meant it.

Finally, it was time to say *arrivederci Roma*. A van pulled up in the middle of the night and they hustled into it for the trip to the airport. Destination: Frankfurt, Germany. The day before, Maria had told Jozsi the papers were reporting on the search for a shady Hungarian and his two translators. Now that they were safely on the road, Jozsi mentioned this to Laci.

Laci's only comment, "Thank God you never gave Alex the safe house address."

Jozsi replied, "I told you before and I'm telling you again, you have to be raised in the city or you have no chance of surviving in this cruel world. Being two steps ahead is not enough."

The van arrived at the U. S. airbase and pulled up next to a plane, which they were hurriedly escorted onto, the CIA not wanting news of their existence and departure noted by anyone. Maria wasn't the only one who had her suspicions about what the two had been up to all spring.

As they sat bleary-eyed, staring into the darkness, more vans pulled up, and other passengers were similarly hustled on board. The plane finally took off, with several intriguing, vaguely dangerous-looking men on board, different characters than Jozsi and Laci had met before. Everyone surreptitiously glanced around, but in this trade, one learned fast to ask no questions and say very little, so that's what they did. Jozsi thought it the quietest flight in history.

15

Toward the Land of Plenty

The van arrived at the Frankfurt U. S. base in the middle of the night. Jozsi and Laci were brought to a building that looked like a hotel, but wasn't. At least they each had their own room and the beds were comfortable, with extra pillows; a rarity. The next morning, the mess hall's almost lavish breakfast impressed them. After they'd stuffed themselves silly, they agreed that American soldiers ate better than most people in Italy had in years. Though Jozsi still missed Adelina, he was relieved to be out of Italy. That country, still struggling to recover from the war, offered no real opportunities for a hungry young man, and he damn sure wasn't going to take a pity job from her father. The general deprivation, the mourning for the dead, the lack of food, clothing, pleasure, all reminded him too much of Hungary. He was anxious to leave loss and lack behind, to move forward into a future of his own making, into a life over which he had some control. The anxiety of waiting for that road to open weighed him down in Italy. Frankfurt had already lifted his spirits. The anxiety, he knew, would not evaporate quickly; years of living in a paranoid Hungary had rewired his brain. He wasn't yet aware of that fact, but in truth it had. The buoyancy of youth and of his own resilient nature, convinced him he could will himself into a calmer, more secure state of mind, he just needed new and better surroundings in order for his nerves to un-fray. An extra pillow followed by a hearty meal felt like a touch of heaven, or would have if he'd believed in heaven.

After breakfast, the base commander took them aside and firmly told them to stay out of trouble until Sandor got in touch; they could hear Sandor lecturing them right through the commander's voice. He directed them toward the PX, and within a short time the two looked like American soldiers, nattily attired in brand new Army-issued uniforms. The commander insisted they wear them immediately so they could go downtown without appearing at all suspicious. Preening, admiring each other, the two men quickly hopped a bus to the city center and walked the streets. They asked passersby where they might find a Hungarian restaurant, and there they happily wolfed down food that felt like home. The restaurant even came equipped with a gypsy band, and for a brief time served as their second home. Laci put an end to that cozy situation with one late-night whisper into the hurdy gurdy player's ear. She was standing at the bar getting a drink when he leaned close to say, "Would you like to turn my crank?" Unfortunately, her boyfriend happened to be standing right behind her and his hearing was excellent. Within seconds he was pummeling Laci with fists the size of baseball mitts. Jozsi reluctantly abandoned a friendly conversation with a sad-eyed woman at the far end of the bar, and dove into the melee. Four of Frankfurt's finest police had them out the door within minutes. They were hauled down to the station in a van already holding a semi-toothless vagrant who was contentedly humming Beethoven's 9th, eyes closed, head swaying.

Jozsi was blasé. "We'll be out of here in no time. The Americans will fetch us."

Unfortunately, Gerhard Weber, the local police chief, was not thinking along similar lines. He saw their American uniforms, he heard them speak what struck him as the English of five-year-olds, and concluded he'd discovered a spy ring in Germany. He saw his name in the papers, he saw the President of the United States pinning a medal to his chest, flashbulbs popping, a promotion to head chief of the Berlin police force. He saw glory. Just to be safe, he called the American armed forces. They had no record of these two Hungarians. His pulse raced. He called Interpol. They too pled ignorance. He could barely contain himself.

Chief Weber called for an interrogator, whose name was not to be used by the Hungarians — they were told to address him as Herr. Jozsi referred to him as Herr Herr, although never to his face.

Herr came to see them, beads of sweat dotting his forehead, a result of the long walk from the building's entrance down a flight of stairs and several hallways until finally he arrived at their cell. His expression was serious as he informed them he could find no record of their being part of any legitimate American or international organization. Thus, he was left to assume they were working for the Hungarian government as spies, or even worse, working for the Russians. He narrowed his eyes and pinched his nostrils as though the two looked and smelled too disreputable for him to abide. He strung together simple German phrases to ensure they understood his meaning. "Confess now and things will go better for you." No need for any 'or else.'

"We have nothing to confess," Jozsi answered with proper German pronunciation and grammar.

Herr clapped his hands together, as though closing a book whose final page he'd turned, and said, "I will return," clicked his heels together and hurried away, the cell door shutting behind him with a loud clank.

Several days of lengthy visits from Herr followed. He never struck them, but the threat was constant — in his eyes, in his fists, which he rhythmically flexed, and from the nightstick, *mannschaft*, he informed them, that swung from a small leather holster on his belt. Jozsi kept offering him a phone number to call, a special number, nothing to do with the Army or Interpol, but Herr refused to place any calls.

"You'd think they'd be tired of putting us up," Laci said, swiping a thin piece of bread through a bowl of what could only be described as gruel.

"It's not like this is costing them much," Jozsi surveyed the food, the board beds covered with straw-filled pallets.

"I should have stuck with Alex," Laci sighed, just to annoy Jozsi, who spit a mouthful of bread in his direction and crossed his eyes.

Finally, a state lawyer appeared and was convinced to call the special number. "Just call and give our names, you don't need to say anything else," Jozsi wheedled. "*Bitte*," he added, to be gracious, though he felt like strangling somebody — and the state lawyer standing right in front of him would do just fine. This whole episode had been absent from his Frankfurt sightseeing itinerary and he resented its addition. Fortunately, the lawyer nodded assent and left.

In the morning, they were shaken out of their beds, and within minutes hustled into a van heading out of the most tightly secured prison Frankfurt had to offer. At the base, they were ushered into a small office where they found Sandor, sitting at a desk, looking so mad it took them a moment to recognize his distorted face. He rose and began screaming that they were assholes for starting a fight over a broad...and assholes for getting arrested...and assholes for not taking advantage of all the good things he was offering them...and assholes for forcing him to rush to their rescue…and eventually he ran out of breath and stood glaring, allowing his lungs to recover. Jozsi opened his mouth and Sandor's arm sliced across the air emphatically. Jozsi closed his mouth. More calmly but no less intensely, Sandor said, "I should ship you back to Budapest." He gave them a minute to envision their futures in Hungary. Then, through grit teeth, he added, "But instead, I'm putting you on the next boat to America. I'm hoping the Special Forces will train the stupidity out of you." They breathed a silent sigh of relief, keeping their faces immobile lest they irritate their savior any further. Sandor sat down and began leafing through a folder, leaving them stoically standing by the door.

When Sandor closed the folder, Jozsi asked, "Can we buy you a drink?" Laci gulped nervously, but it seemed Sandor's rage was spent. He considered the offer for what felt like a week. "All right, as long as you're buying. If you try to stick me with the tab you will be back in Budapest before the sun rises." He was still quite grumpy with them and it took many drinks to jolly him back to normal.

Drunk at sunrise after their recriminatory reunion, Laci stood on a street corner, his right hand over his heart as he slurringly described the sun coming up in the east, shining on their homeland and on the Hungarians who were just now struggling out of their depressing houses to try to make enough money to support their families.

"The stupid bastards didn't know enough to get out of the country when they had a chance," Jozsi countered.

"Like your father?" Sandor said, hitting a low blow. Jozsi turned away in disgust at the low blow, and at himself. He would flee Hungary all over again, never did he regret leaving, but there was still a raw spot inside where he felt himself a deserter, especially when he thought of his parents and siblings still there, weighed down by the crushing Communist sky.

The next day at lunch, Sandor tracked them down in the mess hall. He still looked a little the worse for wear, his eyes lined with red. But he was cheerful, greeting them like long lost relatives, which by now they felt they were. It seemed all their failings were, for the moment, forgiven. "I have plans for you," he crowed. "Tomorrow morning a van will take you to Bremerhaven. The U.S.S. Henry W. Tucker will carry you to America. Reservations, meals, bed, compliments of yours truly. You have bed numbers 118 and 119, flip a coin to decide who gets which. All you have to do is stay out of jail between now and dawn, and try not to fall overboard after that. If you have any complaints about the service, the Navy will refund your money when you dock in New York City." He grinned.

"All the comedians are looking for work and they don't need competition from you," Jozsi muttered.

Sandor, in an unusually jovial mood, continued, "Other Hungarians and refugees of various nations will be joining you onboard. It will make for an interesting voyage, and of course, this will give you time to rest up before your next adventures."

Jozsi wondered what Sandor was so amused by. Most likely the thought of them enduring bouts of military training, but he kept his thoughts to himself as Sandor practically skipped out of the mess hall. Some days he was glad he'd met Sandor, but this day was not one of them.

Shortly after sunrise the next morning, a military van pulled up and soon they were speeding toward Bremerhaven, where they were turned over to the shore patrol and joined by assorted losers, some handcuffed at the wrist, others shackled at the ankles; young soldiers or refugees who had run afoul of the authorities. Jozsi and Laci were stunned to see their fellow Hungarians treated like criminals, although they learned that a few fully deserved harsh treatment having gotten in trouble for armed robbery, or worse yet rape. But many had simply been unable to communicate their stories, and in that moment in time, no one was particularly patient with troublesome young men who spoke no German or English.

Jozsi had a sinking feeling that their accommodations might not be as amenable as advertised, given the treatment their compatriots were receiving. His suspicions were on the nose. The beds — hammocks, really — had to be pulled up and chained to iron posts at either end of the four-layered bed frames. A mere twenty-four inches separated one bed from the other, and the hammocks jiggled when anyone moved or climbed up and down the rungs at the end of each bed unit. No wonder Sandor had been amused.

Jozsi claimed a bottom bunk, thinking he'd gotten a good spot, easy in, easy out. Laci grabbed the one above him and resumed the mantra, "I should have stayed with Alex," which Jozsi chose to ignore.

Once they'd stowed their gear, up on deck they trooped, mingling with the nearly two hundred other emigrants on board. The handcuffs and shackles had vanished, the shore patrol needed them for future miscreants. The Hungarians soaked up news from each other, all seeking out the most recent Budapest refugees with whom they could relax into the comfort of a shared common language and familiar ways.

The giant troop ship had arrived with fresh troops from the States and was now returning close to 1,500 soldiers back home to be discharged, along with this motley group of refugees. This was the beginning of Jozsi and Laci's induction into military life. Mealtime schedules to follow, lights off ten at night, back on six in the morning. Jozsi was so far unimpressed with anything military beyond his uniform, and that pleased him only because it was the best-made clothing he'd worn in months.

Still, you couldn't avoid being excited by the view from the deck of such an imposing vessel. As they passed the English Channel a silence fell over them all. Just the thought of being *at* the Channel was overwhelming. Jozsi began to feel a bubbly joy; finally, he was crossing the ocean to America. Those moments, and the ones as they entered New York Harbor, were the best of the voyage.

After the first evening meal, Laci, uninspired by the mess hall offerings, was unable to refrain from mentioning how very much he was missing a cavalry dinner with Alex. "At least for this we don't have to pay, and it's better than jail swill," Jozsi observed. Soon after, things took an unpleasant turn for the passengers. By then the ship was heading out of the Channel, moving full steam into the Atlantic Ocean. Heavy as the carrier was, still, the increasingly dramatic swell of the waves had an unpleasant effect.

Most of the men availed themselves of the many bathrooms, grateful for a chance to shower, shave, and spruce up after emerging from whatever hellhole they'd managed to survive. Each bathroom was equipped with showers, sinks and toilets and could hold close to fifty people at a time. As Jozsi lathered his face, his nose registered a foul smell, his ears the tortured sounds of retching. Turning to the toilets, he witnessed several of his countrymen green with seasickness. Those with sturdier stomachs laughed, but their turns came soon enough. Jozsi held hard to the sink, just to keep his face in front of the mirror, while his body swayed to the ship's motion. He managed to finish shaving, but lurching his way across the floor, turned white as a ghost, and within seconds had his head stuck in a toilet, looking from behind like a teenager suffering from his first drunk.

The ship steamed ahead at 20 knots and the waves tossed them about, rising and falling a hundred feet through the water, slamming down and careening up. For almost everyone, the trip was a stomach-churning nightmare of puking, while trying to hold down enough water so as not to become dangerously dehydrated. Jozsi's bottom bunk had its drawbacks — those higher hurled from their beds when they couldn't find the strength to clamber down and lurch to the bathrooms.

Eight days into what Sandor had referred to as their "resting" time, Jozsi told Laci, "Now I know why Columbus was famous for crossing the Atlantic." At least by then he was able to speak. The waves had calmed and the soldiers and refugees finally able to stand on deck, relieved to inhale fresh air after having spent most of their time below decks, practically crawling from bunk to bathroom and back.

The next morning, everyone lined the decks, straining to see the New York City shoreline, wanting to be the first to spot the *Statue of Liberty*. The faces of homebound soldiers held eager relief: they were alive; they were almost home. The faces of the emigrants — Hungarian, Bulgarian, Romanian, Czech, Polish and Russian — flashed from expectant, to anxious, to curious as they approached the harbor. When a soldier called out, "There she is," everyone let out a cheer. *Liberty's* copper torch shimmered in the sunlight. A good omen.

Jozsi took his whistle from his pocket and blew hello to the great lady. He wondered what the other emigrants were dreaming of as they neared her. While the carrier majestically plowed into the harbor, smaller boats tooted welcome from closer to shore. Laci tapped him on the shoulder, "Why so serious? We're in America! We're in the land of the free and the home of the brave." Laci's eyes were dancing; he looked like a little boy about to enter an ice cream emporium.

"My friend," Jozsi said, "stop and think for a minute. Look at all these soldiers coming home; they'll be getting out of the Army in the next few months. By the time that we're experiencing that feeling, the kids of these soldiers will be in first grade." He sighed. "We have a long way to go."

They disembarked to the strains of a small military band assembled on the wharf. As they walked down the plank, Jozsi noticed a black soldier being roughed up by the military police. He'd jumped over the rail to hug his loved ones before going through customs. After what Jozsi had been through, the beating did not shock him, he merely wondered if it would have happened to a white soldier. A search at customs, Jozsi learned, was a prerequisite for any returning soldier — they were taken straight to an isolated area where all belongings were examined for weapons, art, drugs, or anything else the government didn't allow. Loved ones could wait. He filed the information away for when it came his turn to be a soldier returning at the end of his tour of duty.

The Hungarians' screening was brisk — most had arrived with little beyond the clothes on their backs. Jozsi, Laci, and a mixture of other Hungarians and Eastern Europeans were loaded onto a bus straight to *Grand Central Station*. Next, they were going to board a train to Fort Jackson, South Carolina.

The men were ravenous, light-headed from hunger and suffering vertigo from walking across dry land after so many days on the roiling sea. At the station, Laci had his first and last experience trying to help a little old lady. As she stood next to him, struggling with packages and luggage, Laci reached for her suitcase to hand up to her after she'd boarded the train. Startled, she began screaming and beating him with her purse. As though someone like him would want to steal her suitcase full of lavender-scented clothes and such, he exclaimed to the policeman who rushed to her side. The policeman let Laci's passionate Hungarian explanation flow, while cuffing his hands. Fortunately, an Army translator hurried over to explain that in Europe it was customary to help the elderly. Jozsi stood to the side, choking with laughter. "Sandor would kill you if he heard about this," he sputtered. Laci promised never again to be a nice guy, and they bordered the train and were directed a few cars down, and also encouraged to stay away from little old ladies.

The train put them in the lap of luxury, or so it felt. It was after nine that night by the time they pulled out of *Grand Central*, and a moonless night, which deprived them of any chance of viewing the scenery they longed to see. But eating and drinking in the dining car made up for the darkness on the other side of the window, and the lull of the train's motion, gave them their first decent night's rest since before they'd landed in that unpleasant Frankfurt jail.

Jozsi awoke early, viewing the peaceful terrain as they chugged past who knew what state; he had no idea where they were. Countryside, then more settled land, then a stop where a few male passengers waved goodbye to their wives before boarding. It reminded him of a book of Norman Rockwell paintings he'd seen at the American Cultural Center, what felt like a lifetime ago. He shared his cultural insights with Laci, who had never heard of Norman Rockwell, and they passed the day watching America through the train windows, soaking in a kind of plenty and wealth and peace they'd been dreaming of their whole lives. At least Jozsi had. Laci tended to want the best of whatever was in front of him, and this was looking pretty good.

They whiled away another evening in the dining car, tipping their waiter generously. He'd served in the Second World War and knew some German, so they could communicate fairly well. He even expanded their English by a few choice phrases, and snuck them extra drinks on the house.

The second morning, the train pulled into Fort Jackson. No band playing, just a few surly officers and sergeants, none of them able to speak German or Hungarian or anything but English. They stood around looking at each other like kids at a high school dance.

"There's no translator handy, we can take advantage of this," Jozsi said. He stepped forward and began shouting to the other 200 disembarked Hungarians to line up, speaking in Hungarian and German, repeating "Okay, okay," to impress the Americans with his English. It had worked well in Italy, he said, they might as well give it a shot here. Laci joined in, directing the puzzled newcomers into four semi-orderly rows. Indeed, the local staff was impressed by their initiative, and made note of their names. Eventually Lieutenant Drake, who had served in Germany after the Second World War, appeared to assist in moving things along, although Jozsi could barely make out a word of the officer's very rusty German.

After another bus trip, the men were issued blankets, sheets, and pillowcases, and shown to their barracks. Luxury, they agreed, to have your very own bedding. Clean bedding.

That night Captain Kessler and Lieutenant Drake stopped by the barracks and invited Jozsi and Laci for a drink at the officer's club. "*A drink?*" Laci said.

"It's a beginning," Jozsi replied, combing his hair into an impressive do for the last time — he'd heard Army haircuts were on the following day's agenda.

That night they were treated like kings, one drink leading to many. Jozsi grinning, murmured to Laci, "I smell something sweet in the air so keep smiling while I do the talking."

"I can see diamond rings and big cars."

"You forgot the girls," Jozsi added, and they laughed happily while the officers nodded in approval, good spirits all around.

They were soon in their cups, the officers trying to teach them English, everyone slurring words and making little headway. By the end of the evening, with a combination of gestures and phrases, Captain Kessler managed to communicate that a recent promotion had placed him in charge of the Tenth Special Forces Battalion. General Stillwell had charged the Tenth with training the Hungarians and their associates. Should there be another Hungarian Revolution, they could go back and win their freedom! Jozsi thought to himself: Kessler must be completely smashed. Two hundred of us wouldn't be enough to make a piss hole in the Soviet-run snow bank of Hungary.

The captain continued on, saying he'd need all the help he could get from them, that it was obvious they had great influence and control over the two hundred trainees. Jozsi eagerly agreed, praising the captain's intelligence and good sense, qualities Jozsi hoped to emulate. If the translating officer could tell Jozsi was brownnosing like crazy, he didn't let on. The captain shared that his success with their battalion might propel him into a promotion from Captain Kessler to Major Kessler, and he liked the way that sounded. Jozsi assured him that as long as they kept things on a friendly basis, he and Laci would guarantee his success as best they could, and that Kessler could hope to be a major by the time their nine months of training ended.

With that, Kessler ordered another round and they drank to the captain's almost certain promotion. Jozsi leaned over and said he might as well start calling him major now because — and he used a phrase Sandor had taught him — "it's in the bag." Kessler and Lieutenant Drake cracked up and ordered yet another round of drinks.

As they stumbled toward their barracks, Laci asked, "What was the name of that school you went to?"

"Alex University," Jozsi answered. Sleepy and content, the two settled into their bunks, pleased at their first full day of life in the Army's America.

16

Training, Travels and Totems

The following day training began. Although Jozsi and Laci had put a lot of effort into helping the refugees in Italy, and extravagant thought and labor into their various schemes and scams, this new, highly structured existence was a shock to the system. Where they'd been used to varied and unpredictable activities, now there was consistency: banal, plodding, one-foot-in-front-of-the-other consistency.

They rose at five each morning, finished breakfast by six, and were deep in training by seven. Exactly twelve hours later, they were free to do as they pleased. After four hours of language school and eight hours of combat training, they were pleased to sleep. They began and ended each day the same: exhausted. They marched through three months of tough training, and their ability to stay awake past eight at night increased incrementally, as their stamina and strength solidified under the discipline of Army life.

The food might not be great, but at least they had enough to eat. After breakfast, it was back to the barracks for cleanup. Bed always looked tempting, but the moment cleanup was done, they jumped into their uniforms, loaded on full gear, transformed into human mules, and marched ten miles. A pleasant enough circular route, if, say, you didn't happen to be weighed down with 35 pounds of gear. The route eventually brought them back to the camp in time for lunch. After which a siesta would have felt like the right next step, but never mind that.

The Hungarians spent the next four hours in English language class. Their initial teacher, Stonewall Baker, a good old southern boy, greeted them the first day, his accent nearly impenetrable. "Ah'm heeah to teach y'all Ainglish," he drawled. Jozsi and Laci shot each other a look but managed not to burst out laughing. Their favorite and inadvertent English teacher was the group sergeant Billy Nolan. His mantra of stupid motherfucker and whatthefuck and kiss my ass and the like provided them an excellent colloquial base for Army communications.

Every three weeks they pulled KP. Before they knew what that was, they'd imagined it a special benefit, like R&R. Learning the truth disabused them of that pleasant fantasy.

"Kitchen Patrol," Jozsi said, with disgust.

"Maybe we get to eat a lot," replied Laci, hanging on to positive thoughts.

Jozsi disagreed. "It can't be good, not a chance."

KP was their first real experience of clear divisions in the Army's caste system. White soldiers peeled potatoes and handled mess hall duties. Black soldiers handled kitchen clean up: scrubbing dishes and pots and pans. Hungarian soldiers did the down and dirty work of cleaning out garbage cans and grease traps and other stinky tasks.

"We are lower than the Negroes," Laci shook his head sadly.

"They were here first," Jozsi observed. "The new guys are always at the bottom of the barrel." Still it bothered him. He, a university student, considered less valuable than the least educated of the whites or blacks. "It ain't raht," he said, imitating Stonewall.

After they'd survived four weeks of Army steamrolling, Captain Kessler invited them to join him at the Officer's Club where General Joseph Stilwell, then Brigadier General of the First Army, was scheduled to appear.

Jozsi crowed about the invitation to Laci. "If we get a chance to brag about Kessler in front of the General, we'll be in fat city for the rest of training. This General is a big deal."

"Will it get us out of training?" Laci asked. "No? Then what's the point?"

"Drinks on the Captain, isn't that good incentive?"

"You are a wise man, *haverom*," Laci nodded. "Alex would be proud."

The day of the important visit, Jozsi and Laci met Captain Kessler at his office where he practiced his speech, and asked Jozsi to prepare a few words to say on behalf of the Hungarian recruits. By this time, Jozsi spoke and understood enough English to be able to communicate fairly well with the Americans.

That night, the Captain picked up the two in his 1957 Chevy Convertible. Laci's grin stretched ear-to-ear, though Jozsi tried to play it a little cooler. But this was their first time in a convertible and it was a thrill. Jozsi felt like he was starring in one of the American movies he'd seen at the Cultural Center in Budapest. All he needed was a buxom babe by his side. The warm, humid Carolina air, the muffled light of dusk, gave the drive a dreamy feel. Jozsi leaned his head back, admiring the tops of trees and clouds as they coasted along newly tarred road. Exiting the car, Jozsi whispered to Laci, "Remember what I said about riding around in big cars?"

His friend squeezed his arm, and spoke under his breath. "For the rest of my life, I'll regret not being born your twin," he looked admiringly at the car. "I say yes to more of this."

Captain Kessler had reserved a table near the speaker's stand. As they took their seats, Jozsi observed officers around the room glancing quizzically in their direction, no doubt wondering what the hell two privates were doing seated at a special table in the Officer's Club. General Stilwell entered to a standing ovation; his thin line of a mouth curving into a smile so brief it was eclipsed in an instant. Captain Kessler rose to welcome the general to their table, and eyebrows went up around the room as the esteemed general was introduced to two lowly privates. Soon all but Laci were deep in a conversation about the Hungarian Revolution, Laci too tongue-tied to do more than nod in agreement with whatever Jozsi said.

General Stilwell admitted that the American administration had badly let the Hungarians down, leaving scores of innocent civilians to die on the streets of Budapest. "If the politicians had asked me about the decision to intervene or not, you young men would still be in Hungary, living free of occupation."

Jozsi told the general that the Hungarian people had great respect for him, and that he expected someday Stilwell would be as admired and honored as General MacArthur. The general wondered how news of his exploits had reached university students in Budapest. Jozsi described his days of soaking up movies at the American Cultural Center — a number of the American war movies shown there had been about China, The Flying Tigers and Stilwell. The General became an icon after the war and by the time Jozsi was a regular at the Center, although the movies were dated, to a young Hungarian man, each film was a magic telescope into a world beyond their borders. Yes, Laci thought, Jozsi's knowing a lot about General Stilwell was coming in very handy indeed.

Stilwell returned the admiration, remarking on the courage the Hungarians had demonstrated in standing up to the biggest army in Europe. Captain Kessler was beaming, pleased at how well the Hungarians were getting along with the general; his spirits lifted also by knowing the other officers in the room had to be green with envy.

General Stilwell wanted to know how they were doing on the base and asked if everything was satisfactory. Jozsi could not believe his ears, the general asking *them* if things were satisfactory! He assured Stilwell everything was just fine, thanks to Captain Kessler, who was going out of his way to make good soldiers and American patriots out of them. Laci finally managed to say a few words in agreement, eventually stuttering his way to silence. The pressure of the General's penetrating gaze was too much for him; he'd much rather be a fly on the wall.

After dinner, the General strode to the speaker's stand, the assembled hushed and expectant. He was known as a tough, acerbic leader, but one who valued and respected the soldiers; one all expected to go down in the history books as an important figure, his leadership and dedication legendary. Even the lowliest, impertinent private knew it wasn't every day you came face-to-face with history, but the officers were especially rapt. Their goal was to be like him, and here he was, right in front of them. Not a word or movement went unnoticed.

As General Stilwell addressed the dining room, he talked about the strength and perseverance of the soldiers, about what the country owed them in times of war and of peace. And then, surprising all, he talked at length about the Hungarian Revolution. He even introduced the two freedom fighters to the gathering, closing with, "In conclusion, gentlemen, this is what we want to be known for: courage and dedication to our country." With that, he motioned for Jozsi and Laci to stand, then led the crowd in a round of applause. Laci blushed, while Jozsi thought of his father and how proud he'd be to see a room full of American soldiers applauding his son.

They saluted the general in parting, he saluted them back, reached to shake hands, and then headed back to his command center, leaving Captain Kessler practically floating on air and in the mood to buy many rounds at the club that evening. They toasted Kessler for the introduction and the drinks, he toasted them for speaking highly of him to the general, and then they quit toasting and got down to serious drinking. Captain Kessler set a good example for the enlisted men by managing to stride gallantly out of the club after imbibing for hours. "Good night, men," he saluted from the door, and carefully marched away, entirely pleased with himself and the evening.

The captain rewarded them for their praise by handing them several two-day passes for weekend trips to Columbia; their master sergeant explained to the others that the two needed to mix with the locals to advance their language skills. The master sergeant also insisted the two bring him a carton of cigarettes each time they returned. A small price to pay Jozsi thought. The sergeant could easily have upped KP duty for them in annoyance at their special treatment but instead chose to benefit himself. Is this the American way, Jozsi wondered? Considering that the two were from a group looked upon as the bottom of the barrel, beneath even the black men, their special treatment raised a few eyebrows, but most soldiers simply shrugged. The ways of the army were more wisely endured, not challenged.

~~~

The months crawled by at Fort Jackson, with one interruption — after three months they were sent to Fort Benning for parachuting school. Jozsi got to re-live his escape experience over and over, with better results this time. He aced the tests. For Laci, who was not wild about heights, it was a nightmare.

"I don't get to shoot and I have to drop thousands of feet," he'd grumble. "What is the fun in that?"

"I have a feeling you'll be going bang-bang soon enough," Jozsi replied.

Eventually, their nine-month ordeal came to an end. They'd survived Special Forces training and were assigned to an infantry battalion, though where they'd be sent remained a mystery. Captain Kessler took them to the Officer's Club to celebrate. He'd grown fond of the two, and not only because they doled out a steady stream of compliments. Stonewall Baker again expanded their vocabulary by muttering "brown-nosers," when he overhead them sucking up to Kessler. Only with his accent it sounded like brown-nossah; it took Laci quite a while to properly finesse the phrase.

Well into the celebration, Kessler asked them where they'd like to go for their overseas assignment; he could arrange to make their dreams come true. Perhaps it was due to too many cocktails, but a poster for a production of *Madama Butterfly* he'd once seen in Budapest popped in Jozsi's mind and his thoughts drifted to the Far East. He would come to wish he'd known a whole lot more about that part of the Far East — specifically about the brutal Korean terrain and climate — because when Captain Kessler said, "In that case, how about Korea?" the Hungarians agreed. Laci looked a little concerned, but when Jozsi said, "The girls will show us good times," he threw his hands up in a 'why not?' gesture and their destination was set.

Captain Kessler had good news to share. General Stilwell was promoting him to major after which he would be heading to Panama. Stilwell would soon be assigned to the Far East, so Jozsi and Laci would remain under Kessler's command. Before they got too bleary-eyed, Kessler handed them an envelope and asked Jozsi to read the contents out loud. The two were being promoted to private first class as of the first of December. Cause for more celebration. Jozsi wished he could share the news with his parents; Laci wished he still had parents to share the news with. They were each glad to have the other.

Within weeks they were on their way to New York to enjoy the Christmas holiday, before heading across the country to their next home: Fort Lewis, in the state of Washington. They hopped off the bus in Passaic, New Jersey, where some Hungarian refugees they'd met in Italy had settled.

They were soon ushered into the *Hortobagy* — the word meant mirage. It felt like a mirage of home, so exactly did the decor resemble any number of dining spots in and around Budapest. The two waved a little money around and made fast friends, buying rounds of beer and leading the crowd in traditional Hungarian songs. Some of the younger men, impressed by their success in the Army, wanted to know what it would take to join. Jozsi's eyes lit up. Within seconds, he had a plan.

The next morning, he and Laci gathered a group of nervous young men and trooped them down to the local recruiting office. They managed to help sign up ten men, co-signing as their character references. For each recruit the two received a hundred dollars. Laci had to admit that Jozsi had not lost his touch. "Alex would approve," he said with a smile while divvying up the loot.

~~~

On a chilly January morning, 1959 the year, they boarded a plane for Washington and gawked all the way across the country. They had no idea America was so big, it felt like they were flying over Hungary again and again and again.

The Fort Lewis company commanding officer welcomed them warmly, relaying that Captain Kessler had called ahead and given them a fine recommendation.

"We have good word of mouth," Jozsi said, glad for an opportunity to use a turn of phrase he'd recently learned.

"Not like in Germany," Laci answered under his breath.

The CO laid out their immediate future, saying he was looking forward to working with the Special Forces. In a couple of weeks, they'd be heading to Yakima Mountain for two months of winter exercise. From there they'd go to Korea with other soldiers from the company.

Jozsi masked his disgruntlement. "The last thing I want to do is spend two months trudging around a mountain range in snow up to my ass."

Laci agreed. "Hey, *haverom*, you're the one from the big city. I expect you to save our ass from snow and cold."

Jozsi tapped his head with a forefinger. "Working on it."

Following the head count at reveille the next morning, Lieutenant Dave Moore, the base recreation officer, stepped forward to ask if any of the soldiers knew how to carve a totem pole. Jozsi half-listened, daydreaming about walking through the meadow with Bandi for some odd reason. The horse came to mind now and then, which always made him worry that something bad had happened at home. Not that he was superstitious, he reminded himself. His ears perked up as the officer said something about totem-pole carving individuals and their inability to participate in the winter exercises. He poked Laci, "Raise your hand," as his own shot up. Laci gingerly raised his hand, his expression asking: what the hell are you getting us into now?

They were the only men with raised hands, which made Laci even more nervous. The officer told them to come to his office after breakfast, over which Jozsi reassured Laci. "Moore wants a totem pole, we'll give him a totem pole."

"What the hell is a totem pole?" Laci asked.

"That is a reasonable question," Jozsi answered, "but don't worry about the details. It's tall, like a telephone pole, and I went to school for that, I know what electricity is all about."

"You don't carve electricity," Laci observed, which even Jozsi had to admit was a good point.

The two sat across from Officer Moore at his desk while he asked what they knew about totem poles. He wasn't aware there *were* such things in Hungary.

Quickly Jozsi said, "We left Hungary many moons ago," which he hoped sounded Native American enough to impress Lieutenant Moore. "What would you like to know? What are your expectations?" he added quickly, throwing the burden of conversation back on the Lieutenant. Moore wanted them to carve soldiers from past American wars, symbolic of major achievements of American history.

That was enough of a lead for Jozsi. He rattled on about his grandfather having taught him to carve animals and faces and spoons and you name it. Old Hungarian tradition, he couldn't believe other Hungarians hadn't volunteered; everyone there grew up whittling and carving at their elders' knees. "It's European to know!" he exclaimed, having learned that tossing the word European into any sentence often had a positive effect.

Indeed, Lieutenant Moore was impressed enough to write orders excusing them from winter training and all other duties expected of soldiers on the base. Jozsi emphasized that the artistry involved in wood carving demanded a huge investment of time. They were told to move their gear to the base's carpentry shop and settle there for the project's duration.

As they lugged their duffel bags to the carpentry shop Laci said, "Oh, Master Carver Budai, one more time, how exactly do you make a totem pole?"

"Beats the shit out of me," Jozsi laughed, "but tonight we can look it up in the library." Laci just shook his head and headed off to find someone who could enlighten them right then. He returned a few minutes later, English dictionary in hand. He could barely understand the definition, but shoved it in front of Jozsi's nose. "I asked a guy on KP behind the mess hall. He gave me this." He paused dramatically. "Jozsi, we are in deep shit." And in Hungarian he described the task ahead as best he could.

Jozsi had to agree. The base library still seemed their best bet, a set of encyclopedias their first stop. From there they ferreted out books about the American Indians of the Northwest, Eskimos, and anything they could find on carving wood.

The next day, Lieutenant Moore summoned them to his office so he could elaborate on his concept. He wanted five soldiers, representing various campaigns waged. Jozsi took notes; Laci nodded approvingly as though he had a clue what Moore was going on about. He did not. The Korean War he'd heard about, his knowledge of the rest was sketchy.

Lieutenant Moore pulled out a sheaf of drawings and somewhat shyly spread them out on a table. Black and white drawings of the soldiers as he hoped they'd appear on the totem pole. Jozsi saw his timidity, and praised his artwork and vision, insisting they'd do their best to replicate these perfect representations. Encouraged by their success so far, if lies and bullshit praise were the measure (though truth be told the Lieutenant was not half bad as an artist) they set off for town to buy essential hand tools the carpentry shop lacked.

"We need an adze," Jozsi remarked, looking off in the distance, sliding back through time to memories of his grandfather's tool bench. "It's like a hoe, I think, only curved. It's a *fejsze*, that's what we need!" he exclaimed.

"I have to say again, I regret always that I didn't go to school in Budapest," Laci said, in awe at Jozsi's ability to pull their feet from the fire again and again. "But don't go on about the big cars yet. We haven't built the thing." They walked on in silence, and just before entering a hardware store, Laci said, "Aren't you going to mention the girls?"

"You know, I couldn't possibly say a word about that without mentioning diamond rings…and that would lead to the big cars." They laughed their way in the door.

That afternoon Lieutenant Moore and a few army engineers accompanied them on a search for the right tree for the totem pole. Jozsi had coached Laci: they had to appear and act knowledgeable as they searched. "Look smart about the trees."

"How the hell am I supposed to look smart about a tree?"

Jozsi demonstrated, walking around an imaginary tree and framing his hands as though sizing up the tree from various angles.

"Anyone looking at you will think you're out of your mind," Laci observed.

Their jeeps followed a rough road through deep woods till Jozsi called for a halt. Hopping out, the two walked slightly ahead of the group and within a short while they'd focused on a hundred-foot tall hemlock. They walked around it several times, holding thumbs up, hands out, putting heads together in conference, pretending to do anything at all that would impress the Lieutenant. They gave an okay to cut the tree down. Lieutenant Moore signaled to the engineers to lift their axes and begin chopping.

After the tree had crashed to the ground, Jozsi clambered over limbs to get close to the trunk and spotted cracks he thought large enough to be called defects. The Lieutenant concurred. This in fact was not the tree for them after all. They hopped back into a couple of jeeps and drove deeper into the forest. Jozsi signaled to stop and he and Laci strode ahead to another large hemlock and recreated their inspection performance.

"What the hell are we looking for? What was wrong with the other tree?"

"If we settled on the first tree they might think we were jerks who didn't know enough. This makes us look fussy, like experts."

Finally, Jozsi waved the Lieutenant and engineers over, pronouncing this the right tree, absolutely for certain. The engineers picked up their axes yet again and felled the tree. Jozsi once again made a big deal of examining the trunk. Yes, this tree was perfect. The engineers began sawing off branches, and Lieutenant Moore, pleased as punch, drove the trio back to the base. Men would be sent back with equipment to get the massive trunk to the base.

On the way, he asked Jozsi to explain what he'd been looking for in a tree. Jozsi nattered on about everything he could remember from an article he'd read in the library the night before, about how they needed to take into account shape and knots and splits and burls. Moore was impressed and increasingly excited by the thought of his drawings appearing in tree form. He wanted this to be a magnificent totem pole.

Jozsi saw an opportunity. He suggested that he and Laci would benefit greatly from a trip to Tacoma to do extensive research on Native American Indian methods of totem carving from Alaska to South America. A couple of hundred dollars for food, lodging, the bus, and possibly a few more chisels and useful books ought to be enough to cover it. The Lieutenant responded just as Jozsi had hoped, saying he could easily raid petty cash and get them on the road the next day.

In the morning, Jozsi sent Laci to pick up the cash, while he directed a group of soldiers placing the tree in a huge Quonset hut near the carpentry shop. Laci returned with the cash and they divided it up.

"Jozsi, you should have asked for more," he said, counting a second time.

"I'm not a farmer, but I think you start to milk the cow one tit at a time."

Laci looked shocked. "I'll shit if you tell me that you used to work on a farm."

"My friend, I'm one of the chosen ones who had to do everything in order to go out in the world and help people less fortunate, such as yourself. Now you know why I'm walking the earth."

Laci rolled his eyes. "Oh, great Master, would this money buy my way to freedom?"

"You may keep your money, my servant. I have big plans…for you to help make me rich!"

Laci faked a punch at Jozsi, and they clasped arms, in good spirits at how well they were doing at Fort Lewis.

~~~

The carving turned out to be easier than expected, and in its way, pleasurable. They spent five hours a day working with the wood, then wet their whistles in the beer hall for another five. "A finely balanced day," Jozsi called it. He'd discovered that you could have a hangover, but as long as you kept an eye on your fingers, the work would not suffer and no blood would spill.

After nearly 60 hours of whittling, chiseling, carving, shaping, painting, and all around tending to the wood, the totem pole was ready to be raised. By that time, Jozsi felt like he was married to the huge hemlock. "She's invading my dreams," he confided to Laci.

"She?"

"I spend too much time touching it to call it a he," Jozsi said as he idly caressed a smooth patch of bark.

The totem pole went in the ground a week before the troops returned from winter exercises. They made sure not to finish their work any sooner than that, lest Lt. Moore get some bright idea to order them to report to Yakima for the final stretch.

They'd used brilliant red, bright white, and shiny black, to outline eyes and figures, and hats, bandoliers, feathers, and any other details needing prominence. The colors gleamed in the sun when they raised the pole. With the help of a large crane, they placed the totem pole in a spot where it would forever commemorate 180 years of the 12th Infantry's battle history. A rifle stretched wide at its peak. The Native American that Lt. Moore had carefully sketched was the highest of the figures, representing the 12th's role in opening the Western frontier. Beneath him, an infantryman from the war of 1812, followed in turn by a Civil War veteran, a Spanish-American campaigner, and a World War Two infantryman parading down the pole to the ground.

Lt. Moore gave Jozsi and Laci the rest of the week off, insisting only that they get back to Fort Lewis before the group returned from Mount Yakima. He wanted the sculptors to witness the soldiers getting their first glimpse of the totem pole. Laci literally kicked up his heels at this news, so ready was he for girls and booze and nightlife. Tacoma was their first stop, but after a couple of days they struck out for the even brighter lights of the biggest city around: Seattle.

"This is more like it," Laci said, eyes bugging at women and bars and shops and restaurants as they wandered the city streets. Within hours, they'd found a tavern frequented by Hungarians who'd arrived in Washington by way of Vancouver. And four of them just happened to be from Budapest. Laci watched closely to see how Jozsi would cope with meeting his equals, at least in terms of city slicker smarts. They settled in to drink and compare notes on life outside of post-Revolution Hungary.

Eventually one of the men leaned close to Jozsi and in low tones asked if he'd like to buy some Hungarian currency: one hundred *forint* bills in exchange for dollars. Jozsi assumed that after the Revolution the Hungarian government might have changed the currency system, but he simply could not remember hearing anything specific. He would be taking a risk. But then, these four probably didn't know one iota more than he did. Laci watched Jozsi's face, saw the wheels turning, but couldn't read whether the wheels were turning happily or with concern.

Finally, Jozsi spoke with an authoritative tone that Laci could never hope to master. He shared that he'd been debating whether to tell the four, but as they were Hungarian brothers, he'd decided to give them the latest inside information. They were all ears. So was Laci.

Jozsi explained: Hungarian currency had already changed and *forints* would only be valuable as collector's items sometime in the distant future...maybe. But then again, maybe not. Having recently won a bit of cash in a poker game and feeling kindly toward these fellow countrymen, Jozsi announced he'd be willing to take the briefcase off their hands for a fraction of its value. He flashed them his "good guy" smile. Laci figured Jozsi had a plan, but for the life of him, he couldn't see any good side to buying worthless currency.

The men moved away from the table in various permutations, talking and arguing amongst themselves, returning to study Jozsi through narrowed eyes, trying to figure the odds. Jozsi pushed back from the table, saying how nice it was to see his brothers in a foreign land, and followed by Laci, bellied up to the bar for "just one more." Laci muttering, "I hope you're about to impress me with your wily ways."

The men at the table continued to argue, then fell silent when the tallest among them rose to step outside. He was back within seconds, toting a weathered leather briefcase. He placed it on the bar stool next to Jozsi, opened it, and told Jozsi to make him an offer. Jozsi reached down to make certain that stacks of cut-up papers didn't lay beneath a camouflage top layer of hundred-*forint* bills. He estimated the pile was worth close to ten thousand dollars, but kept his expression neutral. He reached into his pocket and pulled out five twenty-dollar bills, telling the tall man, "It's the best I can do, considering this money is no longer in circulation." He clasped his hands in front of him like a priest, with a wistful I-wish-I-could-do-more expression on his face.

The tall man turned to his compatriots. They began complaining the deal wasn't good enough and insisted on more money. Jozsi shrugged nonchalantly, still friendly smiles and easy-going charm, tossed down the rest of his beer, walked out the door, waving goodbye and calling out a friendly farewell, *"Viszontlátásra!"* Laci hustled after.

The four Hungarians caught up with them a block later and told Jozsi he had a deal. Jozsi insisted on checking the briefcase one more time to make certain they hadn't replaced the money with cut papers — which is what he would have done, no question. Following the transaction, the four walked quickly back toward the tavern as Jozsi encouraged Laci to walk even more quickly away from it.

Laci muttered, "Have you lost your mind? Why the hell would you want to lug around all that shit money for the next 50 years? I don't want to be part of this stupid deal. At long last, I am seeing you get suckered!"

When Jozsi had had enough of his complaints, he said, "Laci, what makes you think the Hungarian government will change their currency?"

Laci, wound up like a top, shouted, "Jozsi! You told them in the bar they'd *already* changed it!" Jozsi smiled. Laci stopped in his tracks. "Son of a bitch."

"You got it, my friend," Jozsi grinned. "You see, they're from the other part of Budapest, the suburb of Chepel. Once they told me how smart they were, well, let's just say I used to sell people in Chepel old razor blades as brand new and they couldn't tell the difference." Laci shook his head in wonder yet again at his good fortune in having teamed up with such an urban shark.

And as things turned out, the Hungarian government never did get around to changing their currency. Jozsi and Laci began sending money to Hungary every month, Jozsi to his parents, Laci to his uncle and aunt; the equivalent of a month's pay for the average worker. Later, when

Jozsi began to hear from his friend Ferenc — once he'd figured out a way to sneak mail out of the country, unread, uncensored — he learned exactly how much that money had meant to his parents. After Jozsi's escape, Zsigmond made certain that Jozsi's father, Matyas, could never hold onto a job. Matyas would be hired and once Zsigmond got wind of the hiring, bam…a week later he'd be let go for one ridiculous reason or another. Ferenc wrote that Zsigmond had bragged about doing this. It had eased Jozsi's guilt to be able to help them, and ramped it back up to know how Zisgmond was exacting revenge for his escape.

~~~

After a raucous week in Seattle, the two returned to Fort Lewis and the business of getting ready for their journey to Korea. Every morning they reported to the hospital for shots for the trip. Shots so powerful they had to collapse on their beds for the rest of the day in order to recover enough strength and will power to return the following day for still more shots. It was mind-boggling how lousy the Army could make you feel while trying to help you remain healthy.

They dragged themselves to seminars about Korean customs, history and traditions; learned about Korean geography, food, weather, saw pictures of the place they would be stationed. All Jozsi could concentrate on was his stomach and how it would withstand the hell of another ocean voyage. He confessed his concerns to Lt. Moore who calmed him, promising that compared to crossing the Atlantic they'd find the trip across the Pacific a gentle one. "Think crossing the lake to grandma's house," he said reassuringly. Jozsi slept better than he had in weeks, deciding that once in a while it might be okay to admit your fears.

Two days before departure, a new soldier — Texas Hank his moniker — joined the group assigned to the Far East. He'd just been released from jail, his sentence shortened in exchange for agreeing to sign up for the Army's Korean adventure. A hustler, Jozsi thought on first meeting, and sure enough, Hank had been jailed for illegal gambling. By the end of the day he'd asked Jozsi if he could borrow a few bucks, promising to pay it back first thing in the morning, and with interest.

"If I give you twenty bucks, what do you have for collateral?" The soldier aimed his pointer finger straight up, said, "Hold it right there," and sped over to his barracks, returning moments later with a thick book — his stamp collection, twenty years in the making. Jozsi didn't believe that for a second, the guy had probably won it in a card game, but figured it was worth at least twenty dollars no matter what and handed over the cash.

At the next morning's roll call, no Texas Hank. The Tacoma police had nabbed him again. Laci made fun of Jozsi for getting stuck with a fat book of stamps, but Jozsi calmly swore he'd eventually have the last laugh. "Stamps from all over the *world*," he emphasized just to annoy Laci. "Worth way more than twenty dollars."

The morning of May 15th, a warm steady breeze at their backs, the two boarded a bus to Seattle's Navy base where the ship to Korea awaited them. They were a little sorry to leave the northwest after it had been so good to them. What lay ahead in Korea would likely be far less enjoyable. They were not wrong in thinking so.

17

Korea, Exit Left, Solo

The small plane cut through a cloudbank and Jozsi narrowed his eyes to blur the barren Korean flatlands and mountains. They'd had two perfect weeks in Hong Kong, reveling in long nights of carousing, inhaling the abundance of the city, its smells, lights, colorfully dressed inhabitants.

A few nights prior, lounging in a hot tub, waiting for their girlfriends of the night to disrobe and join them, Laci had turned to Jozsi, and earnestly announced, "This is the way life was meant to be for the both of us." He'd thanked Jozsi for the deal he'd made with the firm, for bringing him along, teaching him, looking out for him. "I want to learn," he'd said, "I want to know how to negotiate like you."

"You stick with me," Jozsi replied, surprised by Laci's demeanor, "you'll keep learning. When you're born poor in the city you learn how to survive. It's like eating, like breathing. Streetwise beats professor learning any day. I wasn't born poor, but the war came, we lost so much. And then I met people who scrambled from the start. These kinds of people, they know what they want and how to get it. Most of them, not much schooling, never worked a regular job in their lives, they have their own system of graduating from one level to the next." He had stroked the bare arm of his new companion who was settling into the hot tub, her long black hair pinned up, away from the water. "My friend, there is no short cut for teaching survival. I can only teach you what I have learned from experience. Because you turn a corner, on the next street you find new challenges you never thought of. Such is life."

"I have hope, then, to continue learning at your side," Laci replied, and with that the two had turned their attention to their companions and other forms of communication.

Now, Jozsi's heart sank as the plane began its descent. They flew past a narrow strip of runway that looked like a black hair ribbon stretched across a balding head. Jozsi hungered to see flowering trees, foliage, bushes laden with berries, anything other than this godforsaken landscape. The beautiful women in Hong Kong had been a pleasant distraction, but returning to Korea brought Ulee's dark eyes and graceful way back to the front of his mind. She had been the surprise gift of his life in this part of the world, but that was over, and now he couldn't wait to be free of the 38th Parallel.

Laci leaned past Jozsi to look out the window as the plane circled back to approach the runway. "Remember when we were card sharks on the boat?"

"I was the shark, you were the pilot fish," Jozsi scoffed. You looked frozen with fear every time you bid." He thought back to the blanket they'd laid flat on the deck floor, the piles of nickels and dimes quickly transformed into dollar bills as the two raked in cash.

"That boat trip wasn't so bad; it was a lot better than pounding across the Atlantic." He thumped Laci on the arm. "We're doing okay, so far," and Laci nodded. It was astonishing, the miles they'd traveled since meeting in Gyor three years earlier: Hungary to Austria, Italy, Germany, North America; then Korea, Vietnam and now back to Korea. Jozsi pictured his Uncle Peter at the Budai dining table, holding a mask up, turning it this way and that, telling them about the place it was from, what the markings meant, how the object had come into his hands.

Jozsi closed his eyes, overwhelmed for a moment by how much he missed his family, and the smells, sounds and feel of home. When he opened them, the plane was seconds from touching down. With the jolt of wheels hard-jouncing the ground, he snapped back to the moment, but instead of dread felt a jittery charged excitement, a tingle in his veins as he wondered 'What's next?' Uncle Peter's stories had fed his imagination when he was a child, but now the world did. Who knew what was around the bend, but whatever it was, Jozsi was ready. He'd learned everything he wanted to know about Korea; time to move on. In ten short-timer days they'd be heading to the States.

Back at Camp Kaiser, Jozsi stood before the barbed wire fences separating North and South Korea, relieved he'd never again have to sneak across the border, never again be at the mercy of land mines strewn like crops by the North Koreans. Jozsi's work during his remaining days was to acclimate recent arrivals to the camp, and implant in their brains the best ways to survive excursions into North Korean territory they might have to make. He drilled the new soldiers on assembling footlocker-sized communications kits. He gave them quick fixes for broken equipment, tips on setting up relay stations across the border. He warned them of the brutal seasons and extremes, the result of being at the mercy of all those huge bare mountains. Whatever the temperature, there was no protection. Nothing to cool the blistering heat of summer, when 120 degrees is just another day. Nothing to stave off the shivery bitter of zero degrees but the clothes you layered on your body, and a military fur-lined hat with earflaps. Simply talking about the snow, which he knew was assembling like an invading army in the skies overhead, gave him a chill. The weather seemed colder by the hour as they headed from mid to late November.

Laci's assignment was to improve the soldiers' marksmanship and teach them how to care for their weapons. The weather was always a factor, but winter was the worst. Winter was a steady stream of dangerous problems. From the suffering incurred by numbed fingers, to the negative effects of freezing rain, rimes of ice, and lubricants and oils thickening to sludge on weapons. Bare skin frozen to metal, a gun's sluggish action, snowflakes wheedling their way inside the gun, any of these could get you killed. Under Laci's guidance they learned to pamper their weapons, scouring them for corrosion, because rust was yet another risk.

At night, the two repaired to the PX, a large hand-painted wooden sign — *Snack Bar* — hammered above the entrance. The small patio area in front of the PX, oddly set with cafe tables and chairs during summer, was now empty, abandoned. A lone skinny tree at one end of the Quonset hut stood sentry; a large rock placed in front of it made the tree, from a distance, look like an exclamation point.

As always, the minute Jozsi began walking from the barracks to the PX, various soldiers, especially the Hungarians, would appear from the barracks, or, catching sight of him, trot over from other areas of the miserable camp. By the time Jozsi entered the hut, he'd be surrounded by a small coterie. Jozsi had charisma, one of the Americans told Laci, who'd never heard the word but immediately understood its meaning. Life of the party was another phrase Laci had heard applied to Jozsi. His wit and sparkle, jaunty swagger, and easy smile drew others to him, men and women. Laci would never go after any girl Jozsi had his eye on, he knew better than to waste his time. Early in their friendship, Laci had snapped at Jozsi after watching yet another girl's attention veer away, now forever ripped away from his admiring gaze and hankering hands, "Whatever it is you put out, like bees to nectar, they swarm you." He spat on the ground in annoyance.

For soon-to-depart soldiers, the PX custom was to take the ribbon off the *Seagram's Seven* bottle and tie it on their hats. This signified they were short-timers, days away from heading back to the States. Jozsi wore his ribbon proudly, touching it each day for good luck. But during those nights at the PX, encircled by fellow Hungarians bantering in their native tongue, the liquor flowing, he'd momentarily forget his readiness to leave. He'd always loved to feel at ease among a crowd of friends, and in the warmth of the PX he was in his element. Of course, even blind drunk, stepping into the chilly night would instantly remind him that he wanted nothing more than to get the hell out of Korea.

~~~

A couple of days before their departure date, the two friends sat through a presentation on the benefits they'd receive if they would just re-enlist for one more year in Korea. Over drinks at the club their last night in Korea, Laci surprised Jozsi, who'd raised his glass in a toast to leaving. His running buddy hesitated for a split second.

"What?" Jozsi asked.

Laci gently lowered his glass, looked around, looked down, tugged on his ear lobe, and cleared his throat. "I'm thinking about re-enlisting." His voice was so low Jozsi cupped his ear so Laci would have to say it again, louder. He did.

Jozsi's flash-quick expressions said, 'What the hell?' any number of ways.

"I get another stripe, two-week's vacation in Japan, more money."

"No, no," Jozsi said in disbelief. "Are you out of your mind? You're making me nervous as a whore in church."

"Why not make the service my career? I don't have a trade. What else can I do?" Laci sounded surprisingly practical given his level of inebriation. "What am I good at? Running spies and shooting. Not a lot of openings for that…unless I join the mob. My Italian's almost good enough, no?"

Even Jozsi had to laugh. "But how will you get to ride around in big cars without me? No girls, no jewels, no life as we should be living it."

"I know, I know," Laci sadly shook his head.

Jozsi spent the rest of the night trying to talk his running buddy out of remaining in Korea. He didn't want to lose his friend, his moveable piece of Hungary. They'd been together most every day since leaving their homeland and the thought of not having Laci close at hand filled Jozsi with an unsettled, strangely insecure sensation, not that he'd ever admit it. Instead he kept reminding country-boy Laci how clueless he was, how smart he himself was, how lost Laci would be without him. But as they talked, Laci seemed more and more committed. "This life suits me," he'd shrug.

Finally, Jozsi gave in. He took Laci's hat from his head and untied the *Seagram's* ribbon, carefully replaced the hat, adjusting it just so, patting it in place, gently. And then they sentimentally toasted and hugged and arm-punched the night away until the bartender poured them a final shot, turned out the lights, and pushed the stumbling duo out the door.

The next morning, Jozsi loaded his gear into the Jeep that would take him to the plane. He was glad he'd packed the day before since he was so hungover he could barely stand. Only his great desire to leave Korea got him up and out the barracks door. Laci stumbled outside also, wearing threadbare boxer shorts, boots, and nothing else. He was practically glowing green around the gills. They again thumped and shoved and hugged each other, promising to stay in touch. He stared at the waving figure of Laci as the bus pulled away until, at last, his friend turned back to the barracks.

Once on the plane, Jozsi was almost glad for the nasty hangover, his need to doze so overwhelming it forced all emotion aside. The flight from Korea to Tachikawa, Japan, was brief, not long enough for his head to clear. He shook himself awake from a dream. He'd been at home, in the back yard of his parents' home, walking up from the swimming hole, his father yelling from a window, "Dodi, we have news, hurry." But he had no idea what the news was, because the plane jounced, waking him up. His sadness at leaving Laci seemed to have leaked over to the place inside where he missed his family. He dragged himself off the plane, and walked around the Tachikawa Air Base, hoping fresh air and movement would speed his recovery.

Within an hour, he was lining up to board a turbo jet back to the mainland. The other passengers were Air Force families, with various-sized children in tow, some fussing, some howling, some restless but silent. It felt odd to be among them, unnatural after so many years outside the scope of any kind of normal family life.

As Jozsi entered the plane a red-haired stewardess waved him toward the back of the jet.

"Gives you a break from the little ones," she said, ushering him into a seat in the last row. "I'm Fiona; I'll be your stewardess all the way to Oakland." He could have sworn she batted her eyes at him, but at that moment, all he cared about was getting more sleep. "Stretch out," she said, "I'll be back when I can take a break." She indicated the aisle seat, "Where I get to rest my bottom." She winked. Something to look forward to, Jozsi thought, and with that he scrunched into the two seats and conked out.

He woke occasionally, peering down the aisle to spy Fiona and the other stewardesses serving meals, collecting trash; sometimes pacing the aisle holding a fretful baby. If she needed to sit, she never said. When she'd catch his sleepy eye, she'd merely smile, or, if holding a baby, raise her eyebrows as though to say: will you take a look at this. She had an athletic, almost tomboyish quality — he'd bet anything she had older brothers. Eventually he sat up, rubbed his face, deciding he was clear-headed enough to eat and even to speak. Seeing him upright, Fiona made her way to the back of the plane, rummaged a bit, and brought forth a meal for her new seatmate. She plopped down and chatted companionably sotto voce while he ate.

"I like kids all right, but some of these mothers forget where they are and hand their babies over like I'm the nanny. They're used to ordering their Japanese help around, I guess. I don't think I look Japanese," she laughed.

"Fiona," he said, turning to look her fully in the face. Tiny freckles sprinkled across her nose and cheeks, so faint he hadn't noticed them until she sat close. Her eyes were a sea green color he'd rarely seen, her lips full, smile wide, bosom bountiful. Jozsi was feeling better by the second. He remained upright, leaving the seat available for his new conquest; she'd already begun touching his arm for emphasis, always a good sign. "I've never heard that name before."

"Oh, it was my gran's name. My father wanted to name me Patty, fit in better in America with a name like that, but my ma wouldn't hear of it. She's old country all the way, though she's been in America since she was a wee thing." Then up she jumped to tend to a passenger halfway down the aisle.

As the passengers quieted, Fiona settled in to talk with Jozsi. One thing led to another, and by the time they'd landed to refuel on Wake Island, they'd moved on to what Americans called heavy petting.

After a two-hour layover, everyone loaded back on, pulled down their shades and settled in to sleep through the night. Jozsi practically rubbed his hands in happy anticipation of further exploration, which was immediately forthcoming. By the time that they'd reached Honolulu air space, Fiona had offered to be his guide for the 24-hour Hawaii layover. "A-okay," he said, circling his thumb and forefinger.

After landing, the passengers stood waiting in the hanger while military police inspected duffel bags and suitcases for smuggled weapons or drugs. Free and clear, Jozsi found Fiona waiting at the gate, and within a short while they'd rented a cheap room in a motel off Waikiki's main drag.

That evening, Jozsi attended his first Hawaiian cookout. He thought he'd died and gone to heaven. They sat cross-legged on mats spread out on the sand, a huge bonfire sending sparks into the dark sky. A trio of young men played ukulele, guitar and drum, while lei-wearing beauties in grass skirts and skimpy brassiere-like tops, danced around the fire. Staring into the flames he thought of Jancsi, the grocer's son, and his tales of faraway places where people used tropical foliage as clothing. How had Jancsi even imagined such a thing from the inside of a little market in Hungary? He must have done a lot of reading, Jozsi thought, and then, but I am not reading about this, I am *living* it! He wished he could tell Jancsi all that he was seeing, and also that Laci was sitting nearby, drooling over women and crowing about driving around in big cars.

By late morning the next day, Jozsi and Fiona, both beaming, headed to the air force base to continue their flight to the States. At the plane, they learned it would lift off, minus a few passengers. A sergeant had been arrested for smuggling heroin in his duffle bag. His wife and two children had stayed behind in Hawaii to be near him, Fiona heard from another stewardess. The poor man had served 25 years of active duty and was hoping to put a down payment on a house. It was sad, Jozsi agreed, thinking of Laci for the first time in many hours, wondering where Laci's soldier-forever plans would lead him.

All of this Laci-free time kept sending his mind back to Hungary. He pictured the coffin he'd come to feel certain was Attila's, hidden beneath the branches. He wondered if he'd ever see it again. He pictured Erika with a sudden painful stab to his heart. He had no idea what had happened to her. Sandor, who could usually ferret out any kind of information, had no news. Or, Jozsi suddenly thought, maybe he had news but couldn't bear to share it. Jozsi sat on the plane and concentrated on feeling hope: that she was alive, married, pampering a couple of small, happy children. Non-crying children, he thought, as an ear-piercing wail ramped up a few aisles away.

A sense of childhood nostalgia was no match for Jozsi's one true wish: that Zsigmond had been shot through the head, or beaten to a mindless pulp. He couldn't bear to imagine what might have happened if Zsigmond had somehow learned that she was the Beast of Budapest. He could, however, sum it up, and in just two words: brutal death. Zsigmond's adoration of her would be trumped by embarrassment. And if not that, well, he didn't want his mind to go to alternatives either. The thought of Zsigmond forcing himself on Erika turned his stomach. He finally wrenched free of unpleasant images by compelling his mind to go to a more peaceful place: childhood summer visits to Ura where the most important things in his world were helping Matild, sneaking glances at Rebeka's breasts, and sitting on Bandi while pretending to be a soldier with the *Red Devils* Brigade. He fell asleep to the memory of leading the old horse through the ravine, wildflowers scenting the air, the Bukk Mountains looming in the distance. He awoke to Fiona's lips at his ear.

"Wake up, soldier," she whispered. "We're landing in Oakland soon and I only have a few seconds." She thanked him for the good time in Hawaii, wished him luck as he headed east to Fort Devens, and leaned in for one last kiss. Then she was gone to tend other passengers, his last view, her ass as she leaned down into a row.

Jozsi treated himself to one night in a hotel room so he could remember what it felt like to sleep in a good bed with decent sheets. He liked his room just fine, but he wasn't used to being alone, so restless, he settled in on a comfortable couch in the lobby. Watching people move through the hotel lobby was a relaxing pleasure. No uniforms in sight except his own, no war-weary expressions. With two months of vacation in front of him, he decided to get to know America on the ground. He would travel across country by bus, stopping to visit soldiers he'd met in Korea who'd finished their tours and were home. Jozsi's genial magnetism had reaped all kinds of invitations for "When you're back on the mainland." After purchasing a road map of America, he set about sorting through the invitations and plotting his course. He was more than ready for a break from regimented army life; hungry to learn everything he could about the customs of the country he aimed to embrace as his permanent home.

His first choice was Las Vegas, even though he didn't know a soul there. The guys in Korea told him it was like Mecca for Muslims, and that he must see it at least once in his lifetime. He spent the first day walking around, wandering in and out of brightly, blinkingly lit buildings. Entering a casino for the first time, he thought he might very well forget the rest of America and settle here the second the army let go of him. People were in high spirits; their outfits a circus of colors, ranging from unassuming to elegant, no matter what the time of day. And the air inside, he'd never experienced anything like it. He left the scorching heat of the street behind and entered a kind of physical nirvana, cool air immediately soothing over-heated pores. So, this was air-conditioning. If only they'd had some of that in Korea.

Rooms filled with tables, the sounds of chips sliding across felt, the gentle clacking as they were piled into small towers, the softer shuffling of cards, murmur of bets placed, ice clinking in glasses. It was intoxicating, all of it. He had no idea how to approach the tables, or what to do once he got there, and he did not want to make a fool of himself. He missed Laci; missed feeling the slicker, sharper of the two. He felt entirely off balance, until he saw a slot machine (he'd seen those in clubs in Korea) and his sense of equilibrium returned. Or maybe it was the bar waitress who caught his eye and smiled. He smiled back and suddenly felt on top of the world. Everything was good. He spotted a couple of other soldiers, made friends, and stayed up watching the live shows until three in the morning. They all agreed, this beat any USO tour they'd ever seen.

The next afternoon Jozsi settled in at a slot machine and began sliding silver dollars into the opening. A few spins later ten silver dollars clanged into the bottom receptacle. He tried again, again ten. Regardless of what showed on the slot machine window, his machine delivered ten silver dollars. He sat grinning like the cat that ate the canary, pouring dollars into his little bucket for a good ten minutes. But then two burly guys appeared at his side, as though straight out of a gangster movie. One said, "Soldier boy, it's getting a little too crowded in here. Why don't you take your bucket of coins and head outside?"

Jozsi assured them he was not feeling at all crowded, but before he could say another word, the two put their fingers under his uniform sleeves, twisting them enough to lock their fingers in the cloth. Then they lifted him to his feet, escorting him outside into 100-degree air. Nice way to treat a soldier, Jozsi thought. But he'd gotten the message and was relieved they hadn't taken his bucket full of coins. He counted out three hundred dollars. He could only figure that he'd been fortunate to find a malfunctioning slot machine.

At the next casino, he pocketed some of his winnings, and played the rest, ending up fifty bucks in the hole. He concluded this was a sucker's game and with that the magic of Vegas abruptly vanished. He grabbed his duffel bag and headed to the bus terminal, boarding a bus for Utah. Why Utah? It left in an hour and he was feeling nothing if not spur of the moment.

He wasn't ready to splurge on civilian clothes just yet, and also, wearing his uniform was paying off. Most people were polite to him, respectful, and he'd already had a couple of civilians pay for his meals, citing a son or brother or nephew in the service, offering sympathy for a soldier's tight budget. This must be how it felt to fit in, in America.

The bus drove through the night and he woke to find a troop of six first-time cub scouts and two den mothers piling onto the bus. The boys were drawn to the soldier in the 8th aisle and he was soon surrounded, peppered with questions about where he'd been, what he'd done, and where he was going. The den mothers were taking their little troop to Lake Utah for a weekend camping adventure. After brief exposure to Jozsi's winning smile and his way with the boys, they invited him along. Surprising even himself, Jozsi agreed. The boys were beside themselves: a real soldier who could teach them about survival in the woods, and one with an accent who'd come from across the ocean. This was something they could brag about for weeks. Where the fathers were, Jozsi didn't ask, they'd tell him if they wanted him to know.

An old farmer with a pickup truck was waiting at the bus and delivered them to a wooden shack by Lake Utah, promising to return Sunday afternoon to retrieve them. "If the bears don't get you," he warned, winking at Jozsi, who, for a second, looked concerned.

The boys and mothers settled into the shack with some agitation over who got a top bunk, who a bottom. Jozsi spotted a flat spot under a nearby tree and set about making himself a shelter with branches, and laying out his sleeping bag. He pulled his army hat out of the duffel so he'd look even more soldierly for the kids. In no time, they were studying how he'd put his shelter together, and then began roaming the area to gather wood for a campfire. Jozsi showed them how to trim and clean branches, creating 'v' shaped sticks for cooking their hot dogs. They helped him make a circle of stones to contain the campfire and protect the woods and animals from stray flames. He felt like a light-hearted kid again, as though he'd been sent back in time, to playing with Ferenc and the neighborhood boys, before the war, before the fear, before the communists had put his country in a chokehold.

As the sun fell below the tree line, they began to cook their hot dogs. A few mishaps occurred, hot dogs incinerated on one end, a little too cool and pink on the other, but no one complained. The boys huddled quietly, listening to the snapping firewood and Jozsi's voice spinning out one ghost story after another. Then, making ghostly sounds and letting out an occasional scream, the boys piled into the shack. Jozsi loaded more wood on the fire and stretched out under the starry sky, content to be exactly where he was. It had been so long since he'd been able to relax and enjoy being in the woods. The fear of discovery and the hell of the Korean climate had wiped out all memories of nature as a place of pleasure.

Eventually, Martha, the mother with bobbed dirty blond hair and a slight lisp, joined him at the fire. She wanted to know more about where he'd come from, but mostly she just loved his accent and wanted to hear him say, well, anything. And then didn't he want to watch the moon rise over the lake? And then didn't he want to go for a moonlit swim? She peeled her clothes off and jumped in the lake. He hesitated; she was married after all, her little boy a matter of yards away. But she playfully taunted him from the water and who was he to say no? That would be rude and he was nothing if not a gentleman. He stripped and in he dove, coming up for air to find her at his side, ready, willing and able to assist in his moonlight swim.

Americans are the friendliest people, he thought, once she'd returned to her bottom bunk in the shack. Jozsi lay on his makeshift bed, looking up at the stars, the same stars he used to look at from his bed in Ura. He thought again of the coffin, of walking in the woods with Erika, of the moment he unearthed the corner and brought her hand down to feel the thing he'd discovered. He wondered if she had ever told anyone about the coffin, about where it was. No, he thought. She hated the government as much as he; nothing, not even torture would tempt her to betray his secret, she would take it to her grave. He pictured her, exhausted but fierce, sitting in Zsigmond's apartment, machine gun resting against her knee. He would never meet anyone like her again, that he knew. That she was alive was enough to hope for. If he should somehow be able to see her, that would be a miracle, but he'd seen too much misery to even dare hope for such a blessing.

The camping weekend continued pleasurably, with another late-night invitation from Martha. He felt himself to be a bit of a scoundrel but he was a young, able-bodied soldier, and after all, he hadn't exactly pursued her. Sunday, the farmer returned and trucked them back to the bus station where the boys hugged and then saluted Jozsi, and Martha hugged him too, for a little too long, he thought, but what could he do, shove her away? Her son was too preoccupied to notice anything and the other mother clearly wasn't perturbed by anything that had gone on; in fact, he had the feeling she wouldn't have minded a moonlight swim of her own. Jozsi waved to all as the bus headed west into the sunset and then turned to the task at hand: a ticket for the next bus to Casper, Wyoming, to visit one of his favorite soldiers.

~~~

Yokum, Randall to his mother, had served under Jozsi's command. Not the sharpest knife in the drawer, but a hard worker and a good soldier. Jozsi had been nice to him, regularly allowing access to his little sergeant's office. Yokum would close himself in to write long, heartfelt love letters to his high school sweetheart without being ribbed to death by the others. He'd made Jozsi promise to visit the Yokum family ranch if he ever came anywhere near Wyoming. Jozsi didn't bother to call ahead; he just hopped on the bus, asking the driver to make sure to wake him when they got to Casper. If things didn't work out, he'd simply catch the next bus heading east.

Dawn, Casper, and the driver hollering, "Soldier, you'll end up in Colorado if you don't hop to," and he was off the bus before being fully awake. He waited at the bus terminal till it seemed a reasonable hour to call, dug out Yokum's number and with just enough change to make a two-minute call, dialed. A woman answered, and after struggling to make out his accent, recognized his name.

"Oh, Yokum's friendly sergeant!" she cried. "You're in Casper? You get yourself across the street to the diner and I'll be there in a flash." He had no idea who she was. Yokum had sisters, but Jozsi couldn't remember much about them. Maybe it was his mother. Anyway, she was friendly and on her way to get him, and that was enough. He followed her orders and sat near the cash register at the diner flirting with the counter waitress while he ate. The bell above the door tinkled and someone tapped him on the shoulder.

"Are you Jozsi?" Joe-zee. "Am I saying it right?" He helped her wrap her tongue around his name, instantly thinking lascivious thoughts about that tongue. She was tall, with long, almost platinum, blond hair pulled back in a ponytail. Tanned, fit, a dream girl, he thought, forgetting all about Erika and every other woman he'd ever been with. Yokum didn't look anything like this. Maybe they had different fathers. Anyway, there she was, wearing shorts, sandals, and the kind of striped t-shirt a boy would wear. She wore it well.

"I'm Debbie," she tilted her head. A real American name. Yokum was the eldest, then Debbie, then the two younger girls. No wonder Yokum took to Jozsi, he wanted a brother.

Debbie knew everything about him; Yokum had told her what a great guy he was — he would be so happy to hear his favorite sergeant had come to visit. They were short a couple of hands and Yokum was spending the day out checking on livestock; he wouldn't be back till sunset. "I hope you won't mind hanging around with me," she said, a mischievous smile on her face.

"It will be my pleasure," Jozsi reached for her hand, bringing it slowly to his lips. He could see her melting like an ice cube in a sizzling hot frying pan.

She sighed dreamily, "We don't see manners like that around here." Then she picked up his duffel bag like it weighed nothing, threw it in the back of the truck, and drove them out of town so fast she might have left her shadow behind.

She was not shy; he liked that about her right away. She talked a blue streak and by the time they turned onto the ranch driveway she'd talked him into accompanying her on a trek to check on livestock further out on the ranch the very next day. "Randy will be sore at me for stealing you away, but it's my turn to ride out to the south pasture and I'll bet you've never done anything like that before, and you should because it's really beautiful out there and I'll bet you've never seen anything like it." He was breathless just listening to her. She made everything sound easy and fun and he was more than game for that.

The ranch took what was left of his breath completely away. A huge, solidly built wooden house stood in the middle of nowhere, with land stretching out in all directions. From the backyard, he looked out at majestic mountains hundreds of miles away, the air so clear you could see the snow line. No one was at the house when they arrived. Jozsi immediately spotted his own face hanging on a hallway display of photographs. He stood before an enlarged snapshot: he and Yokum in Korea, standing beside one of the tanks at the 38th Parallel.

"G.I. want ice-cold beer," Debbie imitated a Korean accent. Jozsi turned, startled, to find her holding out a frosty bottle. By lunchtime, when Paw Yokum hurtled down the drive in a black Ford pickup, Jozsi had drunk his beer, unpacked his duffel, cleaned up, and gotten the lay of the land.

"Who do we have here?" In strode a broad-shouldered man with two of the hugest, strongest-looking hands Jozsi had ever seen. The nickname Paw had to have come about because of his bear-size hands. "I know that face!" He reached out a hand, then led their guest out to the porch as he directed Debbie to fix lunch. He told Jozsi to call him Paw, same as everyone else, and thanked him for all he'd done to look after his one and only son in Korea, recounting a whole list of kindnesses Jozsi had forgotten ever doing for young Yokum. "I don't mind telling you, my heart was in my throat the whole time he was away," Paw said. Jozsi thought: I should have done even more for that boy.

Paw dragged Jozsi off after lunch to have a look at the barn, the horse paddocks, livestock pens, everything. The younger girls and Mrs. Yokum came home from running errands in town. They bustled off to fix dinner and set the table, while Paw and Jozsi sat on the porch waiting for Yokum to ride in from the range.

"He'll come from behind the house, but he always rides around front to let his horse graze out this way," he pointed to a paddock off to the right side of the house. Sure enough, as the sun lowered, they heard Yokum talking to his horse as he dismounted and walked him toward the paddock.

"Say, soldier," Jozsi called out. Yokum's eyes widened and he looked confused, like he didn't know whether to salute or give Jozsi a hug.

"Holy smokes," he hollered, "You're here! Hang on there, Sarge, let me get this horse squared away." He pulled off the saddle, threw it on the fence railing, slipped off the bridle, hung that on the saddle horn, and nudged his horse into the paddock, thumping him gently on the rear. He closed the gate and ran to Jozsi, practically knocking him down he was so excited. Hugs, salutes, giddy laughter and a few tears later, Jozsi managed to get a word in.

"It's good to see you, soldier," he whispered in Yokum's ear.

"I told 'em, I told 'em you'd show up one day, just like you did, just out of the blue." Then he raced over to the ranch hand bunkhouse to tell the crew there was going to be a wingding party that night to celebrate the arrival of a special friend.

After supper, all the cowboys and ranch hands made their way over to the big porch to hear stories about Korea. Jozsi felt like a hero. He had long dreamed of driving an American jeep down the streets of Budapest and into his neighborhood, the streets lined with cheering, applauding people. For the time being, this would do. The beers went down easy, and a few cowboys brought out guitars and fiddles and began singing Roy Rogers songs. Jozsi didn't know any of the words, but he smiled as though he did. And when they started playing barn dance tunes and Debbie pulled him to his feet to dance to some crazy fiddling, he gamely hopped about and swung her around, not caring one bit that he looked like a big clumsy fool.

Morning came way too soon. Debbie pounding on the door, hollering, "Hurry up and eat breakfast, we have to get a move on, we have a long ride ahead of us." Yokum only agreed to let her ride off with Jozsi because he'd promised to stay at the ranch for several more days. He brought Jozsi a small pile of farm clothes. "You'll scare the shit out of the horses, you try to mount one wearing your Army uniform."

"I never thought I'd be wearing these just to please the herd," Jozsi laughed, putting on blue jeans for the first time in his life.

Downstairs, he wolfed down leftover steak, along with eggs and home-fried potatoes. Yokum said, "Don't this beat Korea?" looking as pleased as Jozsi could imagine a person looking.

Outside, tied up to a railing in front of the porch, two horses stood, packed and ready for the trail. Jozsi told them he'd never been on a horse as big as the one whose reins Debbie held. She assured him Louie could carry him to the end of the world. Jozsi mounted the horse, dramatically making the sign of the cross. Yokum stood on the porch laughing his ass off. Debbie gracefully hoisted herself up onto her horse, Painter, and off they rode. About four hours into the day, Jozsi asked when they were going to turn around. "We'll never get back before sunset if we don't."

She looked surprised, "Jozsi, this is a two-day trip, remember?" He didn't let on that he *did* remember because his sore ass was begging him to change the plan. Plus, he hadn't seen a cow, horse or buffalo since they'd left the ranch behind. This was nothing like the movies. He felt every bump and jostle on the trail and promised himself he would never try to become a cowboy. This was nothing like being bareback on Bandi. It gave him even more respect for his father's riding life as a Red Devil.

Finally, they stopped to water their horses at a lake. Debbie said, "We can set up camp for the night here. You start gathering wood and I'm gonna ride over the hill there, see if I can spot some cattle." Jozsi was happy to oblige since his ass felt like raw burger. At least building a fire was something he was good at. The sun was setting fast and he couldn't see her in the glare as it dipped behind the hill. He hoped this wasn't some goofy western joke where you get abandoned and have to find your own way back. But soon enough, he saw her silhouette cresting the hill and he relaxed. Steak over an open fire; was there anything more delicious? He didn't think so.

The night was hot and sticky, and Debbie suggested they cool off in the lake. She stripped and dashed to the water, and Jozsi did the same, now firmly convinced that all American girls loved to swim naked in lakes. The rest of the night passed in exactly the way Jozsi had hoped. They dried off by the fire, and began to get more intimately acquainted. They opened their sleeping bags to make a cozy bed, his army camouflage green one on the bottom, her blue one on top.

The next day they continued, checking on cattle even further out on the range, and spending another romantic night by the lake. They took their time heading back to the ranch. Jozsi felt easy with her; they talked, and then fell into companionable silence for stretches. She hoped he'd stay a little longer than he'd planned. Wouldn't her parents mind them messing around? She shrugged; she was a grown woman and if it wasn't in their face, they wouldn't care. He could sneak into her room at night; no one would make a fuss. He mentally crossed a few soldiers and places off his list. He'd feel fine staying on here for a bit.

They got back to the ranch in time for supper and an even bigger gathering. Paw had invited local politicians and ranchers, photographers and storeowners, everybody he could think of, to hear another round of stories about the 38th Parallel.

In the days that followed, Jozsi helped with whatever needed doing. Paw was pleased their guest had farm experience. Jozsi fixed fence posts, learned how to brand cattle, and generally made himself useful. The rest of the time he tried to stay off a horse, his ass remained sore for days.

Jozsi figured Debbie had the pick of the litter in these parts, and Yokum let him know that every eligible and not so eligible bachelor for miles around was after her.

"But she's falling hard for you," Yokum confided. "I've never seen her so gone on anyone."

It was all very seductive: the ranch, the woman, the family. They weren't the Toths, yet he felt embraced and at home with them in a way that reminded him of life with the Toths. But his sore ass and restless heart wouldn't allow him to fool himself into thinking he would return. Yokum suspected as much. "I know you've got more years of active duty ahead of you, and I know you and Laci were involved in some other goings-on that weren't exactly part of normal duty. But if you ever decide this is the place for you, we'll be happy to see ya."

After a few weeks, Jozsi decided it wasn't fair to Debbie to stay any longer. He knew from Yokum she was more and more hopeful Jozsi would want to make a life there, with her. He broke the news to her the morning before he left. He didn't think he could handle looking at her sad blue eyes any longer than that. "I know," said Yokum. "Sometimes you gotta just rip the bandaid." He wasn't as dumb as Jozsi thought. "She's gonna be crying for days, but she'll be all right. Don't you worry about Deb."

Jozsi said goodbye to her in the barn, so she could turn to Painter for comfort as Yokum drove him away. It went hard, Debbie trying not to sob, but finally breaking down, her hands crossed over her aching heart. Paw and Mrs. Yokum didn't seem to hold anything against him, for which he was grateful. "I know you're a good man," Paw stated. "There are things you have to do in this world. I wish you luck." Mrs. Yokum was a practical woman; she gave him a big hug and a bagged lunch so he'd have something decent to eat on the next leg of his journey, and then went to try and talk some sense into her daughter. As she said to Yokum, "At least she had an adventure."

At the bus terminal, he and Yokum said their farewells. Jozsi promised to keep in touch. It was probably best for all that it was a promise he had little intention of keeping.

18

Fort Devens

The bus headed east out of Casper, and Jozsi's mind headed south, across the great ocean that separated him from Hungary, all the way to Ura and the coffin. It occurred to him this was becoming a coping strategy. Think about the mysterious object hidden by branches. Wonder if you'll be able to find it again. Wonder if you'll even be able to cross the border. Think about this object, not the people near it, not your family, not any of that. Sitting alone on the bus, no Laci to distract him, no fellow Hungarians to entertain, no enemy soldiers to capture, civilians to scam, girls to woo, just stretches of long empty time to catch up with himself. In the catching up, he realized that to quell the pain of saying goodbye, he'd immediately think further back to before the momentous goodbyes began, when goodbye meant see you soon, meant *szia*. He'd never minded goodbyes before; curiosity and love for the new made change feel good. And Jozsi did not like sentimentality. Life was what it was; you dealt with it. But fleeing his homeland, saying goodbye with no guarantee that hello would occur any time soon, or ever, had been different. Since then, he had moments where he could feel emotions burbling up, unbidden, from deep inside. Peaceful quiet time would ruin you, he thought ruefully, staring hard at the landscape, trying to turn his brain off. He pressed his palm against the bullet shell whistle that at the moment rested inside his pants pocket.

He decided it would be hard to beat his visit to Yokum, who'd been one of his favorites, not to mention the bonus of Debbie and their fine parents and the beautiful landscape. He mentally scanned the list of other soldiers who'd offered him berth. No more visits, he decided. He wasn't due to report to Fort Devens for six weeks. He'd head straight east to Boston, the nearest big city to the Fort, and figure out what to do once he got there.

When he arrived, after what felt like years on the bus, he lugged his duffel to the first cheap hotel he could find, then walked all the way to the end of Washington Street, just for the joy of walking. Before he had to make a decision about what to do next, he spied the colors of the Hungarian flag, the real one, hanging from the front of a restaurant down a side street. He looked up at the sign: *Nagybácsi Miksa's Place*, Uncle Miksa's. In he went.

He could tell right off that this was no five-star restaurant, but he didn't care that the place looked like it was cobbled together by hard-up refugees desperate to make a go of it, the place felt like home. A few men were spread along the bar, sharing a conversation from their various perchs. They turned as one when he entered, made note of the uniform, nodded respectfully, turned back to their conversation. Jozsi plunked himself on a stool and greeted the assembled. "*Sziasztok*," he said, and with that he was the center of attention. Where in Hungary was he from, how had he gotten out, how had he come to be wearing an American army uniform? And of course, he was not allowed to pay for even one of his drinks. These new friends made him feel right at home, his mood soared.

Upstairs, a room as large as the whole barroom held four pool tables and a few tables and chairs. He whiled away the afternoon between the two floors, sitting at the bar or shooting pool with other refugees who had escaped after the 1956 Revolution. Jozsi hoped to discover among them someone who knew someone he knew. Indeed, soon after five, up the stairs tromped a young man close to his age.

"Tibor!" Jozsi's pool opponent called out. "You're late. I had to start playing with this guy."

Tibor recognized Jozsi immediately, though it took him a few minutes to figure out why. "Were you around the university in Budapest?" Tibor asked. Jozsi was a little suspicious at first, but when Tibor mentioned he'd flunked a class he'd taken with a wild teacher named Alex, Jozsi figured that was a good sign. They laughed long and hard as Jozsi recounted his exploits with Alex in Rome. By the end of the night, Tibor had convinced Jozsi to check out of the hotel and instead come to his little apartment in Cambridge, where Jozsi could rent a bed for his six weeks in Boston.

"Cheaper than a hotel and more fun," Tibor grinned. He was impressed with Jozsi, all his experiences, his smarts and facility with English. "I can see you know how to do more than just survive," Tibor said. "We can help each other." Jozsi saw that Tibor could use help, although at least he was a bit more sophisticated than Laci. Tibor worked around Cambridge, cleaning rental apartments, making carpentry repairs, and doing other odd jobs. He hired Jozsi as his helper. "I don't want to do this forever," Tibor said. "I want more than to barely hang on in Cambridge."

Tibor's girlfriend, who had emigrated to the States from Ireland, wanted him to do more than barely hang on too, but not if that meant joining the army. She was at the age where her parents kept asking when did she plan on becoming "a settled lady." Tibor was kind and strong and would make good babies, she confided to Jozsi, who quickly warned his new friend he'd best be careful or he'd end up trapped in Cambridge forever. Not that Bridget was unappealing, far from it. She was a little plump, but in all the right places, with long thick black hair, and a sunny smile and nature. But since she belonged to Tibor, Jozsi busied himself with Iren, a classically trained pianist, slightly older, who appeared at *Nagybácsi Miksa's* weekend nights to play the upright piano that stood against the restaurant's back wall. She made fast friends with Jozsi the first time she laid eyes on him. She, too, let Jozsi know she was looking for permanence, for marriage. Jozsi pled his youth and lack of experience with women as reasons it was way too soon for him to settle down. After all, in the time since he'd fled Hungary, the many months on the road, in the Army, well, he'd missed out on a lot. Iren told him he could have fooled her, to which Jozsi replied he simply had natural talent. "A natural talent for lying," she retorted, raising her eyebrows, at which all Jozsi could do was nod. After all, she was correct.

The weeks passed happily enough and soon it was time for him to report to Fort Devens, about 50 miles west of Boston. Before he left, Iren worked hard to convince him that she could provide all the experience he needed to become a good husband. On his last morning, she commented that looking back at the night they'd just shared, she had to say there wasn't much room for improvement; he was as ready for marriage as any healthy man would ever be. Jozsi thanked her for the compliment, but said there was always room for improvement, and she needed some too. Iren heaved a solid couch cushion at him and told him to get out and stay out. Since he was on his way to Fort Devens, he was not remotely concerned by her annoyed rejection.

A raucous farewell dinner was held at *Nagybácsi Miksa's* that night, despite the likelihood that Jozsi would be back in Boston soon — Fort Devens was only an hour away. His fellow Hungarians lamented Jozsi's upcoming absence at the bar and pool table; as seemed to happen everywhere Jozsi went, he'd become an instant ringleader. Finally, Tibor and Bridget drove Jozsi to Fort Devens. For much of the ride, Tibor talked about how much he admired and would miss his new friend. Then he announced he'd begun seriously thinking of joining the Special Forces, so that he too could have the Army pave his way to citizenship. He couldn't come up with a better way to improve his situation.

Jozsi was surprised. "You must be crazy. Haven't you paid attention to any of my stories?" He smacked the dashboard repeatedly for emphasis. "All they will teach you in the Army is how to kill, and how to jump out of airplanes in the middle of the night, and how to climb mountains for days without food, and how to spend hot days in the Florida swamps fighting off snakes. Figure out another way."

"But, but, but," Tibor tried to inject himself into the middle of the tirade, but Jozsi was building up steam.

"No buts. The only reason I joined was because I had no other choice. And now Vietnam is next on the agenda. You know anything about what's going on between North and South Vietnam? No easy peace there; it will be ugly. Even the French got the shit kicked out of them. Tibor, I was in Vietnam, trust me, you don't want to go. I told you about Laci; he'll probably end up there. I'm worried what will happen, especially without me to look out for him. I'm sorry to discourage you, but I don't want you to think it's a great adventure when it's not, it's just plain awful." And with that, they fell silent until they reached the Fort Devens entrance, though Jozsi noticed that Tibor looked around excitedly as they drove past army jeeps and trucks, Quonset huts and barracks. It was late, the base quiet but for a few soldiers on their way from the PX to the barracks.

At the base office, Jozsi thanked them for the ride, grabbed his duffel and hugged them each. Bridget whispered, "Thank you," in his ear, grateful for Jozsi's attempt to discourage Tibor from signing up. Jozsi waved them off, pointing a finger at Tibor. "Do as I say, not as I do! And remember, next time I come to *Nagybácsi Miksa's*, supper will be on me." As they drove away he called out *szia*, Hungarian for see you later, and Tibor, having heard, tapped the horn in farewell.

~~~

That weekend, Jozsi hopped a bus and headed right back to Boston, arriving at *Nagybácsi Miksa's* in time for lunch. He settled in at his favorite table by the window for a big bowl of goulash, which Miksa brought him, along with an envelope from Tibor, and a glass of Jozsi's favorite wine.

"Tibor asked me to give you this wine before you start to read his letter." Jozsi had a sinking feeling. The letter was brief: "Jozsi, *baratom,* I know you think I'm crazy to follow in your footsteps, but I admire you and want to make something of myself. I want people to look up to me the way they look up to you. Even if I risk death in trying." Jozsi pressed the note flat on the table and shook his head no, no, no.

Jozsi and Miksa commiserated for a bit. Miksa, too, had tried to dissuade Tibor from enlisting. Jozsi had been planning to stay at Tibor's but now that was out. Miksa promised him a foldup cot could be his if he didn't mind sleeping in the pool room. It beat paying for a hotel room, Jozsi said, so Miksa stowed Jozsi's knapsack in his back office while Jozsi moved upstairs to the pool room to kick someone's ass in the game, the cue ball bearing the brunt of Jozsi's frustration over Tibor's stupidity.

When he next came downstairs, he found Bridget moping at the bar. They secluded themselves at a table so she could pour her heart out to Jozsi. How could Tibor do this? They'd been going out for two years. Had she been crazy to think they'd eventually tie the knot? Jozsi tried to explain how it felt to have to flee your country as Tibor had done, with little command of English and only the skills of a laborer. How it might be too hard for him to imagine settling down so soon when so much in his life had already changed.

"But wouldn't he want stability?" Bridget challenged, "After all he's been through. No, I don't understand." She wiped tears from her eyes, struggling to keep from sobbing.

Jozsi tried again, sharing that at one time he, too, was close to settling down despite fearing he was not even close to ready. If history had not happened, if the Hungarian Revolution had not exploded, he might have gotten married. He felt sad as he spoke, suddenly seeing Erika in Bridget's questions and tears, imagining she felt he'd betrayed their own powerful connection. Had he stayed and married Erika, he might have lost the urge to roam, transformed by love into a satisfied, sedentary man of Budapest. Jozsi's nature was not sentimental but the wine and Bridget's sorrowful face were putting him in a maudlin state of mind. Beautiful Erika, the bravest woman he'd ever met, could have been his wife, and now he had no idea if she were even alive.

But just as he felt tears might begin flowing from his own eyes, he felt a hand on his shoulder. Iren. Apologizing in Hungarian for her ill temper of the other day, promising to make up for it after this night's show. She pulled up a chair and they spoke intensely for a good while. Bridget, who knew only a few Hungarian words, followed their expressions and could see that Iren was pleading but that Jozsi was not warming to her in any way.

Miksha rescued him by giving Iren the high sign that it was time for her to play. As she poured her emotions into a Liszt piano concerto, Jozsi explained to Bridget that things between he and Iren had ended badly but unlike Iren, he did not want to start them up again. He'd like to keep talking but was afraid Iren was going to haunt him every moment she was not playing. He was already feeling bad enough about letting down Erika, who had meant the world to him; he did not intend to also feel bad about Iren who had, from the start, been an affair of convenience, not of the heart. Someone might call him a callous user, he thought, but not someone who'd been in his shoes these last few years. At the bar, Miksha shook his head sadly because the Liszt was not at all setting the right mood for a Saturday night drinking crowd.

Bridget, still wanting to talk about her missing Hungarian, suggested they move to her small apartment, a few streets away. He caught Miksa's eye, calling out that he'd be back later; carefully avoiding the near-exploding eyes of Iren, who, seeing him head out the door with Bridget would have only one large jealous thought in her head. At the bar, Miksa continued to shake his own head because he knew Iren would spend the rest of the night playing music that would make the Hungarians cry in their drinks, instead of tossing them back and ordering more.

At Bridget's, they compared stories of failures of the heart as they worked their way through a bottle of Irish whiskey he'd picked up along the way. Halfway through the bottle, Bridget's heartbreak shifted to outrage, and she began roundly cursing Tibor and continued to do so for the rest of the night. When it finally occurred to Jozsi he'd better head back to the bar before Miksa locked up for the night, Bridget invited him to stay on her couch. The shape he was in dictated he accept, and with rubber-legged relief, fully dressed, and after a quick call to Miksa, he collapsed on the couch.

Sometime later, Bridget shook him awake. "I'm too mad to sleep," she slurred, tugging at his pants. Before he was even half conscious, she'd climbed on top of him, her nightgown shoved above her rump, and was having her way. Drunken lust took over and with no thought of Tibor, Jozsi let her work her heartbreak and rage out all over his body. Eventually she led him to her bed where they fell asleep, her head on his shoulder, arm slung across his chest.

The weekend passed enjoyably, and then it was time for him to catch the bus back to Fort Devens. For all her emotions, Bridget was surprisingly sensible when it came to Jozsi, or so he hoped. She knew he wasn't the guy for her, but while she was recovering from her broken heart she would be grateful for his good advice and comfort — she winked when she said the latter — and if he were so inclined, she'd be happy to offer him a bed in Boston any time he could get away from Fort Devens. With a no-strings guarantee he was, he said, very inclined to return, though when he could not say. They shared a sweet kiss, and he headed out the door to pick up the things he'd left with Miksa and return to the base.

~~~

During Jozsi's first week he'd gotten a handle on all the communications equipment he was responsible for and learned his way around Fort Devens. He returned late Sunday night and immediately fell into bed. The next day, Captain Mayfield, one of his commanding officers, dragged him over to the PX for a talk late in the afternoon, just as Jozsi, still a little the worse for wear after his drunken weekend, was thinking he was about ready for a nap.

Mayfield, a recent West Point graduate, had never served overseas, which Jozsi intuited he felt to be a weakness. The captain quizzed Jozsi on his experiences in Korea and Vietnam, though Jozsi kept saying he had little to share about the latter — his time in Vietnam spent peacefully teaching soldiers how to coddle outmoded communications equipment into continuing to function for just a little bit longer. Jozsi said that both places were hellholes and that he had no desire to return to either... ever. He shared some of the real miseries he'd endured in Korea and then made up a few stories about Vietnam he thought a new officer might like to hear, extricating himself just in time for supper and an early night.

The next day, Mayfield sent word Jozsi should go to General Yancy's residence at 2 pm sharp so Yancy could have a word with him. All this attention from the higher-ups got some of the other soldiers looking sideways at him, but Jozsi was used to that by now. Being in the Special Forces meant no one could quite put his finger on what you were up to or exactly how important you were. But just to be safe, others tended to treat you with at least one kid glove least they rub you the wrong way and thus piss off a higher-placed official you might complain to. Jozsi was ready to take advantage of any Army politics he could, so always tried to maintain enough mystery to keep others on their toes.

Jozsi walked to the residential area on the base, where the officers lived in houses or apartments, depending on their rank. Well-made brick houses and small apartment buildings, trees lining the streets, small front yards landscaped with bushes and flowerbeds. More civilized than Jozsi expected any army base to be.

At the General's house, a maid ushered Jozsi into one of the best-furnished rooms Jozsi had ever seen, a library and office in one. Shelves lined the walls, a comfortable leather couch, large oak desk, and wooden chairs were spaced about the room. Oriental rugs lay here and there, their colors stunning against the beautifully polished oak floor. General Yancy stood looking out the window, which provided Jozsi with a second or two to appreciate his profile. Yancy was tall and trim, with dark gray hair, an aquiline nose and blue-gray eyes, distinguished looking, elegant almost. Jozsi felt a twinge of insecurity, his short stature making him feel a peasant to the lord of the manor.

General Yancy turned slowly, acknowledged the soldier, extended his hand toward one of two plush easy chairs placed by a small table in front of floor to ceiling windows and took the other. Not a word was said. The General leaned forward to offer Jozsi a cigarette from a silver case, extended an old Zippo, lighting the cigarette for him. Jozsi had only seen such things happen in the movies and felt a little like he was being courted. Finally, the General spoke, his voice a bass rumble.

"Washington sent word that I am to extend to you all the privileges of a distinguished non-commissioned officer that lay within my power to extend." Jozsi stared, not sure what to say to such a formally worded statement. He did something with his face that must have communicated thank you, because the General answered, "You're welcome," flicking something invisible from his uniform pants leg. The General looked directly at Jozsi's face. "I'm not used to paying attention to commands like this from the upper brass, but as I'm getting ready to retire, I see no reason to unnecessarily rock any boats. General Stillwell put in a good word for you and he's a friend to me."

"A great man," Jozsi said, feeling those three words within the realm of safety.

"You mark my words he will go down in history as one of the greatest generals of our time."

Jozsi nodded. Without Laci by his side to do the nodding, Jozsi was afraid he'd soon turn *into* Laci. So far, General Yancy had him entirely intimidated and he did not like that one bit.

The maid entered and asked if they'd like a drink. "It's too early to drink," General Yancy's face relaxed into an almost silly grin, "so I'll have a scotch and soda." Jozsi felt relieved. The General had a façade; he wasn't entirely stuffy. "And so, Sergeant, within reason, you can have anything you want, including an early afternoon drink."

Jozsi said, "I'll have the same," to the maid, and to the General, "I only want what the CIA and I agreed on."

"May I ask what that might be?" The General's eyes twinkled.

Jozsi now felt safe enough to tread lightly on what might be considered thin ice. "Sorry, General, but that was one of the expectations, that I not discuss anything. A man in your position understands this, yes? Did they not send a copy of the contract prior to my arrival?"

Again, General Yancy grinned. "Yes, I did receive the contents of your contract. I was only wondering if you were ready to spill any stories I'm not supposed to hear. What I was told was one, that I'd be stuck with you; and two, that you're to work on the communications equipment whenever you damn please; and three, that you're not to work on it whenever *they* damn please."

The maid returned with their drinks, and for a moment the only sounds in the office were the door closing behind the maid, ice cubes clinking, two men sipping. "Ah," the General sighed, "that hits the spot." He put the drink down after a sip that turned into a swallow. "I'll tell you, when I came out of West Point, I had dreams of joining the CIA. Sneaking around doing mysterious but important work for the government. Enjoying the pleasures that go with that kind of job."

Jozsi felt comfortable enough to chuckle. "In my experience, not so many pleasant things happen. I count sitting here talking with you as one of the few."

The General smiled. "Kiss-ass," he said kindly.

"Someday, General Yancy, after you retire, and I am free of my duties, we can get together and talk about all of the…"

"Secret bullshit?" the General interjected.

"Yes, the secret bullshit."

"Young man, you probably don't know this, but I was in Vienna monitoring the refugees coming out of Hungary in late '56, early '57." He frowned. "Ugly situation over there, which we did nothing to prevent." His eyes closed momentarily, as though trying to avoid unpleasant images his memory was stirring up. "Shameful," he added, opening his eyes and reaching for the glass.

Now Jozsi had a clue as to why the General was taking such a friendly tone with him. They looked each other long in the eye, allowing shared memories of the chaos, fear, and despair at the border to hang between them, until Jozsi cleared his throat. "What else were you doing there?" he asked.

"Down the road, that will be my contribution to our discussion. You tell me yours, I'll tell you mine." He reached forward to clink glasses, and they both downed their drinks. General Yancy said, "Let's get down to business. So, what is it you need?"

"I was told the word is autonomy," Jozsi struggled to remember the correct pronunciation. He explained that he needed complete freedom from his company activities at any given time; that there might be periods he'd leave the base and wouldn't be able to account for his absences, possibly for several days at a time. The General nodded. Then there was Jozsi's commitment to manage the lifeguards at Fort Rodman.

"Hellish task," the General shook his head in disbelief. "You must be some wily negotiator to have wrangled that deal."

Jozsi smiled, and continued. He was supposed to pick six soldiers to be trained as lifeguards before the Fort officially opened to reservists in May. They would then watch over the various waves of reserve intelligence officers who'd cycle through during their two weeks of active duty at Fort Rodman.

"I like that," General Yancy said. "Officially, Fort Rodman's under my command, but it sits quiet during the off-season. There are people that tend the property and barracks and whatnot, but that's about all that goes on. Then beginning in June, the reservists start rotating in and out and I have no idea what's going on down there all damn summer. I never get to New Bedford; don't much like fish or Portuguese food." He shrugged. "Major Hunter's in charge in that area and he's no fan of mine. Tight-lipped bastard, he never tells me anything he doesn't have to. You think you can come back with a good report?" Jozsi asked what he wanted the reports to be about. "Names and addresses would be a good start. I'd like to know who the officers are and where I might find them the rest of the year."

"In case they run off with some towels?" Jozsi risked making a joke.

General Yancy raised his eyebrows. "Exactly."

"But, sir, it might jeopardize my career if I gave out names," he said, as straight-faced as he could.

"We both know it won't amount to a piss hole in a snow bank," Yancy shot back. "And it'll help me out," he smacked Jozsi's knee. "I'm sure that matters mightily to you." He laughed.

Jozsi raised his glass. "More than anything, sir."

"Well, I've got a proposition." The General laid out his strategy for their collaborative effort. Jozsi would get an additional fifty dollars a month for hazardous duty starting as of that moment, and would be free of all duties in his company. He'd have private sleeping quarters and not be required to make the morning roll call as long as he checked into the base office during the day.

"The days I'm here," Jozsi corrected.

"Well, you're an exacting son of a bitch," the General chortled. "Yes, the days you're not off doing God knows what that you don't have to tell me about. Agreed."

With that, Jozsi and his new collaborator shook hands and had one more drink. The General offered to have his driver take Jozsi back to the base proper so he'd get back in time for supper. When the post commander's car pulled in front of the mess hall, eyes were glued to the door. Could General Yancy be making a surprise inspection? No, it was just Jozsi, the foreigner, who waved and called out, "As you were." No one knew whether to jeer or salute, so they did neither.

Jozsi took advantage of his connection to the upper brass by regularly mentioning that he'd be speaking with General Yancy (though always at some unspecified time in the immediate future), suggesting that he just might make favorable mention of a soldier or two. This insured him nights of drinks on whichever officer was hoping for Jozsi's praise regarding his outstanding leadership qualities, and led to all manner of friendly exchanges. It seemed he could do no wrong at Fort Devens, an unusual position for Jozsi to find himself in. Milking it seemed the only honorable way to express his gratitude.

During the week, Jozsi instructed young soldiers about radio communications and basic repairs on their equipment, throwing in a little advice about life in general when he felt magnanimous. The soldiers appreciated his irreverent attitude about the army, his humor and general good nature. He intrigued them: the accent, the disappearing, the access to General Yancy. All this set him apart from their more run-of-the-mill sergeants.

Jozsi didn't return to Boston for a stretch of time. For one thing, he was called away from the base by his CIA contacts several times and didn't want to overuse this thing called autonomy. Also, he reasoned that if he started showing up so soon in Boston, lovelorn Bridget might get the wrong idea. He liked her just fine, she was a good woman, and he would be happy to do with her what young, healthy adults do with each other. He just didn't want there to be any confusion as to why he was in her bed. Instead of heading to Boston, he bought a used Ford with money saved from his monthly CIA pay, and made brief excursions to the towns near Fort Devens.

The meetings with his CIA handlers helped Jozsi get his bearings in the northeast: Rhode Island, Massachusetts, New Hampshire, even Vermont. Newly arrived Hungarians were migrating everywhere. Families that were emigrating didn't make the CIA nervous, Jozsi rarely had to keep an eye on them. But single men and women, that was different. Jozsi would be called to meet one or another handler somewhere within a few hours of the base for a discussion. After his assignment was explained he'd be sent "out in the field" they called it, to find out everything he could about this or that emigrant. He felt like a private investigator on the good days, a non-torturing member of the AVO on the bad.

Usually his "research" as he thought of it, lasted but a few days. So-and-so came to the country having filled out "clerk" as an occupation. As the CIA explained, "clerk" was a very nice catchall phrase, commonly used, not always remotely descriptive of a person's actual former occupation. So, when a penniless clerk emigrated, found lodging, and within a short time had a car for transportation, eyebrows were raised. How did the car come into their hands? How did they manage to afford their own apartment? And the most important question: were they in truth communists up to no good?

Jozsi would see if he could find contacts in the area of his search. The Hungarian network was wide, and *Nagybácsi Miksa*'s *Place* had been in business for a number of years, despite its humble ambiance. Jozsi would call Miksa, who would call someone else, and on down the line, until Jozsi had at least a name in the general vicinity of his target. He'd get leads from this person, or just start talking to people: neighbors, storeowners, restaurant owners. He'd try to trace the car, where it had been bought, with what kind of payment. Cash? Instant suspicion. Sometimes he'd follow the subject for a day or more. That could be tricky because any Hungarian would recognize a fellow countryman just by looking at Jozsi. He bought a special homburg to wear, and thick black-rimmed eyeglasses he'd slip on, and when the weather was cold enough, a heavy wool scarf wound up to his chin.

The handlers promised him these people would not be hurt, not tortured like back in Hungary. Jozsi preferred not to think about the probability that his handlers were lying to him. Nothing he could do about it if they were. Then they said that the worst that would happen was they'd be sent back from whence they came. Jozsi knew that if they came from a place anywhere like where he came from, torture would be a very real possibility. But it wouldn't happen in America so the Americans would feel okay about it. As for himself, he'd chosen these shoes to walk in and there was no point in feeling squeamish about a little bit of spying. He'd done worse himself, so much worse. Now and then he would ask himself: am I Zsigmond? No. Then okay.

Over the holidays, he took off for Boston, ready for two weeks away from the monotony of life at Ford Devens, and checked into a decent hotel to treat himself to the luxuries of civilization. The first night, he headed over to *Nagybácsi Miksa's Place* where he was greeted like a long-lost brother. Iren was playing the piano, her back to the room, but she must have sensed something because she suddenly looked over her shoulder and spotted him. Her eyes lit up and the second she took a break, she nudged her way next to him at the bar and tried to cozy up. Civil, but cool, he was relieved when the break was over and she returned to the piano. He could practically smell desperation overpowering her perfume; it was not appealing.

Soon Bridget, hair wrapped in a Kelly-green scarf against the cold, bustled in the front door, her smile stretching ear to ear when she spied him at the corner of the bar.

"You didn't call! Why not?" Hands on hips, head cocked, playful. She was cheerful and soon they were hugging and drinking, catching up with each other. He couldn't tell her about his spying, so instead talked about how boring Fort Devens was. She shared that she'd heard from Tibor. She hadn't completely given up on him, but he was in training and hoping to go to Vietnam, so who knew what the future held. She squeezed Jozsi's hand. She was lonely, no family in Boston, the holidays' making things worse. Wouldn't he just as soon spend them with her? They could keep each other company and enjoy the bright, cheery lights and holiday decorations of the city. Soon they were on their way to fetch his things from the hotel, Iren casting a forlorn look as she watched them leave.

The next day they bought a small fat Christmas tree on Tremont Street, decorating it with foil and cotton, so it looked snow-covered and sparkly. Not quite the same as a tree decked out with Hungarian Christmas candies, Jozsi thought, but it would do. At night, as they snuggled on her couch gazing at the tree, Jozsi was surprised by how content he felt. He pictured himself making Bridget his home base. She would be a good partner, he thought, her sunny nature a definite plus. She loved Tibor, but she was far too practical to let that stand in her way, and Jozsi felt them growing closer as the days passed. But he shook off those thoughts. The holidays could get to anyone, even him. He was probably feeling sappy under the influence of the scent of pine needles mixing with the mellow glow spiked eggnog lit in his head. It would pass.

The holidays ended without him handing her an engagement ring, and he barreled out of there, wondering what was happening to his wanderlust and lust-lust. Could he really be on the verge of settling down? Perhaps the Army was worse for him than he'd thought. Bridget sniffled a bit as he left, promised open arms upon his return, that is if Tibor hadn't shown back up, and looked to be altogether sturdy enough to carry on without him no matter what.

~~~

Winter dragged on at Fort Devens. Jozsi did his fair share of special work for his handlers, and the rest of the time concentrated on making sure the communications equipment would be in excellent shape when he headed to Fort Rodman. The reservists would begin arriving in June, but Jozsi had to be there at the end of March for two months of training.

Toward the middle of March, General Yancy called Jozsi to

base headquarters to meet the officer in charge of all recreation and rehabilitation at Fort Rodman, a young-looking Captain Novak. "The Captain is already aware of your needs, but I want you to spend some time talking about the summer schedule. Come see me at my home office when you're done speaking with him," and with a salute Yancy was gone.

Captain Novak had an unsettling habit of twiddling his ear lobe as he talked, but otherwise seemed a decent enough sort. Jozsi, having locked onto the phrase, "The captain is already aware of your needs," decided to jump in and take the lead by telling Novak just how things should proceed. The captain was very cooperative and Jozsi wished Laci could have seen his deft handling of the situation, just so he could have said, "Stick with me," and launched into his refrain about big cars and diamond rings.

First on the agenda, Jozsi would pick six lifeguard candidates for training. Second, they would begin training at the New Bedford YMCA the beginning of April. They would live at Fort Rodman while they were training. After the first of June, Jozsi would be in complete charge of recreation at Fort Rodman. To all of which, Captain Novak nodded yes, promising to write up the order as soon as Jozsi supplied the names of his six lifeguards-to-be.

General Yancy met Jozsi at the door, and within moments the two were sipping drinks in the general's splendid office. "I want to ask you something, Sergeant," the general said, stretching his legs out, carefully placing one ankle over the other. "Have you ever thought about becoming an officer in the U. S. Army?"

"Never," Jozsi laughed. "Not even once."

"That's too bad. You have all the qualities an officer needs. I'd be personally willing to sponsor you for officer candidate school. It would be my parting gift to the Army."

"That's very kind of you, General, and I'm flattered you think that highly of me," Jozsi said, and meant it. "But no, it's not for me. After Hungary, Korea, everything these last few years, I think I'm ready for civilian life as soon as I'm discharged."

"Hard to find good men," the General said. "Thought I'd try to add one to the stockpile." He reached forward and they clinked glasses and let the conversation range far and wide.

The next week, Jozsi assigned his favorite soldier, Al Accardo the task of finding five other trusty soldiers. "I don't want any career soldiers. Also, they can't be afraid of water, and if possible, I want them to come from New York City." Al looked puzzled. "I have plans," Jozsi said. "In time, you will learn the wisdom of my ways."

By nightfall, Al had rounded up five soldiers to meet with Jozsi. One was from New Jersey, the rest from the New York City area. "Close enough," Jozsi said, when Al apologized for the geographic failure. The next afternoon, Jozsi gathered his troops together, pleased to find that they were all draftee short-timers, dying to get the hell out of the Army. In other words, not likely to run and report infractions to the brass. Al later admitted to Jozsi he'd almost chosen a Mob hit man, an enforcer, for the team. The guy had been sentenced to prison, his sentence reduced in exchange for turning the remainder of his prison time into Army time. Evidently, he was not the first mobster to take that option. Someone tipped Al off about the guy's past just in time.

"We leave for Fort Rodman next Monday and begin training at the YMCA the day after. Two months we train, and then the reservists arrive. You get every weekend off, Friday night until Monday 6 AM." He informed them that they'd be at Fort Rodman from June till the end of October. The men would be housed in barracks, Jozsi would have separate quarters. He'd make the schedule; if anyone had a problem they should come see him. If anyone missed their scheduled time, Jozsi said, "I will find a replacement and send his ass back to Fort Devens. I want this to run like clockwork. No problems, no visits from the higher-ups, we have a good summer."

Wise-ass Levine, which is how he was known, piped up. "Sarge, this sounds too good to be true, what's the catch?"

"Glad you asked, soldier. The catch is I'll be going to New York City every weekend with one of you guys, and you have to get me back on time at the end of the weekend. This Hungarian is past due to have some fun in a big city. Now, you've got all of a half-hour to make up your minds if you want to commit. Other guys are standing in line for a deal like this." He grinned a wolfish grin. "I'll be back in thirty," he said, and strode over to the PX for a beer.

Upon his return, he was greeted with a round of "Count me ins" and "Yessirs" and smiling faces. Marty from Queens even offered a date with his sister. "We're Polish and Hungarian, my grandmother would love to meet you. She grew up in Budapest."

Jozsi had visions of tasty Hungarian pastries and steamy bowls of borscht made by someone who cooked just like his grandmother. "If you hang around with me, boys, you'll be wearing big diamond rings and driving around in fancy cars in no time."

Even Levine signed on. "I'm a skeptical Jewish boy from Brooklyn but I'm beginning to believe in you."

Jozsi, pleased with all current developments, enjoyed his last week at Fort Devens and a final visit with General Yancy, who wished him luck. "I hope Major Hunter doesn't ruin your summer." Jozsi had no intention of letting that happen and told the general so. "Indeed, I thought not," the general chuckled. "In truth, I wager it is Hunter who will need the luck." He clapped Jozsi on the back as he sent him out the door.

19

A Summer Sojourn

Jozsi and his team of water gladiators, as he called them, jubilantly left Fort Devens for their summer by the sea. The "gladiators" settled into their quarters and "Sarge," as the soldiers called Jozsi, moved into the beach house. It was deluxe: fully though humbly furnished, with a kitchen, dining room, bedroom, even a full bath. Jozsi stared at the tub, imagining what it would feel like to take a bubble bath, something he'd never done. He thought: I can manage to live here for the summer, indeed I can.

Major Hunter sent Anibal, one of the Portuguese groundskeepers, to summon Jozsi before he'd even had a chance to unpack his duffel bag. He quickly threw the contents on the bed and retrieved a small envelope, with his name typewritten on the front, nothing more, a parting gift from General Yancy. He'd placed the envelope in a folder pressed flat against the bottom of his duffel and now tucked it away in his jacket's inner pocket. He was looking forward to meeting Hunter, armed as he was with this document.

Jozsi quickly strode to the main building, his gait inspired more by the chilly March air than by any interest in impressing the Major with obedient haste. He paused to enjoy the sight of sea gulls cruising the beach for treats. He inhaled, filling his lungs, not minding the low-tide stench of seaweed. He could just make out a fishing boat bobbing in the distance. A gust of wind slapped his cheek, reminding him of his mission. He turned his back to the water and walked east, up the path to the main building. Anibal was up on a ladder, painting the trim on top of a first-floor window. He pointed his paintbrush in the direction of Hunter's office, careful not to spatter paint on Jozsi's head.

Major Hunter was at his desk, writing on a legal pad, when Jozsi knocked, entered and saluted. He put his pen down and stood, his eyes giving Jozsi a thorough going over. Hunter had the build of a middleweight boxer, which contrasted oddly with his wispy comb-over and pale complexion. He'd sunburn in a second, making this beachfront post slightly torturous, or so Jozsi imagined. They stared at each other, and then the Major sat, without offering Jozsi a similar option.

In as few words as possible he let Jozsi know that he ran a tight base, despite the relaxed seaside setting, and that he expected the lifeguards to adhere to his standards, whether outfitted in uniforms or wearing only swim trunks. "I expect the same of *you*," Hunter said, zero warmth in his voice.

Jozsi couldn't place his accent, though he suspected he was from Kansas, an envelope addressed to a Mrs. Hunter with a Wichita, Kansas address lay flat in a wooden box labeled outgoing mail. "Yes, sir, "Jozsi responded. The business at hand at an end, Hunter dismissed Jozsi, who again saluted and turned to leave, but the motion was just for effect — he had his own business to discuss with the Major. He paused and turned back, startling Major Hunter, who'd picked up his pen and resumed writing.

"Sir, I hesitate to impose on your valuable time, but I feel it best to inform you of a certain sensitive matter."

The Major narrowed his eyes. "Go on, Sergeant."

Jozsi removed the envelope from his pocket with feigned nervousness. "This was delivered to Fort Devens; I do not know by whom." He slowly unfolded a piece of letter paper and read the typewritten message aloud. "'Dear Sergeant Budai, I understand that you are to spend the summer as a recreational officer at Fort Rodman, under the command of Major Hunter. Please mention my name to my darling George and tell him that I still love him and do hope he'll change his mind.' It is signed Lucy." Jozsi slowly refolded the note, carefully placed it in the envelope, returned it to his pocket, and looked at the Major with what he hoped was a concerned yet naive expression.

Major Hunter's eyes narrowed even more, his pale cheeks reddened. He was clearly thinking things over and his thoughts seemed to make him extremely uncomfortable. Jozsi stood waiting. The major sighed, opened his mouth to say something, shut it again. Jozsi waited some more, letting his eyes wander to the wooden box on the desk and the envelope in it. The major's eyes followed Jozsi's to the box. The major stood, leaning slightly forward, his fingertips pressed into the desk. He cleared his throat. "Needless to say," Major Hunter paused, stumbling his way through several false starts, managing finally, "No further than this room."

"Sir?" Jozsi asked, as though unsure of what Hunter might mean, all the while staring at the envelope in the box as though memorizing the address.

"Sergeant, I can assure you, your duty here will be successful, trouble-free, as long as we understand each other."

"Yes, of course," Jozsi answered with an appropriately submissive tone. "Understood..." He paused for a tiny disrespectful moment, "Sir."

Major Hunter's cheeks maintained their flush. Furious, he was using all his willpower to appear civil, nearly shuddering with the effort. "*Dis*-missed," he barked, sitting down with a thud.

Jozsi saluted and turned just before a huge smile broke across his face. He couldn't wait to describe the exchange to General Yancy when next they spoke, it would positively make his day.

~~~

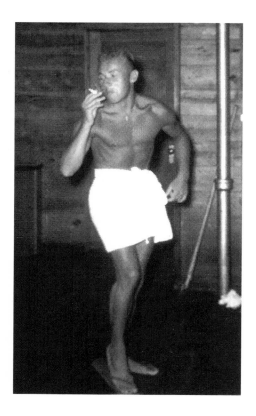

Jozsi and his gladiators settled in for two months of serious senior lifeguard training at the New Bedford YMCA. The ocean was still too cold for anyone without a wetsuit, and wetsuits were hard to come by, an invention too new for non-combatant soldiers to have on hand. Jozsi didn't care what the guys did after hours, as long as they showed up sober enough to keep from drowning. They already knew he was a soldier's kind of sergeant — not in the game to lord anything over them — and included him in their wild parties. When they fretted because they'd heard Hunter was a bastard, Jozsi shrugged it off, saying the base commander was not as much of a stickler as they might have heard. In fact, he wasn't too worried about anything as long as no military police were called. He did not tell them that he had a document proving the base commander screwed around on his wife. Seemed the least he could do for his commander in exchange for a happy-go-lucky summer.

During training, their weekends were free and Jozsi took advantage of his foresight in selecting soldiers from the New York area for this summer assignment. He spent his offduty weekends traipsing up and down the East Coast. Jozsi loved his visits to the fast-paced city, filled with people from all over the country, from all over the globe. New York was unlike Budapest, or Rome, or anywhere else he'd been. But he was also glad to return to the relative peace and quiet of Fort Rodman. Of course, New Bedford did have bars and its own wild side, but to call it a city was a bit of a stretch in his opinion.

Jozsi's picks for lifeguard training were mostly able-bodied and at ease in the water, except for Marty who struggled a bit. "I like the water," he'd say, his nasal Queens voice echoing across the swimming pool, "I just don't understand it." But even he managed to pass his test, and after they'd received their certificates Jozsi invited the whole YMCA staff to celebrate.

Major Hunter agreed to put on one of the biggest cookouts the locals had seen since Fort Rodman first opened, just before World War Two. No surprise, the major, their official host, made only a brief appearance to congratulate the lifeguards and welcome the assembled, then pleading other engagements, departed the base. That night, Jozsi called General Yancy to thank him for all his help. The general roared with laughter upon hearing the description of Hunter's face as Jozsi read him the faked letter. Yancy had bribed a private to find "something, anything," on the major. The private had managed to unearth the name of one of his paramours. "It was mostly for my amusement, but I'm glad it's coming in handy for you," he said into the phone. Jozsi could hear him sipping something; most likely he'd pulled the bottle from his drawer for a celebratory drink. The general wished him good luck, told him to watch his back, letter or no letter, and asked him to keep in touch, especially when he had amusing anecdotes about the major.

Though Major Hunter never betrayed any hint of hostility toward Jozsi, even when they were unobserved, Jozsi knew Hunter would secretly enjoy using his boxer's body to pummel him to the ground, so he did nothing to provoke the major's ire. Soon after their first conversation, he'd snuck out to the beach one moonless night and buried the phony letter in a coffee can at the foot of the furthest of three lifeguard towers. He didn't want his leverage mysteriously disappearing from his room. Convenient thing about sand, he thought, you couldn't tell if it had been disturbed; much less trouble than hiding a big coffin in a ravine.

The first week in June, the initial wave of reserve officers arrived for their two-week indoctrination on military intelligence. Major Hunter welcomed them and ran down the official base and water recreation rules. The lifeguards were on duty from nine in the morning until eight at night. After that the Army would not assume responsibility for anyone's water safety. If they drowned, it was their own damn fault.

"Fatherly of him," Marty muttered to Jozsi, causing him to sputter while trying to stifle a laugh. Major Hunter cast a sharp look in their direction but couldn't tell who'd done what, so continued on. In case of medical emergency, they'd have to contact the nearest Air Force base. Fort Rodman's medical equipment consisted of a cabinet with little beyond basic first aid supplies.

They soon learned it was the major's standard welcome, repeated almost word for word every second Monday to the new arrivals. Shades of Father Richter on the school steps. After the first batch of soldiers, Jozsi added his own medical addendum. Seafood was plentiful, and reservists, particularly those new to coastal life, tended to dive in. Jozsi would threaten them with a barracks enema, to be delivered in front of one and all. It was easier and faster than dragging them to the Air Force base for private medical attention. Lobster turned out to be a particular culprit. Midwesterners couldn't get enough of it and then were sorry, miserably sorry. More than once a fellow lifeguard was called upon to hold the pan while Jozsi helped relieve someone's stomach pain. It was unpleasant but Jozsi had been through so much worse, this barely served as an annoyance. He'd dispense the enema and quickly flee, leaving the lifeguard on hand to deal with what came next.

Jozsi's stint at Fort Rodman was the least soldierly experience of his Army life. In fact, it was a bit of a circus. Many of the officers in their normal lives held responsible civilian jobs and so they arranged to show up with their secretaries, some even brought their wives. All of the women were set up at a nearby hotel because the rule was that the officers had to lodge on base. The wives were suspicious of the secretaries, the secretaries were wary of the wives. The men with secretaries were nervous, the ones with wives were annoyed. Jozsi didn't care about any of it; he had found a New Bedford honey who was happy to come play house in his cozy little lair, and all he cared about was being left to frolic undisturbed in the tub.

Every two weeks, the routine was the same. First thing Monday morning, all hundred officers were welcomed and registered, then had the rest of the day off. This generally proved the busiest night for barracks enemas, since the officers would inevitably gravitate toward town to sample the local fare. The rest of the time they were training, enjoying the beach, and amusing themselves with other pleasurable activities. Jozsi was the go-to guy for information on the area, he'd made sure to educate himself with the help of Anibal's local expertise. The officers were more than grateful for his consideration and often rewarded him with decent sums of money. The ones with visiting secretaries especially appreciated the fact that either Marty or another trusted gladiator took all long-distance calls from their hometowns while they were entertaining their sun-tanned colleagues elsewhere. He didn't know how word managed to spread but new arrivals seemed to immediately sense they could trust Jozsi to cover their butts, and truth be told, he did enjoy the espionage aspect of his concierge duties.

Throughout the summer, Jozsi relished both weekdays and weekends at the ocean and frequent jaunts to New York City. He spent most of his time there at Marty's family's house in Queens. From Queens, he'd venture into Yorkville, known then as Germantown, where he found a clump of Hungarian restaurants and clubs. Keeping up with the language and enjoying the attention of Hungarian women was almost medicinal for him. New Bedford was sorely lacking in Hungarians and he greatly missed his Boston comrades, and even more, Laci.

Jozsi's gladiators were happy because they got to spend every other weekend off-base and he made certain that life on base felt as unlike the army as possible. The six gladiators couldn't believe what a good deal they had that summer and kept asking him how in hell he managed to pull off this kind of shit in the army. Jozsi assured them it was hard work, and he hoped they appreciated all the things he'd done for them. They never questioned his integrity, and he never mentioned how you had to be from Budapest to manage this level of slickness.

But eventually, the days grew shorter and the reservists who still went to the beach stayed on the sand instead of venturing into the water. Their time at Fort Rodman was coming to an end. By the first week of October, they were preparing to close the beach for the season and pull the docks back to shore for storing in a large Quonset hut.

Their final weekend, the lifeguards threw a wild going-away party for soldiers, workers, and anyone they'd happened to cross paths with the day before. They set up a campfire on the beach for an all-day cookout, and hired fado musicians who serenaded them into the night. Surprisingly, Major Hunter deigned to join the gathering and even brought his wife, who had flown in from Wichita for a visit. He did keep Mrs. Hunter away from Jozsi, except for engaging them in the briefest introduction in human history. When Mrs. Hunter began bidding the gladiators goodnight and goodbye, Jozsi approached the major, who with an almost dancelike move guided him away and to a corner of the room for a private conversation. Jozsi thanked Major Hunter for his cooperation throughout the summer and reached out to shake his hand. Major Hunter took it, squeezing very hard. Through clenched teeth he said that he'd spoken with Lucy recently and that she claimed never to have heard of Jozsi, much less written him a letter. Jozsi smiled ruefully, more because his hand was beginning to smart than because he regretted being caught out.

"I cannot speak to that," Jozsi said, turning to look toward Mrs. Hunter who was just then heading in their direction, "and I suspect you'd like this conversation to end."

"Oh, Jozsi," she gushed, "such a pleasure to have met you. My first Hungarian!" Major Hunter, released his hand, smiled grimly, took his wife by the arm and as soon as goodbyes were said, led her away.

The party started at noon and continued into the early morning hours of the following day. When it was over, not a single one of the gladiators was good for anything other than crawling back to their bunk for a few hours of shuteye before rising to pack and leave.

~~~

Back at Fort Devens, Jozsi arranged a visit with General Yancy, who was eager for a full report on Fort Rodman and the reservists who'd been there. They settled in over drinks, the general eagerly absorbing the information and stories about officers who'd cycled through Fort Rodman.

"Information is power," the General said cheerfully, "and getting some from behind that prick's back just plain makes me happy." They talked for a time, the General enjoying all of Jozsi's tales about the gladiators' escapades during the summer. "Sounds like you had a fine time down there. Good you had a break. I've got some news though," he paused and sipped from his glass. "Washington called a few weeks ago. They've got another trip for you now that you're done irritating Major Hunter." One look at Jozsi's face and he added, "Sorry."

A call from Washington meant only one thing: the CIA had a new assignment. "What can you tell me?" he asked.

"Not much," said the General. "You've got a week before you're due in Harvey Point, North Carolina. You're flying from Hanscom Air Force Base in Bedford. That's all they told me, except that you're not supposed to give anyone a heads up about your departure. I'll handle your company commander; you've got nothing to worry about on that end. And you're due a week off, so you don't even have to hang around here. Take a vacation, you've earned it."

Still, Jozsi's good spirits sank and refused to rise. General Yancy plied him with a few more drinks, trying to jolly him up by saying how much he envied him, how much he wished he were young like Jozsi, going to mysterious places to do adventurous things most people only imagined or saw in the movies.

Jozsi finally laughed, saying that some days he wished to do things like that too, "But not today."

The General called the meeting to a close. "Enough of your shenanigans, I've got a military base to run."

Jozsi left, his spirits taking a darker turn. He'd spent the summer feeling almost like a regular person leading a normal life. He'd appreciated the privacy of sleeping in a little house of his own, a woman in his bed, a tub filled with bubbles. Seeing Marty with his family in Queens brought on memories of his parents and his siblings. He must be getting old, he thought, where was his spirit of adventure? He decided to take advantage of his week off and see his friends in Boston; in America, they were as close to family as he could get. He went to the nearest phone and called Bridget, asking her to meet him at *Nagybácsi Miksa's* the next evening. To hell with adventure, what he wanted at the moment was camaraderie and comfort. At 22, he was not *that* old, he decided. It was okay to need touches of home, and at *Miksa's* he'd find them.

20

Old Home Week

Bridget waited at the bar, shouting with joy when Jozsi and his duffel bag walked through *Nagybácsi Miksa's* door. Pool players clattered down from upstairs to welcome their soldier friend and urge him to join their game, they were more than ready to take all of his Army earnings. Hearing the hubbub, Miksa lumbered out from his office and embraced Jozsi as though he were made of his own flesh and blood.

Immediately after Jozsi had called to announce his arrival, Bridget arranged for a week off from work so they could spend time together. "You've saved me," she confided, as they sat cuddling in an upstairs booth along the wall opposite the pool tables. She'd recently heard from Tibor, who said he'd met a girl in the town near where he'd been training. "That's that, I guess," she said, her eyes sad. "I didn't realize how much I was hoping he'd miss me. I've been dark blue since he wrote." She smiled weakly. "First it was the army that took him away, now this new girl. There's no point waiting for someone who no longer wants me." Jozsi gave her shoulders a sympathetic squeeze. She planned to work through the fall and return to Ireland by the start of the New Year. "1960…A good way to launch a new decade, don't you think? I've seen at least this much of the world. Now I'll find a decent boy from my hometown and settle down. You Hungarians are no good," she punched him playfully.

Jozsi nodded in agreement. "It seems to take us a while to settle down," he agreed. "At least the ones who wander away from home."

"You and me could work, you know?" Her expression said she knew that was not in the cards.

"If I didn't owe the government certain obligations, I'd drop to one knee right now," he answered, more to give her ego a lift than to lead her on.

"Oh, go on, liar." Her brogue had thickened since she'd spoken about returning to Ireland.

Jozsi continued, "But this country saved my hide, it's been good to me in the hard times. I keep my word."

"Lord knows, that you do," she laughed. "You told me you had to be a 'no strings' guy and you've been good to your word."

"Two ships passing in the night," he murmured into her ear. "Nothing wrong with that." The stream of dislodgement and relocation caused by war and poverty had throughout human history made an institution of two ships passing. No shame in honoring a connection born of loneliness and longing. No guilt in recognizing it as short-lived. On that they agreed. And so, they bounced from bed to bar during their happy week together, and parted for good with long hugs and melancholy tears that Jozsi tenderly wiped from her eyes.

Jozsi took the scenic route back to Fort Devens at dusk on a Sunday evening, the warm late September air caressing his face as he cruised slowly along roads lined with trees still fully green. Lights flicked on up and down the streets and families gathered for their evening meal. Although he went to sleep thinking about Bridget, he dreamt of Erika, and woke up picturing his holy grail, the coffin whose existence he hoped was still a secret.

That morning, the military police drove him to Hanscom Air Force Base, and even carried his gear and loaded it into a small twin-engine plane. He felt like a big shot and wondered why he was receiving kid glove treatment, at least relative to the way the army generally treated its soldiers. Two hours later the plane landed in Harvey Point, the humid North Carolina air enfolding him like a blanket. He had not been told where he was going or why. He'd heard of Harvey Point but knew little about what went on there. He'd observed that any mention of the place was delivered in very hush-hush tones, significance implied, details mysterious.

As he disembarked, one of the soldiers grabbed his gear, directed him to a jeep, and speedily deposited him at his quarters. Jozsi's room was sun-filled; complete with a comfortable sitting chair, small rug, firm mattress, and a dresser — more like a hotel than any other room he'd been housed in throughout his stint in the army. The soldier told him he was free until eight the following morning at which time he'd be expected in Conference Room 10, and then told him how to find it.

Jozsi thanked him, and though it was still early afternoon, asked where a man could find a drink. The soldier told him to walk two streets over and turn the corner. There he'd find a club that stood open 24-hours a day, complete with a no-cost bar. This too was not the norm. Jozsi cleaned up from his travels and seeing nothing scenic enough to draw him into a walkabout, headed straight for the gratis watering hole.

He entered the darkly lit barroom, standing by the door for a few minutes to acclimate his eyes after the bright day he'd left outside. As he headed toward the bar, he noticed someone alone at a table, sprawled comfortably in a chair. Something about the back of the man's head looked familiar, and Jozsi stepped closer. The man reached for a highball glass, tilting his head slightly as he drank. Laci! Jozsi grinned, snuck close and whispered into his ear.

"My friend, we had better stop meeting like this. People will think you are after my diamond rings and big car."

Laci's mouth hung open as he turned and leapt up in one motion, speechless, tears in his eyes. They hugged hard, like brothers, while Jozsi told him to stop crying, he needed to save his tears for weddings and funerals. They were both alive and that meant it was time to celebrate and catch up.

Jozsi soon learned his own life had been a walk in the park compared to that of Laci, who after re-enlisting had returned to the 38th Parallel for another mission.

"It was shit," he said. "My partner was too green to handle a gun. We crossed the border, but instead of sending the North Korean guard who spotted us to meet his maker, the kid got cold feet. I was in trouble up to my ass getting out of there. Lost track of my partner, nearly didn't make it out myself. You and me could have done it easy, but this was a young kid and everything scared the piss out of him. He's more scared now, if he's even alive. I thought football players were supposed to be tough. That's what he did in high school, he said, he played football."

They sat, heads together, talking on and on, toasting Laci's survival, their friendship, their home country, their new country, whatever they could think of to drink to. Laci entertained him by sharing other more amusing adventures in the Far East, most involving women, food, and booze.

Suddenly a voice from behind interrupted. "Sorry to interrupt..." They sat back to look and unbelievable to both, there stood Sandor, smiling and nodding.

"My God, it's been so long, I thought you were dead!" Jozsi said.

Laci jumped up to pull a chair from another table so Sandor could join them. "In honor of us being alive, we'll buy the drinks, yes?"

"I see nothing has changed," Sandor laughed.

"Yes! In appreciation for all of your generosity in Austria and Italy, we'll pick up the tab. On this we vow," Jozsi insisted.

"I'll have what they're having," Sandor called to the bartender, motioning for a round for the trio. "I appreciate very much your generosity, but since, as you know, drinks are on the house, I'll take a rain check."

"There are no rain checks in this line of work." Jozsi smacked his hand flat against the table. "It's now or never."

After some friendly teasing and several more toasts, their high spirits calmed enough for Jozsi to ask what the hell was in store for them. Sandor told them to hold their horses until the morning meeting when they'd be told about the new deal the company would offer. Meanwhile, he'd been to Hungary in the recent past and had much news to share.

"Erika?" Jozsi asked, afraid of what might come next.

"She's alive, working as a midwife, and married to a man named Vilmos," Sandor got right to the point. Jozsi's heart leapt and sank and leapt again. She was alive, that was the most important thing. Sandor had spent a long lunch with her and they needed to be patient so Sandor could share everything he'd learned.

First to Zsigmond: he had also survived the Revolution and was now a big shot in Budapest, near the top of the Secret Police pyramid, and not hesitant to take advantage of his position. He was constantly on Erika's husband's ass and they figured it would be only a matter of time before he arrested Vilmos for some stupid infraction. Vilmos hadn't even played a part in the Revolution; he'd been far from Budapest, out in the country, working his father's farm. But Zsigmond would never give up, and if he could get Vilmos out of the picture, he'd once again try to win Erika over, or so went Erika's thinking, and no one thought she overestimated his obsession with her.

Jozsi looked disgusted. "He always was stubborn. But start further back, tell us what happened from when we left." Sandor nodded. He'd memorized everything Erika had told him. Having treated the couple to many a meal during their regular clandestine meetings, he knew the strength of their feelings for each other. He knew Jozsi would want to know everything he could about Erika, no matter how many other women he'd loved or bedded in the meantime.

Sandor took a deep breath and shared what he knew of Erika's life from the moment Jozsi walked away from her on the *Margaret Bridge*. Erika had told Sandor she'd hidden in Budapest for a few days, moving from apartment to apartment, waiting for some word that Jozsi had made it out of Hungary alive. In hiding, she'd heard through the grapevine that Zsigmond had emerged from whatever hole he'd crawled into during the worst of the fighting and was back in action, looking for word of Jozsi and Erika's whereabouts.

Meanwhile, the newly re-organized secret police had instructed the Budapest radio station to broadcast messages calling for information on the "Beast of Budapest," and other figures of the Revolution, offering substantial rewards for any information. As expected, the Communists endeavored to turn decent Hungarian people into treacherous informants.

"No better than rats," Jozsi interrupted.

Sandor nodded and continued. Zsigmond even went to the extreme of announcing to the newspapers that he personally offered to match the reward money should someone identify the Beast. She had killed many of his comrades; he wanted no stone unturned in bringing this monster to justice. But no one came forward to turn in the Beast and after a few more days Erika, worried sick about her ailing mother, snuck out of Budapest and headed home to care for her.

Eventually the secret police reported to Zsigmond that Jozsi Budai had tried to escape and been killed by the Russian Army. Soon after, the newspapers reported that just after the Russian invasion, Jozsi's unrecognizable body had been recovered on the other side of the Danube, identified only by papers found in a jacket pocket. The body had been thrown into a mass grave along with those of other traitors.

Erika, knowing how resourceful Jozsi was, had held out some hope that the "unrecognizable body" was not his. She stayed close to home, veering between despair and optimism, jumping at any knock on the door, always on edge, fearing she'd be discovered. Via his spies, Zsigmond had learned that she'd returned to her mother's. He sent one of his agents to her door several times, nearly killing her with anxiety each time they appeared. She expected to disappear into the bowels of 60 Andrássy Street, her body dumped in a mass grave like so many others.

But each time the agent appeared, it was only to give her a message: Zsigmond wanted to meet, any time, any place. No, she told the police. No. She lay low in this uneasy seesaw, veering from dread to terror, for several months.

The neighbors knew her mother felt guilty about having to lean so heavily on her only child; they volunteered to watch Mrs. Simon during the day so Erika could resume her studies at university. Her mother forced Erika to accept the offer, convincing her that it was time to occupy her mind with something besides worry and fear. "You can't hide forever," she said. "Your father would not want you lashed to my side this way." Her mother did not know her as the Beast of Budapest, but she did know that Erika had picked up a gun. "If they haven't come for you yet, they probably never will. It's time for you to resume living your life. If they come for you later, they'll find you no matter where you are." Her voice bitter and pained, she spat out, "And if Zsigmond is good for one thing, it's keeping you alive."

Erika had cut short and dyed her hair before sneaking out of Budapest, hoping she wouldn't be recognized by any but close, trusted friends. Since then, she'd kept a very low profile, rarely venturing out of the house except to hurry to the market, or bring her mother to the doctor. Her body was in high alert the first several times she ventured into Budapest. The AVO was still avidly seeking to unearth organizers, participants, and leaders of the Revolution, and everyone in Budapest was on edge or depressed. Still, it had felt good to be out in the world.

One day after school, Erika was walking toward the stop where she'd catch the bus for her long ride home. An official looking car pulled up next to her and Zsigmond leaned out of the back window and offered her a ride. Time slowed the way it does when something shocking occurs, and for what seemed like too long a moment, she struggled to catch her breath. She decided she couldn't avoid him forever; also, she had to admit to a perverse interest in hearing what he'd say. So, with no hint of warmth, she agreed. Besides, traffic was moving so slowly the bus would take a couple of hours, and she was a woman with a practical nature. She settled in next to him, flinching when he reached to pat her knee in greeting. The traffic was indeed terrible; even Zsigmond's staff car had a difficult time getting through the city as workers struggled to remove rubble from the roads. The Russian army and the Hungarian fighters had between them wreaked havoc on the streets of Budapest.

Zsigmond ordered his driver to stop at the nearest café. "We'll have an espresso, eh?" he said to Erika. "When the traffic lets up, we'll go on." She agreed, though his tone had let her know he was not exactly asking. She could see he'd become very comfortable in his big-shot shoes.

The driver pulled over in front of a café at Lenin Circle, and they sat at a small marble table by a window. Zsigmond wasted no time getting to the subject of Jozsi. "He's dead, you know. Buried in a mass grave with other traitors and scum."

"I know, his parents told me." She spoke tersely, through clenched teeth. Erika's hands were shaking with rage; she didn't dare lift the espresso cup to her lips. She pressed her palms hard against the table. "I attended his memorial gathering. I did not see you."

Zsigmond reached across the table to pat her hand comfortingly, but she pulled it down to her lap. "I know this is hard for you," he tried a sympathetic tack seeing that his position of power was still not winning her over.

"He was your friend, too, long ago," she said bitterly. Thoughts of her father suffering at this man's hands began to overwhelm her, then grief at his loss, followed by even more grief at the loss of Jozsi. But she refused to let Zsigmond see her cry. Instead she stood to bolt from the table before the tears could flow. "He was your *friend*," she said, her voice strangled with emotion, then turned and fled.

Mrs. Simon, her heart growing weaker by the day, was resting in her sitting chair when the front door opened. She took one look at Erika's face and stretched wide her arms. "*Gyere hozzám, gyerünk,*" she called her child to come to her. Erika knelt by the chair and wept into her mother's lap while Mrs. Simon patted her on the back and stroked her head, making comforting sounds, as though Erika were a little girl, upset by a mean playmate at school or some other small misery.

When Erika's tears subsided, she told her mother how much she'd wanted to kill Zsigmond during the Revolution, how sick it made her that he still lived and breathed, how badly she wanted to shoot him straight between the eyes. "I want him to be looking at me when he dies."

"The day will come when justice finds him," her mother said. She, too, wanted Zsigmond to pay for not having prevented her husband's horrific death. To her last breath, she would want Zsigmond to suffer as Dr. Simon had suffered. And then she told Erika a story. Out on the *Puszta*, the vast plains where she had spent her early years, people used to collect special mushrooms to kill a predatory beast or get rid of unwanted animals around the farm. She looked at her daughter significantly. Erika begged her to carefully describe the type of mushroom they gathered, and tell her where she might find them. "The Amanita mushroom is easy to spot. It has red caps with white growths all around the cap," her mother said. "Your cousins can show you where to find them, but tell them no specifics and absolutely do not let anyone see you gather the caps."

"It's not just for papa, it's for Jozsi; it's for all the freedom fighters that bastard had a hand in killing."

"And it will stop that monster from hounding you," her mother added, worried always about Zsigmond and his longstanding yen for her daughter. Worried enough not to care if her daughter caused his death. The war and loss of her husband had hardened her heart too.

~~~

The Christmas after the 1956 Revolution the Budai family invited Erika and her mother to their house for Christmas Eve. It was a melancholy gathering. Everyone avoided mentioning Jozsi's name; the news of his body having been dumped into a mass grave was still too new and raw for them to fully bear. At least no one had to ask why when tears leaked from Erika or Mrs. Budai's eyes. The two sat next to each other, squeezing hands for ballast and strength. The Budais had invited immediate and extended family and other friends who'd lost homes or family or both. Everyone huddled, grateful for a little respite from exhaustion and sorrow. All had suffered; there was no need for anyone to put on a happy face. But the antics of the younger children provided moments of real joy, and Matyas got everyone singing, which lifted their spirits for the moment.

Suddenly a neighbor threw open the front door and barreled into the house. Panting, he shouted, "Jozsi is alive!" At first, they thought he was drunk, but once he'd caught his breath the man described how he'd been listening to *Radio Free Europe* when he heard a message: "Dodi from Rakos is well and in Italy." He remembered Dodi was a nickname for Jozsi when he was a toddler. It had to be him.

Suddenly their fragile spirits grew sturdier, and even the glummest eyes brightened. What had been a sedate gathering turned into a wild party. Matyas turned on *Radio Free Europe* and they listened to messages from refugees, repeated every half hour through the night. Jozsi had used his childhood nickname hoping that his family and neighbors would be listening and would recognize his code. Matyas was so proud and overjoyed he brought bottle after bottle up from the cellar, swearing he would open even more bottles this Christmas Eve than on the night that Jozsi had been born. Most guests present this night had been present on the other, and all were overjoyed to celebrate Jozsi's second life. Everyone agreed that Jozsi must have a guardian angel.

There was soon cause for even more joy, because right after the holidays, Erika and the Budais each received a single postcard sent from Italy. The postcards contained sentences about the scenery, and no signature, but the handwriting was recognizably Jozsi's. Erika felt like an entire building had been lifted off her back. Even if she never saw Jozsi again, he was alive! That he walked the earth was all the consolation she needed.

A few weeks after the holidays, Zsigmond waited in his staff car outside Erika's school and again offered her a ride and a break for coffee while they waited for the traffic to clear. They went to the same café and sat at the same table.

"I have news that will please you," Zsigmond said a little sourly.

Erika, anticipating his news, told him that she already knew — she would not give him even a moment's satisfaction. "And yes, I am pleased."

"Of course, I've seen the postcard." A slight chill ran through Erika's entire body. She should have known he'd spy on her mail. "He is a traitor to our country, and to you," Zsigmond continued. "He left you, he will never return, never. What's more, the Secret Police have proof that he has taken up with a woman in Italy. He may have sent a postcard, but he's deserted his country and he's never coming back to you."

Erika allowed a few tears to trickle down her cheeks. If he thought that she believed Jozsi had abandoned her and his life in Hungary it was all to the good. He tried to rest his hand on hers, but she flinched and yanked it away.

"Erika," he murmured, "we have known each other a long time

and you have always had a hold on my heart." He beat his hand against his chest for emphasis. "I am hoping you'll allow me to help you repair the damage to your reputation. It is not impossible to recover from the mistake you made in siding with the revolutionaries. At least I can protect you from anyone who'd want to do you harm." He reached toward her hand, but again, she quickly moved it out of reach. "In time, I am hoping we can start a life together."

In time, she thought, I am hoping to watch you die. What she said was, "I am not ready to make plans for the future; I am not ready to decide anything about anyone." She put both hands in her lap. They stared at each other, Zsigmond looking much like a dog gazing upon a big juicy steak. Erika could stand the sight of him no longer and said, "I want to go home now." He took her to her mother's and asked if he might call on her again. She nodded weakly, and he drove away, elated at the prospect of seeing her without having to set an ambush outside the university.

He'd allowed a whole week to pass before contacting her, this time via a police officer who delivered a box of chocolates to the house, along with an invitation to supper the following evening. She allowed Zsigmond a few more dates after that. At least, Erika thought, the food was good and he was too nervous to do more than kiss her on the cheek each time they parted. With revulsion in her heart, she allowed him that liberty. At the moment, staying in touch with him seemed safer than turning him away. Especially now that she had the beginnings of a plan for how to do away with him entirely.

On their fourth date, he raised the subject of Jozsi's extracurricular studies. Whatever was he talking about, she asked. Ura and its property records, he said. Zsigmond informed her that records from various libraries indicated Jozsi had been very interested in researching property owner archives in the area around Ura, searching as far back as he could. Erika assured him she had no knowledge of Jozsi's research. He persisted. She'd spent all her free time with Jozsi during those days, she'd even accompanied him to Ura so of course she'd have known what Jozsi was researching. She told him they'd gone to Ura to reconnect with the old Hungarian ways and customs they feared city dwellers were losing. She told him that since Jozsi had spent time in Ura as a child, he was profoundly nostalgic — about his friends and the land.

Zsigmond pressed on, but she held her ground. So as not to antagonize her, he finally let the matter drop.

Their dating life was interrupted when Mrs. Simon's health worsened and she took to her bed. Erika glued to her mother's side, refused all invitations or offers of help from her relentless suitor. Very early one morning, near the end of January, just before the sun arrived to cast a soft pink glow on a fresh layer of snow, Mrs. Simon passed away.

With sadness, but relief that her mother's suffering was finally at an end, Erika planned a trip to visit her maternal relatives. Her mother's family welcomed her with a big Hungarian gathering, inviting all nearby relatives and friends, and a handful of eligible bachelors should she be at all inclined toward meeting a decent country man. Erika felt safe, and as happy as a grieving daughter could feel, but she had something besides marriageable men on her mind: she wanted mushrooms, lots and lots of mushrooms.

During what her uncle thought was an innocent walk on the *Puszta*, Erika pointed out trees and flowers, naming all the ones she knew, inquiring about others. And then, as they walked into a wooded area, she pointed to first one patch of mushrooms, then another. She bent down to pick one from a rotting log, one from the base of a tree, holding each up to inspect it closely. She noticed a cluster of mushrooms with red caps and with her uncle's eyes on her, bent to reach for one. He called out sharply "No, don't touch!" Erika knew she'd definitely found what she was looking for.

"What are they called?" she asked, the picture of innocence, and repeated the name almost lovingly after he answered. "*Amanita muscaria*. It sounds like a good wine."

He explained that the mushrooms were deadly, not to be handled with bare hands, and went on to add a little history lesson: these very mushrooms were used by Ildiko to kill Attila after the invasion of the Huns. Ildiko had dried the mushrooms, ground them up and poured them into Attila's drink. The drier the mushroom, her uncle added, the deadlier.

The next morning Erika retraced their steps, and with gloves she'd taken from the garden shed, she filled a bag with mushrooms to take home and dry. It might take a while for her to enact her revenge, but at least now she had the supplies she needed and that cheered her more than anything had since the death of her mother.

~~~

Eventually Erika moved back to Budapest to be closer to the university and around other young people. She knew it was unlikely that Jozsi would return any time soon, and that even if he did, so much had happened in the intervening years, they'd never be able to pick up where they'd left off. It would be hard to go from being comrades-in-arms with blood on their hands to carefree lovers. He would always hold a place in her heart, but it was time for her to resume normal life. She began dating other men, still allowing Zsigmond to wine and dine her every few weeks. If he thought he had a prayer of a chance with her, she would eventually find an opportunity to kill him. Normal life yes, but she'd never lose sight of that particular mission.

Puzzled following a number of dates with men who said they'd call again but never did, she sought one out and asked why he hadn't called on her a second time; she'd enjoyed his company and thought he'd felt the same. Shamefaced, he admitted that he'd been scared off by Secret Service men who'd beaten him up after the date, then returned to dish out a follow-up drubbing a few days later. The men told him that if he didn't want to end up as fish bait, he should steer clear of Erika.

"I shouldn't be telling you this," he said as they sat at a busy sidewalk café on a balmy spring evening. He looked nervous, repeatedly scanning the other tables and the street to see if anyone was watching them with more than casual interest. Erika now understood what had happened to all of her dates and wished she could find a way to apologize to them without further endangering their very beings. That bastard Zsigmond was going to haunt her forever.

If only she could take back her childhood kindness to her tormenter. He'd latched onto her as the object of his desire in grade school and nothing since had dissuaded him. She could not believe any human being could be so dense, so intractable. It was not just revenge fueling her desire to kill him as quickly as possible. He was, she believed, quite capable of hounding her till she gave in and allowed him to claim her as his bride. She'd just as soon die. But that was not a good or right solution. It was he who had to die, and he had to die soon.

She didn't have to wait long for an opportunity to present itself. He showed up at her apartment a few days later and invited her to dine with him at *Emke*, the most famous restaurant in Budapest. He'd already begun taking liberties, she thought, showing up out of the blue as though she'd be pleased by a surprise visit. Erika accepted, directing him to wait for her in his staff car while she took a moment to freshen up. She freshened up, and also pocketed two vials of the powdered mushroom she'd prepared and stored in a bedroom cabinet: one for Zsigmond, one for herself in case she should be discovered.

She forced herself to be cordial, even as Zsigmond bragged about how the Secret Service not only knew that Jozsi was alive, but also that he was being trained in America to become an elite member of the Special Forces. Cordial even as he smugly reminded her that if Jozsi returned to Hungary he would be executed on sight, without benefit of a trial or even a hearing. Cordial still when he returned to the subject of Ura and what Jozsi had wanted to learn about that area. "He found something," Zsigmond insisted. "He's keeping a secret so I know it must be important, even valuable. I can't put my finger on what it is, but I know there is something to my suspicions. I will discover the truth," he smiled grimly. "You can count on that."

Erika tried to keep her expression neutral, to behave as though hearing Jozsi's name repeatedly fall from Zsigmond's lips did not make her want to climb across the table and claw his eyes out. But finally, she snapped. "You're so obsessed with him, why don't you put him behind you as I've done? A person might think you were in love with him, not me," she challenged.

Offended, he launched into a tirade about Jozsi's feckless behavior, deserting her, taking up with other women, dancing off to Italy and America with no thought of anyone's well-being but his own. "He will never come back for you," he said scornfully. "He's too much of a coward. He knows if he comes back, he's done for."

"Enough talking about Jozsi," she said. To distract, she asked how his other investigations were going. By now it almost amused her that it never seemed to occur to him that she could be the Beast of Budapest. Love truly is blind, she thought. He jabbered on about his frustration at not yet having laid hands on the woman who had caused so many deaths, who had embarrassed and evaded the Secret Police. How Zsigmond had ever managed, stupid as he was, to reach such a level of power in the Secret Police was beyond her. She forced herself not to think about those who had surely suffered at his hands during his hunt for the Beast. She forced herself not to think about her father.

To an onlooker, Erika might have appeared calm and relaxed, though all the while she was edgy enough to jump out of her skin. As the evening wore on, she even prayed for an opportunity to spill the mushroom powder into his drink. But as usual, two bodyguards kept watch throughout the evening, and she couldn't figure out a way to get away from them short of inviting him into her apartment. She couldn't kill him there. She'd just have to be patient and find another opportunity.

Zsigmond kept ordering after-dinner drinks, hoping she might become inebriated enough to allow him a kiss on the lips. He bragged about how helpful he could be to her career; his position put him in contact with many important people and he'd be happy to use his connections on her behalf. She could see he was getting carried away, the alcohol fueling his fantasies of the two of them walking hand-in-hand into the future. Her mood darkened.

Since the Revolution her emotions seemed to have a life of their own, flipping at the drop of a hat. The more he laid out his scenario for the two of them, the less she could stand to maintain even the hint of a charade that his dreams might come true. She feared he wouldn't stop with just a kiss on the cheek for much longer. Erika didn't think he'd force himself on her, but you could never be too certain, and even a kiss on the lips would feel like rape. It was time to set him straight. Whatever it took, she couldn't stand the thought of having to sit across a table from that yearning face again and again. If that meant waiting years longer for an opportunity to murder him, so be it. If that meant he decided to have her killed, so be it as well. She took the plunge.

Erika told him she'd discovered that he'd been scaring off her suitors. He looked shocked. "Having them roughed up does not impress me." With those words, she hoped to protect her past suitors. She explained that although she was getting over Jozsi, she wasn't ready to settle down with anyone, she was just going on dates to feel normal again. He would wait, he said. Erika discouraged him further. Surprising even herself, she looked him in the eye and said coldly, "When I am ready, I do not believe you will be the man for me. We are too much like family and there is too much history."

Zsigmond's face froze in shock, but his eyes kept reacting. In a split-second revision, she decided it would not be all right, 'so be it,' if he had her killed. She felt his despondency, but she saw rage in his eyes. Fearing he might snap, she held out at least a small amount of hope for further contact. "But we can get together now and then, talk about the good old days before all the troubles, all right?" And nearly gagging on the words added, "You are so powerful now, you should not be distracted by me. You have more important things to do." Throwing flattery into the mix she added, "You can have any woman in Budapest. You should aim higher than me." She smiled and ducked her head, the picture of humility.

Zsigmond declared his love was endless, but he would respect her wishes to keep some distance…for now. "But we are meant to be together," he insisted. She should know that he would rush to her side at a moment's notice, always and forever. She knew, she said, and to herself thought: I'm counting on that. She felt relief when they parted. All this anger and thirst for revenge was exhausting. Suddenly all she wanted was to be free of the intensity. She wanted to study, to date, to remember what it felt like to live like a person who hadn't been through hell.

~~~

By the time Jozsi had crossed America by bus, heading toward first Boston and then Fort Devens, Erika had decided to become a midwife, to somehow balance the scales for the lives she'd taken by helping new ones into the world. She then met and married Vilmos, a decent and kind laborer from a small Hungarian village. He was nowhere near Budapest when the Revolution broke out, he did not know the people she knew, or remind her in any way of those exhilarating and heartbreaking days. She told him a little about her life during the Revolution, but underplayed her love for Jozsi, and shared few details about her days with guns or the violence she'd wreaked on men twice her size. They wed shortly before Christmas in 1959 and she vowed to live a life exactly like that of other people her age.

A few times a year, though, she would visit Jozsi's parents to find out if they'd had news. The Hungarian papers had listed his name along with other so-called traitors to the Hungarian government, promising, as Zsigmond had said, that anyone reckless enough to return to the country they'd betrayed and forsaken would be executed. It didn't hurt that she could catch an echo of Jozsi's warm smile when Erzsebet welcomed her, and grin at the sight of Matyas from behind, his shape and walk a mirror of Jozsi's.

Erika's visits with the Budais were precious to her. She told her husband they made her feel close to her mother because the two families went so far back. And this was true. Vilmos didn't need to know about the secret place Jozsi occupied in her heart or how sitting with his parents watered that ground. She loved Vilmos with most of her heart and that would have to be enough.

Matyas and Erzsebet were always happy to see her. Matyas, proud of his son, had a map hidden up in the attic. As best he could, he plotted Jozsi's travels with pins and strings. Every time a package from his son reached him — through indirect routes, often handed over by Ferenc — it was flush with Hungarian forints. Jozsi still siphoning off the haul from the Hungarians he and Laci had scammed in Seattle.

Matyas had given up looking for work and officially retired. What Jozsi sent in one envelope was more money than he'd received as his entire monthly allotment from the Hungarian government. Every day after lunch, Matyas would stroll over to the tavern to visit with other local retirees or otherwise unemployed. He loved to brag that Jozsi, whom they'd all known since he was born, was doing well in the elite U. S. Special Forces. That someday he'd return to do some serious ass-kicking of the useless cowards who'd helped break the hearts of truly patriotic Hungarians who'd tried to snatch their country from Russian hands. And all the men would cheer.

Erika felt safe sharing her loathing for Zsigmond with Matyas who, like her, wanted to see him punished for his vicious brutality. Each visit they would take a walk together and talk about how satisfying it would be to know that Zsigmond drew breath no more. Erika never told him about her vials filled with death, nor did she describe how she wanted to watch Zsigmond's body twisting in his own crud, like a worm on a frying pan. The deadly mushroom powder would keep. After all, the drier, the deadlier.

With those words, Sandor ended his report on Erika. By then it was late, and Jozsi needed silence to absorb all he'd heard, so they called it a night. Sandor reminded them that they needed to be up bright and early and arranged for a wakeup call.

Jozsi tossed and turned his way through the night. Between mentally touching and committing to memory everything Sandor had told him, and wondering what fresh hell Sandor was getting them into now, there was no leeway for rest. At least he knew two things: first, Erika was alive, and second, he had only two more years of Army bullshit. A new life lay at the end of those two years. He thought about that too. And by then it was almost time for him to get up and continue the journey toward that new life.

21

El Delfin y El Fusil

The next morning, Jozsi and Laci managed to find each other and arrive at Conference Room 10 on time, although they were the very last people to enter. Waiting for them, a group of five men. Surprisingly, Sandor was not among them.

A young CIA officer opened the meeting with a roll call, followed by all those present swearing to maintain confidentiality and, of course, to honor the usual company rigmarole. With that out of the way, the young officer introduced Major Shumway who was to brief the Hungarians on the mission they would eventually be undertaking. A ragged scar snaked out from under the major's sharply creased collar, vanishing under an ear missing part of its lobe. Jozsi had instant respect for the man; he'd obviously suffered a serious mishap out in the field.

The major walked to a small raised platform, placed the folder he carried on a podium, opened the folder and glanced down. Then he looked up and for a long moment stared at Jozsi and Laci, taking their stock. Apparently satisfied, he spoke. "A brief bit of background is in order. Robert F. Chiari, the newly elected President of Panama," Major Shumway paused. "Newly re-elected, I should say. President once before, in '49, but that is not essential to this matter. What is, is that we've learned he's in secret negotiations with Fidel Castro's brother, Raúl. Do you soldiers know much about these men?"

Jozsi and Laci shook their heads no. Shumway glared until Jozsi put two and two together and spoke. "No, *sir*. Cuban. Communist. Kicked Batista's ass. That's all, sir," Jozsi said. Then Laci said, "No, sir, nothing."

Shumway nodded curtly and went on in a staccato rhythm. "Raúl Castro was a rebel commander. Captured along with Fidel back in '53. After the Moncado Barracks attack. Sentenced to jail. Released in '55. The brothers went to Mexico, joined up with Che Guevara, set up in the Sierra Maestra Mountains. Batista's forces couldn't manage to smoke the bastards out. Took a while, but eventually there went Cuba." Major

Shumway looked livid, as though the Cuban Revolution had been a personal affront. "What I am saying is that we have serious concerns about Chiari bringing Cuban revolutionaries into the Panamanian realm. Raúl Castro is now the Minister of the Armed Forces and he'd like nothing better than to send his thugs over there, turn Panama into another communist stronghold. Nationalize every goddamned thing they see. Not on *my* watch. And we certainly do not want them starting a revolution against the Americans in the Canal Zone. They'll be looking to seize the Canal before the contract runs out." The Major banged the table with a fist. "I'll be goddamned if we're gonna let something like that happen." He nodded grimly. "Bottom line: we get Chiari out of the political circle. Next, stabilize the Panamanian government. Show the bastards what's what."

Jozsi's mood sunk. This was not going to be anything like shadowing Hungarian emigrants to see if they were doing a little spying for the Russians. No hopping in the car and cruising around the East Coast. It occurred to him he'd grown a smidgeon soft since North Korea. But not Laci, Jozsi could tell Laci's trigger finger was already itching; he'd begun throwing off a shimmery vibration Jozsi recognized from their days in Korea. No question, there'd be guns involved; Jozsi could practically smell the odor of metal and charcoal in the room, Laci's favorite scent.

Shumway interrupted Jozsi's train of thought. "The assigned agents will supply you with further details. You'll remain here on base to receive proper training from our experts. When you're fully trained and we feel it is time to set things in motion, you will leave." Shumway closed the presentation folder. "Any questions?"

Jozsi raised his hand.

"Sergeant?" Shumway indicated with a nod that Jozsi should stand.

Jozsi rose and officially introduced himself. "I am curious to know how many of us will be on hand to execute this order?"

Major Shumway registered surprise. "I thought you two were informed prior to the meeting; the order will be executed by you, and…" he raised his hand, palm up toward Laci.

Laci grinned, jumped up, saluted. "Laci Botlo, Sir."

After an eye-twitch's worth of acknowledgement the major dismissed the Hungarian duo. The others remained in their seats.

Jozsi and Laci walked toward the door, though Jozsi turned and said loudly, "I guess, like you guys say in America, the wife is always the last to know."

Laci flinched and grabbed Jozsi outside the door. "Ballsy of you with the bigwigs in the room."

Jozsi shrugged. "They want us bad enough, they have to put up with us." He wasn't exactly certain what was bothering him so much. He wasn't afraid and he wasn't clueless like Laci's pitiable partner, the Serbian who'd gone missing in North Korea. Jozsi would rally; he'd do whatever they asked. Still, he had been hoping to glide through the remaining days of his stretch in the Army without drama or risk. It was beginning to sink in that no drama, no risk was a fantasy — simply not in the cards.

Laci was all set to head straight to the club to celebrate their new escapade, or at least get a few drinks down before they had to begin the slog of training. Jozsi went along, but his purpose in drinking was to dull the dismay he'd felt set in during the meeting. He'd been tempted to wait outside the conference center until the meeting ended so he could have a word, or several, with the young CIA officer. But really, what was the point? He'd unload on Sandor later on when he wouldn't have to put up a civil front before the others. He knew Sandor would seek them out soon enough. Indeed, after supper he appeared at Jozsi's door with a message from their trainers. "School begins at 8:00 AM," he announced cheerfully, by way of a greeting.

Jozsi braced his arms against the doorway, blocking Sandor from entering. "Figured that. But what type of training are we in for?" he snapped. "You didn't have the balls to tell us what our new swell assignment would be."

Laci darted into the hall from the room next door. "You're holding out on us, spill the beans," he said, happy to find use for yet another of his new American phrases.

But Sandor insisted he himself had had no idea what the task would be. "I recommended the two of you because they said it was a highly confidential mission that needed a small, reliable team. I wasn't given a lot of details; I'll know more when you do."

Jozsi scoffed. "I believe you, and in Santa Claus too."

"No, it's true. You know the firm doesn't tell everybody everything.

Bits and pieces, bits and pieces, strictly need to know. I *was* told that picking a team able to work extremely well together would be a crucial factor in pulling this mission off."

"Whatever the 'this' is," Jozsi retorted. "Thanks for the compliment. Thanks for signing us up when you don't even know what the hell we're in for, if that's even the truth." He shook his head wearily, turned and sprawled in his comfortable chair, arms hanging loose over its arms. Laci, on the other hand, bounced lightly on his heels, looking more energized by the second.

Sandor asked, "May I enter your sanctuary?" And moved into the room as he spoke.

"Like I could keep you out," Jozsi raised his hand in the direction of a wooden chair by a desk and said a bit more warmly. "Make yourself at home." He could only remain irritated with Sandor for so long.

Laci followed and stood by the window. He aimed his hand, gun-style tracking anyone walking.

Noticing, Sandor winked at Jozsi. "Practice, practice, practice."

"Well, that's one thing we can count on if Laci's involved: someone *will* get shot."

Laci nodded an emphatic yes, never taking his eyes off his target of the moment.

Sandor explained he'd been pulled out of Europe to help with the mysterious project. "Guys, it's that important," he said. "Important to the country. Your soon-to-be country," he reminded them. "Whatever the mission turns out to be, it's important to me, personally. My promotion will depend on how things go, so don't screw it up."

That opened the door for much ribbing about miseries they'd endured in order to help Sandor's career. "And what did we get?" Jozsi asked.

"Money, meals, women, adventure," Sandor replied, a satisfied smirk on his face. "And what do you like?"

"Money, meals, women, adventure," Laci said, from the edge of the bed where he'd gone to sit, finally bored with pretending to knock off soldiers walking across the grounds.

"You know, the firm in Langley worries about you guys getting out of control. Sandor continued with a serious expression, "Do you know why you're here?"

Jozsi responded just as seriously, "Yes, because we aren't all there." He pointed at Laci's head, which triggered a fit of laughter from the bed.

Sandor did not look at all amused. "Because you're a good team." He shrugged, "I agree, crazy, but despite that, good." He rose to leave. "Time zones and travel are catching up with me. Be on time tomorrow." He closed the door behind him before either of them could say a thing about the door hitting his ass on the way out.

The two old friends agreed that a short visit to the club was in order, even if they did have to show up on time and coherent the next morning. They settled in at a table to continue catching up with each other's exploits since their time in Korea. Before calling it a night, they returned to speculating about their mission.

"They say this guy's the enemy," Jozsi said, "but I don't know, it feels a lot different than taking out those crazy North Korean border guards. You okay with bumping him off?"

Laci shrugged. "Look at it this way, he's willing to sell his people out to a communist dictator like Castro."

"A traitor!" Jozsi said, yawning. "Okay, I see your point. Enough. Let's hit the hay."

"Hit the hay!" Laci said. "I like that," and he stored it in his memory for future use. "That will be good with girls," he mused, as they rose to leave.

The next morning, their trainers got straight to work. The Hungarians had three months to train. Jozsi would learn to maneuver a small fishing boat retrofitted with two 100-horsepower engines. "Vroom, vroom," Jozsi imitated a revving engine. The trainers were not entertained. Less fun than zooming around, but no less important, he'd also have to learn to maintain the boat in case of mechanical failure.

"Your life depends on this," said the head trainer, who happened to be in possession of a set of bright white buckteeth. Jozsi was sorry, but it was hard to take someone seriously when they looked so much like a chipmunk.

Laci's main task was to improve and practice his sharp-shooting techniques. The twist: he'd be shooting from a moving boat and would have to master hitting his target with dead accuracy at 200 yards. "Better than being on a horse," Laci said cheerfully, unfazed as ever by anything to do with guns.

During the final month of training Jozsi and Laci would have to change roles in case one had to take the other's place due to any unforeseen circumstances.

"Like if someone shoots you dead," Jozsi said helpfully.

"Or you," Laci smiled.

Trainers exchanged glances, surely thinking: these are the best men for the job?

The head instructor informed them that every other day they would study the geography of the area where President Chiari spent weekends. They'd have to memorize different faces from photographs to make certain they took out the president and not his cousin.

"Or grandmother," Jozsi added. "Family resemblances can be tricky."

Buckteeth flashed a momentary, tolerant smile. He could see he'd have his hands full with these two, no point alienating them right off the bat.

Their training began in earnest the following day, and they went over the same things day in, day out, week after week. Fall turned to winter, though in North Carolina this was not exactly a hardship. Temperate though the climate was, the days did drag. Jozsi learned to take the engine apart blindfolded and to shoot the high-powered rifle with dead-on accuracy from the crucial 200 yards.

Laci was impressed. "All these years," he said, "I thought you were just a lucky shot." And Jozsi returned the praise when Laci managed, with great effort, to take apart and then rebuild the engine. In the meantime, he'd thrown many a wrench across the workshop in frustrated rage, so there was much celebrating when he finally accomplished his task.

Jozsi swore that once he was out of the Army and settled down he would never have a gun in his house, not even a slingshot. Laci said he understood, and for his part, would never own a rigged-up fishing boat with two 100-horsepower motors. "I will have a wife with big breasts though. That is a certainty."

They weren't allowed to leave the base for the duration of their training and the only place they could go to relax was the club. There they found a few kindred spirits to trade lies with, but mostly the two stuck with each other. They were used to this, and their old rhythms returned — they managed to stay on good, laughing terms, a jovial club of two. One of the bartenders taught them backgammon. Between that and poker, gin rummy, and any other betting game they could come up with, they traded dollars back and forth, passing their evenings like two old codgers with nothing better to do.

For the Christmas holidays, the bartender put up a small spruce in a corner of the club and everyone took turns gently throwing tinsel on its limbs. That was the extent of the festivities. New Year's Eve passed much like any other night, though with more toasting and a little whiff of apprehension. They knew their time at Harvey Point was drawing to a close. Finally, at the end of the final week of January, they were given the word: next stop Panama. Departure, first thing in the morning.

Packing took very little time. Duffel bags open, belongings shoved in, done. They enjoyed their comfortable rooms and beds even more that night, not knowing where or what their next lodgings would be.

Sandor wasn't around to see them off in the morning, but they expected him to appear at the other end of the journey, a standard Sandor move.

They boarded a small plane and settled in, leaning forward to peer through the windows when they approached Panama, looking for the Panama Canal, soaking in the sight of turquoise water. "This beats North Korea," Laci said.

"This beats any Korea," added Jozsi.

They landed at the Quarry Heights Military base and were met by hot, humid air, and at the bottom of the airplane ramp, Sandor and three other intelligence agents. They clambered down the ramp stairs and Sandor held up a bottle of *palinka* in welcome.

"We could have used this in North Carolina," Jozsi said, grabbing the bottle. They spent some time at the base, during which they changed into looser, lighter clothes to better deal with the heat. They refreshed, they ate, and again studied their maps. They were told they'd be going to a waterfront resort area called Jaque, near the Rio Jaque. The area was lush with immense tropical rainforests spreading out to the east, and the swelling splendor of the Pacific Ocean to the west.

"It looks beautiful," Laci said, with a pleased sigh.

"You're fortunate," Sandor agreed. "In many ways, this will be an agreeable mission."

Jozsi laughed. "Always looking at the bright side. Never mind the shooting."

Eventually they were ferried back to the landing strip to board an Army cargo helicopter that would thwap-thwap-thwap them all the way to Jaque. "Otherwise," Sandor said, "it would take days. No direct route."

"Still beats Korea," Jozsi said, climbing aboard.

They landed at the Jaque Airport, a glorified term for a landing strip in the jungle, Jozsi thought. The whole group was then driven in a tourist bus to a resort motel on the waterfront about a half-mile outside of town. By now Jozsi was resigned to the mission and increasingly intrigued by the setting. More beautiful than the beach in Italy, he and Laci agreed and, Jozsi added, the sand and view incomparably better than what he'd seen in New Bedford. It was indeed looking to be an agreeable adventure; except for that thorny part about taking out the president.

Their motel was one of several strung along the beach in a purely resort stretch of Jaque. The two were housed in a modest suite — two small bedrooms and a central room, furnished with a large round table, two small wooden chairs, and two comfortable reading ones; Jozsi immediately claimed one of those. The front windows looked out on sand and sea. Behind the motel, forest and low mountains stretched out across a great distance. The agents remained bunched near the doorway.

Jozsi whispered to Laci, "These agents seem as nervous as whores in a church." He took matters in hand. "Laci and I need to catch our breath before you start in with us, so how about we all sit on our buttocks until we unwind." He cracked open the *palinka,* inhaled its scent and let out a long satisfied "Ah."

Sandor jumped in before any of the other agents could react, "Sure thing. No reason to rush. Why don't you all step outside for a bit and let them settle in."

"Settle down is more like it," one of the agents said *sotto voce,* but all three turned as one to leave.

Jozsi found a couple of glasses, and Sandor poured from the bottle and led them in clinking, though without a glass, he refrained from drinking. "So, you guys busting their balls for any particular reason?"

Jozsi was surprised when Laci spoke up. "You tell those morons that we call the shots and if they don't like it, they can do the fucking job themselves."

Sandor contained his initial reaction to his eyes, which he closed for a second. Then he went and stood at the window, his back to his charges. "Whatever you need, boys. As soon as the two of you are completely and utterly relaxed, you give me the word. In the meantime, I'll direct the others to kneel outside your door like the three wise men, awaiting a sign from the almighty."

"Now you're being an asshole," Jozsi said, joining him at the window, putting an arm around him. "Send the three monkeys off to find more glasses and a couple more chairs and let them join us for some drinks before the lectures begin."

Sandor complied, and when the agents returned with their assigned objects, he told them to relax, that later they'd get the chance to explain their roles. "You're going to be spending a lot of time together, let's start things off on the right foot."

They squeezed close around the table and made small talk. All lies, Jozsi suspected, including their names: Mike, Stan, Charlie. At last Jozsi lifted an upraised thumb, his signal to Sandor that the agents could begin their spiel. Sandor pointed at the chunkiest agent, Stan, who told them that two bank accounts had been set up in their names, with enough money for them to remain in Jaque for almost six months, at least into early June. He handed Jozsi and Laci each a savings account card. Mike, the one with jet-black hair, gave Jozsi a list with the names of local suspected revolutionaries they hoped would approach the two Hungarians for help in building up their arms and explosives cache.

Jozsi stared at the piece of paper. "I'm missing a step. Are we supposed to carry signs saying, "Looking for revolutionaries, guns for sale?""

Mike explained the plan: they were to make a bar called *Fernando's* their base. "Go in every night, be generous about buying drinks. It's not a tourist hangout; it draws locals and expats who've settled here. Get known in that crowd and soon enough you'll be spotted by the people we expect to approach you."

Jozsi waved the piece of paper. "How the hell are we going to get small arms if one of these Joes does ask?"

Mike assured them that the local American base would fulfill all their needs. He handed Jozsi a small piece of paper. "Call that number whenever you require something. Once you get the lay of the land, figure out a good drop-off and we'll get you whatever you need."

Sandor stepped in to flesh out the directive. The president came to the retreat only on weekends, but they were told to scope out the presidential retreat seven days a week. They were also supposed to mix with the locals, act like two guys with lots of money and connections to American officers in Panama City. "Come up with a cover story to explain why you're acting like a couple of beach bums — but bums with connections. We want you to find out where the revolutionaries are hiding out, who their Cuban advisors are, and anything else we can use to nip this bullshit in the bud."

"I see you've finally been filled in," Jozsi said with a wink.

Next, Charlie handed over a list with the itemized prices they should charge for various types of small arms. The list ranged from a .45 caliber pistol to the latest M16 rifle. Jozsi held the list out for Laci to study, pointing at one line.

"Hand-held rocket launcher?" He turned to face Charlie. "You guys are nuts."

"Nothing to worry about." Charlie answered, "They're special rockets; the kind that'll blow up in their faces if they ever try to use one."

"Good to know," said Laci, wistfully. There went his idea to sneak one out to the jungle for a little bit of fun.

Before the agents left, Sandor handed Jozsi the key for the boat and told him where it was moored in the harbor. "It's painted dark gray so as not to stand out. The boat name is *Delfin,* it's painted on the aft. That's the back, the ass of the boat, okay?"

"Fuck you," Jozsi said. "Three months messing around with that boat, I know what is aft."

"Oh, excuse me," said Sandor, all fake apology. "By the way, *Delfin* means Dolphin in case you were wondering."

"Poetic," Jozsi said.

Sandor ignored him, instead pointing toward one of the bedrooms, telling Laci his high-powered rifle kit was stashed in a corner of the closet. He gave them a phone number at the Hilton, about 10 miles from where they'd first landed. He promised that an agent would be available for them at all times.

"Just a helicopter-hop away," Jozsi pointed out. "Not much help in a pinch."

Sandor shrugged. "The best we can offer. When I'm around, I'll lodge in Jaque, if that makes you feel any better." And with that, he bid them good night.

The two friends settled in on the porch and finished the rest of the *palinka* while enjoying the warm sea breeze. They spoke in the special Hungarian slang they'd developed in Korea to confuse the CIA or anyone else who might be interested in their private conversations. They'd learned to be wary of bugged rooms no matter what continent they landed on.

Laci was in an unusually reflective mood. "We're gonna buy the farm if we keep this shit up."

"Your new philosophy impresses me, *haverom*," Jozsi said. "Glad to see you're coming to your senses. If you want to weasel out of this trip, just tell Sandor. He'll get your ass out of here and back to Korea or Vietnam in no time at all. You're the one who re-enlisted, idiot. I'm just trying to run out the clock till I'm free of this bullshit. I've got two years to go. I figure by now I can screw them over more than they can screw me."

"I know I'm an idiot, I just didn't know what the fuck else to do. But now I'm beginning to think we're pushing our luck. Sooner or later the firm will put us in a situation we can't get out of and I'm beginning to worry that this is that." Laci put his face in his hands.

"To this *not* being that," Jozsi raised his glass and tossed back the last of his drink. They called it a night and retired to their separate bedrooms to sleep their way out of dark thoughts.

In the morning, they explored the area and checked out the *Delfin* for bugs and bombs. They ventured downtown and picked out casual beachwear and swimsuits, trying to imagine what a couple of boys from the States would choose if their rich parents were footing the bill. That day, a check arrived for them, forwarded to the hotel from Boston, purportedly from Jozsi's "grandmother," courtesy of the firm. Another one of the CIA's little touches to add more cover to their disguise as spoiled rich boys.

The clerk had to find the manager, saying she couldn't cash such a large amount without his okay — word of that would get around. The manager brought out the cash, idly asking how long they were staying in Panama.

Jozsi grinned, "All the way through the summer, amigo, as long as you take good care of me and my *campadre*." He tried to lose his Hungarian accent, but failed. But America was the land of immigrants, so who cared what the manager or anyone else at the motel thought. As long as they paid their way it wouldn't matter if they were third generation Americans or first.

By the end of the first week in February, they'd created a solid identity as two beach bums living off family money. At night, they mixed with the natives and bought rounds of drinks like drunken sailors with one night and one night only of shore leave. They easily made friends with their thirst-quenching largesse. They kept booze on hand at the motel and invited people back for a nightcap, always with an eye toward screening possible clients.

Each morning before they headed out to fish, they stopped off at the wharf bait shop to buy bait and beer. They made friends with the owner, wheedling him for information as to where the best fishing spots were. They didn't give a damn about catching fish, but that was part of their cover, so they fished like maniacs and tipped the bait shop owner well for his advice.

On their first fishing excursion, Laci said, "Don't tell me that you and Alex were great fishermen in Budapest."

Jozsi shot back, "Anyone brought up in Budapest knows how to land a sucker. And remember what a sucker is — a fish that lives off the bottom of a river, living in the sludge."

Neither had done much fishing but for their cover story that didn't really matter. If they looked like total screw-ups, it would only encourage the locals to think they were rich fools out for a lark, ripe to be taken advantage of.

They ventured out each day the weather allowed, and inched their way closer and closer to the presidential resort. When they came within a certain range of the resort, the guards would motor out and chase them off. They were hostile at first, while Jozsi sputtered, "We follow the fish, we follow the fish." But after the two had made several incursions the guards mellowed, especially when the president wasn't in residence. They still shooed the *Delfin* away, but without malice. It seemed they'd decided these particular two fishermen were harmless enough.

Jozsi and Laci had been instructed to give the locals most of the fish they caught and within a couple of weeks a group of regulars awaited them at the marina each afternoon. They figured that didn't hurt their image with the guards, either; word getting around that they were good-hearted guys who treated the locals kindly would be a plus.

At *Fernando's* each night, the two paid for all the drinks ordered by any off-duty presidential guards they recognized. The guards never refused a drink and most of them wandered over to their table or place at the bar to thank them for the largesse. After a few weeks, Diego, the night bartender, began putting the guards' drinks on Jozsi's tab, and needless to say, the two generous bums stopped getting shooed away from the presidential retreat entirely.

At night, chatting up the girls at the bar, the two would casually brag about their connections to the local U. S. Army base. It took only a few weeks for Beatriz, one of the regulars, to sidle up and ask if they would be interested in making extra money. She pointed to a couple of men they'd seen a few times before. They were seated at a table on the back patio. She leaned in close, "They have an interesting offer for you."

Jozsi and Laci had rehearsed their reactions to the very thing they hoped would happen. Jozsi feigned outrage, Laci took the calmer role, reminding his friend of certain uncomfortable facts: "Your grandmother is late with the check sometimes and we need to pay bills at the hotel."

Jozsi calmed down, saying he supposed it couldn't hurt to hear Beatriz out, but insisting that his uncle, the general — "My aunt married well," he said in an aside — must never know he was doing anything that wasn't completely aboveboard. Laci headed out to the patio and Jozsi stayed at the bar talking with Beatriz.

Soon, a man with prematurely gray hair entered; he was short but exuded a powerful presence. "*Hola,*" he called to Beatriz when he caught sight of her. She introduced him as Pedro, and within minutes he'd made it clear to Jozsi that he was interested in buying small arms. If Jozsi and Laci could help him with that, he'd make it worth their while.

Jozsi saw Pedro give a subtle nod to the two men on the patio. Jozsi wasn't sure why Beatriz had made sure to separate the Hungarians, but he played along. Pedro was behind whatever Laci was being offered, of this Jozsi was certain. Beatriz was no fool; she'd identified Jozsi as the leader and made sure the two powers could have a one-on-one.

That night Jozsi squeezed more information about local activities out of Pedro than the CIA had managed to gather in a whole year. By the following week, the Hungarians were delivering small arms to their customers. The drop point was close to three kilometers from their motel, and just past the riotous edge of the jungle. An unruly sprawl of bushes that seemed to be awaiting permission to merge with the larger wildness was the first marker. A stone's throw away from there stood a distinctive coral snake tree, its trunk leaning noticeably to the right. The trunk was covered in markings similar to a coral snake's and its leaves swooped down like bird feathers. Twenty feet away, just past the jungle's threshold, was a hole 2-feet deep by 5-feet long, large enough to hold a sizable assortment of weapons. It was covered over by two trap doors; the whole thing disguised by vines and huge palm fronds. Jozsi couldn't help but be reminded of the coffin in Ura.

Two weeks later, they'd built up enough credibility for Pedro to introduce them to the underground organizers of the revolution, the men backing Fidel Castro's brother. Jozsi and Laci managed to convince Pedro that they were completely apolitical and cared more about money and a good time than what any country was up to, including the United States. As obvious émigrés to America, it was an easy sell. The organizers paid after each delivery, and Jozsi and Laci continued to throw money around the bar and live up to their reputation as beach bums with nothing on their minds besides fishing, drinking, and dancing with dames. In other words, it was an ideal vacation for Laci and a tolerably pleasant one for Jozsi, who was counting the months till he could leave the Army and the CIA behind. He felt he'd already experienced enough danger for two lifetimes.

The two continued to venture out on the *Delfin*, becoming better fisherman by the day. As they trawled, Jozsi took to edging the boat closer and closer to the presidential retreat. When President Chiari was there, he rarely came to the docks by the water, and when he did, his bodyguards were in tow. They noted how closely Chiari's bodyguards hugged his perimeter at all times, whether he was strolling the grounds or, as was more often the case, sitting outside on the expansive terrace. Jozsi wondered how the hell they were supposed to shoot someone who was always surrounded, but that was Laci's problem not his. Laci just shrugged, claiming he'd find a way.

Occasionally a guard would offer a desultory wave in their direction, but no one chased them away. When they were further from shore, Laci practiced with his high-power telescope, kneeling in the boat and holding it low so as not to attract attention. At the end of each day they fished, Jozsi made a point of opening the engine wide and racing to a pre-arranged pickup point, making note of the wind, tide, and waves. Back at the hotel he'd record the relevant data. His goal was to make a chart containing enough information to help him move directly and swiftly no matter what the weather conditions.

Sandor dropped in periodically, appearing out of the blue at their door, or the bar, sometimes even at the marina. One day they motored in to find him, bare feet dangling off the dock, sipping a beer at their mooring. He announced that President Chiari would be holding a big celebration at his retreat on Easter, six weeks hence.

The firm wanted to eliminate Chiari on that day, reasoning that the bodyguards would have to give him a wider berth with family and guests on hand. Sandor asked if they were ready. Yes, they were.

Jozsi had news for Sandor as well. He'd overhead Beatriz make an oblique reference to an impeding event. Jozsi took it to indicate that the communist revolutionaries were ready to set the date for taking over the existing regime, and it sounded like they would be ready to act the week after Easter.

"So, I believe this is very good timing," Jozsi said, nodding thoughtfully, thinking it more than likely that the firm had heard this from other sources as well. There was no telling what other people Sandor or another handler might be in touch with in the area. Of course, there was an expectation that this Easter plan, if successful, would result in immense turmoil in such a religious country. There was concern, but it was overridden by the sum of other events. As lapsed Catholics, Jozsi and Laci cared only about getting out of there alive, so a day other than Easter would be preferable, but there was no chance of that.

The two continued to supply Pedro with small arms. Beatriz and her friend Ofella were getting their fair share of the arms money since they helped navigate the exchange of goods. Sandor let the Hungarians keep the money; it simplified his life not to have to keep paying Jozsi and Laci their allowances. He explained that lucky for them, CIA bookkeeping was a little fast and loose.

The women, having also risen to girlfriend status, had no idea that their two gringos were looking for anything other than a good time and easy money. They gradually dropped the names of the leaders of the revolution, and went on to complain about how poorly they were paid by the rebels, even after having found them a source for small arms. Just one more reason Sandor thought it sensible to keep the profits from the gun sales inside Panama. Getting the leaders' names was a large enough feather in Sandor's cap for him to invite the Hungarians over to his hotel at the far end of Jaque. He broke out a bottle of the finest *palinka* they'd ever seen, and filled them in on what he'd learned about certain escapades of the captain in charge of the presidential retreat.

"Mind you, Captain Villars is married to one of President Chiari's second cousins," Sandor explained, laying out a series of photographs of the guard in compromising activities with a stream of very young women. "If these don't come in handy, I'll buy you a bottle of this very *palinka*."

"Deal," Jozsi said. It truly was the best *palinka* he'd ever had.

~~~

In the middle of March, they arranged for Laci to set up a "surprise" birthday party for Jozsi at *Fernando's*. Laci had Ofella invite all of the guards who weren't on duty at the presidential retreat, and as they'd hoped, Captain Villars was to be among the guests. Laci said, "We better bring along those pictures Sandor is so proud of. And a lot of money so we can entertain him and his goons all night." He'd already told Diego to put everything on Jozsi's tab because "grandma" was buying; she'd expressly asked Laci to act as host on her behalf, but insisted the cash come from Jozsi's account, since it was her money in the first place.

He was pleased with himself for this brilliant idea. Jozsi less so, saying, "Laci, I think you learn too fast, especially when it comes to spending other people's money. I'm the guest, I shouldn't be paying."

"Too late," Laci grinned.

On the night of the party, they showed up at the bar and took their seats in a darkened barroom, Jozsi pretending to believe Diego's claim that there was a power outage. Suddenly lights blinked alive and a three-piece band began to serenade Jozsi with a slightly samba-esque version of the happy birthday song. Beatriz and Ofella carried out a huge round birthday cake lit with multiple candles and made Jozsi make a wish and blow. Diego strode out from behind the bar carrying a special wide-brim sombrero that he insisted Jozsi, as the man of the night, must wear.

Laci pointed to Captain Villars. "I'm going to see if I can squeeze anything out of him about the retreat's Easter schedule." He plunked himself down at the captain's table, quickly ordering a round for everyone. Jozsi, sweating slightly under the sombrero, remained at the table, entertained by local girls shaking maracas and singing native songs. Beatriz indulged his flirtation with the girls, leaning in for a sensual kiss now and then.

During a lull between songs, Laci returned and leaned close to Jozsi's ear to relate that the captain was not divulging anything willingly. "I need our secret weapon," he whispered. Jozsi had wrapped the photographs in a piece of paper, tucked inside his pants pocket. He handed the pictures to Laci and turned back to his female coterie.

Around midnight, Laci returned with a shit-eating grin on his face, so pleased Jozsi didn't even need to ask how things had gone. By this time, he knew all of Laci's facial expressions, whether in defeat or glory, and this was definitely a glory grin. Normally, Jozsi would have been the one to wheedle information, so Laci was especially pleased with himself.

By one in the morning, the party was winding down; the locals had to be up and at work by six in the morning. Jozsi paid the bar bill, even though he knew it to be recklessly inflated, and even gave Diego a tip so large he'd have reason to brag about it for years to come.

Laci waited on the porch with a bottle of tequila. Jozsi stretched out in the chair next to his and for a few moments, they sat quietly, enjoying the night's cool breeze.

Eventually, Diego broke the stillness by calling out that he was going up to his room above the bar, and if they needed anything more, they should help themselves, the door was unlocked. "Just shut the door behind when you leave."

Laci poured two shots of tequila. He was still wide-awake; his body buzzing with energy — much like a manic mosquito before it swoops in for the kill.

Jozsi raised his glass and said, "Okay, country boy, tell me about your time with the captain. Use the Hungarian slang," he raised his eyes in the direction of Diego's room above.

Laci recounted all the details of the president's planned activities on Easter morning, minute by minute. They'll be having a *Matanza*, he said, a big party, with scores of people coming. "They kill a pig in the morning and cook it all day, then they eat, drink and make merry."

"You can't have Easter without a crucifixion, but that's a pretty quick turnaround," Jozsi joked.

Laci ignored him. "There will be many tables set up and Chiari will be standing to address his guests at different times. He lights the fire that cooks the pig, and he often wanders from table to table, pouring wine for his guests. Because this occasion is with friends and family, the bodyguards are supposed to lay low. But the best news is that Chiari stands and greets them all one by one, under the arbor near the water."

It took quite a while to recount all of the details, and Laci had to poke Jozsi awake a few times — as the birthday boy, he'd consumed a lot more alcohol than Laci. When the recitation was complete Jozsi congratulated him, "Someday, *haverom*, if you ever return to Hungary, you'll be ready to start up in Budapest right where I left off."

Laci laughed, pleased by the compliment, and responded that from all he knew after his life in Gyor, he couldn't see Jozsi ever fitting in as a country boy, in any country.

The light began to change, sunrise a breath away. As Laci picked up the nearly empty bottle of tequila and they headed back to the motel, their girlfriends having abandoned the party hours earlier for their own quiet beds, Laci asked if Jozsi had ever noticed Pedro's necklace — an Aztec sunstone emblem hanging from a gold chain.

"The damn thing's so big how could anyone *not* notice it," Jozsi said, sleepily.

"I'd give my right arm for that thing. I've offered him money for it, but he turns me down every time. Says it's his good luck charm, handed down from his ancestors. Says he has to die with it on."

Jozsi joked, "We could ask Sandor to arrange that." He wondered what made Laci want it so badly, but was too tired to ask. They polished off the tequila and as the sun pinked the horizon, collapsed in their rooms.

At last horizontal, the exhausted birthday boy, blood racing with booze, could not manage to sleep. He found himself thinking about the poor son-of-a-bitch president and how they'd topple him in a week, and on Easter Day. Unkind, to say the least. He thought of how easily Panama might avoid a communist dictatorship, thanks to Laci's ability to waste a person with one well-aimed round. He had no doubt that Laci would succeed. They might not make it out of there, but neither would Chiari. He asked himself why this situation didn't exist in Hungary; why, during the upheaval after the Revolution failed, the CIA hadn't hired risk-takers as reckless as they? If someone had shot Janos Kadar, the Prime Minister of Hungary, Jozsi might right now be admiring a framed master's degree instead of spending his days trawling for fish he didn't even want, with murder on his mind.

The next morning, they went through the exact same routine as during the previous two months. As soon as they were out on the open water, far from earshot, Laci told Jozsi exactly how he'd squeezed the captain's balls to acquire the details of the president's Easter plans. "When he saw the first picture — that one showing the girl with the red birthmark on her ass — his eyes fell out of his head," Laci exclaimed. I only had to show him that one and he was putty in my hands. I guess Chiari is big on family loyalty and would can the captain or worse if he found out about all those girlies."

"That's funny," Jozsi said, "coming from a guy who's willing to sell his entire country down the river." They cursed communists everywhere and dissected the damage the Russian and Hungarian Communists had done in Hungary. It passed the time between tugs on their fishing lines.

Thinking of Chiari as a communist-in-the-making made them feel slightly better about plotting the man's death. All those weekend sightings of the president had taken a toll on whatever level of chilly objectivity they'd managed when first discussing his demise. Seeing Chiari's glasses glinting in the sun as he emerged from the house, papers in hand, to sit on the piazza and work, watching him throw birdseed, stretch tall and then bend to touch his toes, little things like that, had made him seem too familiar, too human. He was a hard worker, that's what all the guards said, toiling through the weekends, only taking time off to walk in his gardens and socialize briefly with family and other weekend guests. And he treated them decently, the guards said. He didn't sound like a tyrant or an evil man.

As they motored around the bay, Jozsi and Laci talked about their plans following the mission, if they indeed managed to escape. Laci would receive another stripe and two weeks in Hong Kong before returning to Vietnam as a Sergeant First Class in his intelligence corps. He had no other choice, and unlike Jozsi, was content to return to Hong Kong for R&R rather than venturing on to a new location. "I like knowing my way around. I like going back to the bars where they recognize me."

That was the farm boy in him, Jozsi thought; routine bred in from the start. Morning chores, labor in the fields, tending the animals, the same thing every day. The war threw a wrench into the routine, but it was routine Laci truly craved, and in an oddly twisted way, the army gave him that. Jozsi, on the other hand, saw the war and the Russian incursion as explosions that blew the lid off everything he knew; that made him want to race into the future in some other place. But really, he'd always been hungry for change. He thought of his Uncle Peter, and his family, picturing them at the table. He suddenly felt old and alone. Too much time in a boat, he thought, steering the *Delfin* toward the pickup spot and throwing open the throttle, wind pressing hard against his face. Enough ruminating he decided, turning his full attention to the waves and the boat's speed.

They practiced for one more week, and again and again, before they came in, Jozsi made sure to take the boat out to the open sea, to the point where they'd meet the submarine, and in the right amount of time no matter what the conditions. He'd tried to make it look like a regular post-fishing kicking-up-of-heels so as to get the guards used to it. Speed was the only way they'd manage to get away from the Panamanian Coast Guard, which was certain to give chase.

~~~

Two days before the Easter holiday, Sandor showed up with Mike, Stan, and Charlie, the agents who'd first brought them to Jaque. They went over the plan one more time, Sandor running down a punch list to make sure there'd be no screw-ups on their end. They were given cyanide pills, in case something did go wrong and they were captured. Lack of pills allowed for the possibility of torture; torture allowed for the possibility of information extracted. No dignity in that. Jozsi and Laci tucked the pills in their shirt pockets. Jozsi asked Charlie if they had to return the pills if they managed to get out of this alive. "It's not a money-back kinda deal," he said with a Texas drawl. "You get to keep them as a souvenir. Might have you a bad wife someday, need an escape hatch."

"You're a dark son-of-a-bitch," Jozsi laughed. "I like that."

Easter morning came. Jozsi and Laci had restrained themselves for the previous three nights, heading to bed early and sober. They were ready to go into action by six in the morning. They'd cleared their rooms to make sure no physical evidence remained. Laci checked his rifle one last time, and they loaded their belongings into the boat.

Jozsi checked the dynamite, checked the timer, which had been set to make sure the boat blew to hell and back exactly five minutes after they climbed on board the submarine. And as he always did before any significant action, Jozsi fingered his bullet whistle for luck.

As the locals headed to church for the Resurrection services, the two Hungarians motored out to sea. Jozsi told Laci that he should be on his way to church to confess his sins.

Laci laughed. "What sins? I haven't committed any yet!"

"None in Panama, you mean." They exchanged a look, thinking back to their time together in Korea.

Easter morning was beautiful, the water exceptionally calm. As they sliced the boat away from shore and out of the harbor, they reminisced about the Hungarian custom of visiting the local girls early Easter morning, spraying them with inexpensive lilac water, receiving coins in exchange from the girls' parents. Jozsi envisioned Erika, long braids hanging down her back, smiling as he sprayed lilac water above her head.

Moving out on the open water, the conversation subsided as they entered mission mode; each concentrating on funneling mental energy toward the task at hand. They motored steadily toward the waters off the retreat, slowly so as not to attract attention, and as they neared their target area, put their fishing rods in the water, without bait, though no one could tell that from the shore.

Jozsi donned his headset to check in by radio. He received code "Hun," which meant that they were ready and clear; the submarine was waiting for them just outside the bay. Laci assembled his rifle, attaching all of the hardware to his gun, including the telescope and special sight.

They had practiced for weeks and weeks for this occasion and were ready to carry out their mission as soon as the president arrived from Sunday service. Their first and best chance at a clean shot would be when he went to greet his guests at the colorful waterfront gardens on the far side of the vast lawn. He'd walk from the house all the way to the gardens, and then the guests would walk along the shoreline to meet him.

As the two trawled up and down in front of the palace, more people arrived, dressed in their best for the Easter celebration. The bodies gathered in clumps, greeting each other with hugs and kisses. From the water, they looked like multicolored blooms rustled by the wind. Human bouquets, Jozsi thought wistfully. Though this day would be ruined for all of them if things went as planned. Still, better than enduring life under communism.

He kept up a constant communication under their code name, and told Laci word was that the president had just pulled up from the church. Jozsi held his left palm up, then abruptly fisted his hand, the signal for Laci to get ready.

Laci readied himself and his high-powered rifle, looking much like a violinist tucking instrument under chin before the conductor lifts the baton. He double-checked his telescope with tender care and readied himself for the big performance.

They'd killed before, they'd killed together, but killing in defense of your life in the middle of battle or in the course of a kidnapping attempt was a completely different animal than stalking this particular prey.

"Nervous?" Jozsi asked.

"It's not every day I do this," Laci shot back. "Yes, nervous."

Jozsi reminded him that he understood those feelings, and that if Laci had any doubt, to hand over the rifle since he was a pretty good shooter himself.

That was all it took to calm Laci's nerves. No way was he going to give Jozsi the glory. He positioned the rifle carefully, so that he could comfortably keep a steady hold. He was in full hunter mode.

"We were born to live dangerously, *bizal bennem*," Laci said, his eyes never leaving the distant shoreline.

"Trust you? A country boy." Jozsi snorted.

"This is what we are meant to do. I can't see us having lived any differently, not even if we have to die here."

"I don't know when the fuck I'm going to die, but given a choice, I'd rather be stabbed by a jealous husband than shot out of this boat."

Jozsi turned the wheel and made another pass by the presidential retreat, pulling in and re-casting his fishing reel for good measure. They were close enough to hear a local band begin to play native songs as the guests mingled on the lawn.

Finally, President Chiari appeared from inside the house and began to stride across the lawn, bodyguards on all sides of the man. Laci grunted in frustration. He kept his rifle at the ready, and as the front guard trotted ahead to the arbor where the president would stand to greet his guests, Laci pressed his finger against the trigger. There it was, the perfect open shot. No collateral damage in sight.

"Jozsi, prepare the boat to meet the sub." Just before Jozsi began to gun the two 100-horsepower engines, the radio crackled on and he heard their secret emergency code, followed by, "Huns, abort, abort, abort."

A split second before Laci pulled the trigger, Jozsi shoved the rifle barrel down toward the water and the gun went off, hitting the water three feet from the boat. The band's music ensured no one on shore heard a thing.

Laci jumped up, body shot full of adrenaline, and started swearing wildly in Hungarian. Jozsi had never heard curses like that before. Country curses, involving manure and pigs and offal. He'd have laughed if he weren't feeling like he'd just been plugged into an electric chair. Once Laci calmed down, Jozsi, with rat-a-tat speed, explained that the firm had called off the operation, they were home free, they had nothing to confess if they ever again made it to the inside of a church. He felt a level of relief he didn't know existed.

Jozsi and Laci sped back to the marina and clambered out of the boat to find Sandor waiting for them at the dock, calm as could be. He thanked them for the effort they'd put into the operation; the firm had been impressed. Simultaneously the two held their hands out, their expressions pleading for information. Sandor shook his head no. "You win some, you lose some," he shrugged. "You did fine. This wasn't cancelled because of anything on your end." He ran his hand across his mouth, a zipper closing. There would be no more. "Mexico City sound good to you guys? We're treating you to a week's stay if you want it." They did.

The two unwound from their Panamanian months, relieved to be out from under the firm's watchful eye.

The night before they were to leave Mexico City and again go their separate ways, they sat poolside, stretched out on plush patio lounge chairs, sipping piña coladas. They told each other how great they were, how the Americans couldn't do without them.

After a few more piña coladas, Jozsi pulled a gold necklace with an Aztec emblem from his pants pocket. He put it in his comrade's hand and quickly folded his fingers over it. "Remember me as a friend for as long as you have this."

Laci uncurled his fingers and stared down to discover the emblem balanced face up on its clumped chain. He stared as though it were treasure from an Egyptian pyramid. "Jozsi! How in god's name did you manage to get this away from Pedro?"

"Have you ever heard of Ali Baba and the Forty Thieves," Jozsi asked, grinning.

"Yeah, and what does that have to do with this?"

Jozsi sipped his piña colada and smiled like the Cheshire Cat. "Nothing, and that's all I'm going to tell you about how I got it."

Laci put the gold chain around his neck, gently fingering the emblem. "I'll remember you every time I take a shower."

"Oh good, at least once a month then," Jozsi smiled.

After breakfast the next morning, they hugged each other long and hard. They heard each other sniffle. They stood back, wiping away tears. Laci was headed back to Vietnam; Jozsi to Fort Devens to try to resume the military life he'd left many months before.

Jozsi's plane was to depart just before noon, Laci's later in the afternoon. He watched Jozsi climb aboard an airport-bound bus. Jozsi took a seat facing the hotel. They found each other's faces just as the bus pulled away, each raising a hand in farewell. Laci called out, "V*iszont latasra,*" till we meet again, and Jozsi nodded and smiled, though inside he felt sadder than he'd felt in a very long time. The bus pulled away and Laci stood stock still, following it with his eyes till the bus, belching smoke, moved out of view.

22

Chez Ann

Fort Devens looked just the same as it did when Jozsi had headed off for his Panama adventure. He found this almost comforting, his military home unchanged. He stopped by General Yancy's to let him know he'd returned. The General invited Jozsi for a mid-afternoon visit in his study a few days later; he was eager to hear any details of his recent excursion that Jozsi was allowed to share.

Back in his quarters, Jozsi was unpacking when there was a knock at the door. His company commander, Captain Cardelli, politely asked if he could enter. Jozsi thought: what's with him? He's an officer; he can barge in any time.

"Of course, come in," Jozsi indicated Cardelli should take the chair, while he sat on the edge of his bed. After a few minutes of salt and pepper talk, the Captain invited him out for a drink at the nearest plush eatery, *The Bull Run*. Jozsi changed into civilian clothes explaining it wouldn't look good for a mere non-commissioned officer to be seen drinking with a Captain in downtown Shirley, a consideration the captain appreciated.

Cardelli had always treated Jozsi decently, though had never expressed any interest in him or his whereabouts, so the invitation came as a surprise. "Never been here," he mentioned as they parked. The Army doesn't pay me enough to drink in a place like this." He held open the heavy entrance door for the Captain.

"The drinks are on me," Cardelli said, good-naturedly. Soon enough, the reason for the captain's invitation became clear. "I hear you spend a fair amount of time with General Yancy. He seems to have taken a shine to you."

Jozsi shrugged noncommittally and waited for Cardelli to continue. Where exactly was this going?

"I'm wondering if my name has ever come up…"

Ah-ha. Jozsi tilted his head in inquiry, remaining tight-lipped. No reason to make this too easy.

The captain swallowed. "If perhaps he's mentioned me in any of your conversations."

Jozsi replied that why yes, his name had come up; the General had been interested in Cardelli's leadership qualities. It was Cardelli's turn to, with a look, ask for more. Jozsi let one, two, three beats pass, then proceeded to earn his drinks. "Let me assure you, Captain, he's heard nothing but positive things from me. You've been good to me since I came back from North Korea, in fact, you've treated me generously since I joined your company." He continued pleasantly brown nosing the man and the drinks flowed as freely as water over Niagara Falls. Eventually the captain admitted his curiosity had been piqued by General Yancy's interest in Jozsi and that he'd even gone so far as to look into Jozsi's military records, "But a lot of good that did me." He'd kept running into documents stamped "NFYI" – Not for Your Information.

"Captain, if you wanted to know about me, all you had to do was ask! I could have given you the exact same runaround and saved you all kinds of time." They shared a laugh, and sensing he'd gotten on Cardelli's good side, Jozsi relaxed.

"So, what the hell are you doing in the Army?" Cardelli asked.

Jozsi assured him that he was protecting the country from undesirable communists so that Cardelli and his family could rest at night, safe and sound. From then on, they talked easily, though by suppertime, the Captain was close to incoherent; Jozsi had to pretty much pour him into the passenger seat, and then dig around in the glove compartment to find his registration and home address. The Captain snored loudly, his head flung back, as Jozsi drove him home.

Jozsi went to the front door to warn Mrs. Cardelli that her husband was not at his best. "Not again!" she said irritably, insisting that he could not afford for the neighbors to see him stumbling across the lawn. Could Jozsi take him somewhere, get him sobered up so he could at least walk rather than be dragged from the car? Of course, he'd be happy to help.

Back to *The Bull Run* they went. Jozsi ordered food for both, coffee for the captain, more drinks for himself. The coffee made Cardelli talkative in a peevish kind of way. Jozsi heard all about his problems with military life, his financial concerns, his sex life, his wife's ill-humor, everything. He dropped the captain off, knowing he'd be getting exactly no sex that night. He promised Mrs. Cardelli he'd bring the car back first thing in the morning. All in all, it had been a satisfying day, especially since he now had more than a few things to hold over Cardelli should the need arise.

The next morning, Jozsi lay in bed, trying to adjust to a head-spiking hangover before daring to get vertical. He managed to pull himself together in time to return Captail Cardelli's car and make it to a meeting at General Yancy's at 3 PM sharp. Yancy greeted him warmly and told his Jeep driver to take the rest of the day off. The driver, who was relatively new to Fort Devens, thought: I don't know this Hungarian sergeant, but I like him already.

Surprising to Jozsi, the General settled them in the living room, explaining his wife was away, visiting relations down South. "It's us and the maid, and as you may remember, Rita can make any drink on the face of this earth." Soon Rita had supplied them with cocktails, doubles per the General's request, and finger food, and said she'd be back to check on them regularly.

The General saluted and toasted Jozsi's safe return, then leaned back in his chair and said, "Tell me all." Jozsi told Yancy as much about Panama as he was allowed to divulge. The General ate it up, and

Jozsi could see in his eyes how much he envied Jozsi his youth and adventures, from chatting up revolutionaries in the bar to racing around in a motorboat.

As their visit came to an end, the General asked if there was anything he could do to help him. Jozsi spent a moment feeling quite full of himself — a general offering assistance to a soldier didn't happen every day — then mentioned that he was due in Washington to report on his Panama experiences.

"I may be stuck there for a while. I'd appreciate it if you'd notify Captain Cardelli and remind him that no one needs to know anything about my absence." He also asked if Yancy might reassure the Captain; tell him he was doing a fine job. "It would mean a lot to get praise from you." Making friends left and right Jozsi was. General Yancy, in fine humor after their talk, made a note on a piece of paper and assured Jozsi he'd place a call to Cardelli first thing in the morning.

Early the following morning, a rapping at the door quickly brought Jozsi out of the bathroom where he'd been lathering his face for a shave. He threw on trousers, and opened the door to find a sputtering Captain Cardelli. "The base commander, your friend Yancy, called me just now, *personally.*" Jozsi had been hoping Yancy's phone call would have been enough to keep Cardelli completely out of his face — he was a bit of a bore when you got right down to it. "General Yancy told me you've got an important trip coming up and not to interfere with your schedule. He wouldn't say where you were going." The Captain seemed to think they were now buddies enough for Jozsi to divulge his destination.

"Sorry, Sir, 'NFYI'," Jozsi smiled.

"Fair enough," Cardelli replied, returning to the subject he cared about. "And he told me, he said, 'Captain Cardelli, you're doing a fine job with your company.'"

"Very good," Jozsi smiled again.

Cardelli continued practically pissing himself with excitement, "And he recommended my cavalry for duty in Vietnam!"

Running through Jozsi's mind were two questions: how did such an idiot get made captain and how truly awful was his wife? But all he did was grin. "Great news!"

He really was growing weary of the Army. His company commander strutted away, wishing him a good trip, "To the Pentagon or wherever you're going," he said with a wink, revealing he was not entirely clueless after all.

~~~

Before heading to Washington, Jozsi went up to Boston to visit his old haunt, *Nagybácsi Miksa's*. Entering, he recognized a few faces, but the elation he'd expected to feel failed to materialize. The place felt different, the way a schoolroom seems small when you return as an adult. He asked Miksa, "What's changed?"

"Nothing," he assured Jozsi. "The people here, the place hasn't changed, it's you who've changed. You're living a fast life! We sit here on Washington Street while you're off on who knows what secret adventures."

It was good to see Miksa, however disappointed Jozsi was at not feeling more connected to a place that had been, for a time, his second home.

On the way back to the base in Shirley, Jozsi asked himself: am I living a fast life, or are the people around me standing still? His own life seemed normal from the inside, but when he stopped to reflect on everything he'd experienced since World War Two, it occurred to him that from someone else's point of view, his life had been tornado wild. He himself no longer knew what kind of life he wanted. The normal life, staying in one place, having a job, children, a routine had never seemed appealing…until now. He almost wished he'd walked into Miksa's and felt utterly at ease and content to be there, night-after-night, until the end of time. Perhaps he'd been moving so fast, he couldn't see straight. As his release from the Army grew closer, it occurred to him that he'd better spend a little while taking stock and thinking about what he truly wanted in the years ahead. He'd be a citizen; he'd be able to put down roots. But he no longer had a clue how to go about doing that.

The next day, Jozsi took a bus to Washington, D.C., and once there, hopped in a cab to the Pentagon where he'd be debriefed about Panama by the general in charge of the Army Intelligence Corps. This was his first visit to the inner sanctum of the Department of Defense. The cold, impersonal nature of the building put his teeth on edge. He saw numbers of uniformed officers, practically bending from the weight of medals and decorations pinned to their chests. He wondered which battles they'd endured, who of them had held a dying soldier. He'd arrived early and passed the time standing near the entrance, watching generals and high-ranking officers pass by — he hadn't seen this many brass since watching hordes of them marching through South Boston streets during a St. Patrick's Day parade.

Eventually he set out to locate General Clark's office. He asked ten people before finally making his way through the DOD maze to the correct door. The general's secretary, a long-legged young woman, with hair the color of chestnuts, dark brown eyes and a warm smile, ushered him into the office to wait for the general. She explained that certain of the heavy brass didn't appear until at least 10:00 AM. "Due to morning meetings and the like, or so they claim. To me it sounds like banker's hours," she winked conspiratorially, sharing a small state secret.

They looked at each other admiringly, sparks flying as they held each other's gaze. Jozsi introduced himself, telling her he was just in from Fort Devens. She grinned. "Ann," she said, holding out her hand, "and I'm very familiar with Fort Devens. I grew up a few miles away, most of my family still lives there." They made small talk about New England and she mentioned how much she liked the sound of his Hungarian accent. "A nice change from the Yankee."

Before the general appeared, Jozsi had secured a dinner date. Since he didn't know his way around, would she pick the restaurant? *The Capital Eatery* at seven that night. She neatly printed the address on a pink phone message, handing it to him just as General Clark strode in.

Jozsi disliked him on first sight. He treated Ann like a disposable lackey and as soon as Jozsi was seated in his office, did the same to him. General Clark demanded a "pithy" description of the trip to Panama. Jozsi could tell he was only interested in who would get credit for the mission. He then launched into a speech about the competition between Navy and Air Force and "God knows how many other organizations that will come out of the woodwork to claim credit. Tell me what, if anything, was achieved?" A dismissive sneer seemed his stock expression. He looked at his watch every few minutes, so Jozsi started looking at his as well. Two could play at that game.

After he'd given General Clark the briefest of reports on the Panama mission, the general gave him a "so what?" look. Jozsi decided to fire up the general's ass just a smidge, telling him that later that day he had to give an in-depth accounting to the CIA at Langley. If the general had learned all he cared to know, he should feel free to terminate their meeting whenever convenient. In other words, I have more important places to be.

The general looked like a bomb had just exploded under his ass. He buzzed Ann, asking her to fetch coffee and donuts, telling her to hold all calls. He'd decided a more extensive report actually was in order and would rearrange his schedule to allow for a longer conversation. Jozsi gave him a slightly fuller report, leaving out certain significant details; only fair, given that the Navy and CIA had footed the bill for the mission, and had not been utterly rude to him on top of it. After he'd had his fill of coffee and donuts and the general's company, he respectfully reminded General Clark that he had other places to be and that the CIA expected him to be on time.

He leaned in toward Ann on his way out the door, whispering, "See you later?"

"I'll be there," she mouthed, in case her boss was within earshot.

His in-depth debriefing at Langley took several hours, but they treated him as though what he'd done mattered, despite the mission's having been aborted. The agency set him up in the well-appointed Hamilton Hotel through the weekend, handed him a fat packet of spending money, and wished him a good visit in Washington.

At 6:45 he was standing in front of *The Capital Eatery* waiting for Ann, who stepped out of a cab at 6:58, wearing a simple but fetching sheath dress appropriate for the warm spring evening. He convinced her to lead him to a classier place on the Potomac River, "It's on the Firm," he said cheerfully.

They walked to the restaurant, enjoying the sight and scent of cherry blossoms in full bloom, the humidity present but not enough to make one suffer. It was a beautifully balmy Friday night, cirrus clouds floating in the slowly dusking sky.

There was such ease to their conversation that the evening flew by without a moment of uncomfortable silence — no wondering what to talk about next, no wandering thoughts. He was genuinely interested in everything she had to say, and felt intellectually matched in a way he'd not felt since his days with Erika. He could see from the eagerness with which she listened, and the smile she couldn't suppress, that she too was enjoying his company. Yes, she was attractive, but his thoughts were not so much of bedding her as of knowing her, deeply and well. He was not the sentimental sort to call this love at first sight, though that in fact was the feeling astir.

The next day was Saturday, and Ann offered to show him around the capital. They spent that day and the next visiting sights and museums all over the city. Sunday evening, after she'd cooked him a good New England style supper at her apartment — cod, potatoes, peas — it was time to separate. He hadn't yet put any serious moves on her. A gentle peck on the cheek each time they parted, handholding as they walked along the riverside. He gave her his Fort Devens phone number; he already had hers. She promised she'd be visiting relatives soon and would look him up when she was in the area. At the door, she tilted her head, expecting a chaste peck on the cheek. Instead, he took her in his arms and kissed her with 48-hours of built-up desire.

With a touch of the coy, she said, "Well, I may be there sooner than you think."

His thoughts as the bus ferried him toward Fort Devens were all about Ann. Marriage had not been much on his mind since he'd walked away from Erika that day on the bridge. He definitely had not been ready to marry then, even without the madness of war and repression, and his life since had been peripatetic and filled with women of all shapes, sizes, and nationalities. Was he ready to get married now? He couldn't believe he was even thinking these kinds of thoughts. Maybe Ann reminded him of some sentimental American movie he'd seen back in Hungary — *Gone with the Wind* came to mind. Deciding he needed to give his head a shake, he forced thoughts of her away and set his mind in another direction as the bus cruised up the Northeast corridor. The intensity of his emotional state was starting to make him feel a little wobbly. Let time tell him if this was meant to be. No need to rush.

Recounting the stories of his Panama mission at the Pentagon and at Langley had put him in a reflective mood. He started thinking about all that he'd seen and done since leaving Hungary, some moments deeply unpleasant to recount, some sad, some amazing, some funny. His uncle Peter kept popping in mind, sitting at the table recounting stories of his travels far and wide. Jozsi wanted to tell his own stories and decided he'd start jotting down notes. Someday he'd write a book that his children and grandchildren would point to with pride. There it was again: the notion of family, not just the one he had, but the creation of a new one. What the hell was happening to him?

No sooner had Jozsi returned to his quarters and dropped his duffel to the floor than Captain Novak banged at the door, shouting, "Sergeant, I know you're in there. Open the hell up!"

"No problem," Jozsi said calmly, opening the door. Simultaneously twiddling his ear lobe with one hand and jabbing his other pointer finger in Jozsi's face, Novak shouted at Jozsi that no non-commissioned officer ever got him out of the club before, not to run and fetch his sorry Hungarian ass just because the post commander wanted to see it sitting in front of him.

It took a few minutes for Jozsi to make sense of Novak's ranting. Apparently, General Yancy and Novak had both been at the Officer's Club when the general had heard that Jozsi was back from Washington. He'd sent Novak to fetch him. Novak had not taken kindly to being treated as an errand boy.

Jozsi tried to calm the irate young officer. "The general must be in a mood, don't take it personally."

"Well, I'm a soldier not a goddamn messenger," Novak insisted. "He's got a perfectly fine home; I don't know why he insists on coming to the damn club anyway. There's a driver and jeep waiting to take you there. Get your ass out of here before the general gets *my* ass in trouble."

Captain Novak, calmer at last, walked Jozsi toward the jeep. "Do me a favor, Sergeant? Make my life a little easier, find yourself another company, move the hell on."

"Sorry, not my call, Captain," Jozsi climbed into the jeep and as it pulled away, called out, "You'll be heading to Vietnam any day now, you'll be rid of me forever." He leaned out and looked back to see Captain Novak glaring, his middle finger held high.

At the Officer's Club, the military police questioned Jozsi, refusing entrance to an enlisted man. Apparently, there'd been a small personnel shift in his absence; these were new faces who didn't know that this sergeant was an exception to the rules. They were being such hard-asses even the jeep driver couldn't convince them that General Yancy had in fact invited Sergeant Budai to join him. "Get the hell out of here before I arrest you," one of the MPs ordered.

"Let's go tell Captain Novak," Jozsi laughed, and they sped back to where they'd last seen the annoyed captain, then tracked him to his quarters. Jozsi rapped on the door, calling out, "Oh, Captain Novak..." With a grunt, Novak rose from a couch — he'd just pulled off his boots and answered the door in his stocking feet, to find a smiling Jozsi. "Okay, Captain, the MPs told this enlisted man standing before you to get the hell out of there, so I need you to get me in the door."

"Piss on them," Novak annoyed, yawned. "I'm going to kick some ass around here before the base commander kicks mine," he snarled, shoving feet back into boots.

"I'm not sure you've got the balls for that," Jozsi observed, maintaining a good-natured tone.

"Watch me!" the captain brushed by him, jumped in the jeep and yelled, "Let's go!" dramatically pointing the way forward as though leading men into battle. Jozsi barely made it into the back of the jeep before they were speeding back to the Officer's Club. As the jeep screeched to a halt, the more aggressive MP shouted, "Hey assholes, we told you to get the hell out of here."

They hadn't had time to register that a captain was sitting in the front passenger seat. Novak stepped out of the jeep, belligerence incarnate, and yelled, "Who the hell are you calling asshole, soldier? I want your name and service number. After that I don't want to see your face again." The MPs all but had speech balloons saying "Yikes" rising above their heads. They were both new to duty and this was not how things were supposed to go.

One of them, a corporal, started to apologize right quick. Jozsi interrupted. "Soldier boy, I could have taken off and left you to have your ass drawn and quartered by General Yancy."

"Yes, sir," the corporal was all humble apology now. Novak disgusted with everything in front of him leaned back against the jeep and let Jozsi bust their chops.

"You better remember me, because you'll be seeing me again, right here. And tell your MP buddies to keep an eye out for me. I just saved your ass, and the next time I won't be such a nice guy." The poor MPs didn't know whether to salute him or thank him or back away groveling. "As you were, soldiers," Jozsi said, bailing them out again. "I'm Sergeant Budai, and anyone on this base with bars on his chest knows who I am. Now, excuse me, the base *commander* is waiting."

He was finding Novak's biliousness amusing, so Jozsi motioned him over. "If you buy the drinks tonight, I'll bring you along to sit with the general." The MPs stepped aside, saluting both as they finally entered the Officer's Club.

It had taken only an extra half hour, but Novak felt drained. He roused himself, though, at the prospect of sitting with the general. Although Jozsi and General Yancy had met several times, this was the first they'd been in the Officer's Club together — the general didn't venture there all that often — and all eyes were on Jozsi and Novak as they moved through the room. General Yancy practically embraced Jozsi, he was so glad to see him. He acknowledged Novak but quickly sent him away to get drinks. "Give us a few minutes, the Sergeant and I have some things to discuss privately." Novak aimed a killer look at Jozsi, who shrugged with a 'what can I do?' expression. As soon as Novak moved away, Yancy leaned close. "What the hell is going on at the Pentagon? They told me to treat you with kid gloves, like I haven't already. What the hell more can I offer you? Have you been complaining about me up in Washington?"

"No, sir, not at all. I told General Clark that you more than accommodated my special needs and that none of my achievements could have happened without your assistance. They're aware Fort Devens soldiers are high caliber and that your military training and experience create the right atmosphere for those results." Jozsi almost patted himself on the back for such a fine answer.

Captain Novak, practically moving in slow motion, returned with the drinks, looking to General Yancy for a sign that it was okay to come close. Suddenly he wasn't minding being an errand boy. He knew the other officers envied him. Appearing to be having a friendly private meeting with the base commander right there in the Officers' Club was a feather in his cap.

They all clinked glasses, and Jozsi continued with his report, sharing that General Clark sent his best and hoped very much to make it to Yancy's retirement party. The general nodded. All good. Surprising even himself, Jozsi took this moment to introduce the concept of Ann. "I had dinner with his personal secretary, a lovely woman who was raised around here. I hope to see her again as soon as possible, or at least as soon as my allowance can cover a trip back to D.C." Here he had been thinking he'd wait till she showed up in Massachusetts, let time slow things down, but apparently, his heart was in a different gear.

General Yancy winked at Captain Novak. "I see no problem with that. Do you, Captain?" Captain Novak, of course, did not. "So, Sergeant, we'll allow Captain Novak to work out the details, but consider your expenses covered whenever you've a yen to see this young lady in Washington. Anyone impressive enough to capture your interest deserves to be courted."

That night, after the general bid them a good night, Captain Novak insisted on buying drinks like it was the last day of Pompeii. In fact, Jozsi wasn't exactly sure how the evening ended, though he did wake to remember that the same MPs who'd first kicked him out of the Officers' Club had been ordered to return him to his quarters and practically tuck him into his bed before going off duty.

~~~

At first, Jozsi struggled to get back into his Fort Devens routine. He hung out with his Hungarian buddies on base and for the first few days restrained himself from calling Ann. He was still coming to grips with the intensity of his feelings. His request for money to go visit her whenever his schedule allowed had panned out well. Now he had to take stock. One weekend with this woman whom he hadn't even slept with and he was already begging money to see her again. What the hell? He kept his feelings close to his chest; his pals would scoff if they knew how hard he was struggling not to call her until he felt a little calmer.

After almost a week had passed, he downed a couple of stiff drinks at the PX and huddled in the day room's wall-hung pay phone, a pile of coins at the ready. She answered and the joy in her voice at finding his on the other end of the line filled him with an almost fizzy feeling. They talked until he ran out of coins; it felt as though they'd known each other for years, not days. She was delighted he'd be able to come see her soon. "I hope you won't think me a brazen floozy, but you might consider skipping the Hamilton Hotel and instead checking in Chez Ann."

"By all means," he whispered, anticipation lighting a little fire in his groin.

He was by her side the following week, and in her bed moments after putting down his duffel bag. Throughout the spring and summer, they took turns visiting each other. When she came east for the 4ᵗʰ of July holiday, she introduced him to her parents and sisters, whose early suspicions of the foreigner evaporated under Jozsi's charm. Soon they were treating him like one of their own, though they kept him from meeting the extended family for a while longer, wanting to make certain this relationship was going somewhere.

Jozsi had the occasional small mission away, mostly tracking suspicious characters, possible spies and the like. Between these four-to-six week long trips, his visits to D.C., and to Ann's family nearby, he wasn't at Fort Devens for long enough stretches to get sick of it.

During his off-duty time on base, he and the guys would head to *Jack's Bar & Pool Hall.* Jozsi would saunter in at the head of a pack of guys, clearly the ringleader. Jack would call out, "Al Capone's in the house!" and all heads would turn in greeting. Everyone knew Jozsi. Big spender, big tipper, even if it was with other peoples' money, as in, "Your turn to buy a round, buddy," and "You gotta tip more than that!"

Jozsi had communicated with his family in Hungary via postcards for the most part. Short messages, no details; just enough information to let them know he was okay. That summer, he'd mentioned a young lady he'd been spending time with. He knew his mother would be beside herself with joy at the thought that he might be contemplating marriage.

In the fall, Ann decided to move back to Massachusetts to be closer to her family and the man she now hoped to marry. By the end of the year, Jozsi had asked her parents for Ann's hand. On Christmas Eve, he'd bent on one knee, holding an open velvet-lined box in the palm of his hand, a modest diamond ring glittering against the midnight blue velvet. They'd set the date for the following May.

Certain of Ann's friends and family members needed a little convincing as to the wisdom of her choice. What about a local boy, they asked: someone whose family was known, whose character and history had witnesses, whose trail through life had evidence. Ann insisted she wasn't looking for someone who'd worked in the mills all his life. It didn't matter if Jozsi was from a distant country, it didn't matter that she'd never met his parents, or seen where he'd grown up. She didn't need or even want to know everything there was to know about him. She loved him and that was enough. What she didn't tell them was that in D.

C. she'd had access to all of his records, and since the CIA had recruited him she already knew plenty about what kind of man he was. He had character; he was brave, resourceful, intelligent and funny, and he had suffered and survived great loss and hardship. She'd been dreaming of just such a man all her life.

Jozsi's friends reacted to news of the engagement with utter disbelief: their ringleader about to settle down? No! Their bon vivant, the bigtime ladies' man, a true girl magnet, lower his wattage? No! How would they find girls without him? No more raucous nights, no more fun! They were distraught and did everything they could to talk him out of it. This amused him for a time, but one night he drew the line. "*Be happy* for me," he ordered. He ordered, they obliged. There was no more talk of her not being right for him, or pretty enough, or fun enough. She was suddenly treated like a minor deity. It was that or they'd lose Jozsi, no question about it.

During the winter of 1962, Jozsi had to leave Fort Devens for a couple of months, during which time Ann concentrated on wedding plans and selling her man to everyone in her life.

Finally, the day arrived. Ann, in a traditional gown, with lace sleeves and veil, hair neatly bobbed, white lilies of the valley in hand, walked down the aisle toward Jozsi. He wore a white tux with black bowtie and pants, a rose boutonniere in his lapel. They wed in a small chapel, Jozsi's closest Hungarian buddies standing in as family. It was everything Ann had dreamed of, and as long as she thought it perfect, so too did he. For their honeymoon, they drove to the Berkshire Mountains. A weekend's worth of honeymoon, and then it was time to return to Fort Devens. His discharge was imminent, their new life together about to begin.

23

From Home to Home

Jozsi settled down with Ann in May of 1962, his eyes focused forward. Two months after the wedding, he became an American citizen. Ann was at his side, her mother Eleanor, beaming, served as witness. The judge handed out tiny American flags and Eleanor presented Jozsi with a gift that was wrapped in red, white and blue striped paper — an American baseball glove. He had managed to charm her silly. She'd promised to bake him an apple pie, so after the swearing in, they went to the house Ann had grown up in and spent the afternoon waiting for, and then devouring, that very all-American confection.

This was his country now; he took citizenship seriously and considered the right to vote sacred. He followed news of current events closely, paying particular attention to anything related to the Bay of Pigs. Jozsi had been invited, as he put it, to participate in that fiasco, but his impending marriage provided him the perfect excuse for bowing out. By then, he wanted nothing more than to get on with his life; after his Panama excursion, he'd had enough of boats and islands and guns to last a lifetime.

In the United States, Freedom Riders were traveling through the segregated South, being harassed and beaten, but unwilling to turn tail and run. Although the only black people he'd come to know were from his time in the Army and he'd never known them well, Jozsi respected their struggle for equality. He knew a little something about being a second-class citizen in your own country. Overseas, construction of the Berlin Wall was beginning in earnest, and the Soviets had managed to be first in sending a man into space. Jozsi wasn't surprised, given the weight the Russians placed on science and technology. In a sense, he had them to thank for any hope of a career in America; the training he'd received during their occupation provided him with a trade he could ply anywhere in the world — the language of electronics was international.

But at first, it was rough going. Without access to his papers, Jozsi had no way to prove he'd received a fine education. His thick accent marked him as a foreigner, regardless of the proof of citizenship he carried at all times. Supervisors made fun of his speech and lack of familiarity with American customs and ways. He swallowed all humiliation, convinced he'd prove himself and move past the bullshit, no matter what that took. He particularly loathed the coworkers who hadn't been GIs; he thought of them as soft, but he kept it to himself. They had no clue what he'd had to do to survive. Contending with their disdain was child's play, although he did grit his teeth when anyone questioned his loyalty to the United States. It was tempting to drop little hints about his CIA service, but mention of that work was strictly forbidden, so he bit his tongue and worked even harder. Jozsi landed a job at General Electric, a beacon of stable income in those days, but was first assigned to work out in "the yard" because he didn't have the proper security clearance to be allowed near the company's machinery. The irony did not escape him.

After six months, a state senator helped Jozsi get his papers from Hungary, which, though unintelligible to most employers, did prove he'd graduated from an institute of higher learning. With those and his citizenship papers in hand, Jozsi found work at a newly started computer company where he quickly proved to be a valuable asset. The owner's parents were foreign born so the man had no prejudice against a thick accent, valuing competence, skill and a can-do attitude above all. Suddenly, increased responsibility and raises leap-frogged Jozsi forward faster than he could ever have imagined.

But he and Ann continued to live frugally, siphoning all excess money into their savings account. Ann wanted a baby and a house as soon as possible, and almost to his own surprise, so did Jozsi. Daniel was born a year after they wed, his name chosen from the *Book of Daniel*, a name they associated with kindness, strength, and faith. Ann had always loved the story of Daniel in the lion's den, and felt its real message was that if you believe with your whole heart that you will survive a misfortune, then you will.

~~~

By the time that Dani could walk and string words together, they were in their own home with a yard and a white picket fence; not too far from and not too close to other members of her family. By now Jozsi had won over everyone in Ann's world. His charisma made him popular, and everyone could see how happy he made Ann. The mysterious wandering foreigner had attained a new home.

What no one knew about was something Ann was just beginning to adjust to: his nightmares. She'd been aware of them before they married, but was now coming to witness them intimately. She assumed they stemmed from the Revolution, the stress of fighting, hiding, sneaking, and lying. Sometimes he shouted into the dark night, triggered by disturbing images and memories his subconscious dredged up when he wasn't paying attention. Ann knew very little about the Hungarian Revolution before she met Jozsi, and although she was curious, he resisted talking about those days, or the days of the Nazi occupation during World War Two. She learned an occasional detail in the wee hours when he woke, thrashing and moaning, wide-eyed, sometimes sweating, cursing or crying out. Long-suppressed memories from his childhood would surface, things he hadn't consciously thought about in years.

When Jozsi was eight the Nazis had taken over their town. He remembered the townspeople being forced to gather in the town square. The mayor had been ordered to introduce their new "leaders," and in an aside, had tried to convey to the invaders that the people of Rakoskeresteur were a community. He stressed that every person was considered part of that community regardless of religion or race. "We respect and support each other, we get along," he had said. After which the Nazi commander had immediately shot him in the chest, and insisted the body be left in the town square. The mayor lay where he'd fallen in the dirt for a full week to emphasize that it was a new day in Rakoskeresteur. The horror of this display weighed on everyone; a new day indeed.

Another night he awoke thinking of his uncle Ganix, a tank commander who'd taken it upon himself to save a number of Jews from the Nazis. He'd hidden them in his tank and snuck them out of occupied territory. Eventually a local shop owner turned his uncle in. Ganix had been dragged down the street to the man's shop so the shop owner could identify him. Ganix spit at his betrayer and said, "When I get back I'm going to hang your ass from a streetlamp." Then he'd been beaten by his captors and eventually sent to Siberia. Amazingly, he'd survived and returned five years later to do exactly as promised. The townspeople had stood by Ganix, their attitude summed up by the mayor who'd simply announced, "That man got what was coming to him."

But often Jozsi would wake in a state of terror, not remembering any particular dream or incident, just fear — virulent, invasive, unrelenting. He'd reach for Ann, "Talk to me." Ann wasn't exactly at her most quick-witted in the middle of the night, so she made it a point to have something planned. She started telling him about the American Indians, a fascination of hers. "Yes, talk about the Indians," he'd say. She might relate how smallpox and typhoid fever were introduced to Indian communities, or talk about the Cherokee and their Trail of Tears, or the work of Mohawk shamans. She realized these weren't always particularly uplifting stories, but thought that hearing about the tragedies Native Americans had endured might somehow distract him from his own suffering past.

In happier waking moments, Jozsi sent his parents photographs of his wife, his son, his home. At last he had a place to put the newly framed photographs his parents and siblings sent from Hungary. Jozsi's focus on making a life with his family outside the Army had kept thoughts about

Attila's coffin on the back burner for some time. But seeing his family's faces gazing from a side table in the living room and watching his son grow, brought on waves of memories — of his childhood home, of the Toths' farm, of Bandi and the ravine. He'd told Ann a little about finding the mysterious object and of his suspicion that it might be Attila's coffin, but like Erika years earlier, she suspected his memory was perhaps just a little bit melodramatic and didn't give the story much due. Someday, he promised, they would be able to travel to Hungary and he would show her. It was only a matter of time.

~~~

Hungarian buddies he'd met at Fort Devens would make the drive to visit now and then, amazed by their former ringleader's rapid domestication. They agreed he was a good advertisement for marriage — happy, and more content and relaxed than they'd ever seen him, yet still able to drink them under the table and entertain with stories and wisecracks. Other regulars were the Hungarian friends he'd made at *Nagybácsi Miksa's*, who traveled from Boston and other nearby communities to gather for a cookout, or a few drinks at Jozsi's table. They reminisced about their hometowns in Hungary, trying to imagine how much had changed since 1956.

After Ann had met several of his less well-acclimated Hungarian friends, she felt even prouder of Jozsi for how well he managed to deal with his traumas. Some of the men she met were emotionally shut down and never managed to develop a close, loving family. There was an odd group of four men who'd moved in together and spoke only Hungarian in the house. The kitchen held an unsettling number of Hungarian wine bottles, lined up like soldiers along the base of the walls. Although there were many things Jozsi couldn't explain to Ann, or later to Dani, they each knew he loved them, was there for them, and that they were the center of his life. He was grateful for everything he had, that was very clear. And just that, Ann believed, was a major achievement for a man who'd seen and done the horrific. She and Dani learned to read his face for those moments when some part of him seemed unreachable — his eyes might be open but they'd hold a certain look, known by soldiers as the "1,000-yard stare," and they learned, in those moments, to give him some space.

Regardless of their differing emotional states, all of the Hungarians shared a yearning to go back "home," if only to visit — not just family but the land: to inhale the scents of the earth they'd first trod, see the native plants change colors with the seasons, hear everywhere the language in which they'd formed their first thoughts, and be not *a* Hungarian, but simply *Hungarian.*

~~~

Finally, in 1966, a full decade after the Revolution, Hungary opened its borders to Hungarians who had served in the U. S. Special Forces. The Hungarian government notified families that their offspring were no longer being considered traitors, enemies of the Socialist Hungarian government, or criminals. They would all receive amnesty and were welcome to return for a visit, as long as they obeyed the law of the land. The news came as a shock. Jozsi opened a letter from Matyas, read a few lines and sat silent.

"Is everything okay?" Ann asked anxiously.

He nodded yes, dazed, and under his breath whispered, "*Azta,*" Hungarian for wow. Then took her hand and tears forming explained, "I can go home."

The first of their group to make the trip was Eduard, now Americanized to Edward, known as Ed. He'd also been in the Special Forces. He planned to go alone, saying he was too nervous to risk bringing his family on this first trip.

They held a going-away party at *Nagybácsi Miksa's*, everyone envious of the pioneer journeying homeward. The men wished him luck, the wives and girlfriends wished him safe return; secretly relieved it wasn't *their* man making the trip. Jozsi talked with Ann about traveling there the following year. As long as Ed came back safe and sound, she said.

Ed drove to New York to catch the plane that would bring him to Hungary for the first time in ten years. Three weeks later he returned to America. His Hungarian friends surprised him with food and wine to celebrate his safe return, eager for news of the homeland. Ed told them about changes that had taken place, and regaled them with stories of reunions with old friends and classmates, and of how wonderful it was to hug his mother, and of the tears of joy she shed. No, he'd had no trouble crossing the border; yes, it really was safe to return. He showed them souvenirs he'd brought back from the famous *Herend* porcelain factory. Ann especially liked the iconic statue of a Hungarian cowboy holding the reins of a bridled horse as he leapt wildly into the air. Jozsi explained it captured the wildness of the *Puszta*, the prairie, where his ancestors had lived since the time of Attila the Hun.

Ann could practically taste Jozsi's envy of Ed, and as they drove home suggested they start planning a trip. His parents were still alive and she badly wanted to meet them. She also hoped it might improve his emotional balance to see them.

"Maybe it will help you get rid of all those bad dreams," she said.

Jozsi said he'd been thinking about returning and appreciated her understanding what a visit could mean for him, though grimly added, "It won't stop the demons."

Ann was a doer, and within weeks, they had passports, including one for three-year-old Dani. "No, I'm not leaving him with my parents," she insisted when Jozsi expressed concern. "*Your* parents would never forgive me!" He argued they should wait, bring Dani on a second trip. Headstrong she pushed back: either they all went or Jozsi went alone. Which is when he learned you never argue with a woman who has a wooden spoon in her hand. She waved it emphatically and he caved. In truth, he couldn't wait to see his mother holding Dani in her arms, his father parading him around on his shoulders the way he'd once carried

Jozsi.

They scheduled the trip for the middle of July, in time for the wedding of his sister Susan's son. Each night Jozsi read to Dani from a Hungarian picture book — Dani already knew as many Hungarian words as English. That spring, Jozsi sent their visa applications to the Hungarian Consulate in Washington, D.C., and they soon received visas, stamped with a seal of approval. Without mention to Ann, Jozsi sent copies to the American Embassy in Hungary, with their date of arrival, and their itinerary, just in case any problems arose. Ed had made it sound easy, but Jozsi couldn't shake memories of fear he'd experienced in the past. He didn't want Ann to worry, but he definitely wanted his new country to know exactly where he was going when he visited his old one.

~~~

The three of them flew out of Logan International Airport in Boston one July night on a Lufthansa 747. A German television crew took pictures as they taxied along the runway. It made Jozsi anxious for no reason he could name, the cameras, the feeling of being tracked. But as soon as they were aloft, the captain announced that the plane, the first 747 bought by Lufthansa, was making its maiden voyage — the cameras were merely recording this momentous takeoff. The stewardesses fawned over Dani and the flight was smooth, uneventful; a good start to their trip.

They landed in Vienna early the next day, checked into a hotel, and after cleaning up set out to visit the sights. This was Ann's first time overseas and she was eager to soak up as much as possible. By the end of the day, they were exhausted. The next morning, Jozsi woke his family and brought them out on the terrace to watch the sun rise into a clear blue sky. They had espresso brought up, and a banana for Dani, and gazed at the city before them. Jozsi had chosen that hotel and requested a specific room because of its view — he and Laci had at one time spent a great deal of time at the hotel, though he shared none of those details with Ann since girls and wild behavior had been a definite part of the activities in those days.

They packed up, loaded suitcases into a rental car, and soon were on their way to Hungary. Jozsi could not put into words all that he was feeling and Ann didn't ask him to. She squeezed his knee occasionally, and pointed out buildings and trees and animals to Dani, who insisted on sitting on her lap. The three of them in the front of the car, snug together, felt good.

The border was only thirty miles away, and as the miles ticked down to single digits, Jozsi thought his heart might erupt. What if they recognized him from the past? What if they detained him? He wasn't even sure who *they* might be. He spoke with intensity, "If anything happens at the border, you turn around and go back to the hotel with Dani. I don't want him scared." He assured her that no matter what happened, he'd more than likely make it back to the hotel before they did and welcome them with hugs. Ann appreciated his bravado, but also noted he was biting his lower lip, something he only did when stressed.

Ann placed her hand on his. "Ed had no trouble, so, why would we? It'll be fine."

As they waited in line to cross the border, they watched guards processing tourists entering Hungary. There were two lines leading to separate gated corrals. The first gate opened, a car entered, then that gate closed, securing the car between two shut gates. After papers were checked, a guard would give the okay for another soldier to open the far gate leading into Hungary. Occasionally, the guard would ask a driver to get out, then wave to a soldier who would hop in and drive the car to a secured zone. Whoever was of concern would be escorted into the station while the other passengers waited in the car. They saw this happen a few times, the last time to a car full of young men. The soldiers made two of the group walk into the station, but within a short time the men were back in their car and on their way. The lines moved slowly as Jozsi and Ann waited silently, watching.

Finally, it was their turn. Jozsi handed the guard their passports. He examined them closely, lingering over Jozsi's. He looked at a logbook clamped to a clipboard. After a few endless-seeming minutes, the guard motioned for Jozsi to get out of the car and escorted him into the station. A soldier hopped in the car and drove them to the secured lot. Ann didn't want to alarm Dani, so she told him she thought Jozsi had gone to buy souvenirs for *Nagy Papa*. The guard said nothing to Ann beyond, "You wait," in heavily-accented English, and left with the keys to the car. That made her even more anxious.

Inside the station, he was led to a stall and ordered to disrobe. The guards weren't hostile, just formal, so Jozsi's racing heart slowed a few beats. But until he held his passport in hand, with his wife and child by his side, all was not well no matter how mild the guards' behavior.

Everything in Jozsi rebelled, but he swallowed hard, fending off memories of the Nazis, the Russians, the deluded Hungarians who believed obeying a foreign overlord was more important than honoring your countrymen. If he rebelled in any way, these guards could make things harder on him, so he said nothing and quickly disrobed.

He wasn't worried about what a search of his clothes and belongings might reveal. Through the stall window he watched the guards methodically finger his clothing and knew that out of view, there were other guards pawing through the rest of their luggage. He was relieved Ann and Dani were not enduring the same search. Although the guards were soon finished with his clothing, they left him standing naked for a good while longer. Finally, he heard a door creak open and a voice called out, "Okay, he can go." Free to go. Free to enter Hungary. These guards had no idea what those words meant to him. Ten years of wondering if he'd ever be able to return. Be able to look his mother and father in the eyes, hug and laugh with his siblings, be in the land of his birth, and maybe, just maybe get his hands on the mysterious coffin that he hoped still lay beneath brush and tumbleweed and dirt.

When the guard opened the stall door, Jozsi turned and thrust his bare ass toward the captain. "You want to poke around, see if you can find a transistor radio up there?" He immediately regretted the childish impulse.

The guard scrunched his lips tight, then spat out, "Get dressed. The security officer wants to talk to you." They weren't done with him yet. His gut tightened. The guard led him into a room with a small square table, with two chairs facing each other, and told him to wait for the officer. A wave of almost vertigo-inducing fear flushed through him; the room reminded him too much of 60 Andrássy Street. He struggled to keep his wits about him as flashback images of dead freedom fighters splayed on Budapest streets bombarded him. He pictured Ann in the car, worried sick, but trying not to let Dani feel her fear.

A half-hour passed. He checked his watch, concentrating on the second hand as a way of grounding himself. Finally, a tall, well-muscled security guard walked in holding his passport and visa.

"Are you Jozsef Budai?"

Jozsi snapped. "If you can read, you can see that on my papers." Not wise, he knew, but again words flew out before he could trap them behind his teeth. He'd screwed up with this insignificant officer, but decided to let the chips fall where they may. He reasoned that since they'd let him get dressed, they were going to let him go, though not until they'd spent more time fucking with his head. The officer glared, cheeks reddening. They stared at each other for several seconds, each knowing that in a different time and in a different place, they'd likely have been trying to kill each other.

"You know my name," Jozsi finally said, as calmly as he could manage. "And what is *your* name? I want to spell it accurately when I write an article for the *New York Times* describing my pleasant welcome at the Hungarian border."

The officer said he had no time to waste and would get right to the point. He inhaled deeply, stood up and started screaming. Jozsi had a big pair of balls coming back to Hungary. The government knew who he was, a hooligan who had tried to destroy the country in 1956. He paused for breath and resumed at a slightly lower decibel level. "Now you're coming back to enjoy the Motherland that we saved from pig scum like you." Spittle gathered at the corners of his mouth. "All your Special Forces training and here you are, begging to come back in when you thought you'd be able to return like John Wayne and kick us out."

Jozsi concentrated on breathing, knowing he couldn't afford to lose control again.

"Well..." the guard growled, having screamed himself out. "What the hell do you have to say?"

Jozsi answered as calmly as he could manage. "I'm here without a fight. I want to see my family, that is all I want."

"Mr. Budai, I have no choice but to let you go. The new law demands it. But let me inform you, you're the first pig who has had the balls to come home. You risk having your ass strung up from the nearest tree. We have not forgotten your crimes against the country. Today is your lucky day. Not all soldiers have my level of self-control." He handed over Jozsi's documents and opened the door. As Jozsi walked down the hall, the guard yelled, "We will be watching your every move. Step out of line and the police will be on your ass like flies on horseshit."

Just before turning the hallway corner, Jozsi felt he could risk one more comment and over his shoulder called out, "For some reason, you guys really like shit. You've eaten so much communist crap you can't think straight." Then sped toward the entry guard, who directed him to his car in the secured parking lot.

Ann's face showed the relief he expected to see. She knew he hadn't been an altar boy during his final years in Hungary, though she did not know all of the details. And she had complete confidence that he could get himself out of any kind of fix. Still, his momentary detention had been a test — she didn't quite trust his mouth to obey his instinct for self-preservation. After they embraced, he turned the ignition key and saw the guard open the gate. He sighed with relief, and they headed to Budapest to see his parents...moving at a respectable speed. He had no desire to give officials any excuse to stop him.

Once he'd calmed down, he started thinking hard on a comment the guard had made. *He was the first guy from Special Forces to visit the country*. But Ed had been the first guy to step up, risk taking shit from the border guards, cross the border. And he'd had no trouble. According to Ed. Someone was lying; he hoped it was the border guard and not his friend, but he had a bad feeling. Jozsi did not mention any suspicions to Ann, but quietly fumed. He would never have brought his wife and child with him had he known this nonsense at the border would happen.

Thoughts of security guards and Ed vanished as they drove along the shores of the Danube, and he told Ann about the history of the area. As they neared his parents' house, he had to pull over now and then to elaborate. "This was the place where..." "This looks just like it did when..." At last they arrived...home. Jozsi felt he'd lived many lives in the past ten years, but amazingly, the house looked very much the same. His parents had aged, but the place was as he remembered — he could have managed to navigate blindfolded, there was so little change.

Matyas was the first to spy the car as it pulled up to the house. He'd been keeping vigil at a window for some time. He threw open the front door and quickly moved toward them, arms thrown wide, chanting his childhood nickname, "Dodi, Dodi, Dodi." He grabbed on, rocking Jozsi side-to-side, tears in both their eyes. "My boy," he murmured, holding him by the arms, moving him slightly away so he could stare at Jozsi's face, as though he could absorb the impact of all that his son had experienced during his years away. Erzsebet was busy welcoming Ann and meeting Dani. Susan came running from the kitchen where she'd been helping her mother prepare a feast, laughing and crying and waving her hands excitedly. "You're really here!" she gasped. Bouncing up and down on her toes until Matyas relinquished Jozsi's body to the others. The rest of Jozsi's siblings would be arriving soon, along with all their children. They would all miss *nagyanya* Alida.

After an extended flurry of hugging and kissing and crying and more hugging, Jozsi indicated he needed a few moments to catch his breath. He picked up Dani, and guided Ann out to the big acacia tree, down to the river, and all around the big yard that had been the launch pad for many a bicycle adventure in his youth. Matyas, Erzsebet, and Susan stood on the back terrace watching as they wandered, exchanging emotional glances and squeezing hands. When they were all together again, Erzsebet and Susan commandeered Jozsi's wife and child to show them around the house. His father sat Jozsi down at the kitchen table and poured them each a hefty shot of *palinka*. Matyas toasted to life, "*Egeshegedre,*" he said, looking deep into his son's eyes, and they clinked and drank.

Throughout the day and evening, relatives and neighbors appeared, and Jozsi was so overwhelmed there were times he couldn't remember names. He'd point across the room and whisper to Ann, "This is another relative but I can't remember their name!" Ann spoke even less Hungarian than Dani, and Jozsi felt sorry for her, though his relatives kept urging him to translate: tell her about the Nazis in the square, tell her about rescuing American pilots from the burning planes, tell her, tell her, tell. Others had different agendas: they had relatives in America, did she know them?

Jozsi studied his father as people arrived, watched his generally intense demeanor shift to warmth and affection at the sight of each new and welcome guest. Matyas had always been a favorite friend, neighbor, relative of anyone in his circle. He was extremely well read and intelligent, and could be relaxed, charming and witty at gatherings. Others came to him for advice and valued his opinions on politics, business, and life in general. He was a leader. Jozsi was relieved to see that despite the years of oppression and hardship, his father's true nature remained unaffected. Where others had cowered, or broken, Matyas had managed to stand his ground. His soul was intact.

Eventually, the crowd dispersed, leaving Jozsi's new family to get better acquainted with his old one. Tears of joy hovered in his parents' eyes throughout the day, and they couldn't stop staring, first at their son, then grandson, then Ann.

A few days later, preparations began for the huge old-fashioned Hungarian wedding of Susan's eldest son. Ann had only heard about such events from Jozsi so was delighted to be a part of this ritual, soaking up all she could of her husband's culture. She endeared herself to Erzsebet and the other women by diving in to help clean, chop and do whatever else was needed, and for being interested in all the things they wanted to teach and share with her.

A local farmer arrived with a huge slaughtered pig, bled out and ready to be prepped. Immediately the pace picked up as everyone went into high gear. Ann couldn't believe how much work it took to get ready for a pig roast. First Jozsi and the men moved furniture out of the way. They set up sawhorses and created tabletops from hastily nailed together planks of wood. They chopped wood for the roasting, gathered kindling, set up chairs around the spit and otherwise prepared the cooking site. And of course, fueled their labor with copious amounts of alcohol.

Meanwhile, under Erzsebet's direction, the women cleaned, skinned and gutted the pig, preparing sausages from the innards to reinsert in its gut during the roasting. Just about every part of the pig was used for something. The hocks were considered a delicacy, the ears dried for use in soups, main dishes, and as appetizers. Ann sat this part out, it was just a little too intense, and she had to admit, the pig looked pretty unappealing at first. But as the pig, hand turned on the spit, began to warm and brown and smells emerged, she began to appreciate the feast to come. Their labor done, the men gathered by the fire to talk and drink, occasionally spritzing the pig with apple cider vinegar to keep its skin from splitting.

Exhausted, Ann and Dani retired early. As she drifted toward sleep she could hear Jozsi going on and on and on from the fire pit. He was wound up like a little boy. He'd been waiting ten years and he wasn't going to miss a minute.

Ann shook him awake the next morning — the men in his family demanded he rise and help, laughing the whole time because they knew how much he'd had to drink the night before. Jozsi had had only a few hours' sleep and was pretty much still drunk as far as Ann could tell. He sat up, confused, and started speaking Hungarian.

"Hello, you remember me? Your wife who speaks no Hungarian? You made an ass of yourself last night," she said, laughing. "Hogging all the conversation by the hog." He was too groggy to notice her play on words.

"My grandfather always used to say, 'If you go to a party and the next morning you have nothing to regret, it was a dull party.' Just wait till this afternoon when the real party starts," he crowed.

She rolled her eyes. "I can hardly wait."

The wedding followed the old traditions. The groom and his family marched down the street to the bride's house. The best man knocked on the door and asked if any young woman there wanted to marry the young man standing at the door. The father came outside and inspected Susan's son, while a crowd waited in the yard for him to approve. The father finally waved his hand and loudly said, "Yes, we have a bride for this young man!" Then the visiting crowd entered the house and appraised the young bride, dressed all in white.

After consuming polite amounts of *palinka*, the wedding party strolled down the street to the church, and after the ceremony, to the house for the party. A gypsy band played, drinks were drunk, the pig roasted, and Jozsi kept busy translating for Ann as guests recognized and greeted him.

At one point a couple of younger men sought him out. They'd somehow seen him on a television news program, demonstrating for new recruits in Vietnam how to cook a poisonous snake in the jungle in order to survive. Jozsi downplayed his Vietnam experience, saying in truth, he had never even carried a gun while there and was in fact scared shitless of snakes. He blew a hole in their fantasy of shootouts on the streets of Saigon, but they figured he was holding back on sharing his true exploits. Because Hungary was still under communist rule, they understood that he was on thin ice even having crossed the border, which of course made him seem even more heroic.

The party revved up as platter after platter was hustled out of the kitchen — 50 different Hungarian dishes, one right after another. The kitchen was a hub of bustle all night, small plates of food handed out to help restore flagging energy as the evening wore on. Jozsi's memory surfaced a history book description of Ildiko's father having a harvest party on his farm, the wives lading the table to show off their cooking skills.

After dark, the rooms were cleared of tables, and then the gypsies leaned into their violins, playing the old Hungarian music people remembered from their childhoods. Jozsi reminded the musicians that he was paying, and the deal was that if they quit while anyone was still dancing, there would be no pay. If they lasted the night, they'd get a big tip. Erzsebet pulled little Dani into the middle of the room for a special dance as the crowd watched, many with tears in their eyes. Ann finally took Dani to a cousin's house next door so they could get some sleep. She said she was fine with Jozsi staying on at the party, she knew it was the best medicine he could have, even if he felt like death the next day. "I can't stop you, anyway," she said, winking.

As one day crossed into the next, guests took naps in chairs, later bouncing back up to rejoin the festivities. The exhausted band begged to be let go before the sun started to rise. Jozsi relented. He paid them well and asked if there was at least one violin player who could stay until the sun inched higher in the sky. A young man, Marcus, volunteered — he knew he'd be well rewarded.

The serious partyers and Jozsi grabbed bottles of wine and gathered under the acacia tree, while Marcus played emotional, heart-wrenching songs. Soon they were singing with tears in their eyes. Marcus even played a number of the forbidden songs bemoaning the homeland Hungarians lost to the Rumanians in the Second World War. The singing kept on, though this person or that faded away or simply fell asleep under the tree, until finally Jozsi put his head down mid-song. Marcus lay his violin down and within seconds was sound asleep like the others.

Suddenly Jozsi was being roughly shaken. His sister Susan, with a grin, told him Ann was looking for him. Jozsi surveyed the scene — bodies stretched out or collapsed across tables, and over by the cherry tree, bottles strewn everywhere. By then Marcus was awake and again reaching for his violin. Jozsi promised him the party was finally over, and handed him a big wad of American money. Seeing the amount inspired Marcus to rosin the bow anew.

"No, no," Jozsi shushed him. "We have to keep quiet now. My wife has a certain drive for sex when she hears music so early, and I am too tired!"

Susan laughed. "Your wife is in no mood for sex with you. I can see that in her face!"

Jozsi stumbled his way back up to the house, and forgetting she'd made peace with his wedding wildness, made all kinds of excuses to Ann — the custom is this, he had to stay up with the hard-partying boys, he'd been cleaning, had no sleep since the day before, jet lag, and on and on. Ann rolled her eyes, patted him on his back, guiding him toward a bed just to shut him up. Laughing, Susan said, "Watch out, some day she will learn to speak Hungarian and then your goose will be cooked."

~~~

After the wedding, they spent time with Jozsi's family, relatives appearing in ones and twos, and Ann continued soaking in everything she could about this part of her husband's world. They visited and ate and simply existed together. Erzsebet taught Ann how to make special Hungarian dishes, Matyas taught Dani Hungarian words and games. Susan teased Jozsi and Jozsi teased her back. Slowly everyone caught him up on all that had happened while he was away.

The following weekend his old friend Ferenc came with his wife and daughter, Jolanka, who was close to the same age as Dani. While the men sat on the back veranda, enjoying being together and catching up, the bell at the front gate jingled. Jozsi heard Susan call from the kitchen that she'd see who it was. Jozsi noticed Susan didn't utter a warm, *"Üdvözöljük!"* There was no sound of welcome. Suddenly, his gut tightened.

Seconds later, Susan turned the corner and moved hurriedly toward the terrace with a flustered expression, and right behind her came Zsigmond. Everyone recognized him except Ann, but she could sense that he was an unwelcome guest. The silence grew loud. Finally, Jozsi, his mind an explosion of memories, made the decision to fake a certain amount of hospitality. He spoke as evenly as he could manage, "Ann, this is Zsigmond. We went to Catholic school together. He, Ferenc and myself all played together out there," he gestured toward the yard sloping toward the river. To Zsigmond, he said, "My son, Dani, over there, is playing with Ferenc's daughter. Funny, no?"

Zsigmond, civil, but chilly, shook hands all around and asked Jozsi if they could have a brief walk around the vineyard. They strolled away from the gathering on the terrace, now silent, watchful.

When they were out of earshot, Zsigmond said, "You are not welcome and I don't need to tell you why that is. I expect your visit to be brief and limited to the designated areas you were told you could enter. I want no problem from you while you are here. Do not underestimate my power."

"It's hard to believe we were once friends, real friends," Jozsi said, an unexpected twinge of melancholy taking him by surprise. Being home, being reminded so powerfully of his childhood, for a second he forgot all about the destruction and terror Zsigmond had wrought. "It means nothing now that the fighting is over?"

Zsigmond lowered his eyes and almost shuddered. When he again met Jozsi's eye, something in his face had softened. "It cannot be like before." He drew his shoulders back, stiffened his spine, turned on his heel and headed back to the house, stopping by Ferenc's chair. "I hope you will bring up your children in the right way. We need to build our socialist country strong enough to repel all foreign invaders." He looked at Jozsi. "Keep in mind what we have talked about, and understand that we will be watching your every move."

Susan rose to walk him out, but he motioned her down, "I know the way." He stalked back around the side of the house, missing Ferenc and Jozsi simultaneously giving him the Hungarian middle finger.

"You know that photograph of my eighth-grade class we have at home," Jozsi said, putting his arm around Ann, who suddenly looked just a little pale. "Zsigmond is in that, he's the boy standing behind Ferenc." He paused. "He used to be human." Ann felt a chill. Something in Zsigmond's manner had scared her even more than the incident at the border. For a moment, she wished they could pack up and leave right that minute.

~~~

A few days later, Erzsebet and Jozsi's sister Susan took Ann and Dani into Budapest to sightsee and shop. Jozsi took the opportunity to drive to Ura and spend the night with the Toths. His quiet plan was to first check on the coffin whose image had flitted in and out of his mind these many years.

He pulled over by the side of the road, parking behind a group of trees in order not to call too much attention to his presence. He walked across the *Puszta*, just as he had twenty years ago, thinking of Bandi and missing his large, comforting presence. Nothing much had changed, except that weeds had totally taken over and it took him awhile to find the spot where the land dipped down to the older section of the ravine. His secret location was completely covered in thick thorny briars and overgrown bushes.

He cleared brush from a large flat rock and sat at the edge of the drop, enjoying the peaceful quiet. He had been wondering about this spot for ten years and was relieved to find it completely untroubled. His mind went to Erika and the time they'd spent here, and to Ulee, whose visits to this spot existed only in her imagination. He thought of all the strange places he'd been and the stranger things he'd done these last ten years, and yet here he was again, sitting just where he'd sat as a boy. For a minute, he looked around and felt thrust back in time, as though everything had stayed the same and it was just about the right moment for him to get up from a midsummer daydream and bring old Bandi back to the barn for a carrot or apple.

If the coffin laying a few yards from where he sat was Attila's, millions of dollars of treasure could be within his reach. But the shadow cast by Zsigmond's words told him not to disturb anything just yet. Treasure, yes, and 1500 years of history, Hungarian history. He didn't think he'd been followed, but he couldn't be certain. And he felt he had no right, nor did he wish, to expose Attila's grave to a callous communist apparatchik like Zsigmond, a man who'd abandoned his true heritage to serve at the whim of the Russians. Jozsi could picture Zsigmond racing to hand over his findings, just to gain the advantage of some trivial recognition and a cheap May Day medal pinned on his uniform in Moscow's Red Square.

Jozsi sat, watching the sun move lower in the sky, anticipating his visit to the Toth family as though it were a delicious savory dessert he wanted to spend time imagining before indulging in the actual pleasure. Just before sunset, he returned to his car and headed for their farm. As he got close, he sensed a black car following, although it disappeared once he turned off the main road. An involuntary chill flashed through his body. Zsigmond had warned that his every move would be watched. Well, so be it.

Matyas had alerted the Toths that Jozsi was coming. When he arrived, the gate was open and within seconds, the whole family poured out of the house and barn to welcome him as they had when he was a little boy coming for a summer visit. That night Mari cooked a feast and treated him as though he were the King of Hungary. After supper, the dishes cleared away, out came bottles of *tokaji* and *palinka,* and the family again gathered around the table on the back porch, hungry for stories about Jozsi's life during the years he'd been away.

Late in the evening, after Jozsi's very selective telling of his adventures wound down, he fell silent, staring into the kerosene lantern, thinking of some of the more horrific things he'd not wanted to share. Mr. Toth asked, "With all your traveling around the world, what did you learn?"

Jozsi smiled at the question; it was exactly what his father had sometimes written to ask him, and indeed had asked his first night home. But Jozsi continued staring at the lantern, everyone's eyes glued on his face, waiting for his answer. The porch was so silent they could hear mosquitos buzzing and moths flitting around the light. Finally, he leaned over and grabbed Toth's arm, "The most important things I learned in life I learned right here on this farm when I was just a boy."

Matild, by this time so nearly blind she had to feel her way around the table, made her way to Jozsi, leaned down and gave him a hug. "That is one of the most beautiful compliments we have ever received."

But of course, he had learned many, many things out in the world. The youthful view he'd had from his vantage point in Hungary had been expanded ten times over. He'd met people from many different countries, of many different skin hues, speaking a wide range of languages. He'd learned much from the histories and backgrounds of other humans. He was beyond happy to be sitting with the Toths, and to again be with his Hungarian family, but he knew there was no way he could ever return to the narrowness of life there. That was over.

Soon, most of the family made their way to bed, but Toth led Jozsi out under the old berry tree for one more drink. Jozsi smiled, remembering the years he'd heard adult conversation late into the night as it drifted through the air from under that same tree.

Toth was in a mood to reminisce, launching into stories about the old days, traveling back to the First World War when he first knew Matyas. He'd served as Matyas' servant when he rode with the *Red Devils* regiment. He remembered Matyas as a dashing cavalry officer, traveling through the Carpathian Mountains from the Ukraine to the

Black Sea. Toth hadn't had much education, but he was a hard worker and knew horses. He'd been assigned to Matyas to care for his horse and uniform for eight years during the war. The last horse Matyas had, of course, was Bandi. Toth had been impressed from the first by Matyas's physical strength and stamina.

"Your papa was quick on his feet and precise with his sword," Toth said, nodding at some particular memory. "You did not want to have that weapon thrust in your direction. He was merciless when necessary," he added, "but merciful and just the rest of the time. The *Red Devils* under his control were devoted to him. He commanded attention; he had such a presence, such an authoritative air, but not in the cheap meaningless way of an *apparatchik*. You met him, instant respect," he snapped his fingers. "Anything went wrong, you looked to him. Nothing ever rattled your father. He's always had that way about him, a sense of calm and control."

As Matyas came to know and trust Toth, they'd shifted from master and servant to comrades who shared their history, observations, fears and hopes. "He was not a braggart," Toth emphasized. "Never taking advantage of his power, never stepping on anyone's shoulders to forward himself. He shared credit always with his men. And since our time in battle my respect has only grown. His intelligence, his confidence, fairness and generosity, all these things about him are why I am so loyal to this man. You are fortunate to have him for a father, and I see how you are now, grown, and I see him in you." Jozsi was almost in tears by this time, but a quick shot of *palinka* kept him from losing control. His father would not have wept at such praise, so neither would he.

Far into the early morning hours, Toth told stories about the war his father had never shared. He described how Matyas had rescued Bandi from a swamp by using his blanket so the horse could have something to step on. Matyas had been up to his waist in swamp muck, bending to tuck the blanket under the horse's hooves. He told Jozsi about being grabbed by a group of furious men at a local Sarajevo market — Serbians looking to hang Toth from a lamppost. They called to other Serbs to come watch the hanging and soon a crowd gathered. Matyas got wind of Toth's predicament, and with his fellow officers charged straight to the market, swords drawn, slicing through the crowd until they found him. "Once they saw the cavalry coming, those fatherless *szemeteks* fled, leaving me tied to a post. Your father did damage to the men who'd tied me up, cut them up pretty bad. He grinned, "That market emptied in a flash. Everybody knew the *Red Devils* took no prisoners."

Jozsi was grateful to Toth for sharing these stories. Another rite of passage, he thought, another sign he had a new status. He felt a lump of pride rise into his throat and swallowed hard. He had always looked up to his father. Though he could be stern, with piercing blue eyes that when fixed on you could freeze you in your tracks, he was fair. If you had an explanation, he'd hear it out, think it through, evaluate all sides, and judiciously settle whatever matter was at hand. All of Jozsi's friends had liked him because he understood that children needed to be children. Though stern, he was often indulgent of their antics and always made them feel like they truly mattered. When you spoke with him he paid full attention; he always left you feeling good. Unless, of course, you had screwed up, and then you felt you had failed him personally and miserably. Jozsi remembered the sting of those moments, the shame. He was glad they were few, and looked forward to getting back to the house so he could experience yet again the rush of joy it gave him to lay eyes on Matyas. He would take him aside and thank him for having been such a strong man and father.

Jozsi might be viewed as a grown man, but to his pleasure, the Toth family still remembered the boy in him. The next morning, as they prepared to leave, Toth said, "You go open the gate one more time before you leave." And the Toths all grinned, remembering it as Jozsi's boyhood job during his summer visits. He left feeling injected with knowledge and love, and hurried back to his childhood home, his spirit so much lighter than when he'd arrived. He didn't care who was following, he was happy.

~~~

They spent another week visiting with relatives, dining on special Hungarian meals prepared just for them; a different house every night. At each gathering they were given Hungarian gifts to take back to America. Their three weeks of vacation came to an end and for a final supper, they went to Ferenc's. Dani was happy because he could play with Jolanka and try out the new Hungarian words he'd learned, along with the sign language they'd relied on during their first meeting.

After emotional farewells, they took a scenic route to Vienna, the ride silent as a flood of thoughts and feelings overwhelmed them. Jozsi kept turning back to see his parents waving as they drove away. This parting was bittersweet, though not heartbreaking. After all they'd been through, at least this time he knew he would be able to see and touch them again. They were part of his life now, not a memory behind an impenetrable perimeter.

At the border, Jozsi underwent the same hostile treatment he'd received upon arriving. He drove across it with immense relief; he had been afraid the police would fabricate something and keep him for questioning, just to rattle him one more time.

He was wrung out from all the tension, so when they arrived at their hotel, he asked Ann to take Dani outside to burn off a little energy before supper. Poor Ann — Dani had *lots* of energy, they walked and skipped and walked some more. But she understood the impact of this momentous trip, and that her husband needed to have a little peace and space to catch up with his thoughts and feelings.

Jozsi took a long hot shower, hoping it would pummel the tension out of his body. He'd still not told Ann that he believed Ed had lied about his trip, he saw no reason to share anything stressful until they were far from the Hungarian border. He left them a note and went to sit in a dark corner of a restaurant. He ordered goulash and a bottle of wine, and fumed about the danger they'd been exposed to by Ed's dangerous tall tale. So many worse things could have happened at the border, and Zsigmond could have created terrible problems during their time in the country. In fact, Jozsi wasn't sure why Zsigmond hadn't harassed them more. Not out of decency, that much he knew — Zsigmond had lost his humanity long ago.

They re-entered the United States and Jozsi felt like hugging the customs officials. The family was punchy with exhaustion by the time they arrived at their house. Erzsebet had given Dani a handmade blue crocheted blanket that he clutched tight as he happily climbed into his own bed. Jozsi and Ann fell into theirs, exhausted and relieved to be safely home.

The first thing Jozsi did the following morning was to call Ed. "I want to tell him all about our trip," he explained to Ann, still not revealing Ed's betrayal. He arranged to meet Ed at a local bar that night.

Jozsi arrived early and sat in his car, watching for Ed to pull into the parking lot. Spotting him, Jozsi strode toward the spot Ed had parked. Ed, smiling, held out his hands in happy greeting. Jozsi smiled back; right up to the moment he drew close enough to knee Ed in the balls. Ed gasped and fell to the ground.

Jozsi dragged him upright and shoved him back against the hood of the car. "You lying son of a bitch. I almost had my ass arrested because of you. You put Ann through hell!" He yelled, "I could have lost my family, lost everything because of your bullshit." He let Ed slide off the hood and when he'd reached the ground, kicked him flat and stepped on his throat. He lifted his foot and watched Ed groan, roll over, try to crawl away. Then Jozsi grabbed him and flung him sitting against a car tire. Legs splayed, Ed looked pathetic. Jozsi slapped him hard just once, then stood back, trying to get a grip on his rage. "Explain," he said through clenched teeth. "Explain or I'll beat you dead."

Ed sputtered and coughed out the story. He had a serious gambling problem and hadn't made it any further than New Jersey where he'd spent three weeks gambling. He'd blown a few thousand dollars, managing to hold onto just enough to buy his wife and friends a few souvenirs at a Hungarian gift shop he'd tracked down. "How did you know?" he finally had nerve and breath enough to ask.

"The AVO told me I must have a big pair of balls to be the first Special Forces-trained traitor to come back. You dick-less bastard, stay away from this bar and any other place I might go. If you don't, what just happened here will feel like an embrace." Jozsi then drove off, leaving Ed on the pavement, hurting something awful.

When he got home, he leveled with Ann, at least about Ed's lies. He did not exactly own up to how badly he'd beaten the man. "We're safe," Ann murmured, holding him tight. "We're safe and we're home."

24
Operation Hemingway

Ann had hoped Jozsi's visit to Hungary might ease the nightmares; that seeing his family, his childhood home and haunts, could alleviate at least some of his anxiety and fear, and to a certain extent there actually was a difference. His violent dreams, the ones that made him break into a sweat, thrash and cry out, came less frequently. But still, many nights he'd be restless and moan, a haunting agonized sound that tugged at her heart.

The comfort and joy he'd felt at being in the cocoon of the Budai family cheered him for many months. But eventually Jozsi started grumbling about how frustrating it had been to return and find Hungary still under communist control. "I didn't finish the work," he'd lament late in the evening after many drinks. "The communists should be done, gone, Hungary a free country, you do what you want. We didn't accomplish that; we didn't make the important thing happen." He'd shake his head sadly. "I go back and in so many ways, it's the same rat hole as before."

"Someday," Ann would murmur, massaging his shoulders as he slumped, depressed, in his chair. "We'll go back and it *will* be truly free." But her comfort and encouragement made no difference when he was in these dark moods.

Jozsi was adamant that Dani must learn to speak Hungarian fluently, so Jozsi spent many nights with Ann, teaching them both; first words, then phrases. As time passed, when Jozsi's Hungarian friends came around, Dani could communicate with them better than Ann could, at least about the things adult men would want to discuss with a small boy, such as trucks and trains and lions and tigers.

By the fall of 1966, Jozsi's engineering job at a computer firm regularly involved trips around the country as he met with and approved subcontractors for his corporation. Ann was used to the rhythm of his travels, enjoying her time with Dani, and a chance for peaceful sleep; Jozsi's dream agitation kept her on edge many a night.

~~~

Their life was consistent through the end of that decade, although America's was not. Each upheaval in its political and cultural life — the assassinations, the riots, the wild music, the drugs, the crazy clothes, even the walk on the moon — led Jozsi to love his adopted home more, although it was not with unfettered adoration. He didn't like a lot of what the young people were up to, he didn't approve of Negros tearing apart their own cities. He understood why they felt as they did, but he could not fully accept that they saw themselves as having had it so much worse than the Jews, Chinese, American Indians, Poles, Puerto Ricans, even the Irish. If someone mentioned slavery, he'd counter with the horrible things North Americans had done to Native Americans.

When it came to giving a helping hand to those less fortunate, he shrugged. "People are made one way or the other. There are hard workers and then there are shirkers — professional shirkers who will take and take." When Ann demurred, he'd grow even more adamant. "You give a hand up, some people take it as a hand out and just want more. They don't want to work hard; they want to la-la-la through life on the backs of the people who *do* want to work." From when Dani was too young to comprehend what was being said, Jozsi would tell him, "Make sure when you grow up you *do* something. You can be a trash collector, I don't care. It's a job and it's important. But try to be the guy that owns the trash truck, it's always better to be the boss."

He never forgot the deprivations of his childhood and sometimes Ann would struggle with him over what he saw as excessive abundance. Dani did not need brand name clothes, or more than one pair of shoes and two pairs of pants, Jozsi insisted. "Well, then *you* do his laundry," she'd retort. "It's just not practical." Ann would win, but he would continue to grouse about the excess.

Jozsi had no patience with idleness, or with protestors. "It's a free country, but it costs like hell, and all of them, they should be working," he'd insist, "not waving signs and throwing bottles." He saw protest as a luxury activity. When Ann would remind him that he'd done plenty of protesting during the Hungarian Revolution, he would answer, "But we had *real* reasons, it wasn't over bullshit." He'd read the paper and mutter, "We would have been shot for that," at some of what Ann described as "the shenanigans of the young."

But while he didn't want to see a revolution, at the same time, he did not want the war in Vietnam to go on one second longer. What he appreciated most was that he knew what was happening, the truth of it, at least that's how "the news" felt to him. Even the words "the news" came off his tongue with a special emphasis, as though it were a sacred phrase.

After having escaped a cesspool of deceit and oppression, to *know* what was taking place meant a great deal. To be able to speak openly, to disagree and still co-exist, meant everything. Jozsi never took for granted his ability to live "the American dream." He had gone through hell to get to a place where he could finally have good dreams along with the bad.

~~~

The February of 1970 was a miserable, cold month and Jozsi was happy to fly away from Boston and land in Los Angeles for a few days while evaluating the purchase of capital equipment for his company. After a ten-hour day, he was equally happy to take a seat at the bar of *The Black Horse Tavern*, which was attached to the Redondo Inn, a lodging he favored when in the area. It was already too late to call Ann. He decided to have a couple of drinks, swap lies with the bartender, eat, and fall into bed, knowing the following day would be equally demanding.

The bartender was the child of Hungarian immigrants, which was part of the place's appeal for Jozsi. The young man had been there a few years, just killing time, he claimed, till he became a Hollywood movie star. He had an audition the next day and between drink orders was practicing his audition piece. Jozsi was a willing audience. Suddenly a tap on the shoulder and a voice he recognized.

"Long time no see."

Sandor. Jozsi knew who stood at his shoulder before he even turned his head, a wry smile on his face. Sandor too was smiling, his teeth bright against a tan. Jozsi gave his head two shakes at the shock of finding Sandor inches away.

"What the hell? If you didn't have that bathing beauty tan, I'd think this was a visit from a ghost! I thought you were dead. I even sent flowers to the Langley whore house!"

Sandor smirked, "Jozsi, you'll never change, and if you do, I'll resign from the firm and the two of us can buy a farm outside Akron. We can raise pigs in the Hungarian way, with loads of fat on them." Sandor ordered a round while Jozsi found a corner table for their private conversation.

"You skipped out before the bill, as usual," Sandor handed Jozsi a drink.

"Well, my treasury is a little low and I can't afford to carry you. Besides, you did the ordering."

"Ah, it is like we parted only yesterday, old friend. And why is it you always end up with cash in your pocket after we meet? Don't worry, I'll take care of the bill...for the 500th time."

"For a minute, I was feeling good about you cornering me here in the land of fools and big dreamers," he nodded toward the bartender across the room. "But now that you're offering to foot the bill, I better squeeze my legs tight. I'm getting a bad feeling because I know that somehow, some way, I'm gonna get screwed." They laughed and talked into the night, dining in the bar. How strange, Jozsi thought, to feel as though Sandor were an old friend. He'd engineered Jozsi into more and riskier adventures than he could count, but he'd also helped get Jozsi out of Hungary and eventually into America, passport and all. The vicissitudes of life provided them a strange, intense connection.

Just before parting in the lobby, Sandor spoke seriously, "Jozsi, I'm sorry, but I have to ask you to do just one more job for me. After that, I swear I'll leave you alone for the rest of your life."

Jozsi's face flashed: curiosity, puzzlement, irritation, resignation, back to curiosity. "Seriously, I thought you were out of my life. Out in the Akron hayfields by now, a beautiful girl helping you load a trailer.

"Jozsi, you know my life is not that simple."

"What, you are homosexual and not ready to come out of the closet?" He raised an eyebrow.

Sandor laughed. "No, no. I'm still working fulltime for the firm; I have no time for marriage. And anyway, I like a little variety." Jozsi checked his watch and started walking toward the motel, but not before agreeing to meet again at *The Black Horse* the next night. Jozsi scolded himself for indulging in another conversation, but his interest was piqued.

Jozsi worked hard the next day, but a tickle in the corner of his mind kept him wondering, "What could he want now?" When he entered the lounge, Sandor was already seated at the same corner table. He pointed at the bartender as soon as Jozsi came in, and seconds after settling in his seat, a double Manhattan, two cherries, was staring up at him.

"Uh-oh," Jozsi said, "Now I know you need something big from me." He took far more than a sip of his drink. Sandor raised his glass to Jozsi's health and took his own long swallow.

Sandor spoke about Los Angeles, about his time there, about this, about that, ordering round after round. When he got around to asking about Jozsi's day, Jozsi decided enough was enough.

"Son-of-a-bitch, you're asking about my day like a wife when you could care less. One drink, twenty, same difference. How about you cut to the chase now."

Sandor nodded. He explained that the CIA had information out of Hungary that a young team of agents was being sent to Cuba. From there, they would travel to Puerto Rico and then enter the United States. Their goal: to access the latest computer technology in order to share it with the Russians.

Jozsi cut in, "Why in God's name do you still think of me for this kind of thing? Here's what I'll do for you, I'll give you James Bond's phone number. Better yet, I'll send you to Boston. You pick out a mental institution and check in for a few months. Your brain is broken."

Holding up an index finger, Sandor asked Jozsi to just hear him out. "Your company has set up a manufacturing site in San Juan. According to our sources in Hungary, three agents will arrive in Cuba about two months from now--"

"I get it! I'll be waving the Hungarian flag somewhere on the shores of San Juan and I'll invite them to my hotel room, and serve them *palinka* and say, *Hogy Vagy* and--"

This time Sandor cut him off. "The president of your company is aware of our concerns and understands that if he cooperates in this project, there will be more government contracts for his corporation in the future. He has agreed to help. All we need is for you to cooperate and we're ready to go."

"You've set me up good." Jozsi, suddenly serious, said, "I need to think this over. I have a family now; I like my life the way it is. I'm sick of the Cold War, I'm sick of all war, all subterfuge, the games, the lying, all of it. If I thought this was going to help get the bastards out of Hungary, I'd jump, but what difference will it make?"

"Just think about it on your way home," Sandor said. "It takes many acts to shift the balance of power." He rose to leave, dropping one final nugget of information. "Jozsi, these infiltrator agents, they are working for Zsigmond, they are directly under his command."

Jozsi's eyes widened, almost cartoon-like. Now he didn't know whether to punch Sandor or kiss him. A chance to get even with Zsigmond was an entirely different proposition. He sat, nodding his head up and down thoughtfully as Sandor left.

He flew back to Boston thinking about the risk he'd have to take, of what it might mean to go after Zsigmond one more time. He didn't mention a word about any of this to Ann. He needed time to think things through.

When a week later his manager, John, a good-natured, friendly sort, invited him to lunch, he was innocently pleased. Nice restaurant, chance to chinwag with the manager. John did that now and then. But the minute John took his glasses off, placed them on the table, and started rubbing his eyes, Jozsi grew wary. John usually removed his glasses when you'd screwed up badly and he was going to have to deliver an uncomfortable lecture. Jozsi couldn't imagine what he might have done wrong, but steeled himself for trouble.

John said the company's vice-president wanted Jozsi to take a job in their new plant in Puerto Rico. "You don't have to live there," John stressed, "just be available on an as-needed basis. The manufacturing startup needs experienced engineers to help open the plant, keep an eye on it, insure the production capabilities meet all the corporate requirements." Jozsi immediately understood exactly what was being asked of him, and realized that John had no idea what the assignment was really about.

That night Jozsi disappeared into his basement workshop where he often tinkered with old clocks and radios, fixed household items and created contraptions. He'd even designed an electric pig-roasting device he was quite proud of, much to Ann's amusement. He'd explore computers and new-fangled gadgets when digital equipment companies introduced them. Firing up the soldering iron and taking something apart to then put it back together always gave him a sense of peace and calm. Ann could read his moods and saw that he was preoccupied by something weighty; she kept Dani occupied so his father could putter undisturbed.

Earlier he'd prepared stuffed peppers, a favorite of his; he loved the smell wafting down the stairs to the workshop. He'd called up to Ann, "Put on the *Csárdás*," a tape of traditional Hungarian dance music he sometimes listened to. And a moment later, "*Kérlek*," please. She was surprised, because hearing that tape usually made him homesick. Between the music and the stuffed peppers, she knew he was grappling with something from the past. "Let me know when you want me to start warming up the peppers," she called down, and pressed "play" on the tape.

He sat at his worktable, but dimmed the light. He was not there to work. He let his mind venture back to Hungary, to the time leading up to the Revolution. Immediately an image of Erika sobbing about her tortured father flashed through his mind. The kind doctor had been starved, his fingers broken by the smash of rubber hoses, his teeth punched out of his head. Nothing unusual in that, not in those times.

Jozsi's mind flooded with horror stories. He remembered Arpad, a frail man he'd met in a bookstore, his left arm jutting out, frozen at a peculiar angle. It was a time of intense paranoia, when you watched your words among strangers, never knowing who might turn you in for some infraction, real or manufactured. But the bookstore owner, trusted by both, introduced them at the counter, and in the otherwise empty store, they had spoken honestly.

Arpad had told them about his time at the AVO prison headquarters, where prisoners were dragged down to the cellars beneath street level, two floors of shrouded space. Arpad was a rare survivor, a factory worker ratted out by another plant worker. His crime was that he'd grown tired of seeing the Russian flag everywhere — he missed the sight of the Hungarian colors flying high — and he had been foolish enough to say that out loud.

Arpad described weeks trapped in a solitary cell, enough room for only a narrow cot. No windows, just a steel door with peepholes and a single bright overhead light that never shut off. He'd been told to sleep flat, hands above his blanket; told that if he rolled over, he would be shot. Fed scraps, given a rare sip of water, always dirty. The guards had assaulted his mind by stealing his sense of time — a day could be 20 hours, a night three; there was no way for him to tell the difference, they told him whatever they wanted.

After many weeks, he'd been dragged by his arms down another flight of stairs to an even smaller space, not room enough to lay or even sit. He'd been forced to stand for what he guessed was three days, no food, no respite. When he relieved himself, he had to stand in his own excrement. Later, he'd been forced to eat plates of greasy food, then salty food, and totally deprived of water, he'd become violently ill. And still he had to stand. After that he'd been beaten with rubber hoses. Throughout his stay the screaming and humiliation were a constant. He'd been accused of all manner of crimes against the state — for that single sentence about the flags. And he'd once been considered one of the good ones, a Csepel Island factory worker. They were among the first groups won over to communism by the Russians when they began enacting their deadly mission: to engineer Hungary into a satellite plantation for the Soviet Union.

Arpad wept as he recounted the torture of others. He spoke of rifle butts smashed against insteps, knees, heads. Of men forced to stand on one foot for hours in front of a row of bright lights — if a foot came down or you fainted from the effort, everyone *else* would be savagely beaten. Of men kept standing in a clammy cell, in a tub, cold water up to their knees. Of men ordered to carry a 100-pound rock up and down a ladder 15, 20 times. If it dropped, everyone else would be beaten mercilessly. Even a pencil could be used as an instrument of torture. A favorite of the guards was to face a man to a wall where bright light shone directly into his eyes — a pencil point pressed into the man's forehead, the eraser end against the wall. When this happened to Arpad, he'd been told that if the pencil fell to the ground, he would be beaten to death. Jozsi noticed the indentation in his forehead. "When they finally did pull me away from the wall, the pencil stayed sticking straight out of my head," Arpad explained.

Deemed ready for interrogation Arpad had been taken to 60 Andrássy Street, the House of Terror, where he'd endured further tortures. That he was alive and able to speak was a miracle. He'd been released finally, too damaged for anyone to consider him a threat. His arm jutted out at a strange angle, left to heal on its own after breaking when he was dragged down the prison stairs. Again, nothing unusual. Jozsi would often see men like that on the streets of Budapest, legs or arms askew, pronounced limps, vacant stares; an air of brokenness and vast internal flatness of spirit. Ghosts on the streets, gutted of life.

Sitting in his basement, the smell of stuffed peppers evoking his mother's kitchen, the sounds of the *Csárdás* tugging at his heart, Jozsi put his head down and did something he almost never did. He wept.

~~~

A few days later, Sandor showed up unannounced at his office door. "Free for lunch?" At the restaurant, he wasted no time. "Are you in? Will you take the job?"

Jozsi, having recovered his equanimity shrugged, maybe yes, maybe no. "Tell me more," was all he said, pleased to let Sandor hang wondering a bit longer.

"Zsigmond's infiltrators will be on their way to Cuba next month. The team is one man and two women. Their story is they're studying Hemingway for the Hungarian University of Art."

Jozsi snorted. "Really? Who will believe that?"

Sandor chuckled, "Hemingway, Cuba, his sympathy for communism. It connects just enough. Once they get to Puerto Rico, they'll be looking for a sucker to sponsor their entry into the good old U. S. of A. Our agent knows where they'll land. He'll meet them on the shore. He'll guide them to the *Mayaguez Hilton*. And that's where you come in, my friend. You'll meet as fellow Hungarians, you'll offer to help."

Jozsi nodded. He had already decided. He was in. Zsigmond's infiltrators, Zsigmond's agents. If he could stop the agents, thwart Zsigmond's plan, well, at least that would mean something.

Yes, he would go. Ann would have to understand, even if he didn't tell her every single reason for wanting revenge on Zsigmond. In fact, he decided to hold off on revealing the true goal of this mission until it was over. She had met the man, he'd given her a chill, and she was aware of a steamer trunk worth of history between the two. Better not to mention his name at all. Indeed, Ann took in stride his sudden travel to Puerto Rico to help manage a new plant, not pressing too hard for details. She just hoped she could go along next time, she'd never been.

~~~

Three weeks later, Jozsi flew to Puerto Rico to visit the plant, arriving at the *Mayaguez Hilton* in the early afternoon. Within ten minutes he had his bathing trunks on and lay prone on a lounge chair by the pool. He relaxed in the tropical sun, catching his breath. He was almost asleep when he felt cold water dripping on his stomach. Sandor. Again. "For Christ's sake… I suppose when I'm in hell, you'll come around with ice cold water and an even icier Norwegian broad, friend that you are."

Sandor ordered piña coladas. "After all, we're in the tropics, and I want to celebrate," he said, responding to Jozsi's look of surprise. "I have big news. Our new Hungarian friends are in Cuba, waiting for transport to the shores of Puerto Rico. Even the Coast Guard knows to let them land. It may be another couple of weeks before it happens, but things are in motion."

Jozsi felt the internal churn that always came at the start of a new mission. Sandor explained Jozsi should make sure the hotel staff knew he was a Hungarian-born engineer working for one of the largest computer corporations in America. "Bragging," Sandor said, "is something you know how to do."

"What else should I be? Maybe I'll tell them I'm a hay farmer from Akron, instead."

"Funny, funny man. You're making me sorry I ever mentioned Ohio. If you don't want any helpful advice, I'll just shut up."

Jozsi said, "That's about all I do know, that you're from Ohio. All these years and I don't know really know squat about you. What makes you tick? I have no idea if you're doing this kind of work for kicks or patriotism or are you just deranged? And were you *ever* married? I don't even know that."

Sandor's expression was both amused and puzzled. "Why do you want to know, after all this time? You writing a book about the spooks or you just nosy all of a sudden?"

Jozsi shrugged. "Sandor, I don't really give a shit about your past, but we've got time to kill and you already know more about me than my own mother. It's your turn: tell me your story, or make one up."

Sandor waved to the waiter and ordered more drinks. "So, Jozsi, how much time do you have?"

"Today?" Jozsi looked around the pool. A good-looking Spanish girl stretched out on a chair, her breasts about to escape a too-small bikini top. "If that beauty decides to ask me to go to bed with her, I've got no time."

"Long odds," Sandor said. "And if your wife found out…"

"For once, I agree with you. My conclusion, then, is that I've got all the time in the world, especially as long as you're buying."

Sandor laughed. "Many times I have wished to have your boundless humor, tedious as it can sometimes be."

"You are not the first to comment so. What makes you think you don't have boundless humor? You get my jokes." Jozsi thought if Sandor had seen him weeping in his workroom, he'd have been shocked.

Sandor sipped on his drink. "Well, you have nerves of steel and don't seem to be disturbed by going through crazy shit and having no control over your life. I'd have given up long ago if I were you. Even your buddy Laci once said to me, 'Jozsi looks at the world like it's a big joke. And in his eyes, we're the comedians.'"

"Sandor, did I ever call you a clown? I don't think so."

"No, you never did, but you sure as shit made me feel like one, and more than once."

This acknowledgment was such a surprise to Jozsi he apologized. "If I ever made you feel that way, I'm sorry. Sometimes — and don't repeat this, I'll just deny it — I can be an asshole."

Sandor tipped his tall glass in Jozsi's direction. "Apology accepted."

"So, tell me why a guy like you is working for the CIA all these years. We're far enough away from the bartender so you can speak Hungarian, then no one else can follow. Jozsi leaned back in his chair. "Tell me all."

To Jozsi's surprise, Sandor did just that, starting with his senior year in college, where he'd majored in political science. He spoke of his first visit from the firm some months before his graduation. When, later that night, his story arrived at the present, Jozsi assured him it was a fascinating tale and suggested he write a book. "Just don't use my name. I have a lot of connections with intelligence, and no disrespect, I'm not talking about the CIA."

Sandor shook his head sadly. "Did you not understand when I said you look down on me like shit before you flush? Well, brother, you've just done it again." Again, Jozsi apologized. "Well, you are an asshole," Sandor said genially, "but I guess you can't help yourself."

For all their joking, Sandor grew serious when speaking about the Hungarian Revolution. Sandor had been assigned six agents in Hungary. When Jozsi asked where they'd ended up, Sandor looked down at the floor for a long moment before lifting his eyes. "You are in front of me and Laci is in Vietnam. Had you heard he was promoted to Sergeant First Class for his bravery a few weeks ago? He's probably on leave in Hawaii, getting laid as we speak." He took a deep breath. "The other four are smelling the roses from the bottom up." He looked genuinely pained.

"I'm sorry, my friend," Jozsi said. They sat silent for a bit. "So, now, what is it *you* want?" Jozsi asked. "To be the head of the CIA or just another field information-gatherer, retiring after decades of dedicated work without ever taking a sick day?"

"What do I want? Zsigmond was part of the group that took those four agents down and I want his ass so bad I can taste it. The firm holds what happened to those agents against me, but no more than I hold it against myself. And you, Jozsi, are one way to make my wish come true." He excused himself to go to the bathroom, as serious as Jozsi had ever seen him.

Sandor had never shared any of this with Jozsi, who was impressed by how skillfully he'd concealed his losses and frustrations. Jozsi also wondered how Sandor could drink all those piña coladas and remain coherent and walk a straight line to the bathroom to boot. Jozsi reached over and took a sip of Sandor's drink. Milk. Pure milk. Of course. Tricky bastard. Even when pouring out his heart. He hated when Sandor played with loaded dice, but he was clearly getting rusty, he shouldn't have been at all surprised. He'd show Sandor, shock him out of his sad reflections. Just as he'd been shocked by how much Sandor had shared. But he couldn't help feeling like he'd also been worked — Sandor opening up for some reason. To prime the pump? Jozsi was already all in and Sandor knew him well enough to know he wouldn't back out. It irritated him even more that he couldn't just appreciate the man's honesty, but that was what dealing with the CIA did. Nothing ever clean and clear, all continually murky and shifty.

Sandor returned and plopped onto the lounge chair, telling Jozsi how drunk he was and how he may just have revealed some things he shouldn't have. Lying bastard, Jozsi thought. He'd revealed exactly what he'd wanted to. The waiter, who Sandor must have paid off to fake his drink, appeared with the bill, which Sandor paid, and then they were alone in the moonlight by the pool.

"Thank you, Jozsi, for offering to help get Zsigmond by the balls. But I'm plastered. I better head to my room and get some rest."

As he got up from the lounge chair, Sandor lost his balance and Jozsi took his arm to steady him. "Thanks, friend." Jozsi thought: he's really laying it on thick.

As they passed the middle of the pool, Jozsi suddenly stepped aside and shoved Sandor into the water, then knelt and grabbed him in a chokehold. Jozsi dunked him a few times, then let his sputtering handler go. Sandor clambered out and stomped away, dripping wet. Jozsi shouted after him in Hungarian, "You lying bastard, take your milk with you, you'll need it to warm up!" Sandor reached his arm back and gave Jozsi the finger as he walked back to his room, coughing up water and leaving big puddles in his wake.

The next morning, Sandor invited Jozsi to breakfast. They met on the terrace overlooking the pool, Sandor's expression hard to read. After a few silent minutes, Jozsi spoke. "I'm sorry about dunking you. I've pulled the same fake-drunk shit on my share of people. I was pissed it took me all night to realize it. You know, I thought for a minute we were being real." He held out his hand, "We're okay?"

Sandor sighed. "I'm okay, you're an asshole." They shook. Sandor waited a beat. "I felt like talking about it is all. It was real. And fake drinking, well, force of habit."

"Okay," Jozsi replied, wanting to believe him in that moment. "Now, how can I help you nail Zsigmond and appear a hero to the top of the firm's food chain?"

They spent the rest of the day working on the plan. Sandor explained that in Puerto Rico, the Cuban government was sponsoring a group called the Armed Forces of National Liberation, known as *Los Macheteros*, "The Machete Wielders." The CIA was keeping a close eye on their activities through an agent they'd succeeded in planting within the group.

Once the Hungarian trio of agents got to Puerto Rico, they'd check into the *Mayaguez Hilton* and Sandor would alert Jozsi, who could easily arrange to meet them by chance; all he had to do was be anywhere near them when they spoke Hungarian — lobby, elevator, pool, didn't matter. The hotel staff would already know him as "a rich Hungarian," which would help support his story for Zsigmond's young agents. Once Jozsi had made contact, Sandor would arrange to get the three agents to New York City. After that, the FBI would be in charge of tracking and capturing them.

Jozsi tended to his official work duties and flew home at the end of the week to await further developments. Ann picked him up at Logan Airport, and they headed north on Route 93, stopping off at a favorite restaurant along the way. She caught him up on Dani's activities, and he told her a little about his trip. He let her know he'd likely have to return to Puerto Rico in the near future, but that as soon as the manufacturing plant was in operation, he'd bring her along to see that beautiful island with her own eyes.

~~~

Three weeks later, Sandor placed a call to Jozsi's house saying only, "New guests have arrived," and hanging up. Within a few days, Jozsi was again signing in at the hotel's front desk. The check-in clerk remembered him and cheerfully mentioned that he was no longer the sole Hungarian in residence; two women and one man had recently booked rooms and were looking forward to meeting him. "I told them about you," she smiled. "It's a happy coincidence, having another group of Hungarians registered."

Perfect, Jozsi thought. "Tell them I'm back and would be delighted to speak with fellow countrymen. In fact, if you would be so kind, please extend an invitation for them to dine with me tonight — on the terrace at eight."

Before Jozsi had a chance to unpack, he found Sandor on the other end of his phone line, informing him he'd placed money in the hotel safe so Jozsi could afford to treat his new friends like old friends. "Just like long lost relatives," Jozsi said. "Not to worry."

"Keep the receipts for a change, okay?" Sandor added. They were back in their usual groove.

"Of course. All expenses will be accounted for. Even the milk."

Sandor swore at him in Hungarian and hung up.

Jozsi had reserved a room overlooking the pool, so he had a full view of everyone on the terrace. He peeked out from the curtain and spotted the three agents at the far end. Probably five to ten years younger than he, they sat waiting, looking casually, but carefully around.

Jozsi studied them for a good fifteen minutes, trying to analyze each person by their body language. He'd always been quick to read people, learning long ago, you didn't always need words to get the gist of a person's character. Finally, he emerged and made his way to the now crowded terrace. Upper class Puerto Ricans and tourists occupied most of the tables, and in the background a band played Latin American music. The maître d recognized Jozsi and after introducing him to his guests — Agnes, Nadine and Bela — escorted the group to their table. Small talk was made, drinks were ordered, and phase one of the plan was off to a good start.

Jozsi apologized for his tardiness, blaming the inexperienced corporate jet pilot who'd flown him in from San Juan. They'd missed the airport twice and had to circle Mayaguez for fifteen minutes before landing. Lies came to him as easily as flies to horseshit, he thought, grateful for his quick wit and lack of compunction.

In turn, they told him about their experiences exploring the island. One fib followed another, he knew, but he feigned interest as he carefully watched them interact, still trying to get a solid bead on who was who in the group in terms of power and smarts.

Jozsi then asked them about Hungary and what changes had taken place since he'd left the motherland. As they ate, they took turns talking about how wonderful life in Hungary was, and how homesick they already were after just a short time away. Jozsi kept quiet, only occasionally prodding for more information. As his grandmother used to say, "You cannot learn anything if you do the talking." She'd never know how often he'd relied on that advice. The three spoke of Budapest and Margaret Island on the Danube. The girls told of nighttime romantic walks on the island, and in that they made him think of Erika and their long walks along the Margaret Island trails on hot summer nights. They'd often escaped the stuffy apartment to enjoy cool breezes wafting off the Danube as they strolled along its shore.

Finally, Jozsi asked, "So, what brought you to this beautiful island?" They answered as expected. They'd been attending school in Budapest and had entered a contest to do research on the work of Ernest Hemingway. They'd been selected out of three hundred students. He remembered to look impressed. Their assignment was to return with an extensive presentation for the school, which would later be published and shared throughout the Hungarian university system. It was a great honor. Jozsi had to admit they were convincing.

He asked if there was anything he could do to help them. Well, they said, they were very eager to do some research in New York City before returning to Hungary. Jozsi said he wasn't sure, but that he might be able to help arrange their trip. It was the least he could do for fellow countrymen; he'd try everything he could to make it happen.

After bidding them good night and tentatively arranging to meet them late the next day, Jozsi reported to Sandor, who said he'd be flying to the island as soon as possible and expected to be at Jozsi's door first thing in the morning. Then Jozsi took a shower. He had just stepped out of the bathroom when he heard a knock. He walked over to the door in his towel, expecting to find Sandor — it would be just like him to pull that kind of stunt — but instead found one of the Hungarian students.

"Oh, hi Agnes," he said, obviously surprised. She was wearing a summery dress that exposed a good deal of cleavage. Must have been shopping at the hotel store, he thought. It was not a Hungarian agent kind of a dress.

She smiled, eyeballing the towel. "Oh, pardon me, I see I should have called ahead. May I come in anyway?"

"Well, I'm turning in early. I'm expecting a colleague first thing in the morning. We're going to discuss viable ways to arrange some kind of student visa sufficient to get you onto the mainland."

Shocking him, she leaned forward, lightly caressing his bare, damp chest. "If you need me for anything, just call." She tilted her head and smiled.

His eyes popping, he assured her he would, and with relief closed the door before she could see the slight lift in the towel. He went to sleep amused that despite his being an older married man, he still had appeal. Amused also by his own disinterest in thinking her motivation driven by anything more sinister than pure attraction. No one had ever said he was humble.

In the morning, he waited for Sandor on the balcony, gazing out at Mayaguez Bay in the distance, and at the hotel pool below. When his handler arrived Jozsi entertained him with the encounter.

"Send her my way! I have never been laid by a young Hungarian student studying Hemingway and am ready to service her in your stead."

"You'll have your chance after I leave the island. For now, let's work out the details so I can go back home and enjoy my family. Something you should think about trying, *haverom*."

"Trying your wife? How generous."

Jozsi punched him lightly on the arm. "You're getting to be entirely too funny for your own good."

They settled down to review the details. Sandor would serve as the "corporate representative" and provide the trio with student visas so they could continue their research in New York City. He'd already had business cards printed with a fake name, Mr. Campbell, and a phone number tied to the local CIA, just in case they called to check his status. Jozsi gave Sandor the three wine glasses he'd paid the waitress to set aside after last night's dinner. Sandor left to take the glasses to José Rivera's place. Rivera, a retired agent, was ready with his dust and tape, and within a short while handed over expertly lit photos of the agents' fingerprints, for the record.

Meanwhile, Jozsi packed, anxious to leave. The adventurous CIA life had seriously lost its appeal; he was propelled solely by his hatred for Zsigmond and took little pleasure in the scheming and deception. He wanted nothing more than to be sitting on his back deck, watching Dani dash around the yard. Sandor returned, seeming excited as a teenager having his first whorehouse experience, thought Jozsi. Sandor reported the students wanted to celebrate their good fortune that night.

"As long as you have the money, we can celebrate all night long, but I'm still leaving first thing in the morning."

"No problem," Sandor replied. He was thankful for Jozsi's help, and anticipated that the "boys in town," as he referred to the CIA, would appreciate their work, and might even give Sandor a promotion.

"Counting your chickens a little ahead of time, aren't you?"

Sandor ignored the dig. "My suite is on the first floor. I'll order in food, we'll drink. And if I play my cards right, I have a feeling I might get laid tonight. Agnes seems to have survived your rejection and moved on," he smiled. "Also, my agent told me that Bela called their group's agent in Ponce and told them what a pushover you are."

Jozsi had rarely seen Sandor so effusive. "I didn't know you'd brought other goons with you."

Sandor put his arm around Jozsi's shoulder. "My friend, you can never be too careful in this business. By the way, last night, Ann complaining about her cold? Might be a good idea to buy her some flowers on your way back home." His thin lips turned up at the corners, a smile suppressed.

Jozsi was aware his phone was tapped, every time he picked it up he immediately heard a brief click — a standard precaution he'd actually have been surprised not to find. What did irritate him was that when they were with the agents, he'd occasionally had to pretend to translate for Sandor's benefit. The Hungarians didn't speak perfect English, or chose not to. Sandor spoke Hungarian fluently, but didn't want to let on since he'd told the trio he was from California. Jozsi and Sandor had to stay on their toes, especially once the *palinka* started flowing — they couldn't manage to fake it after asking that an entire bottle be brought to the table. Earlier in the day Sandor, Mr. Campbell to the Hungarian "students," had provided the bartender with a good bottle of *palinka* to serve, another way to ratchet up the Hungarian connection.

Jozsi excused himself early, citing truthfully that he had to be up at dawn. The students thanked him, saying they hoped to someday treat him to the finest chicken paprika Budapest had to offer. Agnes looked a little wistful. Sandor, in magnanimous corporate personnel mode, ordered another round for the trio, and announced he'd accompany Jozsi back to his room to confer on a few more details related to ensuring the students' visit to the United States was trouble free. They should wait for him at the table, he would soon rejoin them for further celebration.

Instead, the men went straight to Sandor's room, where he plugged a recorder into the wall socket and clicked the receiver to record the students' conversation at the table. He let Jozsi have the headphones, motioning for him to share the gist of what he was hearing.

Bela's was the first voice. "I told you girls, these guys are stupid. We could sell them the *Brooklyn Bridge*." The women agreed, relieved.

"But still you failed to get Jozsi into bed," Bela said, matter-of-factly, adding, "I would never turn down someone like you." She raised her eyebrows; he'd been dropping hints left and right since they'd left Hungary. They went on to discuss the meal, their plans for milking their new friends for as much assistance as possible; perhaps they could convince the two to offer some financial support to aid them in their studies, loyalty to Hungarians, a gift to the motherland.

Eventually Jozsi wearied of their fanatic commitment to the Communist Party and handed off the headphones because he'd had enough of the day and was ready for sleep. Sandor called in one of his agents to carry on listening, so he could rejoin the students. "Hoping Agnes will want to land a corporate American, just for kicks?" Jozsi asked.

Sandor shrugged. "If she's looking to rub up against someone, I'm ready." He walked away, over his shoulder adding, "But I'll take Nadine in a pinch." Jozsi had never seen him so frisky.

The next morning, Sandor called early to invite Jozsi to breakfast before he headed to the airport.

"No luck?" Jozsi asked, joining Sandor on the terrace.

Sandor shook his head ruefully. "I guess I don't have your special magic. I struck out all around. Probably because they think I'm an American."

They went on to review the previous day's events. "When the hell did you install the transmitter under the table anyway?" Jozsi asked.

"Remember when you got them up to look out at Mayaguez Harbor, pretending to get all choked up because it reminded you so much of looking down at the Danube from the Buda side of Hungary? Your speech was good, I almost bought it. But you really are out of practice; you should have figured this out yourself."

Jozsi said that although he wanted to be done with the spook's way of life, he hoped the mission went well, and that Sandor would get his promotion, and most important, that Zsigmond would get his ass kicked or worse. "And now I have a favor to ask of you. My family is expecting us to return to Hungary this coming summer and I want some protection during our visit. It was a little dicey last time and Zsigmond made it clear he'd love to get his claws on me." He couldn't help but be concerned that somehow word would reach Zsigmond that he was trying to interfere in Hungarian matters from the island of Puerto Rico. If that should happen, the risk factor would rise even more when Jozsi returned to Hungary. He supposed he should also worry that Zsigmond's hate for him might even cross the ocean and touch his life with Ann and Dani, but that was an unbearable thought.

25

Operation Magyar

The plan was for the family to spend three weeks in Hungary that July. They would have the chance to see all of the relatives, and spend time vacationing with Ferenc and his family on Lake Balaton. Dani and Jolanka had kept up a friendship by mail, with help from their parents, sending each other funny little kid drawings, since at their age neither of them could quite manage to wax eloquent on paper.

The week before departing, Jozsi reached out to Sandor and they met for lunch. Sandor handed over a few special phone numbers and passwords to provide to whomever answered. He didn't think Jozsi had too much to worry about. For some time, the Russians had been pressuring Hungarians to lay off intimidating foreign or returning expat visitors. Why? Jozsi wondered. Sandor explained: the Russians' new tactic was to urge collaborating Hungarians to recruit their returning countrymen as spies. "Loyalty and guilt," Sandor nodded. "Their thinking is that the Revolution was long enough ago for peoples' memories of violence, of the horror, to have dulled. If the current situation in Hungary appears calm to those who once fled, if they feel safe to return, they might be motivated to help in the country's recovery; they won't think too hard about who is in charge. If you're lucky, perhaps Zsigmond will try to recruit you," he added slyly.

"Who knows, Sandor? I could become a double agent and sell my story to Hollywood." They shared a big laugh, and parted with slaps on the back and good wishes, jollied by the thought of bringing Zsigmond down.

~~~

As the plane approached Vienna that July, Jozsi wondered how he would react if Zsigmond dared try to reach out to him. He wouldn't put it past him: Zsigmond would do anything to make points with his Russian masters. Though he despised the man his childhood friend had become, there were moments when he remembered the thin, hungry-for-a-pal boy Zsigmond had been. It was hard to hold both versions in his head at the same time. He wondered if Zsigmond ever felt the same nostalgia. He doubted it, and Ferenc agreed, saying Zsigmond had lost his soul and felt absolutely nothing, nothing real anyway. At Jozsi's behest Ferenc agreed to see their old friend whenever he chose to reach out. Zsigmond still liked to brag to people from the old days and when the mood stuck, he'd call Ferenc, treat him to dinner and share all his recent news — only the good news, of course. Ferenc played along, always feeling that he needed a strong bath after sitting across the table from his host. Ferenc cautioned that Zsigmond could easily turn up at the Budais' door with a smile instead of a threat if he thought it might get him somewhere. As though everyone would have sudden amnesia about the years of misery and hate and destruction associated with his name.

This trip they were able to fly directly to Budapest, where Ferenc and Jolanka picked them up. At first, Dani and Jolanka were bashful with each other, but that lasted only moments and then they were deep in what constitutes a conversation for small children. Ann squeezed Jozsi's arm and whispered, "Look! Young love." Jozsi said nothing, but had a flash memory of sitting behind Erica in class, her beautiful thick braids tempting him to tug them day after day. Ferenc had written to Jozsi with news of her whereabouts, at last. Ferenc related that Zsigmond periodically had his goons trailing her, in such an obvious way that she'd be sure to notice and know at whose bidding they served. The letter ended with "Just keeping his hand in. That bastard will never give up."

His sister Susan had invited them to stay with her. Their first days in Hungary were a blur of visiting and being visited by countless relatives. On several occasions, when they were out driving, Jozsi noticed cars trailing them. He knew better than to think he was being paranoid. He purposely avoided returning to Ura because Ferenc had told him Zsigmond was still suspicious about Jozsi's interest in the area.

One Sunday afternoon, Susan invited friends and family over for an outdoor gathering. It was a beautiful day; sunlit, although thin, fleeting clouds provided momentary breaks from the bright light. She gussied up the yard so thoroughly it looked as though a wedding were about to take place. Dani translated for Ann whatever his four-year-old mind could grasp; all the relatives had the same questions so it got easier as time passed. They lingered at the table, leaning back after too much food, enjoying the sight of each other. The front door bell clanged. Susan walked through the house, dismayed to find Zsigmond at the door, two bodyguards standing watch by the car. He held forth a bottle of champagne.

"A peace offering," he said. "I heard Jozsi was here again and wanted to extend a more cordial welcome than last time."

Susan couldn't believe he was apologizing. What was going on? But she led him to the terrace. Jozsi's head was bent toward Dani, who stood by his chair excitedly nattering on about what he wasn't exactly sure. Looking up he saw Zsigmond standing at the end of the table. Ignoring him, Jozsi leaned down and tucked in Dani's shirt, mostly to give himself a moment to get his bearings. A moment later he stood and said calmly but firmly, "Zsigmond, you were not invited to this party, and if you don't mind, I'd like you to leave. It's a family gathering. You understand, I'm sure." Such rejection was ill-advised, but it felt good to speak without thinking five steps ahead for a change. Some day he might turn into a regular American guy; they seemed to have no problem saying whatever popped in mind.

Zsigmond, to the shock of all, apologized for dropping in uninvited. "I only wanted to welcome you and your family back to Hungary. Much has changed," he said, as Jozsi warily walked him back toward the gate. The sight of Zsigmond's goons did nothing to put his mind at ease, but Zsigmond continued to appear friendly. Would Jozsi consider having a drink with him before he returned to America? There'd been so much bad blood; it was time to put it behind them.

So, Ferenc had been right, Zsigmond was playing nice, but Jozsi would apparently have to wait to learn exactly why. Jozsi balked — their last meeting had been so hostile Zsigmond wouldn't believe it if he reacted with anything other than suspicion. "Where is the 'or else' behind this bullshit invitation?" he snarled. Zsigmond kept up the courtship. He was sincere, his mother had died not long ago, he was feeling reflective, he wanted to connect to his past. Zsigmond had become a good actor, Jozsi thought, so convincing Jozsi half believed some part of his yearning to reconnect was real. Okay, one drink. But he insisted on picking the time and place: one o'clock the following Friday at the old railroad station tavern. The intervening days would give him a chance to scope it out before they met. He hoped Janos, the owner, was still in charge.

Back at the table, Jozsi was met by Ann's anxious expression, and fear on the faces of his sister and family. Dani babbled on about how nice it was that Papa's friend from school had come to see him. "Just imagine," Ann said nervously, "they weren't much older than you when they met and here they still know each other." All faces turned expectantly to Jozsi.

"Eh," he shrugged the intrusion off, "he's just trying to muddle my head. I told him to get the hell out, but I did keep this." With a flourish, he opened the bottle of champagne, noting it would likely be the first and last time the Communist Secret Service bought him a bottle of fancy bubbles. Susan whispered into his ear, "You've got a lot of balls, brother." And after toasting and drinking, they returned to their happy, contented state, as though Zsigmond had never rung the bell.

Friday came, and after lunch Jozsi explained to everyone that he was off to meet an old friend. Not exactly lying, but not telling the entire truth either. Ann was content to put up her feet and do nothing for a few hours, and as long as Jolanka was on hand, Dani was happy about everything. Jozsi took Susan aside and confessed the name of the old friend. What?!" she nearly yelled. Jozsi shushed her. "That's madness," she whispered. Why did you have to tell me? I'll be worried sick until you get back. I won't be able to look Ann in the eye. Damn Zsigmond."

"Thanks for keeping the secret, Susan. Don't worry I'll be back. Perhaps with another bottle of champagne. . .or with Zsigmond's head. We could bury it in the back yard." There was an edge to his laugh.

Jozsi walked down the old road toward the railroad station. The road wasn't used much any more, the train no longer stopped there — public transportation to the city had grown efficient, and more people had cars of their own. As he made his way to the tavern, he remembered walking this road with Matyas the summer war had worsened near Budapest and he'd been sent to Ura for safety. Jozsi crossed the Rakos River. As a child, the river had seemed so big and fast. He stood at the bridge and looked down on what seemed a stream, compared to his memories. Downriver he could see a small bay, resembling the big swimming hole where he'd spent many hot summer days, listening to stories of faraway places from Jancsi the grocer's son. Here he was again, and for a second, he could still hear happy screeching from the swimming hole and see the faces of all his friends, even that of Zsigmond.

Feeling melancholy, he continued on. The tavern was close to a hundred years old and beginning to show its age. The old-timers were loyal though, feeling more at home here than at newer bars. As Jozsi approached the building, he saw a Russian car parked outside. Must belong to Zsigmond, already inside and hopefully drinking. The driver sat behind the wheel, alert to every face that entered or exited.

Inside, Jozsi spotted Zsigmond, leaning against the bar. He quickly held out his hand in welcome. Jozsi took his time reciprocating, approaching slowly, as though Zsigmond's arm were a snake, the hand a head poised to strike. He figured it best to refrain from seeming amiable for just a bit longer. They sat at a table on the terrace, away from the few customers at the bar.

Zsigmond ordered *Hubertus* for them both. "We're celebrating and I'm buying."

"Well, this is good news for me," Jozsi replied cautiously, "but may I ask exactly what there is to celebrate?"

Zsigmond said he'd heard that three special Hungarian students were well established in New York City, thanks to Jozsi's assistance, and that he appreciated such generosity.

"It was the least I could do for fellow Hungarians." Jozsi remembered to act surprised at Zsigmond's awareness of the trio. "But how do you know about them, about their project? You've developed a sudden interest in literature?" Simultaneously poking him and offering an opening to brag, which he knew Zsigmond would relish.

Zsigmond puffed out his chest. "This is my job, to be aware of where all Hungarians outside the country travel, to know what people they meet. Our national security is crucial, you know, so I take all precautions to protect Hungary and good Hungarians from undesirable people and activities."

Jozsi merely nodded and excused himself to go to the bathroom. He couldn't appear to be impressed or relieved or anything but reserved too soon. Later, he'd allow Zsigmond to think alcohol had loosened him up. Passing the bar, he nodded to Janos. A few days earlier, Jozsi had stopped in for a visit and let Janos know he'd be meeting Zsigmond, and that he had a favor to ask. Jozsi wanted whoever was bartending to pour tea in his glass each time a round of drinks was ordered, and to pour doubles for Zsigmond. Janos had hated Zsigmond for years and was happy to oblige. Jozsi picked up fresh drinks on his way back to the table.

Janos whispered, "If his bodyguard wasn't outside, he'd be floating down river to the Danube." Jozsi winked.

"We can't hold it like we used to," Zsigmond observed, then offered a toast to their years of friendship. Jozsi, a slightly kinder tone in his voice, asked how Zsigmond's mother had died. For a few minutes, they were just two people who knew the same people, two people who shared a childhood. It gave Jozsi the bridge to warm up his chilly hostility as they talked about Ferenc and other schoolmates. It was surreal having this kind of conversation, but it had to be done. Then Jozsi asked how Zsigmond's job was, knowing this would lead to much boasting about power and influence, which it did.

Joszi listened intently, filing away useful information, appearing to be impressed, but eventually Zsigmond ran out of accomplishments to brag about. Then, to throw him, Jozsi took a sudden shift in tone. "So, all bullshit aside, Zsigmond, what is it you really want to talk about?"

Zsigmond was momentarily startled, but quickly recovered. "You want me to get to the point. Good. Your job and what you can do for this country, *your* country." He went on to explain that he knew all about Jozsi's responsible position in the engineering department of a fast-advancing computer company. And in that position, Jozsi could do something very important for his people. "Your brothers need help catching up with western countries in the technology arena. We're lagging so far behind we're at risk of ending up an undeveloped country."

Jozsi nodded. "There are others you could approach. Why me? And don't tell me you miss me. We can talk nicely, but let's not pretend the bad blood never existed."

Zsigmond stiffened. "We have been on different sides, but you are here in Hungary so I thought you might want to help. Your family is still here and you say you love your country. I thought you might want to make up for," he paused dramatically, "all of your past transgressions."

"I will think on it." He looked down at the table. What he was thinking was, did he dare bring up Erika? He couldn't stop thinking about what Ferenc had written. A restless Zsigmond watched Jozsi, who continued staring down. Finally, he spoke. "What am I going to get out of helping you, beyond the good I do for my country?"

"I'd think that would be enough, but go ahead, name your price."

Jozsi nodded and chose his words carefully. "All right. First, I ask that you leave Erika alone. I hear you're sending men to trail her. She's married now. Just leave her be."

"And you are married," Zsigmond muttered, but nodded. Jozsi knew he wouldn't honor the agreement, but never mind. He just wanted Zsigmond to know he knew about Erika. "Second, I need hard cash up front so I can grease the wheels. Valuable information doesn't come cheap you know? I want the money in hand before I pass through customs." He knew Zsigmond wouldn't agree to give him all of it, but the demand was a good place to start.

"How much?"

"Depends on what kind of currency you have in mind."

"But you're aware, I'm sure, that we are limited on western currency. Hungarian currency is another story. After you return to America, I can deliver western currency."

Jozsi laughed. "Good try. You're sending students overseas to learn about Hemingway, but you can't come up with some decent currency to move Hungary forward. All right then, give me ten thousand dollars-worth of *forints*, up front. I will need more, but that's a start. I want it in hand in the next two days or there is no deal."

Zsigmond squirmed: the government had strict rules about moving Hungarian currency in or out of the country. Jozsi would have none of it. "You've told me how much power you have, yes? I have no doubt you can arrange for the airport guards to skip inspection of my luggage."

More drinks arrived as they discussed the details. Jozsi was impressed with Zsigmond's ability to drink endless amounts of alcohol; he'd yet to reach incoherence, but it was only a matter of time. Jozsi emphasized the delicacy of undertaking this mission. "You realize you're asking me to spy on my company. A good company, that provides a good income. I support my family well...two cars, summerhouse on a lake, and still I've been able to save more money than you'll ever see. How the hell can you do better? You ask me to put a lot at risk." He paused, weighing his next words carefully. If he seemed too acquiescent Zsigmond wouldn't believe him, but go too far in the other direction, same problem. "You want me to put all of that at risk when it involves you? I must point out that you haven't exactly honored our past connection in recent years."

"We've had our differences, but I will not apologize for doing my job. Under the laws of the time, you were a traitor. But we move forward, yes? You have family here, friends. You want to help the country, yes?"

Jozsi nodded, noting the repetition of the threat: you have family here.

"Your parents, your siblings can use help, and your wife maybe wants a new kitchen," Zsigmond continued. "Maybe you want a honey on the side, or a good education for your son. The extra money can help with many things."

"What you say makes sense," Jozsi said, since there was nothing Zsigmond liked better than gratuitous praise. "How much are you willing to pay?"

"I can't commit to an exact figure without conferring with my superiors, but believe me, it will please you."

The only thing Jozsi could think of that would please him was seeing Zsigmond behind bars, or at least condemned to a life spent digging holes in Siberia. "You give me your word?" Jozsi stared into his eyes.

"Of course," Zsigmond answered, but his eyes slid down and away, he couldn't quite hold Jozsi's gaze. He wasn't *that* good an actor. "I know you are scheduled to leave a week from today. I'll meet you at the airport before departure to confirm our arrangement. The final amount will be delivered once you are back in America." They agreed on a down payment to be brought to Susan's house within two days, along with word of the final figure. Holding out his hand to shake on the deal, Zsigmond said, "Enough of that business, now let's drink for the pleasure."

"Yes," Jozsi said, leaning in closer. "So, tell me, how does it feel to be such an important figure?"

Zsigmond beamed. "I have power; in certain areas, more than others. Even judges in courts cannot override my decisions."

"Doesn't that make you a dictator?"

"Not yet," Zsigmond answered, without batting an eye. "I have power and I'm collecting information." He paused, as though hearing a cautionary alert, but boastfulness got the better of him. "If I can gather enough evidence against the present parliament, I'll move in and arrest them. But don't bother breathing a word of this to anyone, no one will believe you."

"And what then?" Jozsi asked, stunned by Zsigmond's reckless bragging. Though it was still early afternoon, Zsigmond seemed a mere drink away from slurring his words.

"What then? Then I am in charge. The KGB will be behind me."

Jozsi began to focus in a particular way — filing away details to relate to Sandor, making sure he had them locked firmly in his head. "Are you telling me that you're spying on your own government?" He suspected all of this was a figment of Zsigmond's ambitious imagination or that he'd drunk so much he was losing his mind.

Jozsi could see that Zsigmond was weighing whether or not to reveal more. Good sense lost and he blurted out that he was working hand-in-hand with the KGB. "They will be ready to take over the country in the event parliament moves toward western values. It is not common knowledge, you understand, but it is true."

Jozsi understood. He was disgusted, but steeled himself to continue stirring the waters awhile longer. "This is information you've been collecting for a long time?"

"You know," Zsigmond interrupted, "There is one American I admire very much."

"I cannot fathom who that might be."

"J. Edgar Hoover." Jozsi was taken aback and it showed. "You think my knowledge of the world is limited to Hungary, but it is bigger," Zsigmond continued.

"Well, I am impressed that you know of him," Jozsi said, remembering that the year before, Hoover had been awarded the State Department's Distinguished Service Award for his service to the FBI. It had been big news. "So, you think he's admirable."

"He is a brilliant man. Look, he has information on every leading politician or important person in the United States."

"They call that 'the goods,' in America. He has the goods."

"The goods," Zsigmond repeated and smiled. "And if he wanted to be president, he could be president. That's how much he has 'the goods.'"

For just a second, Jozsi remembered how it felt to like Zsigmond. He recognized the boy he'd once known in witnessing Zsigmond's pleasure at using an insider American phrase. There was something innocent in that. Then he remembered everything else he knew. "I better be on my way, the family is waiting." He stood, thanking Zsigmond for the drinks, reminding him of the down payment delivery date. Jozsi headed toward the men's room as Zsigmond called for the tab, paid, lurching slightly as he headed toward the door. His driver leapt forward to be at the ready for the last few yards to the car. He'd begun to look a little wobbly once he'd gotten outside. Jozsi watched from inside, while thanking Old Janos and handing him extra money. "Whatever the tab, he didn't give you enough."

Janos insisted Jozsi have a drink with him and the other old-timers at the bar. They were pleased to be a part of any scheme that might cause Zsigmond trouble. "Someday, sooner or later, someone will get him," Janos nodded sagely. The others' heads all bounced up and down in agreement. They wanted more than anything to be liberated from Russian occupation and if, for the moment, Zsigmond was their only way of sticking it to the Russians, so be it. It was better than doing nothing. Janos sipped at his wine. "He may be from our town, but he is not *of* our town." Yes, they agreed, he was no longer one of theirs. Jozsi may have moved away, but he was still their brother.

Feeling nostalgic, Jozsi took the old trail toward his sister's house, thinking about Janos' words. "Someday, sooner or later, someone will get him." He could think of one person who would like to be that someone: Erika. He veered off the trail to take a slight detour down a street that would bring him to her former neighborhood. He stood across from her old house, staring at the long rows of acacia trees lining the street, their full golden bloom a sight of beauty. As the cherry blossom is to the Japanese, so the acacia is to Hungarians. He felt emotional, as though under the sway of Hungarian gypsy music and too much *palinka*. He was suddenly thirsty for a cold beer. He'd drunk an immense amount of tea, which he didn't much like. When Susan's house came into view, he shook off all thoughts of his past with Erika, not wanting them to distract from the present.

~~~

Two days later, Susan responded to the clang of the gate bell and called out that Jozsi had a visitor. A clear sign that the visitor wasn't one she was willing to invite inside. At the gate Jozsi found a man with the form and presence of an ape. He was holding a cheap briefcase.

"Yes?" Jozsi said, motioning for Susan to go back in the house.

"You Jozsi? This is for you." The man held forth the briefcase. "Sent by Zsigmond. You keep the whole thing."

Jozsi discretely checked the briefcase, found a convincing wad of *forints* and a piece of paper with a very generous figure scrawled in pen. He clicked the briefcase shut. "Tell your boss I look forward to meeting him at the airport." The ape left.

Susan stood just inside the door. "Well? What is inside?"

Jozsi gave her a look that would have silenced a teething baby. "Someday I'll tell you, that's all I can say."

Later that night, the house a vessel of slumber, Jozsi stole out to the workshop to carefully count the *forints*. He was pondering where to hide them when Susan cracked the door. "I saw the light. What the hell is going on? If you tell me I might be able to help, I might even save your ass." He knew she'd pester him all night, so he gave in and told her the gist of his meeting with Zsigmond. Plus, it was important to hide this money quickly and she could definitely help with that. He knew better than to try to bring this much money out of the country. "Who knows what Zsigmond will do? He could plaster my picture all over Hungarian television as a spy and a thief and haul me off to jail."

Although all his words made her nervous, Susan did love a good scheme. She thought for a moment. "The back chimney. Since we switched to electric heat, we don't use the back one at all. If we hang the bag inside from the top, it should be safe."

Jozsi was pleased. "First we make a few fires in there to dirty it up so it looks like it's still being used." He knew without looking it would be clean because Susan would never have left it sooty. They wrapped the money in cleaning rags, put the bundles in a large sack, burned a little wood, and then up went Jozsi with work gloves, rope, a hook, the bag, and nerves of steel. "When the time is right," he said once back on the ground, "it's all yours, every penny."

Susan shook her head in disbelief and gratitude. "When will you learn to live like the rest of us? I really thought you had settled down. Please, you must be more careful. You have a wife and child, and then the rest of us, and we worry."

Jozsi grabbed the end of the hose and climbed back up to rinse his scent from the roof in case Zsigmond showed up with tracking hounds. Somehow, no one awoke during all the activity. They opened a bottle and sat in the kitchen drinking and talking into the early morning hours. She wanted to know if what the communist papers had said about him was true. He shared what he could safely share, which was enough to astound her.

"Those papers weren't that far off," she said, made nervous by the things he'd done. "If you had it to do over, all those awful things…"

Jozsi just smiled. "You never asked me about the good parts. We'll save that for another time." They hugged good night and good morning, dawn a heartbeat away. Five days to go before his date to meet Zsigmond at the terminal.

~~~

Ferenc and Jolanka drove them to the airport, Jolanka and Dani poking each other in the back seat the whole way. Ann snuck amused sidelong glances at their innocent flirting, and Ferenc made small talk, while Jozsi stared at the road ahead, his mind on his upcoming meeting. He moved into a state of high concentration: he needed to be alert, there were a number of ways this could go down, and predicting the outcome would be a fool's game. Suddenly he was furious with himself for involving Ann and Dani in this scheme. He had not been thinking carefully, that much had become painfully clear. He had single-mindedly ignored the presence of his family in this scenario. He could have figured out a different way, sent them home ahead. He'd slipped back into a CIA mindset — all that mattered was the goal. He felt deeply ashamed. Ann could see he was off somewhere in his head; her eyes asking what he was thinking, but he didn't register her expression, didn't respond.

As they pulled close to the airport terminal, Jozsi noticed what seemed to be a larger than usual number of police officers, along with a smattering of photographers. His survival instincts told him he might very well be the reason for their presence. Outside the terminal, everybody hugged, and then Ferenc and Jolanka drove away.

Jozsi and his family went inside to check in. He felt terrible for not telling Ann there might be trouble, but it was too late to give her cause for alarm now. Customs officials took their luggage. Jozsi kept his eye on the ticket agent as she examined their passports. Then she looked up and across the room, blinked twice rapidly, turned to Jozsi and said, "Please, sir, bring your luggage to the back room." Ann looked only slightly concerned as they followed a police officer to a nearby room.

Jozsi turned to look through a window in the door and saw Zsigmond gathering photographers around him. He'd appeared out of nowhere. Jozsi guided Ann ahead of him, blocking her view of the window in case she turned around. If she saw Zsigmond, she really would worry. The back room held several long tables and a number of fold-up chairs. The police instructed them to empty all their belongings onto the table and take seats against the wall while officials pawed through their things. Jozsi knew they'd find nothing amiss, but still had a knot in his gut. He watched the two officers carefully in case they tried to plant something, though he realized catching them in the act wouldn't do him much good. Ann cast worried looks his way and he returned reassuring smiles, squeezing her hand. Their search at an end, the officers told them to repack their bags and return to the lobby.

As they rejoined other waiting travelers, Jozsi heard someone call out his name. Zsigmond. Ann flinched at the sight of him.

"There you are!" Zsigmond was all fake cheer. "Let's have a word before you leave."

Jozsi pointed Ann and Dani toward the boarding area. "I'll be back in a few minutes," he kept his voice neutral. He followed Zsigmond back into the room with the long tables, silently rehearsing what he'd planned to say.

"Apologies for being late," Zsigmond said.

"Cut the bullshit. Now that you've had to send those photographers away, you must feel like an asshole. I felt like an asshole waiting for the upfront money you promised. Two days came and went, no word, no money. But you show up here like nothing is wrong."

Zsigmond's face paled. "What? You never received the money?!"

"If I had that money, I'd be taking it with me. You were supposed to keep us from being searched. Instead, you stood watching through the two-way mirror over there," he pointed dramatically at a wall mirror across the room. "You bastard, you were going to have my ass arrested. Did the reporters laugh at you, asshole? J. Edgar Hoover wouldn't let you lick the bottom of his shoes."

Zsigmond, slightly flustered, bypassed the insults. "No, no, no. The plan was for me to meet you, as agreed. The photographers were here for an important foreign visitor, but his flight was cancelled." Jozsi had to hand it to him, quick thinking on his part. "There will be hell to pay for the search. I specifically told them not to search you! But if they'd found the money, I would have stepped in and smoothed things over. Jozsi, I want this plan to succeed. I sent a courier to give you that money and was told it had been delivered."

"Then you have a lot to learn about your workers." Jozsi put his arm around Zsigmond sympathetically. "You remember what my *nagyanya* used to say? 'If you pay with peanuts, you get monkeys.' You should remember that, old friend."

Zsigmond looked perplexed, even slightly rattled. "I will have his ass in a sling. Trust me, I put Hungary's future progress above all and I want our arrangement to work. I'll get this nonsense straightened out. An operative will contact you in the near future and--"

Jozsi interrupted. "No down payment, no word about the final amount approved for the information. And you want me to believe you?"

Zsigmond leaned forward to whisper a figure in his ear. "That should please you. And the down payment will be added to that in the first payment. When you are contacted, the password will be *Magyar*. All right? It will happen soon."

"Zsigmond, for the sake of this country, I hope you are telling the truth." Jozsi held his hand out and they shook and parted. Ann was kneeling next to Dani in front of a large window in the boarding area. "Everything is okay," he said, bending to put a comforting hand on her shoulder.

Leaning back in his airplane seat, he thought all and all, he'd handled the situation correctly. He was sorry for the ass-kicking the courier would get, but anyone who worked for Zsigmond was likely to be a scumbag, so he didn't feel all that bad. If the courier somehow managed to convince Zsigmond that Jozsi had lied about the money, Susan's house might be searched. That was a risk. But Jozsi hoped Zsigmond would instead forge ahead with the technology scheme. If he couldn't manage to arrest Jozsi, then using him to score valuable information might make up for that failure. Jozsi hoped so.

When Sandor heard about the deal he'd made with Zsigmond, he was pleased. Revealing a surprising level of excitement, he said, "If we can pull this off, we'll have that bastard shoveling snow in Siberia by Christmas. His Secret Police career will be kaput!" He instructed Jozsi to alert him as soon as Zsigmond's agents got in touch. "We'll talk again the day before you're set to meet his agent. I'll make the arrangements and be on hand to see things through." He drummed his fingers on the table, grinning happily in anticipation.

~~~

A couple of weeks later, Jozsi heard from one of Zsigmond's agents. He gave the password and arranged to meet Jozsi the next day — shortly after five o'clock at *The Rusty Scupper* in Acton, Massachusetts. Did Jozsi know it? Yes, he knew it well. Click, silence. Seconds later, Jozsi reached Sandor who told Jozsi to meet him at three the following afternoon at a park near the restaurant.

In a van parked some yards from a large apple tree, he wired Jozsi with a small transmitter and tested it out. Sandor walked a couple of hundred yards away while Jozsi talked to himself. He didn't realize a mother pushing a stroller was approaching from behind. She cast a concerned look his way as she hurriedly sped past the tree. Sandor returned, amused by the worried mother and pleased with the transmission. "We're good," he said, and they killed time watching pigeons and squirrels rustle through the crunchy fall leaves.

At four-thirty, Jozsi pulled into *The Rusty Scupper* parking lot, and spotted the van. How he'd managed to get there first was beyond him. Inside, Jozsi went upstairs to the cocktail lounge area, past Sandor, who was chatting up the bartender. Jozsi sat at a corner table, removing a chair so there were only two. He sat facing the bar, so he could see Sandor. Nothing happening. He ordered a drink from a waitress, and noticed Sandor glance toward a door leading to the restrooms and a stairway. Jozsi followed his gaze and saw a man in a blue pea jacket standing there, scoping out the room. His drink arrived and a few minutes later, the man approached the table.

"*Hoagy vagy, Magyar?*" he said.

"Sit down, my friend, if I may call you that," Jozsi said.

"Antal," the man answered, by way of introduction, casing the room once more before sitting down.

"Antal, would you like a drink?"

"No, I only have a few minutes," he said, matter-of-factly. "I'm going to leave a shopping list from Zsigmond. This is what he wants." He pulled a thin envelope from an inside jacket pocket and pushed it across the table toward Jozsi, who pushed it right back.

"I'm not even going to look at this until I see money. Zsigmond screwed me out of the down payment. I expect a big fat wad of cash right this minute or you can tell him where to shove the list."

"Wait," Antal said. "I have what you want." He reached inside his coat pocket and pulled out a fatter envelope, which he pushed across the table, followed by the slim one.

Jozsi quickly slid the bigger envelope into his lap and fingered through packs of $100 bills. "Sorry to make you wait, but…" He continued flipping through the currency, quick as a bank teller. "This better be $10,000 dollars. If Zsigmond wants me to pilfer company secrets, it's worth far more than what I've agreed to." He glanced up, saw Sandor surreptitiously snap a couple of photos of them at their table and then head for the exit. Sandor must have gotten all the conversation he needed on tape. Now he'd be heading out to set up and shoot pictures of Antal walking to his car. Jozsi slowed his counting. Antal squirmed, anxious to be on his way. Finished, Jozsi put both envelopes in his coat pocket. "Call me in two weeks," he said. Antal nodded and left without uttering another word.

When Sandor returned to his seat at the bar, Jozsi passed close on his way to the bathroom. Sandor joined him a moment later. They waited for a couple of customers to empty their bladders, and then checked under the stall doors to make sure they were alone. Sandor clapped Jozsi on the back. "You were perfect. I have pictures, the recording came through clearly, I've got everything I need. We'll have Zsigmond's ass broiling in no time at all." Jozsi handed over the shopping list and the money. Sandor pulled out a couple of hundred dollar bills. "Let's celebrate. You earned a steak dinner and all the drinks you want. For a change, I'm not buying. This is on Zsigmond, may he rot in hell."

26

Scuttled Plans

Jozsi returned to his daily routine with a little bounce in his step. He had truly wearied of anything to do with the firm, but couldn't deny a thrum of anticipation, a jolt of the old excitement. The lull between planning and acting had always given him a certain kind of charge. Holding a secret, readying his mental and physical muscles before springing into action, an almost pure animal heightening of the senses. He had to admit he never felt that particular thrill in his normal work life. But the satisfaction of negotiating, evaluating, and problem solving did feed another part of his soul. And the joy of stability and family life more than made up for any lack of adventure. He paid attention to savoring the thrill before his final action for the firm, at least he hoped it was the final one, you never could tell. And he recognized another thrum in his veins: guilt about how easily he'd put his family at risk. If Zsigmond was even half telling the truth about his own connection and value to the KGB, any retaliation could get very ugly. The KGB was capable of just about anything. And apparently, so was he. It unsettled him to realize this gigantic, reckless oversight — the possible threat to his family here in America.

~~~

Ten days later, Sandor reached Jozsi at his office. The information Zsigmond sought had been gathered and was ready for delivery. Another two weeks passed, then Antal called him at work. Did Jozsi have a present for him? Yes, he did. They arranged to meet at *The Rusty Scupper* at five o'clock the following day.

Jozsi called Sandor, who suggested they get together to kick a ball around. Jozsi knew what that meant. Go to the edge of the soccer field in a local park. There he again put a wire on Jozsi. "I want you to keep him at the bar till we are certain everything has fallen into place. We can't waste this opportunity. No false steps. From what I know, that shouldn't be too hard. He's not a monster, just a lost soul they got their hands on early. He wants to be liked, he wants to be praised," Sandor explained. Then added, "You know if that good-looking bartender will be working tonight?"

"You're thinking I'm a pimp now?" Jozsi snapped. He figured Sandor must be in the midst of some kind of mid-life crisis, he didn't remember him ever being so blatantly randy. "Make your own dates or I'll start charging the firm for matchmaking time." He excused himself to run an errand. It was payday and he usually brought Dani a new matchbox car to mark the day.

"I still can't get used to this new, domesticated version of you," Sandor said, saluting Jozsi, who returned a salute of a sort, by raising his middle finger.

A short time later, when Jozsi pulled into *The Scupper's* parking lot, he spotted Antal's car, unoccupied — he'd been shown a photo of it when he'd met with Sandor. Inside the lounge, Antal was nowhere to be seen. Sandor, however, was seated at the bar chatting up a young woman with long bangs and large hoop earrings. Jozsi would have to compliment him on his adaptability.

A waitress approached, carrying a tray with two highball glasses — scotch from the smell that preceded her by a millisecond. Jozsi was about to say he hadn't ordered these when Antal loomed behind her shoulder.

"I hope you don't mind, I was in the mood for a stiff drink," he said, raising his glass to their good health.

Jozsi studied him, imagining the story behind how he'd come to be sitting on the other side of this table. "You were *Kisdobos*," he asked? Yes, Antal had been a "Little Drummer" as a child. When Mátyás Rákosi ruled as General Secretary of the Hungarian Communist Party, he'd brought in Socialist teachers, trained at schools in the Eastern Bloc. They'd been known as "The People's Teachers." Their job: indoctrinate children early on. Beginning in nursery school, once a week, little boys and girls donned white shirts, dark pants or shorts or skirts, and pretty blue neckerchiefs. By drumming into their heads socialist values from the start, the communists hoped to deepen and strengthen their hold on the country. The highlight activity for the children had been to march around the schoolyard singing the praises of Comrade Rákosi. They were special, dressed in their outfits, a community of believers, even if they were too young to understand what these beliefs really were. Groupthink was the important thing, and obedience.

As Antal warmed to Jozsi's interest in his past, he stopped checking his watch and ordered another round. "It's good to sit sometimes, eh?" They clinked in toast. "So much running from here to there in my life."

Jozsi pegged him as a competent errand boy, reliable and ultimately dispensable. He felt a little sorry for him; his life was about to change in the worst possible way for someone as wedded to the system as Antal appeared to be. But Jozsi got back to business and pretended to regret some of the choices he'd made that had led him away from Hungary. Antal admitted he'd be lost without his country, his brotherhood in the Communist Party. Jozsi reminded himself that the poor mope willingly worked for Zsigmond and that helped stifle his sympathy. He chided himself inwardly: not only was he getting slow, he was getting soft.

Sandor headed toward the men's room, a sign that it was time to begin the exchange. "Well, Jozsi said, "I've enjoyed this, but my wife will be irritable if I'm late for dinner." He reached behind to remove a manila envelope from his coat, which was slung across the back of the chair. The pockets were roomy enough to hold the large envelope, now folded in half. He fumbled around, allowing Sandor time to get his camera ready for shots of the exchange: the final cash installment for the information. Antal had already slid his envelope of money toward Jozsi.

Jozsi waved for the waitress to bring the check, his signal to Sandor that the transfer had begun. "You ordered, but I'll do the paying. Bring him one for the road along with the check. I'm good," he held up his hand. When the waitress turned away, he laid his envelope on the table. Antal slipped on his pea jacket and tucked the envelope partially into his pants, then buttoned the jacket halfway up. Jozsi held up the smaller envelope before dropping it to his lap for the count.

"I'm going to shoot this down and be on my way," Antal said as the waitress returned with his drink.

"Not until I'm done," Jozsi cautioned. Under his breath, he counted, just loud enough for the transmitter to record. "Ten thousand, on the nose. Okay, you can scram." He was amusing himself; he'd seen a Jimmy Cagney movie not long before and had adopted the word scram.

Jozsi raised his glass in farewell. "I'll sit a few minutes longer."

"Yes," Antal agreed. "Better I leave first." He gestured a salute and strode away. Sandor motioned for Jozsi to join him at a table by a picture window overlooking the parking lot. A graceful line of hills in the distance was clearly the point of having a view at all given that the parking lot itself was an eyesore. But for them, the view of the parking lot was ideal. They looked down in time to see Antal open his car door, only to be grabbed from behind by a trio of FBI agents who leapt out of nearby unmarked federal cars.

"They keep those guys in good shape," Jozsi observed. The agents were as swift, their movements as choreographed, as those of a dance team. A handcuff clamped Antal's hands behind his back and within seconds he was guided into a large black sedan with dark-tint windows. The car sped away. "The charge?" Jozsi asked Sandor.

"Conspiracy and spying against the United States." They toasted each other.

"What about the students? Still studying Hemingway?"

"Funny you should ask," Sandor said, checking his watch. "Within the hour, they will be locked up under similar charges, along with several other people who've been helping them in New York." He turned to face Jozsi, "On behalf of the firm, I want to thank you for your cooperation." He bowed with a wry smile. "They did ask me to say that. But no bullshit, we just spoiled one of the biggest Hungarian spy rings out there. This is a big deal for me. And it will be for Zsigmond too." He grinned, a rare occurrence. "The KGB will beckon him for a little visit, very soon I think."

Jozsi's fingers made 'come hither' movements and they both cracked up. "He'll be lucky if he gets out of their offices alive."

"I'll get a promotion and he'll get his ass kicked if he's fortunate, if not..." He ran a finger across his throat.

"I have to ask, what's in it for me?" Jozsi asked.

"Beyond the great satisfaction of messing with your boyhood pal? You name it! If I can make it happen I will. I've been waiting for you to say 'And what about me?'"

Jozsi had thought long and hard about what he wanted and was ready with the request: the complete layout of the town of Ura along with the government's future development plan.

Sandor's eyebrows rose high, and he looked pleased, Jozsi wasn't sure why. "Jozsi, you will have it, and the names of the people who manage the project, in case you want to squeeze them for whatever reason. I'll get you information on their background, too, go as far back as their grandmothers. That should set you up just right."

Jozsi had never seen him in a better mood; entirely pleased with the world at large. He ordered steaks and an expensive bottle of wine. It wasn't until they were relaxing over after-dinner brandies that Sandor dropped an unexpected aside. He'd seen copies of Jozsi's records from the Hungarian Secret Police; he'd found something interesting in Jozsi's past, something new to him.

"What is that? I was an altar boy and they discovered money missing from the collection box?"

Sandor chuckled. "No, more surprising than that. And it has to do with the request for information about Ura, you sly dog, you." The records reflected Zsigmond harbored a suspicion that Jozsi knew of something valuable buried in the Hungarian countryside. "Loot, gold, a treasure chest--"

"No magic carpet?" Jozsi interjected.

"He was convinced you knew about something of worth and it looked like it had become a bit of an obsession." Sandor related that Zsigmond had assigned a lackey to travel to Ura and photograph anything of interest in the area, research the town history, even find town elders and arrange for them to come in for a "conversation." Zsigmond had traveled to Ura to conduct the interviews himself. He'd also assigned someone to follow whatever could be found of Jozsi's research trail.

Jozsi shook his head in disbelief. "That man is stupid and crazy. As for you... would I be sitting here talking with such an insignificant lackey as yourself if I knew about a big fat fortune waiting for me to dig it up."

Sandor stared at him, eyes crinkling with amusement. "And your interest in Ura? What do you care about development plans in that area? Do tell."

Jozsi matched Sandor's smile with one of his own. "Oh, my friend, long ties to the area, childhood summer memories, close family friends still living there. Did I ever tell you about Bandi?"

Sandor snickered. "Please, Jozsi, you don't have to tell me anything."

"You'll find out anyway," Jozsi laughed.

"Well, yes, there is that. But really, I wanted you to be aware that Zsigmond had mentioned it repeatedly. Regardless of what happens to him, those notes live in your records, so be careful."

"But according to you, Zsigmond will be busy getting spanked by the KGB for his failed spy network in the States. Who will believe anything he says now?"

Sandor just kept smiling. "I might."

They had time to kill, waiting for word that all had gone according to plan, and Jozsi saw no reason not to tell Sandor about his find at this point, so he did. Starting with his childhood discovery while riding Bandi the summer the war worsened in Budapest.

"You just had to tell me about that horse, didn't you," Sandor laughed.

"Well, he was a fine horse," Jozsi insisted, then continued recounting his years of off and on research, and the odd twist of fate that had brought Ulee into his life. "And I don't want to get back there and find your footprints anywhere near Ura," he added.

Sandor grew serious for a moment. "Don't worry, you are one person I would never stab in the back. It's hard to have friends in this business, but with you, I believe I have come close."

~~~

At 2 AM Jozsi woke to empty his bladder and then quickly fell back to sleep. Meanwhile Sandor snored peacefully in the ear of the young woman with the bangs and big earrings. And six hours ahead, in Hungary, Zsigmond's secretary Vilma rotated her stiff neck before reaching for the ringing phone: a KGB security officer calling to speak with Zsigmond Maksai. "Not in yet?" Icy tone. "Inform him he is to report to the office of the station commander. It is urgent." Vilma immediately rang Zsigmond at home, but there was no answer.

Unaware of all, Zsigmond had risen early and showered, lingering under a cold-water rinse at the end to clear away his hangover, then shaved and dressed. He'd called his driver Peter, ordering him to arrive early so they'd have time for a brief cruise around Budapest. Inspired by his good mood, and the clear, crisp fall weather, he wanted to savor a few morning moments before heading to the office. Like a potentate surveying his empire, thought Peter. They drove along the river. Zsigmond opened the car window, inhaling the smell of car diesel from the rush of morning traffic, the aroma of coal and oil from Danube barges, and the rich smell of the great chestnut trees, heavy with nuts. Damp air radiated off the Danube; the cool breeze flowing from the north reminding all of the wintry chill soon to arrive. It pleased him to see the number of barges. Business was good, fisherman trolled the shores, people walked briskly toward their workplaces. There was hustle, there was bustle, there was the feeling of progress.

He directed Peter to head away from the river toward the city streets where vendors were peddling sausages and prepared foods, their odors floating through the streets, mixing with the rich scent of smoked meat coming from butcher shops, and the nourishing one of baking bread coming from small bakeries. Trolley cars squeaked along their routes, occasionally accompanied by the plaintive vibration of a gypsy violin.

Zsigmond did not notice the many beggars scattered along the sidewalks, each tending a small section of turf, hoping for the kindness of shoppers entering and exiting the many markets. But Peter did. Nor did Zsigmond register the beauty of ancient architecture standing firm in defiance of the years of human conflict, though Peter did. Likewise, Peter noticed the buildings scarred by the Revolution. Bullet holes flecked upper windows, rows of bullet holes five-and-a-half feet off the ground in walls and buildings. Execution holes. Peter had known many who'd chosen to fight the regime, their blood spilled against some of these very walls, their breath cut short on the upper floors of these aged buildings.

Peter veered the car toward the business quarter of *Lipótváros*, cruising past large banks, government ministries and office buildings flanking the ostentatious Budapest Parliament on *Kossuth tér*. Then it was on to the office. Zsigmond arrived promptly at nine and Vilma leapt up to meet him. Before she could begin to share the officer's hostile summons, Zsigmond had swept her into a hug. Never before in 40 years of secretarial service had any officer hugged her. This was puzzling enough, but next he was promising to bring her a dozen roses. She tried to get him to understand exactly how un-celebratory the voice on the phone had sounded. But he ignored her, hurrying off to wait out front for Peter to bring the car around yet again. Madness. Perhaps her hearing was flawed and she'd misread the caller's tone. Zsigmond seemed so certain this was going to be a good meeting.

Peter flicked on the car's blue flashing light and they sped across the city. Zsigmond sat smiling in the back seat of the homely but sturdy Russian-made *Pobjeda*. Thinking of Antal and the Hemingway students gave him a warm feeling. A promotion would follow, of course, but to what? A fancier car, he hoped.

An orderly brought Zsigmond into Commander Andropov's outer office. "Sit, Comrade, the Commander will be but a moment." He rapped twice on Andropov's door. Moments later, Andropov uttered a sharp, *"Belép,"* and the orderly ushered Zsigmond into the inner sanctum, then left, shutting the door behind him. Andropov sat at his desk. No pleased crinkle around the eyes, no vodka toast, no suggestion that Zsigmond take a chair. All of this managed to pierce Zsigmond's happy haze, and like a pin-stuck balloon, he abruptly deflated.

"Comrade Zsigmond, I will be brief. I do not want to keep you from your work, such as it is. The facts are these: the Hemingway Project is dead; last night the FBI arrested our three agents and their support group. And also arrested," his voice rose higher, "the revolutionary network in Puerto Rico. All…of…them." Andropov shook his head back and forth several times in disgust. "So," he held one finger up in front of his face. "An entire network." Two fingers. "Good agents gone. Those students and all the work that went into training them, a complete and utter waste." A third finger. "And the support group, well entrenched in the Bronx ... *where are they now?"* His voice rose to a guttural shout and he slammed his hand on the desk. "Vanished! Being interrogated no doubt. We have discerned from witnesses that a large black van appeared in front of the storefront. We arranged to buy that tailoring shop to serve as a solid base. All of the agents were in the back workroom, meeting. Papers were out on the table."

His voice rose. "Boxes of records have now been *removed.* Do you know what this *means*?!" He held his hands out as though to strangle Zsigmond. They shook with fury. "And Puerto Rico, a very useful transfer location for access to our enemies on the mainland…" He paused again and Zsigmond could actually hear his teeth grind. "Two nabbed at dinner at some *kibaszott empanadilla* food stand on the street." Andropov spat out the curse; it was rare for him to use such a word. "The rest picked up where they worked, their cover stories totally blown. Two dragged from their houses. *Szar, szar, szar!* He screamed out the word for excrement again and again. Outside the office eyes were raised at the tantrum-level rage on the other side of the door.

Inside, Zsigmond stood immobile, his face a study in shock and dismay, his labored breathing audible in the sudden silence.

"And there is more, and worse," Andropov said, struggling to regain his composure. He pushed his glasses back off his nose and glared at Zsigmond. "Antal was arrested as a spy. The FBI grabbed him in a restaurant parking lot. This very much pains me. I am waiting for more details, but the ones I already know are *extremely* disturbing."

Zsigmond's head involuntarily shook back and forth, no, no, no. How could this be happening? He felt his brain might explode. He could not seem to hang onto a clear thought. He gulped.

"We believe your school friend Jozsi Budai was in the middle of that disaster. Obviously, he set Antal up, he was arrested right after their meeting." Teeth clenched tight enough to sever rope, he continued. "And earlier, helping the students in Puerto Rico. A sham is what that was," he said sharply. "He completely fooled you."

Zsigmond concentrated on breathing evenly. He just had to get through whatever came next. He could survive this. He wasn't handcuffed or chained; a positive sign.

"Failures such as these are not acceptable. You have been a loyal comrade for many years. But that will not save you next time. One more mistake and the KGB will pressure Comrade Kadar to find you a more appropriate position, commensurate with your qualifications, such as they are." He bestowed a look that said: I expected roast pheasant and here I lift the lid and find a stinking turd. "You are dismissed. I suggest you leave the building and stay away from your office for the day. *No one* wants to look at you." He lowered his head, inhaled and exhaled deeply, and then put his head in his hands, pressing fingers hard against his temple.

Zsigmond backed out of the room, feeling quite wobbly, and ordered Peter to take him immediately to the *Rozsa Virag*. This, Peter knew, meant something had gone horribly wrong and his boss would spend the rest of the day on a barstool, drowning his troubles in a torrent of alcohol. But desire for revenge overcame the desire to forget every word that had come out of Andropov's mouth. Muttering profanities about Jozsi, Zsigmond left the tavern after only a few hours. From the car phone, he ordered Vilma to contact the Bulgarian Embassy for a meeting, next day if possible. He had a plan.

The next morning, Peter arrived at Zsigmond's door expecting to find his boss not too wrecked since he'd been delivered to his residence at a reasonable hour. But it was obvious he'd done more drinking once he got home; he looked terrible, and at the office, Vilma's disapproving expression reflected just exactly how terrible. She muttered that Zsigmond bore a resemblance to a poorly done corpse at a wake. And noted that he hadn't brought her the promised roses. When he arrived at work this hungover, she could get away with saying anything. More to the point, he simply did not intimidate her. She'd known his mother and seen his pecker when he was a newborn, a fact she reminded him of on the rare occasion he tried to get uppity with her.

"The Bulgarians confirmed they will arrive at ten, Sir," she sniffed. She did not like Bulgarians. Trash. Nonetheless, when they arrived, she greeted them like they were dear friends. "Comrades, welcome," she said all cheer and good will. "Would you care for coffee? Perhaps some fine Hungarian *palinka*?"

Zsigmond felt superior to the Bulgarians, which helped perk him back up. That and a quick slug of *palinka* he snuck before Vilma brought the group into his office. He leaned back in his chair like the CEO of a large corporation, rolling his pencil with one hand, speaking in a strangely ponderous manner. "As you are aware, the KGB and CIA spies have an unwritten agreement not to assassinate one another. Disrupts the work flow." He waited for the Bulgarians to smile at his joke. They did not. "Since the Americans use the Mafia to do their dirty work, it's only natural that some of the Warsaw Pact countries, including the Soviet Union, have been using other means to deal with certain undesirable individuals. Hit squads, so to speak." The Bulgarians were known to be ruthless, fearless, and thorough. "Your group has this kind of experience?" The three Bulgarians sat stone-faced. "If this is so, I may have a job," he concluded, looking expectantly at the trio. After a long silence, he added, "Well?"

"Interesting proposition," Penko, the group leader, said nodding. "But we only get involved when a political situation or a traitor interferes with our mission to spread the communist ideology. We are not mindless thugs," he added emphatically.

Suddenly Zsigmond felt insulted. Was Penko implying that he

himself was that kind of thug? He was, however, too single-minded to appreciate the incongruity of a thin-skinned, defensive, hit man. "In this case, that is *exactly* what is taking place," he exclaimed, and gave a detailed description of the situation. He did selectively edit facts to make himself appear less of a dolt.

Penko said he knew of Jozsef Budai, that he was reported to be smart and dangerous, and not an easy target. He asked to know his address and workplace. "To check if it's real. Agents of this type often have more than one residence, sometimes more than one wife even. Makes it harder to nail them. We need time to observe and verify. There is a minimum fee for these services, and more if we take on the contract — to compensate for our risk."

Zsigmond nodded assent.

"We know he is wily, has been around — Vienna, Hong Kong, Korea, South America. And for one like him, we must take extra precautions. We do not want to tarnish our reputation by failing."

Zsigmond flinched, afraid of what was coming.

"We have also heard about certain of your. . ." Panko paused as though searching for just the right words, "excruciating fiascoes."

Zsigmond clenched his teeth. Sometimes you have to eat shit. He wanted Jozsi dead or too crippled to move, that was all that mattered. "How much?"

Panko looked at the ceiling for a long while, whistling now and then as he calculated, or pretended to do so. Finally, he spoke. "I estimate about a half a million dollars, plus the expenses of our agents. In installments of course," he threw his hands up disgustedly, like he'd rather have it all at once, but would deign to put up with installments.

Zsigmond silently fumed. How could Jozsi be worth that much money? But he agreed, without a thought as to checking with his superiors. He'd get the money somehow. "How soon will we hear of his funeral?"

The leader bristled. "Comrade Zsigmond, you cannot put us on the spot. We have to do our research, carefully study his daily routine, pick the right time and place to make this thing look like an accident. You have emphasized how difficult he will be to corner. We cannot afford to rush. You do want it to appear accidental?"

Zsigmond wearily agreed. He just wanted it over. But Penko had more to say. "Comrade, we are experts and we will cover our tracks, and yours. As soon as we receive the first installment, our agents will begin the work. We understand you must bring this to your superiors for approval. You know how to reach us." And with that he bowed his head and rose, the others leaving as they'd entered, without having said a word.

The next day, after an anxious, sleep-deprived night, Zsigmond appeared in front of the finance committee to ask for money to do away with the Hungarian traitor and informer responsible for the loss of several agents. The committee listened respectfully, but Zsigmond soon discovered that the KGB had already given them a report card on his recent catastrophes.

The chairman said they appreciated his concern about Hungarian national security and that they'd bring his request to the Politburo for discussion. If they approved it, fine. The chairman did note that the more than $20,000 already spent on this failed project had not been forgotten. He pointed out that Zsigmond was now requesting an inordinately large amount to eliminate one man, a man he himself had arranged to work with in the first place. The chairman ended the meeting, saying he'd be in touch with Zsigmond in two weeks with word of a decision.

It would be a long two weeks, Zsigmond thought. He had no interest in returning to his office where everyone, including his own Vilma, had been scowling at him. He told Peter to take him to the *Rozsa Virag*.

"Comrade Zsigmond," Peter ventured, "although this is none of my business, it seems that many times lately we have stopped there early in the day. Do you think perhaps you might need some help? For the sake of your career."

He was not surprised when Zsigmond snapped at him. "Mind your own business and do what I tell you or I'll turn your ass in for the young boys you entertain in your apartment."

Peter blanched and raced straight to the tavern, clearly Zsigmond was in urgent need of the comforts of alcohol. Peter sat in the car until a waiter stuck his head out the door and motioned for him to come pick his boss up from the table upon which he'd chosen to nap. Desperate times, Peter thought, feeling just a little sorry for the jerk.

~~~

Two weeks later, Zsigmond heard from the committee chairman. He was told to appear in the hearing room at three that afternoon. Fortunately, word had come before he'd had a chance to go to the tavern. At three he appeared, looking better than he had in weeks. The politburo had convened around an oval table and the chairman, Comrade Kovacs, asked him to take a seat at the far end. Without the calm and assurance alcohol brought, Zsigmond was one raw nerve. Appearing before the Politburo had a way of going very badly for the guest. That you'd leave 60 Andrássy Street alive after a meeting such as this was not a given.

Comrade Kovacs cleared his throat and launched into a speech. "After careful review of your request, we have approved a transfer of funds to the Bulgarian Embassy. Protection of our communist interests in the world market is essential and the man you seek to eliminate has caused enough damage to warrant this expense. We trust that past errors in judgment will not be repeated and that you will achieve your stated goal." Zsigmond practically glowed with relief. The committee members stood and coldly congratulated him and wished for success.

One look at Zsigmond's face as he left the security building told Peter the meeting had gone well. He had mixed feelings, since seeing Zsigmond fail was immensely satisfying; he was such an ass. "To *Rozsa Virag's*?" he asked the happy warrior.

"No, today we are going to stop by Erika's apartment and wait for her to return from work. On the way, we have to pick up some good champagne. She won't know what she's toasting, but I will."

Peter knew there was no chance in hell Erika would have anything to do with Zsigmond, she was more likely to scream than lift a glass. He could not understand his boss's demented obsession with a woman who seemed to hate the very air he breathed. But he picked out a good bottle of champagne, all the while pondering the occasional rumblings on the grapevine that Erika was in fact the Beast of Budapest. He couldn't see that. During Zsigmond's monitoring, he'd heard about and observed enough of her sedate life to have a hard time imagining her picking up a rifle. And he had no intention of ever mentioning such rumors to his boss. Jobs were scarce and he needed this one, despite an aversion to his loathsome boss's activities. He'd witnessed Zsigmond mentally torment Erika and others. He'd witnessed worse done to others, lives ruined, lives taken. He knew the same could happen to him.

Peter watched Zsigmond carry the bottle toward Erika's residence. He stared out the window, watching two squirrels play tag up and down a nearby tree. He looked at his watch. Five minutes had passed. Just then, Zsigmond rushed out of the building, mad as a hornet, cursing her and the whole world.

"Peter, you can have this champagne to drink with your little boys." Peter knew better than to say a word, he just grabbed the steering wheel and headed away from the building as quickly as possible.

That night, Zsigmond drank himself into a stupor, raving drunkenly about how once Erika heard that Jozsi was dead she would see that being on his good side was the wisest course. He would win her over then, finally and forever.

27
After the Sting

Following their success — the arrest of Antal and the Hemingway students — Jozsi put his mind back on family and work and life in America. He believed Sandor's report that the KGB had questioned Zsigmond. Jozsi fervently hoped to hear that Zsigmond had been exiled or at the very least demoted; ideally stuck directing traffic in some bereft countryside excuse for a town. Many months went by and he heard nothing from Sandor, but that wasn't uncommon in that line of work. Since Jozsi wanted to be out of "that line of work" a part of him hoped never to hear from Sandor again. In one way, he thought of Sandor as a friend, but he knew the ropes — if Sandor needed him he'd call, otherwise not. No happy birthday, no calling just to say hello. Sandor had appeared to believe and accept that Jozsi's desire to disconnect from the firm was genuine. Of course, that would not stop him from reaching out should a need arise. Everything fell before the needs of the firm if you were a real "company" man.

Jozsi was determined to become a different kind of company man and devoted himself to his job: engineering manager. He had responsibilities and endured his time stuck in the office; it was made bearable by long stretches of independence — he routinely traveled the country, visiting various plants for his company. He loved owning a house and tinkering and sawing in his basement workshop — fixing appliances, replacing gutters, shingles, sills. Caring for what belonged to him. He savored afternoons outside, chopping wood, or roasting a pig in the old country way — the day passing in a relaxed haze while turning the browning and smoking pork, minding the fire, his thoughts left to drift. Feeling ease was a rarity in his life since…forever ago, another lifetime. Childhood, which had felt carefree despite war and fear and want, when he'd been unaware, except on a primal level, that the adults around were never at ease.

By the time his father Matyas sent word that Zsigmond had, unbelievably, survived another major screw up, Jozsi felt detached enough to suffer only a week's worth of inner aggravation. Granted, during that week he was outraged, obsessively so. Ann gave him space to grieve the failure to take Zsigmond down, keeping Dani occupied with play dates and other outside activities. There was a force field of unhappiness surrounding Jozsi and she didn't want Dani to absorb too much of it.

Jozsi finally pulled his head out of the darkness by conceding that his efforts had caused Zsigmond a good deal of grief, at least there was that. Eventually he'd get what was coming to him, and if Jozsi wasn't involved, well, at least he'd tried. It was never easy to turn his back on the past, his history clung to him, "like shit on a shoe," he often said. That was the curse of the emigrant. You could flee, but wherever you happened to land, the pulsing reality of your homeland, your family, your stories and memories, moored you forever to the place you'd left, and to every single one of the reasons you'd left in the first place.

When dark thoughts overwhelmed, he had learned to focus on Ann and Dani, on their home and life, and to celebrate his good fortune — he'd not only survived, he'd thrived. He had a good job, he'd been able to return to the land of his birth, to see his parents and siblings, to sit at a table laden with Hungarian specialties, with people who'd known him since he was first on this earth. His nightmares ebbed or swelled, depending on his mood, the news of the world, the moon. He could never predict what kind of night he'd have, or day. His mood swings could be severe, but he did his best to protect his family from them, and he had stretches where he felt content and even occasionally joyful. The simple living of life had its own way of soothing wounds and smoothing scars.

Every few months, Jozsi returned to Puerto Rico to ensure that manufacturing was on schedule and delivery commitments would be met. Although he'd begun that work under a ruse, it was still a real part of his job, and he enjoyed being there. Every few trips, Ann would hand Dani off to her parents and join Jozsi in exploring the island and visiting employees for home-cooked Puerto Rican meals. They missed their son, but it was good to have time together, just the two of them, to remember the lively pleasure they'd found with each other years ago in Washington, D.C.

In 1970, Dani entered second grade, and with no new baby on the way — they'd tried, but another pregnancy just hadn't happened — Ann pondered a return to working part-time, though she wasn't sure at what. She hadn't told Jozsi of her thoughts, wanting a clearer direction before broaching the idea. He was old-fashioned in certain ways and took pride in his ability to support the family; and he liked knowing she was free to mind the home fires. But she'd been working when they met and she expected him to understand that her active mind would hunger for stimulation once Dani settled into his school routine. She hoped when the time came he'd have a positive attitude.

They were deep into fall, wind gusts ripping leaves from trees, heavy winter coats at the ready. It was Wednesday. She'd picked Dani up from school and dropped him off for time with grandma while she drove to Logan to meet Jozsi — his flight from Puerto Rico scheduled to arrive close to five. Normally they'd sit out rush hour traffic at a restaurant they favored on the way home. But tonight, she already knew she'd be making the drive home alone. Disappointing, because she'd been looking forward to his return, glad he'd be back in time for the weekend. There were leaves to rake and wood to chop, a table to refinish, and also, she'd simply been eager to have him home. Given his moodiness, his road trips could be a relief. But he'd been in a more relaxed state lately and she missed the jovial, charismatic version of her husband.

When Jozsi walked off the plane, he saw Ann standing in the waiting area as usual, although this time she had a small suitcase in hand.

"Are you leaving me?" he teased.

"You don't have to worry about that…not yet," she pulled him close. "No, tonight you're the one leaving, straight back to Puerto Rico. John booked you on a flight heading out at eight." Jozsi's supervisor had called moments before it was time for her to pick up Dani. He'd said there was a problem at the plant in Puerto Rico and they hadn't been able to catch Jozsi before his flight had taken off. John was sorry, but they needed him to return for a few days. She'd hurriedly packed clean clothes for his trip back, gotten Dani to her parents and made it to the airport on time. At least they would be able to catch up over a meal at the airport.

"It's not fine dining," Jozsi apologized.

"It's fine enough. You're here," she smiled. At the gate, they kissed goodbye, and she rushed off to pick up their son — already it would be close to his bedtime by the time she reached her parents' house.

Jozsi sat in a first-class seat, enjoying being catered to by the stewards. As the plane gained altitude, moving from dusk to dark, he had a clear view of the traffic flowing out of Boston, or wanting to at least. On Route 93, heading north, Jozsi could see cars backed up to the tunnel. He hoped Ann had managed to get clear of the city before getting stuck in that bottleneck. He leaned back in his seat, unbuckled, relaxed, feeling at peace and full of gratitude for so many things in his life: his wife and son, satisfying job, cozy home, his good American life. He was grateful to the firm as well; his connection to it had led to all of these gifts. Still, he felt no regret at having retired from his affiliation with the CIA. He saw it as a new phase in his life, this attempt to live a completely normal life.

~~~

Zisgmond's plan to have the Bulgarian hit squad murder Jozsi had been sidelined, simmering on the back burner for close to two years. The day Zsigmond had pleaded with Comrade Kovacs for money to hire the Bulgarians, another very important finance committee member had been absent, undergoing surgery. Upon his return, he was informed of the plan and the amount of money called for, and he put up an enormous stink, insisting they not allow Zsigmond *any* special project funds. If "that idiot" as he called Zsigmond, didn't make a mess of anything for a good long while, then, perhaps he could be entrusted with a special venture. Till then, he had to toe the line. Zsigmond spent those two years' tenser than he'd been in years. Yet, surprisingly, most days he managed to suppress his urge to drink massive amounts of alcohol. He was that determined to exact revenge. His driver Peter had never been happier: an irritably un-sloshed Zsigmond was still easier to deal with than the slobbering drunk he'd grown used to shepherding.

Finally, the day came when the committee relented and gave Zsigmond grudging permission to reach out to the Bulgarians a second, and final time, emphasis on final. The team personnel had changed, except for Penko, the leader, who was the only one who ever spoke anyway. Apparently, their cover had been blown on a complicated job and they'd lost two operatives. Zsigmond didn't take time to offer sympathy. He wanted the job done as quickly as possible, understanding, of course, they had to proceed with caution. He wanted to forestall another "We are experts" lecture from Penko.

~~~

Penko and his small crew had spent several weeks monitoring Jozsi's home phone to get the rhythm of his comings and goings. They were now ready to carry out their assignment. When Jozsi called Ann from Puerto Rico that Wednesday morning, assuring her he'd be arriving at five, Penko intercepted the call. He silently raised a fist in the air. The Bulgarians, huddled in their motel in Winthrop, 15 minutes from Logan Airport, began packing up and reviewing their plan one final time. They were dissassembling the monitor, just prior to leaving, while Jozsi dozed on the plane. At the same time, Ann heard the phone ring and found John on the line with a request that she bring Jozsi clean clothes, along with his apologies, so sorry he had to send her husband right back.

"If you need him, you need him," she replied. She was used to last minute changes; that was the nature of their life together. She was so proud of Jozsi. Just a short time ago he'd had nothing but an attractive swagger matched by an uncommon sense of confidence, so different from the young men in West Groton, and his down-to-earth manner so dissimilar from the self-important men she'd met in D.C. Jozsi had accomplished much in a relatively short time. Despite his many absences, despite the nightmares, the bursts of temper, the dark moods, she regretted nothing. Her life with him was what she wanted; she was more than satisfied.

Late that afternoon, the Bulgarians dropped one of their team off at the airport's central parking garage. Filip's job was to spot Ann when she arrived, and from the car phone call Penko, Ivan and Vasil at a diner close to the airport. They would then head to a spot just past the Sumner Tunnel where they could catch sight of Jozsi's car as it headed onto 93 going north. They knew his license plate and could easily spot his car with its darkly tinted window; conveniently for them, dark windows were a new feature few cars had. The sluggish Friday traffic was helpful, too, in terms of identifying the car and maneuvering close — everybody would be crawling. They could follow unobserved until traffic thinned and it was time to make their move — either before or after Jozsi and his wife stopped at the restaurant where they regularly ate on airport trips. They'd timed Ann's pick up trips. She always parked and walked to meet Jozsi at the gate. He never checked his luggage, so they'd go directly to the parking lot, get the car and head north.

Filip spotted Ann on her way to the airport and, assuming the couple would proceed as usual, placed the call, then drove to a restaurant where the others would meet him after the job was finished. But things were not going according to plan. Jozsi and Ann ate sandwiches at the airport while watching planes taxi down runways. The Bulgarians waited restlessly, taking turns as point men, eyes tight to the road. Something was up, but they were patient. Lost luggage perhaps? Some such snafu. Filip had definitely seen the Budai car enter the parking lot and that same car would eventually have to leave it and travel this way. Unless, Penko joked, Jozsi had had a heart attack, in which case they could call it a day and head back to their base in New York.

While Ann and Jozsi said their goodbyes at the departure gate, Filip paced the parking lot where he was to meet the others, and Penko, Ivan and Vasil checked their watches, grumbling at the delay. Ann reached their car and exited the parking lot, feeling melancholy. The traffic was slow, but she made it through Sumner Tunnel without hitting any logjams. She moved into the middle lane, cruising at fifty miles an hour, a good traveling speed for that hour. She turned on the radio, heard Elvis Presley crooning "Are You Lonesome Tonight?" and smiled. This was a favorite of theirs. She'd have liked Jozsi to be by her side instead of high up in the air above, but he'd be back soon enough. She sighed, wishing she were already home, tucking Dani into bed. The song ended and she turned the radio off, wanting the longing in his voice to linger in her head.

Ivan spotted the car. He was driving, Penko riding shotgun, Vasil in the back seat. Ivan eased onto 93. They caught up to Ann, then trailed her from a few cars behind for a number of miles. "Oh, shit," Penko said. The car passed in front of a street light bright enough to show a vague shape behind the tinted windows. Seemed to be just one. Was someone lying down? Not feeling well? Bending to reach down? Questions flew around the car. Simultaneously it occurred to them that the vehicle might literally be carrying only a single passenger. Why? They couldn't begin to guess. Since it was impossible to be certain who was in the car, they decided to go ahead with the hit. If they killed only the wife, so be it. Collateral damage. It would mess with Jozsi's head, which Penko hoped would be revenge enough for that asshole Zsigmond, an inept poser if ever he'd seen one. He'd spent enough time thinking about this job, he wanted to get it done and get paid. All they needed to hold up their end of the deal was to force a body in that car to stop breathing. That would be their attitude, regardless of whose body it was.

After a few more exits, traffic eased; they fell back slightly and continued trailing for another five miles. "Ready?" Ivan asked, hunching forward, his concentration intensifying. The passing lane cleared and Ivan slipped over to the left lane, accelerated, and in a flash, they were on their target. Vasil aimed the Uzi through his now open window. He fired until his gun was empty.

"*Go!*" Penko shouted. Ivan stepped on the accelerator. Their car bucked forward, speeding ahead as Ann's car turned right, crashing hard into a guard railing where it came to an abrupt halt, dislodging a mass of leaves that burst up, then languidly floated down to wither on the now smoking car.

Four miles past the crash site, a three-car rear-ender had slowed traffic, drawing a couple of patrol cars to the area. Two officers stood on the road directing the stream of cars as tow trucks pulled damaged vehicles off the center lane. Within minutes of the hit, Ivan had to slam on the brakes, halting the car with a dramatically loud screech. Which caught the attention of one of the cops on the road — he decided that a car of burly Eastern European men speeding recklessly warranted further attention. He waved them over. His partner, still in their squad, heard dispatch squawk something about armed and dangerous men fleeing on 93. He reached for his gun and called out to his partner, who was at that moment walking toward the Bulgarians' car.

The Bulgarians were in shock. "Shoot the fucker!" Penko spat out, then noticed two other cops, guns drawn, jogging toward their vehicle. *"Drive!"* he screamed at Ivan. Vasil was reloading the Uzi, so Penko reached for his handgun as a chorus of sirens squalled, coming closer and from multiple directions. He calculated the odds. They might take down a cop or two but they'd never get away. Penko dropped his gun and held up both hands; Ivan and Vasil followed his lead. Cursing the foulest of Bulgarian obscenities, they surrendered to the police without further gunfire. The police handcuffed and squeezed all three into the back seat of the squad, and drove away. Within hours, the FBI had Filip in custody as well. The highway patrol had been riled about having to call in the FBI — they hated handing over this big a catch — but once they realized the international aspect of the crime, they realized they had no choice.

At midnight, the phone rang in Jozsi's *Mayaguez Hilton* hotel room. It was John from work.

"What is it?" Jozsi asked, groggy.

"Jozsi, I've got bad news. Something's happened to Ann, an accident coming from the airport. You have to get back, quickly."

"How bad?" Jozsi managed to ask, as shock settled like a shroud.

"I don't know. She's at *Mass General.* I've got you booked in the morning, first flight out."

"Dani?" Jozsi said, breathless.

"He's okay. He doesn't know anything. His cousin is staying with him at your in-law's house, her parents are at the hospital. They asked me to reach you." Jozsi dropped the phone in its cradle and curled up on the bed, sick to his stomach, feeling a kind of panic he'd never experienced. He veered from icy calm to fearing he was losing his mind, perhaps had lost it already. His head ached from the strain of trying to absorb the news.

He pulled himself together long enough to pick up the phone

and reach his in-laws at the hospital. Ann was in intensive care after emergency surgery, it was touch and go. Hurry.

After Jozsi arrived at Logan the next morning, he grabbed a cab to *Mass General*, ran through the front entrance to the reception desk, and then to the ICU. In the waiting area, he found Ann's parents, surrounded by other tense relatives. Dani sat at a table in a corner, focused on a big box of crayons, a coloring book open in front of him. For Dani's sake, all of them were trying not to cry, but the effort wasn't going well. Dani had been told his mother was hurt after an accident and doctors were helping her. A nurse told Jozsi a few details. She was still alive, she was hanging on. For more information, he'd have to talk to the doctor. Dani looked up, saw his father and ran to him. Jozsi held his son close, speaking with reassuring calm, Dani couldn't see the panic in his eyes. Working hard to control his voice, he brought Dani back to his coloring book. "I'm going to see your mother," he kissed Dani on the head, and followed the nurse into the ICU.

Ann looked small and shockingly fragile, swaddled in bedding and bandages in a nest of beeping machines. He sat holding her hand, murmuring in her ear. Could she hear him? "We love you," he cried softly. He tried to comprehend what he'd heard and now could see. Internal injuries. Face uncovered, bruised and badly swollen, but recognizable. Bandages around the back and sides of her head. Her head had been injured. How bad? Too soon to know. Tubes. Sterile gown. Mask over mouth. His heart hurt. After a while, he went to the waiting room, to reassure Dani while Ann's mother went to her bedside. Only one visitor at a time. Seeing her so diminished was too much to bear, so it was all right that they had to take turns, it gave them each a chance to recover.

Jozsi could see Dani was scared and made plans for him to leave the hospital and spend the night with relatives. If she makes it through the next 36 hours, the doctor said, they could breathe a small sigh of relief. Till then, he was sorry to say, prayers were in order. The doctor also told him they'd found a bullet in her shoulder, and graze burn on the back of her neck. Jozsi could barely absorb what that might mean, and didn't try to. He put all his energy into willing his wife to survive.

Ann clung to life for several hours, vital signs weak, but steady enough to give them hope. Jozsi thought she squeezed his hand. He dozed off, his ass in the chair, his head resting on her mattress. His right hand arced around his head, his fingers resting under hers. That's what he thought woke him, pressure from her fingers. He felt cool air as someone entered the room, felt a presence at the foot of the bed, heard the soft rustle of pages being turned. Must be a nurse checking Ann's chart. Jozsi stayed still. He didn't want to know anything; he just wanted to rest here, by his wife, just like this, until she sat up. Ann's fingers felt cool and still on his hand. The nurse draped a blanket over his folded form and he drifted into uneasy sleep.

When he next awoke, it was because of Ann's labored breathing, no doubt about that. Halting, rasping, gurgling. He sat up. He stumbled to the door and into the hallway, yelling "Nurse!" over and over, until one came running. Soon there were other nurses and then doctors. They huddled around Ann, sending Jozsi out of the room, his mother-in-law's arm around him. He was barely breathing, as though for him to inhale deeply would rob Ann of the exact amount of air she needed to survive.

Eventually, they brought him back into the room. He talked to Ann, he begged her not to leave them, stroking her hand, repeating her name like a mantra. The number of people in the room ebbed and flowed, and then ebbed. The doctor told Jozsi to prepare himself, things were going very badly and there was nothing more they could do.

More time passed, he had no idea how much, and then it was over. Jozsi asked the nurses to leave him alone and they left him to his grief. He sobbed on Ann's chest, where her heart had given out. He stroked her arms, caressed her cheek, still warm. After a while he went to the door where her parents waited. They each kissed her one last time, and then the hallway filled with tears. At least that's how he came to remember those moments when family and friends gathered to prop up her parents and husband as they left Ann's still body in a hospital bed.

~~~

A few mornings later, Jozsi and Dani were in the kitchen cleaning up after a solemn pancake breakfast. Jozsi had taken time off, realizing that he was in shock, useless at work, and that his priority need to be helping Dani deal with their loss. When the doorbell rang, Jozsi answered to find two FBI agents. He recognized them from Antal's arrest in *The Rusty Scupper* parking lot. They were sorry to intrude but they wanted to speak with him about the Bulgarians. This was the first he'd heard anything about any Bulgarians. He hadn't had the heart to do more than keep Dani fed and occupied as much as possible. His mind wandered to the bullet the surgeon had told him about, but he hadn't been able to focus on its source. Knowing nothing was going to bring her back had taken the wind out of his sails and at the moment, he had no stamina to care about anything other than that she was dead. That wasn't like him, but suddenly his life wasn't recognizable, so he shrugged and took one day at time. But now he had to focus. He told the agents that if they had something to tell him, they could go ahead, he was ready to hear whatever they had to say.

The agents informed him that it wasn't an accidental car crash, that it was definitely a hit, nothing random about that bullet. They'd arranged for agents to guard his house for the time being. Good undercover guards, Jozsi thought, he'd had no idea. Could Ann have been hit by mistake? Could Jozsi have been the actual target? The agents told him that the Bulgarians involved had been under the protection of the Bulgarian Consulate. And that western intelligence operations agents knew that Todor Zhivkov, First Secretary of the Bulgarian Communist Party, was sponsoring the Bulgarian hit squad — it had become a valued commodity for all Eastern Communist countries. In return, the dictatorial First Secretary received money and favoritism from the Kremlin. But, the agents added, fortunately, Filip, the conspirator they'd grabbed at the motel, thought he could save his skin by blabbing. With all of the evidence they'd collected, supplemented by Filip's cooperation, the Bulgarians would be put away for a long time. Jozsi nodded blankly and thanked them for coming. Any new information his brain absorbed felt beamed in from outer space and like it might take light years to register. He'd think about all of it later. First, he had dishes to do.

~~~

The day after the Bulgarians attacked Jozsi's car, the phone rang in Zsigmond's office. Vilma picked up to find a KGB apparatchik on the line: Comrade Zsigmond must come to KGB Headquarters immediately. She felt anxious, but when Zsigmond arrived, he bounced on his heels excitedly, summoned Peter the driver, and expectantly set out for headquarters. He'd heard nothing directly from the Bulgarians, but assumed this call must be about their mission. The Bulgarians had a high success rate, so he felt certain the mission had to have gone well, and was absolutely convinced that this time he'd be welcomed and praised. He began composing gracious words for when Comrade Andropov shook his hand in congratulations. Peter, glancing in the rearview mirror, caught Zsigmond mouthing the words of his little speech.

But moments after he arrived Zsigmond's spirits started sinking. The security guard left him waiting in the lobby instead of quickly ushering him into Andropov's office; they were treating him as badly as they'd done two years earlier. Actually, it was worse: he wasn't sitting in Andropov's outer office, he'd been deposited in the lobby. Even Lenin's picture on the opposite wall stared at him like he was a criminal. The lobby was quiet; he watched the second hand move around a large wall clock, his anxiety building until he broke into a cold sweat. Finally, the security guard returned and escorted him to the same conference room he'd entered the last time. The same Russian officers were seated around the table. No one invited him to sit. He stood at the end of the table, knowing without a doubt that he was in big trouble once again. How could that be?

Andropov looked up from the papers he'd been leafing through and wearily shook his head. But his voice was not weary, it was ice cold and firm. "Comrade Zsigmond, the last time you were here, we warned you not to underestimate your childhood school friend. We cautioned you against making further foolish mistakes. You have again underestimated his capabilities and in so doing have made a grave error. Your plan to have him assassinated by the Bulgarians has failed. And worse than that, our comrades have been arrested *by the FBI*." Andropov paused to let the news sink in. "If their resolve and loyalty to the party should weaken they might choose to benefit themselves by talking." He shook his head back and forth, and then spoke with increasing rage. "Do you understand what an embarrassment this would be for the Soviet Union and other Warsaw nations?" He slammed his fist on the desk. "And now we will make a full report of your mistakes to the Hungarian Secret Police. You are their problem and they will decide your future. But know this: we do not expect to see you in this building again. Ever. Comrade Zsigmond, you are *dismissed*."

Zsigmond backed away from the table. Andropov angrily straightened his papers, looked up again and shouted, "This little game of yours has cost your government a half a million dollars. To have someone's *wife* assassinated." He shuddered. As did Zsigmond. He hurried down the hall, anxious to get out of that building and away from those icy, furious eyes.

Outside, he looked for Peter but both he and the staff car had vanished. This was the first time Zsigmond had had to take public transportation since before the Revolution. Too dazed by this terrible turn of events to think about drowning his sorrows in drink, he returned to his office and found it locked. A security guard posted by the door told him to report to the National Security Office immediately.

"Where's Vilma?" Zsigmond managed to croak.

"She has been reassigned," the guard replied. "I'm sorry, Comrade," the guard seemed almost apologetic, "but I have to ask you for your service revolver."

This was worse than Zsigmond had feared. He had been useful to the party over the years and still held out hope that those in the National Security Office would remember his successes and have pity; taking his gun did not at all align with this scenario.

He was ushered into a conference room where his superior officers awaited. Once again, he was told to stand at the end of the table. This time Lenin's picture stared at him from the far end of the room. He was beginning to hate Lenin. Yesterday had anyone said a wrong word about Lenin, Zsigmond would have had the miscreant sent to hard labor camp for twenty years. That was yesterday.

The head of the Hungarian Secret Police sat directly beneath Lenin's portrait. He wasted no time with formalities. "Comrade Zsigmond, we're sorry to inform you that you are no longer in charge of the Budapest Security Office. The embarrassment you've caused our Russian allies, the *shame* you've brought to our own organization, forces us to remove you from your current duties. It is only because of your past loyalty and efforts that we do not punish you more severely. Instead, we demote you to the position of an entry-level police officer in your hometown of Rakoskeresztur. You are to report to Captain Pasztor promptly at 8 o'clock tomorrow morning. You should consider yourself fortunate. Comrade, you are dismissed."

As he walked away from any hope of forgiveness or allegiance, Zsigmond very much wished he still had his revolver. The future looked to be, in a word, grim.

~~~

Time passed, Jozsi returned to work, Dani to school. Ann's parents and family cocooned the two as best they could. After allowing Jozsi a moat of grief, local divorcees began appearing at the door with special suppers and attention. He took to dimming lights and closing the curtains each evening to discourage casual visitors. He helped Dani with his homework, prepared simple dinners, and they carried on — the big and little man holding back their tears as they adjusted to a life without the warmest heart in their home. When Jozsi had to travel out of town, Ann's parents or siblings took care of Dani. He got used to packing his away bag, an easy traveler just like his father.

Winter arrived, although they barely noticed. The family passed the holidays in a near catatonic state, still reeling, still grieving. By early spring Jozsi managed enough energy to take Dani for weekend visits to their country cabin. The change of scenery was good; they roamed the woods, played catch, went fishing. Dani was old enough to want to be Jozsi's little helper when he launched into making repairs around the property. Each night he was home, Jozsi lay next to Dani and read aloud, something Ann had always done, and in those cozy moments they talked about her and comforted each other.

Late one May evening, Sandor called Jozsi at home. He was in the mood to spend a weekend in New England. Would Jozsi invite him to the cabin so they could catch up? Jozsi agreed, with the proviso that Sandor could not bring any more people into his life who might want to talk about Hemingway, or any other famous American, including Walt Disney. Sandor was relieved to hear him make any kind of humorous comment given all he'd been through. They agreed to meet a few weekends later. He started giving Sandor directions to the cabin. "No need," Sandor interjected. "I know where it is. You really are getting rusty!" Jozsi laughed, of course Sandor would know. He probably knew exactly what cans were in the cupboards, which brand of toothpaste in the bathroom. Jozsi sent Dani to spend the weekend camping with his cousins, so he could speak frankly with Sandor.

They met at the cabin on a Friday evening and built a campfire on the shore. Sandor opened a special bottle of *palinka* as they settled down to talk about the good old days, when risk was their everyday routine. Eventually Sandor brought them back to the present.

"I'm sorry this isn't just a friendly visit, but I have two difficult things to tell you."

Jozsi held his gaze, nodded, then looked away, waiting.

"First, your friend Laci."

Jozsi closed his eyes briefly, guessing what would come next.

"He is gone. Vietnam. A mission that went very wrong." Sandor reached over and gently touched Jozsi's shoulder. "Do you want the details?"

"Not yet," Jozsi murmured, lowering his head, elbows resting on thighs, hands squeezed tight as though in prayer. They sat without talking for several minutes. Eventually Jozsi looked up. "And the other thing?"

Sandor apologized for not telling Jozsi sooner, but he'd felt it best to wait while Jozsi grieved. "It may have already occurred to you," Sandor prefaced his unfortunate news, "but I know for a fact that Zsigmond is responsible for Ann's death."

Jozsi reached for the bottle and refilled his glass. "I know," he said, looking ominously into the fire as though envisioning Zsigmond burning before his eyes. He revealed that his friend Ferenc had written him after seeing Zsigmond directing traffic in Rakoskeresztur's town square. Ferenc had done a bit of investigating and learned that Zsigmond had majorly screwed up an overseas operation. Putting two and two together, the old friends figured out what must have happened. Sandor only confirmed what Jozsi already had learned but was too emotionally drained to rage about. All these years worrying about Zsigmond harassing Erika and now this, Ann destroyed at Zsigmond's instigation. The final barbarity: Zsigmond hadn't even been after Ann. The arc of this conversation having landed them in a mud hole of misery, they called it a night.

The following day, as Jozsi rowed them out on the lake for a little fishing, Sandor shared further news: he had significant information about the government's long-range plans for Ura. Over the course of the next two years, a hydroelectric plant to provide power to Budapest would be built in the area. Once local residents had been relocated and the plant built, the area would be flooded. Sandor was distantly related to the executive secretary for the director in charge of constructing the plant. "Aliz. A charming young woman, very bright. She is interested in moving to America and happy to help me out since she knows I can be useful in getting her here."

They listened to water lap against the wooden rowboat as they floated, waiting for fish to investigate their lures. After a time, Sandor spoke, "I know nothing about your special secret in Hungary, but something tells me you should think about returning there before Ura becomes a lake. Go to Hungary and visit your family. It'll be good for you to see them. And your special place in Ura."

More silence. Jozsi stared out across the lake at his little cabin, nestled in a circle of maple and pine trees. He pictured Ann in her sturdy straw hat, waving at him from the doorway. "A change of scene might be good," he said. "And Dani would get to see his Hungarian family. But what about the government arresting or harassing me — punishment for spoiling their operation here?"

"I'll put out feelers and find out where you stand. This could take a little while, but I'll get something. I have a couple of strong connections inside the Security Office, more than that I can't say."

Sunday afternoon, Sandor left for parts unknown, but took the unusual step of giving Jozsi his new phone number in case he needed him for any reason. "Even just to talk," Sandor said solicitously. He'd never been so gentle, not even in the midst of the Revolution.

"Should I be worried? You think I'm in such bad shape you have to be sweet to me?" He laughed bitterly.

Sandor did not respond with a wisecrack. "No, I am not worried, but I am used to you, and after so many years I want to know that you're all right...and be of help if you are not." He patted Jozsi on the back in farewell. "It will take time," he said, seeming to refer to everything — Jozsi's moving through grief, the situation in Hungary, the woes of the world. "I'll be in touch when I have news for you," he said, squeezing Jozsi's shoulder before leaving.

~~~

Several weeks later, Sandor surfaced on Jozsi's office phone with word that it seemed safe for him to return to Hungary. The complete failure of the western intelligence operation was such an embarrassment that no one wanted to speak of it, or of Zsigmond or anything Zsigmond cared about — the annihilation of Jozsi, for example.

He and Dani flew out of Logan on a humid August evening, glad to be leaving the muggy air behind. There were no problems coming through customs, to Jozsi's relief. Ferenc met them at the airport with warm hugs and brought them straight to Susan's house, where Jozsi's parents waited to comfort their heartsick son and his little boy. Though he'd planned on going to Ura, once he landed in Hungary, he was overcome with inertia. He stayed close to the family and to friends. They kept Dani busy and allowed Jozsi his first chance to completely collapse. He hadn't realized how exhausted he was from trying to keep everything together for his son. He slept and slept, took long walks in the woods, revisited his childhood haunts and tried not to think too hard about anything. Returning to Hungary without Ann was much harder than he'd imagined. The visit was bittersweet; there was no way around that.

After he'd floated through a series of uneventful days Ferenc surprised him with an invitation to dinner at his house, with a special guest...Erika. Jozsi's heart clutched. It had been 12 years since they'd parted at the *Margaret Bridge*. Ferenc said she'd moved back to town and bought a small house after her husband died from a sudden heart attack a year earlier. She'd heard that Zsigmond was directing traffic and now that he'd lost power had no fear of him. She asked after Jozsi any time Ferenc spoke with her. She was very sorry to hear about the death of his wife.

Jozsi took a day to mull it over. He wanted to see her, though maybe not this trip. But his sister Susan had recently seen her as well, and counseled that he'd benefit from spending time with his old love. "She is as strong and kind as ever," Susan reported. "You've both suffered through so many things. It will be good to lean against each other, even if it's only for one dinner." He told Ferenc to set a place at the table, he'd be there.

Given all that she'd experienced and done, Jozsi was shocked by how little her appearance had changed. A few wrinkles, a little heavier, but her hair, again long though attractively pinned up, shone as it always had, and her eyes flashed with life and curiosity. They were shy with each other at first, eyes lowering and raising as though too long a gaze might be more connection than either could bear. Ferenc and his wife carried the evening for a bit, until the DNA connection of their shared history eased the conversation into a comfortable flow. They talked about the old days, although everyone avoided saying Zsigmond's name. Jozsi shared a few of his adventures out in the world, and she relayed news of her less dramatic activities after the Revolution. They spoke about their spouses and the depth of loss they were each experiencing.

By the end of the evening, there was such ease to their rapport they both felt comforted and said so. Ferenc and his wife busied themselves in the kitchen so the two could have a moment alone. They agreed it was good to see each other again, but sadly time was short: Jozsi and Dani would return home in a few days, and they had family activities and dinners lined up until the moment they left.

"When will you return, Dodi?" Erika asked.

Hearing his childhood nickname from her lips did something to his heart. He reached for her hand saying, "As soon as I feel better about the world around me." They parted with a brief tender kiss on the lips. She promised to write. He promised to write back.

On the plane back to America, Jozsi's mind became its own little theater, screening images from the past: Erika as a child, a playmate, a lover; Erika as a loyal daughter, a fierce warrior, a symbol of the Revolution. It had been a good trip, although he regretted not managing to get to Ura. He would have a chance to get back before the land was flooded, and now, after seeing Erika, he had a different, equally compelling reason to return.

28

Return to Ura

Summer drew to a close with Jozsi and Dani continuing to spend weekends at the country cabin where the loss of Ann was somehow less acute. Dani entered 4th grade and Jozsi worked, still routinely traveling, which gave Dani special time with his cousins and grandparents. They gradually adjusted to their new life. Jozsi saw women on the side now and then, but never brought anyone home to meet Dani. There was no reason to; none of these women meant anything more to him than a distracting and pleasurable respite from the chasm of an empty bed.

Soon after their return from Hungary, an envelope from Erika arrived; a brief, but heartfelt letter about how much it had meant to see him again, and how wonderful it had been to meet his son. Jozsi wrote back, she responded, and soon not a week passed without their corresponding. The ability to communicate with someone who truly knew and understood him helped fill an aching cavern inside his chest. Taking root down in the darkness now was a sprig of green, this feeling of closeness and acceptance. There was no talk of the future; rather their letters traced the navigation of their daily lives as they each healed from the upheaval of loss and change.

As winter receded, Jozsi began planning a return trip to Hungary. He was due vacation time and intended to spend most of the summer near Budapest, with, of course, a side trip to Ura. He contacted Sandor, asking to be put in touch with his young relative, Aliz. Sandor had already prepped Aliz to help Jozsi in any way she could, including providing him with an identification card that would allow him to enter the town of Ura. A temporary dam had been built, and the town had been evacuated save for a few people with authorized access. The area was slated for flooding late that summer.

When writing to Erika, Jozsi knew better than to remind her of the secret he'd long ago shared with her — the government was no doubt reading his mail — but he knew that as soon as he was able to speak freely, if cautiously, on Hungarian soil, he could depend on her help in retrieving what he hoped was Attila's coffin and the treasure it might hold.

Ferenc also wrote, keeping Jozsi current on goings-on in Ura, and with Erika — since their reunion she'd become friends with his wife Jola. He mentioned that Erika occasionally agreed to dine with Zsigmond, who still did his best to haunt her, despite his fall from grace. She never explained why she put up with him, especially now that he had no power to seriously disrupt her life or hurt anyone she cared about. Jozsi knew she had her reasons, still hating Zsigmond for what he'd done to her father, though she never mentioned anything about Zsigmond in her letters. What neither Ferenc nor Jozsi knew was that Erika's secret poison mushroom capsule remained intact, stashed in a small container under a stack of folded kerchiefs.

Now that Zsigmond was a lesser political being, shamed and discounted, she imagined she could eventually dispense with him, at least do something to avenge her father's death. Whenever they did meet, she tucked the container in a corner of her purse just in case an opportunity arose. But each time, she failed to take action. He'd go to the restroom, she'd think about reaching for the capsule, but always some image stopped her. It could be a memory — a shotgun blast, a body falling before her, a tank rolling over an unarmed Hungarian resister, a small child running to the street to throw himself on his dead father's body. It could be Jozsi reaching for her in bed, her father smiling from across the room, her mother affectionately stroking her hand as they sat by the fire. Whatever it was would delay her just long enough for Zsigmond to return before she could act.

She realized that her hesitation stemmed from having separated some inner piece of herself from that violent stretch in her life. She'd avoided killing even a fly since that nightmare time, that aberration in her nature. It was as though two Erika's struggled inside. A realist, she valued and respected both. Back then, the circumstances had been dire and she had responded in like manner. Still, she did not want to return to the insanity of that rage. And yet, she wanted to see Zsigmond die in front of her. She wanted to watch his body twisting in agony while she spat on him. She wanted to remind him of what she'd learned about her father — that he had begged for an end to the torture he'd endured at 60 Andrássy Street. *Begged.* The thought still doubled her with grief. She wanted him dead, she wanted him dead by her own hand, and still she hesitated.

In May, Zsigmond arrived early to pick her up for a dinner date. Erika would never offer to cook for him, she didn't want him inside her house that long, but she allowed him to come in and wait while she finished getting ready. She'd left an envelope with an American stamp sitting on a side table and Zsigmond spotted it. When she was out of the room, he slid the contents out, and scanned them. He learned that Jozsi was returning to Hungary for much of the summer and wanted to know if she could take time off and accompany he and Dani to Lake Balaton to enjoy the waters. Ferenc and his family would be coming too. Zsigmond grit his teeth and shoved the letter back into the envelope, but in his haste, a corner stuck out just a bit, though all Erika registered was that his face was flushed. Too much drink, she guessed. As usual.

During their meal, Zsigmond mentioned Jozsi. Did she know when he was returning to Hungary and for how long? He knew she'd seen Jozsi, of course — shunned as he was by higher-ups, he still had inroads to the Secret Police, and he wanted her to know that. Something clicked and she realized she'd left Jozsi's latest letter on the table. Perhaps Zsigmond had seen it. She decided to go with the truth. Why yes, he was coming to spend time with his family. For how long, Zsigmond inquired. Was he thinking of doing some traveling?

Erika saw an opportunity to rattle her stalker. "Well," she sipped her wine, dragging out her reply. "I believe he's coming to do some research as well."

"In Ura?" Zsigmond blurted.

"Why no, why would you think that? No, no, he's hoping to find out exactly who is responsible for sending the men who killed his wife. He is convinced the orders originated here in Hungary." She sipped again, watching Zsigmond stifle his anxiety. "From what I understand, he has some connection within the government he thinks will be helpful. And when he finds out who is responsible, I imagine he will put his Special Forces training to good use."

Zsigmond's face paled slightly, though he said nothing. But as soon as they were seated at the restaurant, he began gulping *Hubertus*, and by ten that night, Erika left him drunk in the restaurant, no Peter to ferry him home, and hailed herself a cab. She instantly regretted that she hadn't poured the mushroom poison into his drink. There had been a moment, Zsigmond gone to the restroom, no eyes on their table, but again she'd hesitated.

For the next few days, Zsigmond thought about what he managed to remember of their conversation. He nosed around to see if he could unearth any information from the local authorities. In past years, the police had been notified each time Jozsi applied for a visa, and his travel agenda while he was in Hungary had been shared. But this time the government had relaxed their rules and there were no restrictions placed on Jozsi's ability to come and go as he pleased.

For a time, Zsigmond was too mortified to call Erika and dig deeper. The restaurant manager had been stern. "When he sobers up, tell him not to come back. This place does not need such embarrassment, especially from someone in a state uniform." He was no longer important enough to put up with.

Jozsi might be doing exactly what Erika had surmised, seeking those responsible for his wife's murder, but he could also be looking into whatever seemed to compel him in Ura. Either way, if Zsigmond could catch him doing something wrong before Jozsi had a chance to discover any facts concerning his wife Ann's death, he could manage the situation — damage Jozsi before Jozsi had a chance to strike against him.

Zsigmond hunkered down with the copious files on his prey, which he'd managed to get copies of even after being exiled to Rakoskeresztur. He'd made an inventory of all the items Jozsi and his family had brought through customs on their visits to Hungary, but didn't discover anything particularly suspicious. *Herendy* porcelain horses and books about Attila seemed nostalgia items. He searched for clues and references to Ura and whatever it could be that Jozsi was after. He'd even checked into the Toth family, but the Secret Police insisted the family were hard-working peasants who'd never been in trouble and weren't really capable of causing any.

Zsigmond continued asking questions, annoying his contacts in the Secret Police and irritating the local constabulary as well. No matter, he pressed on. But days and then weeks passed with no break in the logjam. Thwarted at every turn, with Jozsi's arrival drawing closer, Zsigmond's mood darkened. He simply had to figure out what Jozsi was up to. He felt in his gut that if he could unearth the secret, he'd have a shot at returning to the state's good graces. He wanted nothing more than to climb his way back to where he'd once been, standing firm with the powerful elite. He *deserved* to be there, he avowed, soused at his kitchen table night after night.

Erika alerted Jozsi to Zsigmond's likely having read his recent letter, and described their conversation in the restaurant. He thanked her, with assurances that he was not particularly concerned — Zsigmond was no longer powerful enough to interfere with him in any but the most insignificant way. He was looking forward to spending a lot of time with her and she shouldn't trouble herself about anything to do with Zsigmond.

~~~

In early July, he and Dani arrived at *Budapest International Airport*, made their way through customs, and were greeted by Ferenc and Jolanka, who, having shot up several inches was suddenly looking older than Dani. Nonetheless, they were instantly sitting close in the back seat, whispering in each other's ears. They'd declared themselves best friends, corresponding by mail through the months that passed between visits.

That night Susan held a welcome party in her back yard, with harvest tables arranged on the grapevine-covered terrace. Erika was waiting to greet Jozsi, shyly, warmly. By ten that night the assembled were singing traditional Hungarian songs and toasting those they wished were still among the living. Jozsi's parents, older and frailer, lasted as long as they could, but by midnight, they, along with several other relatives, had returned to their homes. Erika also left, holding onto the feeling of Jozsi's arms around her as he squeezed goodnight. "It is so good to see you," she whispered. He sighed into her ear, and they kissed tenderly and gently, alone together in the dark by her car.

Jozsi and Susan sat up late, catching up on family news, so happy to be in the same room. They made plans to get the hidden money down from the chimney, thinking enough time had passed for that to be a safe move. Jozsi wanted Susan to use it to help their parents and her own family. He finally shared the information about his Ura discovery with Susan, who said, "I can't believe you kept this a secret from *me* all these years." Excited, she insisted on going with him to unearth the coffin. She was a good driver, and though it might be dangerous, he knew he could trust her courage, she'd always had strong nerves.

During the next few days, Jozsi and Dani visited all their relatives, tasted all their favorite dishes, and sampled homemade wine, though only tiny sips for Dani. Some of the wine was good, some less so. Jozsi explained to Dani, "Like our lives, sometimes good, sometimes not so good." At night Jozsi made his way to Erika's house where between increasingly passionate kisses, they plotted what to do with any treasure he might find. She offered her basement as a hiding place — there was a secret passage former owners had carved out during the Nazi invasion. And one night he told her the information he'd held back for so long. She'd been sharing with him how much it still ate at her that Zsigmond had done nothing to help her father. Jozsi steeled himself and said, "His true responsibility is even worse." And in a few agonizing moments told her the full truth. At first, she simply clenched her fists and sounding strangely reasonable said, "I think deep inside I knew this." And then she stood, threw her head back, and howled until she had no sounds left to utter. After which, she collapsed in Jozsi's arms.

The next night, after supper at Ferenc's, Jozsi took his old friend aside while Jola and Erika cleaned up the kitchen. They drank wine on the veranda and Jozsi shared his suspicions about the coffin. Would Ferenc be willing to loan Jozsi his truck? Would he be willing to help? Absolutely, Ferenc said, pleased to be included in this adventure. He wondered of Jozsi, "With all of your traveling around the world, here you are again, sitting with the same people all these years later. Me, I've never been anywhere, I've always wanted to stay here no matter what insanity we had to deal with. But tell me, with all the dangers and hardships of these adventures, was it worth leaving?"

Jozsi sat silent for a time. "Yes," he said finally. "Worth it, and I'd do it all again. The evening isn't long enough to tell you all of the pleasures and sufferings I've had through these years. But I wouldn't have missed any of them." He pictured Ann smiling as he walked through the front door, laughing with Dani, reveling in the beauty of a spectacular sunset. "Not even with the biggest loss of all. I would not have missed my life with Ann for anything." They raised their glasses, toasting Ann without a word. And then they toasted to new adventures.

Jozsi had met with Aliz to receive his identity card and she was willing to provide two spare permits, allowing access to Ura by Hungarian residents. She'd informed him that an unusually rainy spring in Ura had raised the water levels so high that the temporary dam couldn't hold much longer. She knew she was jeopardizing her job by giving him these papers, but Sandor had convinced her it was in a good cause, even though he wouldn't tell her exactly what that cause was. She thought Jozsi might want to think about going soon; a major storm was forecast and there was a chance the dam would fail and deluge the area before it could be formally flooded.

Jozsi, Susan, and Ferenc started out that Friday afternoon in Ferenc's truck. Erika stayed behind to prepare her secret storage area. The trio laughed all the way to Ura, teasing each other in ways only those who've known each other since childhood can. The sky was blue when they set out, but soon storm clouds appeared and then the rains came, first showers, then downpours, then utterly relentless sheets. As they traveled through small villages lining their route to Ura, they could see even blacker storm clouds moving in from the Bukk Mountains. They passed farmers shepherding livestock into covered shelters, and everywhere people closing shutters, gathering loose tools, buckets, even wheelbarrows from yards to batten down or store inside. From generation to generation, this kind of storm was looked upon as a curse from the time of Attila the Hun — the rain thundering down to wash his sins off the *Puszta*.

After many hours, the three reached Ura. Just before entering the town, a security guard pulled them over to check their permits and warn them that the area would be permanently flooded within a matter of days. He cautioned that given the wild weather, the temporary dam might reach crest by nightfall. From behind the wheel, Ferenc swore they'd be making a quick turnaround; they were visiting for sentimental reasons — wanting to see the area once more before it vanished under a torrent of water. The guard shook his head at their foolishness, "This is not the day for a trip down memory lane," but let them through.

Driving toward the Toth farm, they passed one empty house after another. Jozsi recognized the milk collection building. It had been years since he'd even thought about it or the many summer nights he'd lugged milk inside. When they arrived at the Toth's, they found the main gate open. Jozsi hopped out and walked around the back yard one final time; childhood memories overwhelmed as he touched the walls of the outside oven. He wandered through the rooms of the unlocked empty house, pausing often. Susan watched sympathetically. She knew how special this place was for him and how sad it made him to see it for the last time. The Toths had been forced to relocate, old Mr. Toth dying soon after the move. Matyas insisted that he'd died of a broken heart. She thought Matyas would be glad to know that Jozsi was here to say good-bye for them.

As they'd been setting out for Ura, Zsigmond had managed to put at least a couple of pieces of the puzzle together. He'd finagled a retired policeman into keeping an eye on Jozsi's activities. When the man reported that Jozsi, Ferenc and Susan had headed out of town in Ferenc's truck, Zsigmond had a feeling Jozsi might be going to Ura.

Zsigmond pondered making a case for a small reconnaissance mission to trail and intercept Jozsi before he could get to whatever he was after. The "pro" was that Jozsi was known to be a clever, potentially dangerous troublemaker. The "con" was that the Security Police cringed when Zsigmond's name came up. But what harm could there be in sending a few policemen to check things out? The area would soon be flooded and whatever Jozsi might be after more than likely was within the flood zone. Zsigmond reasoned that Jozsi wanted to get there before it was too late. This all sounded convincing to him, so he downed a quick shot of *Hubertus* and placed a call to the Chief of the Security Police. It took him awhile to get through; he had to overcome resistance from at least two underlings before Comrade Bela agreed to take his call.

Speaking quickly, Zsigmond admitted that he had no idea exactly what Jozsi was up to, but given his years of keeping track of "that traitor" he knew his hunch was good. Comrade Bela, eager to get Zsigmond off the phone and half hoping he would fail miserably, ordered five policemen to be placed under Zsigmond's command. There was, however, a caveat. "Are you listening carefully?" he asked. "If nothing comes of this excursion your days as a traffic cop will be over. You will spend the rest of your life sweeping the streets of Budapest. Do you understand?"

"Yes, sir," Zsigmond answered, now anxious to get off the phone.

"And you will be deemed a traitor to the communist regime for squandering precious resources...*again*."

"Yes, sir."

"And, the Secret Police will cite you as an example of a once promising career gone to shit. You will be known as a traitor, a failure, a wastrel."

"I understand, sir." The only sound that followed was the dial tone, Comrade Bela having quietly hung up. Despite that, Zsigmond was elated. This was the big showdown. If Zsigmond could nail Jozsi he'd be able to escape his traffic cop world, work his way back to being a Secret Police big shot, and perhaps finally convince Erika that he was a worthy partner. She'd lost her husband and she wasn't getting any younger; now, finally, with Jozsi imprisoned or forever banished from Hungary, he might stand a chance.

He hurried to the station to take command of his very small army. On the way to Ura, he had the driver swing by Erika's. Through a window, she caught sight of the bright yellow police van — a *Russia-Volga Gaz M22* — blue stripes running down each side. She clenched her fists in alarm, fearing her friends had been arrested. It would be just like Zsigmond to drag them here for display, like a cat proud of its mouse kill. She peered from behind a curtain as he strode down the walkway, pelted by heavy rain. He rapped on the door; she took a few calming breaths and answered.

He had prepared and practiced his words. "Erika, I'm here for just a moment to let you know I am close to arresting Jozsef Budai. I'm going to solve a mystery of many years and bring to justice a terrible traitor to our people and land. I know you have a fondness for him, but he is a dangerous traitor and any association with him will come to no good. Look what happened to his wife."

It took all of her self-control not to go for this throat, but she inhaled through her nose, lips pressed shut, and stared at him, feeling rage she'd not experienced since the Revolution. She thought: I could pick up a rifle and shoot you in the head and I'd feel nothing. She stood silent.

"I hope tomorrow evening you'll join me in celebrating this achievement. Until then," Zsigmond saluted her, turned on his heel and marched smartly back to the police van.

Erika could barely draw breath, much less speak. She closed the door, leaned against it, sank to the floor, and sat for some time, staring at her feet. When she rose, she went straight to her dresser drawer and put the mushroom container in her purse. If Zsigmond succeeded, tomorrow night there would be at least one dead person at his celebration. If she herself had to die to make that true, then there would be two.

The storm raged as Zsigmond and his crew set out. The roads were a mess, and the towns they passed through difficult to navigate through the torrential rain and morass of wheel-sucking mud. His police crew was not thrilled by this adventure, repeatedly suggesting they pull over and wait till the storm had passed. They all seemed aware that Zsigmond was on thin ice, so although technically he was in charge, no one was treating him with anything approaching the respect he felt was his due. When the van got stuck, they dragged ass digging out. They were getting paid whether they did anything or not, and sitting in a dry van was preferable to getting wet. He could not afford a mutiny, or a return with bad reports on his behavior. He held himself in check.

Jozsi knew his way to the ravine by heart and despite the pelting rain blurring the windshield, they managed to head straight there. Ferenc wrestled with the mucky road, his truck wheels able to spin out of some gloppy holes, shovels needed to dig out of others. Between one obstacle and another, it was nearly evening when they reached the large meadow. Jozsi had Susan get behind the wheel. "If you see high waves of water, lean on the horn so we'll know to get the hell out. Then head up there," he pointed to a section of higher ground several hundred yards away.

The two men ran across the meadow and clambered down the side of the ravine, crowbar, shovel and hammer in hand, to where Jozsi thought the coffin was buried. They heaved aside mounds of piled brush, racing to find the hole. Blinded by the rain, water sluicing down their cheeks, they relied on their hands to feel the way. By now it was night, although it was hard to tell, the stormy skies had been dark since afternoon.

Just as Jozsi touched something hard and metallic, a bolt of lightning flashed and he could see the coffin's corner. "I've got it," he yelled, but thunder drowned him out. He waved wildly until he hit Ferenc's leg. Ferenc handed him the crowbar. He had little trouble moving the cover off the silver coffin — the bomb from the Second World War had blasted half of it to the side. He worked hard to move the gold cover off the casket, knowing they were racing against time; the guard's words lingered in his head. He knew it was not an idle warning. Under the tremendous pressure of all that water the dam could give way.

With all of his strength, Jozsi finally shoved the cover a few inches sideways off the gold coffin. His were the first hands to touch it in 1,500 years. The last had been those of the Syrian slaves who had placed their slain leader at the bottom of the dry riverbed. Shortly after, they too had met their deaths. Herceg had given a command to his soldiers and within seconds, a host of arrows were discharged in their direction. Their work done, the dead slaves would keep the location secret forever.

By the roadside, Susan honked the horn, screaming that the dam had crested. But thunder and rain drowned out all other sounds, as though they were in the midst of a climactic scene in a Wagnerian opera. Lightening flashed, casting an eerie light on the coffin. Ferenc reached down to grab Jozsi, who was bent over the coffin. Water began cascading down the side of the ravine and within moments their ankles were covered. They bellowed ideas for what to do next, but water began flooding the the ravine and the coffin shifted as the earth beneath it crumbled and washed away. Jozsi kept digging, hoping to grab something, anything to carry off before they had to flee. Soon, the water rose high enough to dislodge the coffin. At first, they waded along beside it but soon were hanging on as it floated through the ravine.

"Now!" Ferenc yelled, waving an arm toward higher ground. Jozsi reached inside one last time, his fingers thrust into a pile of metal. He grabbed the smallest thing he touched with one hand and let go of the coffin with the other. With that, Attila's coffin and all its treasures careened away.

Though they'd drifted a good way from their starting point, Jozsi knew the land deep in his blood. He led them toward the high ground where they made their way to Susan and the truck. She leapt out when she saw them stumble through the storm and they grabbed onto each other in relief, water plummeting off their bodies. Susan had packed extra clothing, so they managed jigsaw puzzle-style to get into dry clothes in the front of the truck. The physical contortions to make room for each other had them laughing hysterically. They slept sitting up as best they could, waiting for sunrise. They needed daylight to find their way out of the now forever altered landscape.

Zsigmond and his police squad had spent hours driving and walking through the storm and mud, searching in vain for a sight of Jozsi. Eventually his men convinced him the search was fruitless and they should wait for morning. They'd made their way to the van and hunkered down for the night. He was annoyed, but unconcerned, certain that Jozsi would be trapped, just as they'd been, by the storm. The guards at the town border verified that three travelers had headed toward the ravine. It was just a matter of time, he gloated.

By early morning, the crimson sky brightening in the east, it was clear that a beautiful day was dawning. Jozsi reached into his pocket and pulled out the most beautiful ruby ring he'd ever seen. He held it up toward the rising sun, the sparkling, colored reflection danced on their faces. Susan oohed while Ferenc said, "Let me hide that." He handed Jozsi an oily cloth from the floor of the truck, wrapped the ring, and jumped out. He climbed into the truck bed, and tucked the precious bundle under loose nails and small chisels in the corner of his crammed mess of a toolbox. It would look like a useless rag if anyone opened the toolbox. But he changed his mind and tucked the bundle in a back pocket of Jozsi's discarded wet pants, burying them under the rest of the soggy, muddy clothes piled in the back of the truck.

The three of them stood on the shores of a newly formed lake to watch the sun rise. Which is where they were when a bright yellow van pulled up. Zsigmond ordered his squad to surround them, rifles at the ready. "Hand it over!" he demanded, hysteria in his voice.

"It?" Jozsi asked, stunned to find Zsigmond in front of him, astonished that he still had enough standing to talk his way into obtaining a van and crew. "What it?"

"I know you have something, you bastard," Zsigmond yelled. "You men, search the truck," Zsigmond ordered, pointing to three of the officers. "The rest of you, keep an eye on these traitors." He stood watching, nearly panting with anticipation, despite the truck bed holding nothing but a mess of bedraggled clothes and a toolbox. Soon the toolbox contents were dumped on the ground and picked through. Ferenc watched anxiously, relieved he'd changed his mind about the hiding spot, though still on high alert. Meanwhile, a different policeman squatted over the sopping clothes, patting them without enthusiasm or full attention. Zsigmond kept his eye on a third officer searching the cab of the truck and didn't register how lackadaisically the clothes were examined.

"Nothing here," the policeman handling the toolbox jumped down, leaving its contents strewn on the truck bed floor.

"Here either," the one standing over the pile of clothes said, wiping damp hands on his pants.

Jozsi, Ferenc, and Susan tried not to look concerned about any single thing in the world.

"Take it," Jozsi said, "Whatever *it* you can find. But do me a favor and let me know what it is, because whatever the hell you're looking for is a mystery to me." Rage erupted inside him, he wanted badly to lunge at Zsigmond's throat, but he restrained himself. If he made a move the police would kill him, plain and simple. He had to stay alive to take care of Dani. After leaving the Special Forces, he'd hoped never to need to kill another human being. Not even Zsigmond really — somewhere inside, he still carried an image of him as a lonely awkward child. But if he could in any way contribute to the complete demolition of Zsigmond's career, he'd feel at least some small satisfaction. Jozsi suspected that if Zsigmond returned from this expedition empty-handed, things would not go well for him. He could hope.

The policemen looked bored and restless. Zsigmond, on the other hand, was revving to a tantrum. "Where is it, where is it, *where*?" he screamed at the top of his lungs.

"I told you, there is no it," Jozsi said as calmly as he could manage.

"Then what the hell are you people doing here?" Zsigmond carried on at full pitch.

"Well, we belong to a new religion, old friend. One of the requirements is that we watch the sunrise each Saturday morning out on the *Puszta*. Hungarians by blood, more than some can claim," he looked pointedly at Zsigmond. "Being born in this land of the Magyars doesn't make you a true Hungarian." A final dig that he just could not resist. Susan shot him a look that said go easy. All three travelers were aware that Zsigmond could go completely mad and order them shot on the spot. They didn't think the policemen would comply but still...

Instead, Zsigmond leaned against the yellow van, head down, looking shell-shocked. "Get in the van," he ordered the police officers, his rage spent. He pulled himself together, stood ramrod straight and pointed at Jozsi. "I don't care what happens next, but I will get even with you, *sunyi gazember*."

Susan put her arm on Jozsi in an effort to keep him calm. "Sneaky bastard, my ass," Jozsi muttered. Zsigmond slammed the door and the van pulled away, leaving the three to stand in the warmth of the rising sun. They were happy to let the yellow van get a good head start before heading back to Budapest themselves.

~~~

Zsigmond had no desire to explain anything to Comrade Bela. He'd be summoned there soon enough. He had the van stop at his apartment, released the officers from duty, and trudged inside. It was early afternoon and before the day was out, he would be mincemeat. He ran a tub so he could at least warm up and clean off the mud. He might as well appear presentable for the moment the ax finally fell.

That morning, after a mostly sleepless night, during which she'd prepared chicken paprika and side dishes just to keep busy, Erika rose early. By late morning she'd taken a seat in a café from which she could keep an eye on the car entrance leading to 60 Andrássy. Her stomach clenched; she felt desperate for news. What she did know was that Zsigmond had gone after her friends; it made her sick to imagine what might have happened. The return of the yellow van could tell her what she needed to know. Anyway, she couldn't stand waiting around any longer. The police would show up at Andrássy with or without Jozsi and company, and then either way she'd at least know something concrete. She'd placed the mushroom poison in her purse just before walking out the door, ready to act if given the opportunity.

She slowly sipped a cup of tea, then ordered another, and still another. Finally, she saw a couple of yellow vans pull up to the entrance. She realized she wasn't thinking very clearly. She had no idea how many policemen had gone with Zsigmond, or if any of these vans were the right one. Officers climbed out before the vans entered through the large arched entryway. She did not see Zsigmond. She grew nauseous, panicky. Maybe she should go home. Then a mud-spattered van arrived. Four officers casually exited and then the van disappeared through the archway. Again, she did not see Zsigmond. But all of that mud spoke to a long journey through the countryside and she had a feeling it was the right vehicle. And if Jozsi and the others had been arrested, the van would likely have sped inside immediately. She felt hopeful. She was now so tired, she could have fallen asleep at the table, so she decided to head to Zsigmond's apartment. The air would revive her, and if he'd been dropped off at home, having failed to accomplish anything, he'd be in low spirits and happy to find her at his door. She should have been afraid to try poisoning him in his own home, worried someone would see her enter or exit, but sleepless and stressed, she felt reckless enough not to care. She was weary of carrying the hate. If he died, she reasoned, so too would the hate.

She stood on his corner as though waiting to meet someone until there were no passersby or cars; she prayed no one was peering out a window. If she could come and go unobserved, she had a chance of surviving. She hoped that Zsigmond was such an embarrassment to the state that no one would work too hard trying to nail his killer. She pulled a scarf tight around her head and ran to the entrance hoping he was inside. She was so very tired of waiting.

Zsigmond came to the door, wearing a crisp clean uniform. His pale face flushed with pleasure at the sight of her, he'd been afraid the doorbell meant that someone from 60 Andrássy had come for him.

"You look exhausted," Erika said kindly. "Let's have a warm cup of tea together, shall we? Can you put the kettle on?" She didn't want to touch anything with her hands if she could help it. An exhausted and discouraged Zsigmond let her direct him around the kitchen. He laid out cups and saucers, and filled two tea strainers with fresh tea leaves, placing them on the counter next to the stove. He also poured himself a small glass of *Hubertus*. She did not ask if he'd found Jozsi and he did not offer to enlighten. He simply said it'd been a long, wet, tiring trip and he was glad to find her at his door. He could hardly believe this: Erika in his apartment, being kind.

"You sit in the front room," she said, "I'll serve you." He took his glass and obediently left the kitchen. The kettle came to a boil; she grabbed a hand towel to pick it up and filled the mugs, putting a large amount of honey in his. Her purse was on the counter. She quickly looked behind to make sure he wasn't watching and reached inside. She brought the mug and saucer to him, using the same hand towel. God willing, she would burn the towel in her fireplace later. In the meantime, it would fit easily in her purse.

Zsigmond had settled on the sofa. She placed the tea on a side table and he motioned for her to sit opposite in a chair. "I want to look at you," he sighed.

"Have some tea, I'll get mine. The cups are so hot I can't carry both at once," she explained, trying to mask her apprehension. She knew it would take some time for the poison to impact his system, and for a few moments steadied her nerves in the kitchen. She returned and sipped her tea, watching carefully as he drank his own.

"A bit bitter," he pursed his lips.

"Old leaves, I expect. Let me add more honey." She did, and then sipped repeatedly from her own mug, encouraging him to do likewise.

"It's better now," he nodded.

She distracted him with talk about their early days in school, before the war interrupted normal life, though nearly gagged when he made a comment about her parents. After about thirty minutes, she noticed little beads of sweat breaking across his brow. She returned to the kitchen to brew more tea. She lingered.

"Erika" he called, a few moments later. She moved to the doorway and began humming an old song she'd first heard at the American Cultural Center.

"What is that?" he asked, smiling.

"Just a song I know. Do you like it?" she went back to humming "Who's Sorry Now?"

"It's a pretty tune." He took another sip, leaned his head back, enjoying the sight of her in the doorway. Let the ax fall, at least he might finally have a chance with her. Whatever had happened before, she was here now, solicitous and humming for him and him alone. She hummed on.

He started to tell her that he'd found Jozsi but hadn't been able to bring him in. "I am disappointed, but no matter." He suddenly rubbed his eyes hard and blinked several times. "It's no matter," he repeated, shaking his head as though to clear it. He blinked some more. "Is someone here? I thought I heard the door."

Erika shook her head no, and hummed on. He was imagining things. Good. The poison was beginning to do its work.

Zsigmond put a hand on his stomach, his eyes widening. He swallowed hard several times, broke out in a sweat, then spit on the floor and shook his head again. "I can't see straight," he muttered. He clutched his stomach, doubled over, vomited, started shaking uncontrollably. "My stomach," he moaned. He looked down at the vomit, and then up at Erika, "Sorry, the mess."

"Something you ate?" She asked helpfully. "I'll clean it up." She went into the kitchen again, sat down and inhaled deeply several times to steady herself.

After a few minutes Zsigmond called out, "Where is your tea? It's getting cold in here."

Good, she thought, he's losing it. Delusions, nausea, vision affected, convulsions, she ticked off symptoms in her mind. Soon he should get drowsy. She moved to the doorway, no longer humming. Within minutes Zsigmond gasped, leaned back against the sofa and began moaning. He looked a bit like a mad dog, a thin foam of saliva forming at his lips, confusion in his eyes. "I'm so tired," he whispered, clutching his stomach again. His eyes seemed to be rolling back in his head. "Cold. Is the door open? I need a blanket," he said, shivering. His head lolled to the side, but he shook himself awake. "This is wrong." He leaned sideways, his head seeking to rest on something soft. Finally, involuntarily, he tipped entirely onto his side. "Help me," he whispered.

Hearing his plea pleased her; she felt not an ounce of pity. She did stop humming however, and moved closer to him, looking down with hatred. He whimpered and clutched his stomach. "Not right," he murmured drowsily. Then, "Is she here?"

Erika needed to speak before he completely lost it. She pointed at him. "I know that you tortured my father. I know he begged you for mercy. Don't talk to me about pain. No," she barked. Her voice intensified with the years of suppressed rage. Erika was ready to unload her own final best torture. "You kept that a secret from me. Now I have a secret for *you*. I am the Beast of Budapest, you bastard." Zsigmond was distraught, but she saw in his eyes he could still make sense of her words. "Jozsi and I looked everywhere for you, to kill you." She paused. "But of course, we couldn't find you because you hid like a rat in the sewer pipes." He stretched his hand toward her but she kicked it away. "I swore to God that I would kill you some day. I've carried poison with me for years waiting for the right moment. *This*," she snarled, "is that moment."

"No," he pleaded.

"And know this before you die, you pig. I still love Jozsi." She picked up his mug with the hand towel, backed out of the room, leaving him writhing, foam trickling from the corner of his mouth. In the kitchen, she washed and rubbed dry the mugs and saucers, and put all the tea makings away. When she returned to the front room he was still twitching but unable to do more than whimper. She waited and watched. Finally, he was dead.

Erika hurried back to her apartment, heart racing. She opened her front door and heard sounds from the kitchen. Her body flooded with relief. She could hear Susan rummaging around in the kitchen, ordering Jozsi to grab plates and utensils and set the table. She heard the sound of water running from the bathroom and of Ferenc whistling as he washed up. Erika remained at the door for a few moments, soaking in the sounds.

Jozsi came out of the kitchen and gasped, then ran to the door, wrapping her in his arms. "He is gone," she said. Somehow, he knew exactly what she meant. "How?" She whispered in his ear.

"You took such a risk," he murmured, holding her close. He would show her the beautiful ring later. It rested in his pocket, next to the whistle, and he hoped to one day place it on her finger. His sister and dear friend quietly watched them from the kitchen doorway as they embraced.

A soft tap at the door broke the stillness. Ferenc gently moved the embracing couple aside, peeked through the keyhole. "Jozsi," he spoke low. "Come, look."

Jozsi held onto Erika's hand as he peered out to see...Sandor, holding aloft a bottle of *palinka*. "I don't believe this," he chuckled. Eyes wide, he turned to Erika, "Our guardian angel appears. I think he's even grinning."

"*Hogy vagy?*" Sandor asked, entering with a flourish — he bowed and presented Erika with the bottle.

"We're doing fine. And by the way, what the hell are you doing here?" Jozsi was amused, annoyed, and generally overwhelmed by the events of the past 48 hours.

Sandor ignored him, focusing solely on Erika. "Our beast," he murmured. "I've heard there's a police car parked in front of Szigmond's place. Seen him lately?" He winked, but seeing Erika's sober expression, leaned in to pat her softly on the arm. *"Jól vagy?"*

"I'm okay...now," she nodded repeatedly, trancelike.

"Good." Sandor backed away respectfully. Her need for space seemed to have created a moat around her.

She moved to the couch. "You go back in the kitchen, I just need a moment here." Jozsi thought he understood. She would want to sit with her parents in her head, telling them that the tormentor could torment no more.

Ferenc and Susan moved into the kitchen and Jozsi took the *palinka*. He handed Erika a small cushion, he wasn't sure why, but she clutched it to her stomach as though it might help hold her upright. They held a gaze, then she tilted her head slightly, signing for him to leave. Jozsi leaned close and whispered. Erika nodded and squeezed his hand.

Sandor motioned to the door, "Come...for a little night air." Jozsi followed him outside and instinctively the two moved to the side, away from the outside light.

Erika leaned back, closing her eyes, feeling her mother next to her. They'd sat side by side so often, through fear and mourning, as history ground forward. "It's over," Jozsi had whispered in her ear. Their Hungarian Revolution that had all too briefly caught the world's attention had, in many ways, been over for years. But not for her. Not until now. Even Sandor had understood how powerful this moment was for her, had known she needed a moment to herself. Erika pictured her father as he had been, whole and unbroken. She could finally let go of the haunting images she'd carried for years, him beaten into agony, suffering, afraid. Her body felt lighter, and even the air in the room suddenly seemed clearer and fresh. So many feelings flooded in. She was grateful for this quiet moment alone where she could savor one very welcome feeling — knowing she had kept up the fight to liberate her homeland. Even knowing that Zsigmond no longer had real power had not been enough to lift the weight on her heart. Now, finally with Zsigmond dead, she felt the shackles around her spirit falling away. Erika could actually imagine feeling free.

Susan and Ferenc talked softly at the kitchen table, elated, relieved, exhausted. They had each suffered through the worst years and borne witness to the destruction brought by the communists. They had fervently supported the Revolution, but hadn't experienced Erika's pain or survived Jozsi's many risky exploits. They were honored to share their secrets, to bear witness to this moment.

Outside, Jozsi and Sandor stood silent for several minutes, as though in a trance. Then Jozsi opened the *palinka* and took a big slug. "No need for us to stand on ceremony," he wiped the top and handed it to Sandor.

"Agreed." Sandor drank and handed back the bottle.

"So, you've been here for a while?"

"Just landed yesterday. But I've had eyes on you since you landed, and also on Erika since you headed to Ura."

"Ah, you're here now because you missed me."

Sandor almost laughed. "Of course. Dreadfully."

"It's been quite a run, you and me."

"I'll say." Sandor studied Jozsi's face in the moonlight. "Erika is some woman," he added. "Never gave up her mission."

"Agreed."

"The relief will take time to feel real. So many years to find any kind of peace. But you know, there are still struggles, important ones."

Jozsi reached for the bottle, took a long slug, and with a satisfied sigh said, "Of course there are, *haverom*. Always there are."

"You could still be..." He turned to look directly at Jozsi.

"What?" Jozsi's expression was suddenly alert and wary.

"Very helpful at times, you know?"

Jozsi took another slug. Maybe it was their history of shared experiences, or that Zsigmond was gone and Erika could finally find peace, or that being back in Hungary had stirred up intense feelings of patriotism, for both his new country and his old. Whatever it was, Jozsi, handed the bottle back and said, "I haven't seen the firm's invitation to my retirement party yet, so I kind of figured you might darken my door again."

"You and I, we never say goodbye, just *későbbtalálkozunk*."

"Yes, see you later..." Jozsi shook his head ruefully. "But you know how I feel. This was one last hurrah, because now I'm not just a father, I'm all Dani's got. So, no more risking my hide for the firm. I think we are even, no? Let some young buck full of balls and stupidity have a crack at it."

"I had to give it a shot," Sandor shrugged. "Because, hell, I know you, I know how you work, and who the hell wants to break in a new you?" He shuddered.

Jozsi chuckled. "I see your point, but no. And shit, Sandor, you're getting up there. You should be slowing down, too."

The door opened and Erika poked her head out the door briefly. "Enough talk, you two. Time to eat. Come inside."

Sandor spoke, suddenly intense."Jozsi, Laci left some unfinished business in Saigon, at a god damn high price to pay." He glared and said no more, knowing he had Jozsi's full attention.

They moved toward the door. Jozsi started to let Sandor thru the threshold ahead of him, but then gripped his arm, halting him."No more talk of this tonight. Let's just eat and be together. Erica needs some peace to unwind."

"Understood."

Through clenched teeth, Jozsi muttered, "There will always be messes to clean up, but I want out, I mean that. But for Laci..." He relaxed his grip. "All I'm asking, *haverom*, is for a time to just *be* in Hungary, for a little time to inhale this freedom."

Made in the USA
Middletown, DE
21 December 2018